The Constant Companion

Eknath Easwaran

NILGIRI PRESS

Second edition, first printing September 2001

The Blue Mountain Center of
Meditation, founded by Eknath
Easwaran in Berkeley, California,
in 1961, publishes books on how
to lead the spiritual life in
the home and the community

For information please write to
Nilgiri Press, Box 256,
Tomales, California 94971
Web: www.nilgiri.org

Cover: National Gallery of Canada, Ottawa
Gift of Max Tannenbaum, Toronto, 1979

Library of Congress Control Number: 2001091795

Printed on recycled, permanent paper.
The paper used in this publication meets the
minimum requirements of American National
Standard for Information Services –
Permanence of Paper for Printed
Library Materials,
ANSI z39.48–1984

Table of Contents

The Thousand Names of the Lord

MOST OF THE world's major religions have a tradition celebrating the Holy Names of God. Muslims have the *Most Excellent Names;* Christians have litanies and commentaries like that of Saint Bernard. Jewish tradition preserves several lists of the Divine Names, which Jewish mystics have made the focus of meditation. The Holy, the Merciful, the Compassionate; Truth; the One: these are names which appear in each religion, emphasizing that however we call him – or, as in some parts of my native India, *her* – the Lord is always the same.

In Hinduism, one of the most popular of these litanies is *Sri Vishnu Sahrasra-nama Stotram,* the "Thousand Names of Vishnu." Since no concept can ever describe the Infinite, Hindus believe that the Lord has many forms – Shiva, Ganesha, the Divine Mother, and so on – shaped, so to say, by the inner needs of those who worship him. The *Thousand Names* praises God as Vishnu, the preserver and sustainer of life, worshipped all over India in his incarnations as Krishna and Rama.

I must have heard the *Thousand Names* recited a thousand times while I was growing up. My grandmother, my spiritual teacher, would place a lighted oil lamp in front of the image of Sri Krishna. Then an uncle who was a Sanskrit scholar would chant the names of the Lord one by one, with the sacred word *Om* before each name and the word *namah* after it. "*Om Vishnave namah!*" It means "I bow down to Lord Vishnu," "I worship Lord Vishnu," much like the Christian or Jewish "Blessed art thou, O Lord." With each name my uncle would take a fresh lotus petal, touch it to his heart, and offer it at the feet of the Lord. This is *japam*, repetition of the mantram or Holy Name, as it has been practiced throughout India for centuries.

I was not a very devotional boy, and I have to confess that rituals meant little to me. But after an hour of this kind of recitation at dawn with my family, the *Thousand Names* used to echo in my mind for the rest of the day. Even without reflection, the meaning went in. The Lord is *everything*, everywhere; he dwells in every heart:

> Om! I worship Lord Vishnu,
> Who has become the universe and pervades all.
> Lord of past, present, and future,
> He has made and supports all that is.
> He is Being and the essence of all beings;
> He is the pure and supreme Self in all.
>
> He is all, and the beginning of all things.
> He is existence, its cause and its support.
> He is the origin and the power.
> He is the Lord.

He is the One from which creation flows.
His heads are a multitude, yet he is the Self in all.
His eyes and feet cannot be numbered.
Many and mighty are his forms.

His soul is revealed in light; as fire he burns.
He is the rays of the moon and the light of the sun.
His forms are many, but he is hidden.
He has hundreds of forms, hundreds of faces;
His face is everywhere . . .

Even for a child, then, the Thousand Names were a constant reminder that there is a spark of divinity in everyone. It prompted us to be a little more considerate, a little more kind, a little more selfless with those around us – which, I suppose, is just the effect these rituals are supposed to achieve. Filling your mind with the thought of God is not primarily an esthetic experience. It has a very practical purpose; for what we think of constantly, we see wherever we look.

Later, as an adult, I discovered that ritual is not necessary to achieve this goal. The most effective form of *japam,* in fact, is the silent repetition of the Holy Name in the mind: *Jesus, Jesus,* or *Rama, Rama,* or *Allah, Allah,* or whatever formula has been sanctified by tradition. This form of prayer has been taught in every major religion, and in my experience it is second only to meditation as a tool for transforming consciousness.

In the following pages, I have chosen a fraction of the Thousand Names and added a practical commentary on what each name means in daily living. These comments are based on the eightfold program for spiritual growth which I have followed in my own life and have taught in this country for more than thirty-five years. Meditation is the heart of this program, as it is of my life; so I refer to it constantly in the pages that follow. What I mean by "meditation," and how I differentiate it from the repetition of the mantram, are explained in the brief summary of my program at the end of this book.

The Thousand Names

The "Thousand Names of Vishnu" comes from the *Mahabharata*, an ancient epic poem which is a vast treasury of Hindu legend and literature – including the best known and most universal of the Hindu scriptures, the Bhagavad Gita. In this epic setting, The *Thousand Names* is given to the philosopher-prince Yudhishthira by the great sage Bhishma. The prince asks his teacher a question that must find an echo in every heart: "How can I find joy that will always be with me, satisfying my deepest desires?" Bhishma's reply is to reveal the Thousand Names, with the assurance that if they can be repeated in the deepest reaches of consciousness, this continuous "prayer of the heart" will fill the mind with joy.

Each of these names carries significance. Some refer to the power and beauty of the Lord; others recall some incident in the vast mythology of Vishnu, whose compassion sustains the world. As Vishnu, "he who is everywhere," God has entered into all creatures as their innermost consciousness. He upholds the cosmos from within, as its ruling principle, and establishes and embodies *dharma,* the indivisible unity of life.

In Indian mysticism, which has a genius for clothing the Infinite in human form, Vishnu embodies the source of beauty and order in creation. His body is the dark blue of limitless space, and the galaxies hang from his neck like innumerable strands of jewels. His four arms show that he holds sway over the four quarters of the world. His are the qualities that draw forth love: forgiveness, beauty, and a tender compassion for all creatures.

Vishnu's image is found in temples, shrines, and homes all over India. Usually he is represented as a handsome man of divine radiance who holds in four hands the symbols of power and beauty. A necklace of precious gems adorns his neck. When he travels he is carried by the cosmic eagle, Garuda, or rides a chariot drawn by four spirited horses. In rest he reclines upon the serpent called Infinity, floating in the cosmic waters in perfect peace, dreaming the dream of the world. Though benevolent, he is noted for a mischievous sense of fun. He is universally kind, always approachable, understanding, and serene. The imagery surrounding Vishnu is of light and peace.

Vishnu is also God the protector, who rescues humanity in time of need and supports and strengthens us from within when other resources fail. He is infinite, but from time to time throughout history his love for his creation is so great that he allows himself to be born as a human being to show the world a way out of evil and suffering. Rama and Krishna are the best loved of these divine incarnations. Krishna, in fact, is so completely identified with Vishnu that the two can be regarded as one and the same – and I do occasionally in the pages that follow.

The name *Krishna* is said to come from the root *krish*, meaning to attract. Krishna is God with a human face, and his enchanting smile attracts all things. He is usually portrayed as a youth, in the years when he was a cowherd boy in the idyllic village of Vrindavan. A peacock feather shimmers with beauty in his long hair, which flows around his face like the blue-black rain clouds that blot out the tropical sky during the monsoon. With his body gracefully bent and his arms holding a flute to his lips, he plays an irresistible song. He wears yellow silk, and a garland of wildflowers swings from his neck; on his chest dances a sacred jewel.

This is how Krishna is painted by his devotees as an incarnation of Vishnu. The imagery is specific, but the beauty and compelling attraction of this Lord of Love is universal. Krishna is the spark of divinity in every heart, constantly calling us to return to him. As long as we are alienated from the Lord within, we will be restless and unfulfilled, for this divine spark is our deepest nature, the innermost core of our being. The Lord of Love, present in every human heart, is our real Self.

Swami Ramdas, a very appealing saint of South India whom my wife and I had the privilege of meeting many years ago, used to say that the name of the Lord *is* God. This is a dramatic way of emphasizing that when you have realized the full significance of the Holy Name, you have realized the unity of life. All your desires will have merged in the love of God, whose presence you see in everyone around you. In this sense the Holy Name is a key that can gradually unlock the prison of separateness which confines and isolates every human heart. It can lead us to the discovery of our true personality – eternal, immutable, infinite, and pure.

In Indian mysticism the Lord is said to be *satyam, shivam, sundaram:* the source of all truth, all goodness, and all beauty. When we open ourselves to this source of glory within, a part of it pours into our life. But in order to do this, we have to get ourselves out of the way. We have to learn to defy and eventually to extinguish all the passions by which we make ourselves separate from others: anger, greed, lust, self-will.

This is a tremendous challenge, but repetition of the Holy Name is an infinitely powerful ally. As the mind fills with the thought of God, the heart becomes pure; for as Bhishma says in the *Mahabharata,* the very name of the Lord is a purifying, transforming influence. Anger gradually turns into compassion, greed into generosity, lust into love.

All this Bhishma explains to Prince Yudhishthira, so that he can hear each Holy Name with full understanding of its significance. Then, having prepared Yudhishthira to receive them, Bhishma says, "Now, O Prince, I shall recite the Thousand Names. Listen carefully, and they will remove fear and evil from your life."

He Who Is Everything

WE ARE APT to think of the universe as something apart from God, as a product that has nothing to do with divinity. But the *Thousand Names* reminds us from the outset that the Lord is the universe. He has entered into all things. At the core of creation, in the heart of every creature, is the Lord, the very basis of existence.

In this sense the world is not so much the creation of the Lord as an emanation *from* him. The Upanishads, India's most ancient scriptures, say that just as a spider spins a web out of itself, so the Lord has spun this entire universe out of his own being.

Imagine a spider sitting in the middle of her web. She doesn't go away once she has made it; that is her home. This is the analogy the Hindu mystics use, only they take it one step further. At the end of time, they say, the Lord will draw the web of the universe completely back into himself. Christian mystics use similar language: we come from him, we rest in him, and to him we shall return.

Because we have come from the Lord, all we have to

do to see him is to look within ourselves and discover who we really are. This is the ancient cry of Socrates – *Gnothi seauton*, "Know thyself" – and in spite of the progress of modern civilization, it is a cry we still need to hear. The human condition is to look just the other way: outside, away from ourselves, to find meaning and fulfillment in the world of the senses. This is the subject of a beautiful passage in Browning's poem *Paracelsus*:

> Truth is within ourselves; it takes no rise
> From outward things, whate'er you may believe.
> There is an inmost center in us all,
> Where truth abides in fullness; and around,
> Wall upon wall, the gross flesh hems it in,
> This perfect, clear perception – which is Truth.
>
> A baffling and perverting carnal mesh
> Binds it, and makes all error: and to know
> Rather consists in opening out a way
> Whence the imprisoned splendor may escape,
> Than in effecting entry for a light
> Supposed to be without.

Today it is almost impossible to believe that the source of joy could lie within us. But no human being can really be satisfied for long by going through life mechanically, picking up a little pleasure here and a little prestige there, while everywhere insensitive to the needs of those around.

We are so conditioned to believe that happiness can be gained by accumulating money and manipulating others that we can't see how ridiculous a belief this is. If gourmet living were the source of joy, then it would follow that the more we eat, the happier we would be. If money were the source of security, then the more we had, the more secure we would be. To be honest, I don't know of anyone for whom this is quite true. Yet we go on believing that somehow, someday, *we* will break the pattern and find what we are looking for outside us.

VISHNU

He Who Is Everywhere

IN THE VEDAS, the ancient source of the Hindu tradition, appears the great saying, "There is no one in the world except the Lord." If we take it seriously, this is a sobering thought. At no time can we get into our car and drive to a place where we can afford to be selfish. Everywhere we go the Lord is present. If extraterrestrials arrive from the far reaches of the Andromeda galaxy, we may not know anything about their language or civilization, but we can be sure that the Lord lives in them. If we go to Moscow and listen to a speech in Red Square, however fervently the speaker might insist that life obeys no law but dialectical materialism, we can be sure that the Lord is within him, listening to his words with an amused smile. The Lord is the Self, say the mystics, and the divine ground of all existence. Life is one and indivisible in him, and a place where he is not is inconceivable.

It takes a lifetime to grasp the significance of this simple truth that the Lord is present everywhere. But as it seeps into our consciousness, we gain a new respect for all creation. When we *know* that the Lord lives in everyone, for example, violence is out of the question; it is a violation of the unity of life. Like Mahatma Gandhi, we may feel impelled to take up battle against violence and war, beginning by setting a personal example.

Similarly, when we see that it is the same Lord who lives in Africa and Asia and South America, we see that the welfare of other nations is part of our own. If we see people going hungry in other parts of the world, we will be incapable of hoarding for ourselves. Sharing the resources of the earth generously with everybody becomes an aspect of spiritual living. No one has put it more eloquently than Jesus: "I was hungry and ye gave me meat; I was thirsty and ye gave me drink. . ." When we are feeding the hungry we are feeding the Lord, and when we use more than is necessary, we are depriving the Lord. Realizing that the Lord is present everywhere thus impels a gradual simplification of our life. It not only benefits others; it brings us too a new degree of health, security, and freedom.

Many centuries ago in India, in the state of Madras, lived an eminent woman mystic named Andal. On one occasion Andal had spent the night in the home of some devotees, and when the woman of the house came to wake her up, she found her guest lying with her feet toward the north. She was shocked and confused, for in some sections of Hindu society the Lord is considered to dwell in the Himalayas and pointing or touching with the feet is a sign of disrespect. But Andal only replied: "In what direction shall I point my feet? If I point them to the north, true, the Lord is there. But if I point them to the south, is he not there? He is also in the east and west. Shall I sleep standing on my head?"

Similarly, there is nowhere we can go to leave the Lord behind. At no time can we afford to lock ourselves in a closet and say, "He is not here, so I can be selfish. I can do whatever I like."

Often we are so concerned with the activities of the day, the little things that irritate us or the little pleasures we desire, that we lose our sense of proportion. We forget there is anything beyond the breakfast on our plate. Here the mystics try to remind us that "he who is everywhere" is not only enshrined in our heart, but pervades the entire cosmos.

Here we see the real magnificence of this name Vishnu. On the one hand, we human beings occupy a speck of a planet around a very ordinary sun out in the suburbs of the Milky Way galaxy, whose billions of stars make a great wheel about a hundred thousand light years across. Astronomers now believe there are billions of such galaxies in the observable universe, and no one can say what lies beyond the threshold of our observation. Yet no matter how far we extend our frontiers, the Lord will still be there, reaching beyond the farthest we can reach and still remaining in the hearts of all.

Maker of All Beings

ALL OF US, whatever our past, are sons and daughters of the Lord. That is why Jesus taught his disciples to begin their prayer with the words "*Our* Father." When we eliminate every trace of separateness from the Lord, we find ourselves united with one who is not only our Father but also, as we say in India, our Mother too.

This is not merely union but a reunion. Like the prodigal son, we have returned to the Lord after many years of wandering, to find the peace and security which can only elude us when we look for them outside. "There is no joy in the finite," the Upanishads say; "there is joy only in the infinite." Our capacity for joy is infinite, and anything less than infinitude can only leave us hungry and unfulfilled.

Meister Eckhart, the great German mystic, explains this vividly. All of us, he says, have the seed of God within us. Just as a farmer has to plant the seed, water it and nourish it, weed around it and protect it, so we have to develop our spiritual potential by systematic hard work. If we watch an apple tree over many seasons and see it producing thousands of apples, we can say that the potential for these apples was in the single seed from which that tree sprang. In the same way, we should remember that the God-seed is in all of us, waiting for the water and warmth and proper soil to quicken it into growth.

This makes everybody special. We all have a little label inside us, "Made in heaven." Through years of self-centered conditioning we may have almost rubbed it out; but if we look carefully we can make out a few letters: "———h——ven." If we haven't quite made the best of our lives, it can be very reassuring to remember that nothing we or anyone else can do can take away this label of innate goodness. But at the same time, the point is that this label is in everyone. If we say "I am special," or "My family or race or country is special," the innuendo is that everyone else is second class. In fact, everyone is special, because we are all the handiwork of the Lord.

This vision can be extended to animals too, and in that lies the basis of vegetarianism. When you have become aware of the unity of life, you see that the calf and lamb are as precious as your dog or cat. You see them as companions to be loved and cherished, and their safety and freedom become yours.

William Blake wrote:

> The wild deer wandering here and there
> Keep the human soul from care.

Deer often wander across our property in the country, even grazing right outside my window in broad daylight. Gradually they are losing their fear and discovering that this is a place where they are safe. The sight fills me with delight. When I see these gentle creatures finding refuge here, I think of a monastic friend in India who used to tell us that sometimes, when he was meditating alone on the slopes of the Himalayas, he would be so still and peaceful that deer would come and rub their antlers against his shoulders. This is how far the unity of life can go. When we see the unity that joins us to what we are pleased to call the "lower creation," all creatures sense that awareness. This is the truth Saint Francis was teaching when he preached to the birds or converted the wolf of Gubbio.

The Support of All Creatures

THE LORD WITHIN is our true support, our only real source of security. This has tremendous implications for personal relationships. As long as we do not know our real Self, our inner foundation, we are always likely to be grasping at others for security. When we do not have a sense of security within ourselves, we easily become agitated when others say or act contrary to our desires.

One of the surest signs of spiritual growth, then, is losing the desire to possess people. Relationships improve immediately, because this desire to possess is what damages personal relationships. Nobody likes to be possessed. Imagine putting a little stamp on your boyfriend's collar: "Name: Romeo. Owner: Juliet, Verona." When I see that stamp, I know it is only a matter of time before that relationship falls apart, unless Romeo and Juliet learn new ways of thinking. No one really wants to possess and be possessed. Our real need is to be one, to be united. This is the meaning of love and romance, which possessiveness misunderstands and misapplies.

When we realize this, we relate to others in a completely new way. Instead of looking for our own fulfill-ment alone, we begin to look for the good of those around us as well. When people act negatively, we have the support within to be more patient, more loyal, more understanding. This is how we gradually erode the walls of the ego-prison of selfish desires that separates us from others. When the walls are gone, we are at home with everyone; nothing can shake our security.

PARAM-ATMA

The Supreme Self

THE LORD IS the essence of every person in the universe, what Emerson called the Oversoul. Here we must understand two aspects. Even though God is one and indivisible, he lives in every one of us; so he appears to be many. Yet at the same time, this supreme Self is not contained by any individual or any created thing. The cosmos itself cannot contain him. In the Bhagavad Gita, by far the best known of India's scriptures, the Lord says, "I am in everyone, but no one is in me." God dwells in everyone, so we must respect his presence in all life; but at the same time we should remember that he transcends his creation completely. In the terms of theology, these are the immanent and transcendent aspects of the Lord.

The Self in Every Creature

THIS WORD *atma* or *atman* means simply "self," and I know of no better name for the Lord in any language. He is our innermost personality, the divine spark that is dearer than our very life.

This name reminds us that the Self within us is the same in all creatures. In the climax of meditation, when all the selfishness that divides us from the Lord is dissolved and we discover this Self in the depths of our consciousness, at that moment we see the Lord in every other creature as well. These are not two different discoveries, in other words; they are different aspects of the same realization. To find out who I am, then, is to find out who you are – and who everyone else is, too.

EKA

The One

THIS IS ONE of the simplest names for God in any tradition. The Upanishads say that God is *eka eva advaitam:* "one without a second." The Lord is the only one in the universe; he doesn't have any competition. Who or what could compete with him? He is alone, though masquerading as the many.

Herbert Benson, a medical doctor who has studied the health benefits of using the mantram, has published a book recommending the repetition of the word "one" in meditation because this is a word without any religious connotation. In fact, not only Hindus, but Christian, Jewish, and Muslim mystics, have used this simple word as a name of God, and Plotinus preferred it almost exclusively. So although most of us would find it rather dry, it is not without spiritual significance.

The name *Eka* reminds us that there is nobody who doesn't have a spark of the divine within. When we act or speak unkindly, it recoils on ourselves: we are being unkind to the Lord, who dwells in the hearts of all. Jesus says, "As you have treated even the least of these, so you have treated me."

The Many

WITH THE NAME *Eka,* the Lord tells us to call him "One." Then he comes through another door and we don't recognize him. We ask again, "What's your name?" And he says, *"Naika"* – *na eka,* literally "not one," which is a Sanskrit way of saying "many." So the Lord is up to his usual tricks. He is one and everyone all at once.

This apparent paradox is the result of looking at the same reality from different points of view. From one perspective the Lord is the one reality underlying all of life. But when we view this supreme reality through the senses, the mind, and the intellect, which can only deal with separate objects, we see only the superficial appearance, and unity appears to be many.

This is called *maya,* the illusion of separateness, or *lila,* the divine game that the Lord of Love plays, in which the One appears as the ever-changing, ever-varied multitude of creatures. He plays as five billion human beings, but that is not all. He plays as the beasts of the field, the birds of the air, and all the other creatures that inhabit this universe.

The Hindu tradition has many stories to remind us

of the value of every creature, no matter how humble. Many of these stories tell of figures like Ganesha, whose elephant form personifies the Lord's power to remove obstacles from our path, or Hanuman, the powerful monkey who was devoted to Rama, an incarnation of Vishnu. But there are also many stories about lesser creatures which don't get such a good press. In the *Ramayana*, the great epic poem in which Hanuman is almost as much the hero as Rama himself, there is a heroic eagle who gives up his life in an attempt to rescue Rama's wife, Sita, from the demon king. And when Rama goes to get Sita back, he is accompanied by an army of monkeys and bears.

There is even a wonderful vignette in this story about a squirrel, who sees Rama grieving over the loss of Sita and is so moved that he wants to help. At that point Rama's forest army is engaged in building a bridge of huge boulders across the ocean, and everyone would have understood if Rama had replied gently, "What can a little squirrel do?" But Rama knows that everyone has a contribution to make. One by one, the squirrel brings his stash of nuts and tosses them in among the boulders. Rama was so touched by the "squirrel's mite" that he stroked the back of the tiny creature with his divine fingers – and that, they say, is why the Indian squirrel to this day has three stripes down its back.

VISHVA-KARMA
Maker of All Things

THE LORD IS the cosmic architect, the universal builder – the designer, the contractor, the blueprints, and the building development too.

I like to interpret this name playfully as the cosmic carpenter, who has built this house, the cosmos, not only for us earthlings but for billions of galaxies to share. Unlike ordinary building projects, this one is ongoing; there is always something to do. Every morning Sri Krishna goes out the front door with his carpenter's tools and a hefty box lunch. "Don't expect me till late," he says. "Some of those galaxies still need a lot of work." Why not? Jesus was a carpenter too. The point is that we don't need to pay homage to the bricks and mortar and two-by-fours for housing us so expertly; we would do better to thank the builder. "Everybody praises the building," says Sri Ramakrishna, a towering mystic of nineteenth-century Bengal. "But how many seek to know its Maker?"

The Essence of All Beings

IT IS WORTH a few moments of reflection to grasp what it means to say that God has become all things. In an age that tinkers with genes and speculates about the first three minutes of creation, we may forget to wonder about the world we live in and how little of it even our sciences can grasp.

We know, for example, that light travels at about 186,000 miles per second. We know that fact, yet it is quite another thing to understand it. Imagine, as young Einstein did, that you had a long ray of light like a commuter train, and that you could sit astride this ray as you sit on the five-fifteen express and travel at the speed of light. It would take only a second and a quarter to reach the moon; one blink of an eye and you would be there. In eight minutes–the time it takes to get to the nearest supermarket–you would reach the sun. Yet you would have to sit there on that magical ray for four years to reach the nearest star, and you could travel that way for one hundred thousand years and never get out of our same old Milky Way. Imagine the expanse! Then for two million more years it is just empty space–no gas stations, no Holiday Inns–until you reach the nearest neighboring galaxy. There are believed to be two hundred billion galaxies within the *observable* universe, each of them containing perhaps a hundred billion suns. It's not even the whole picture, yet we still can't grasp it; we can't absorb what these figures mean.

Suppose, one science writer suggests, that you are willing to work eight hours a day, seven days a week–no days off to tend to the yard–counting at the rate of one number every second. It will take a month to reach one million, a relatively small figure on our scale. If you want to understand one billion, this writer says, keep counting in the same way–no coffee breaks, no vacations, no union slowdowns–until the end of your life. I said to myself, "Yes, sir, I get the point."

Most intriguing, perhaps, is why astronomers are so careful to say "the observable universe." It doesn't mean only "That's all we can see for now," as if someday, with more powerful telescopes in orbit beyond the moon, we might be able to see it all. If Einstein was right, as a good deal of careful observation still bears out, then we can never "see" the whole universe. The speed of light itself limits us to a kind of bubble of observation in space-time, beyond which we simply cannot perceive. No messages can reach us from beyond that bubble, and none can be sent. But that does not mean there is nothing beyond; these are merely restrictions on the delivery service.

Worse yet, as soon as we start looking any significant distance into this bubble, we find we are seeing things not as they are but as they were. Wherever we look in the starry sky, we are looking quite literally at the past. One star appears to lie next to another, but actually we see each of them as it was when that light set out on its journey. One of those stars might have been destroyed centuries ago in the explosion of a supernova; we cannot know. We devote special attention to a star, analyze its spectrum to see what it is made of, guess at its past and future evolution, and while we are guessing, that "future" has happened and the star may be gone! If it is a thousand light years away, the news of its death would not reach us for a thousand years. The Crab nebula represents the remains of a supernova explosion observed by Chinese astronomers in A.D. 1054, but the actual explosion took place about 3000 B.C. Even the constellations whose names have come to us down the ages may suffer from severe generation gaps: the stars in them may be separated by thousands of years, as we measure from here on earth. Space and time, bound together, inevitably limit and distort the validity of what we can say about the universe.

But these dimensions do not apply to the Lord. In the Hindu scriptures we find the provoking statement that this vast cosmos is one thought of the Lord. That is as long as our universe lasts: one thought.

The Eternal Law

IT IS AN AXIOM of mysticism and science alike that this vast, complex universe, so impossible for the mind to grasp as a whole, follows one set of laws. The universe is a unity, so the same laws hold everywhere: and that unity, the source of all law, is another aspect of the Lord.

Wernher von Braun has said that outer space is not a hostile place but very friendly, so long as we know and observe the laws that apply there. Similarly, this essential, law-abiding unity of life makes the cosmos a friendly place, so long as we understand its rules. Until recently, it seems, many scientists accepted the view that we are isolated here on earth in a barren, hostile universe. They pictured our planet traveling forlornly through empty, alien space. These attitudes have changed. What takes place a few thousand miles over our heads is anything but meaningless for human life. You don't have to travel to the moon to pick up a moon rock: just pick up any old rock; it is made of the same atoms as a rock from the Crab nebula, the same atoms as your own body. The depths of space are ruled by the same forces which govern life on earth. "A planet capable of sustaining life," as one German scientist commented, "did not come into being independently of the rest of the universe."

The cosmos is not only vast; it is also dizzyingly complex. Our earth, to take just one example, rotates on its axis in four minutes less than twenty-four hours; and while it spins it is revolving in its own six-hundred-million-mile orbit around the sun. On top of that, the earth wobbles as it performs these feats; its axis slowly gyrates through one turn in about twenty-six hundred years. Then we are told that the sun itself is hurtling along toward some inexplicable rendezvous in the Milky Way, while the whole Milky Way galaxy whirls majestically about a center of its own–and, in addition, does its best to move away from all other galaxies with ever-increasing speed. It reminds me of circus gymnastics, like those feats where a woman in spangles gallops around the ring straddling two horses while she juggles torches in a circle of fire.

Yet in all this complexity there is complete harmony. Everything follows dharma, the basic principle that all of existence is one whole. The cosmos is like a huge dance floor where everyone is Ginger Rogers or Fred Astaire; nobody gets out of step. Every body in the cosmos–galaxies, quasars, quarks, black holes, suns, moons, stellar dust–quietly moves in harmony with the cosmic order, which is the same here on earth, on Mars, around Alpha Centauri, everywhere.

This is a serious business, for even the slightest disequilibrium could destroy us. How many times do we hear ourselves saying, "Put out the trash? I just forgot. I'll do it tomorrow." Suppose the earth felt that way about its responsibilities. "You can't expect me to remember everything. I was trying to get the precession of my nodes just right and, well, I just forgot about going around the sun!" The Lord says simply, "This won't do." Everything has to obey his laws; that is a condition of existence.

Lord of Past, Present, & Future

THIS IS A REMINDER of the law of karma, which no one has stated more succinctly than Jesus: "With whatever measure ye mete out unto others, with the same measure it shall be meted out unto you." The Lord is ruler of the past, present, and future because it is his law, the law of life, that whatever we did in the past has to shape our present, just as whatever we do today must shape our future. Just as there are laws governing the motions of heavenly bodies, there are laws that apply in our own lives, laws which we can break only at our peril. To maintain good health, for instance, we have to learn to use our bodies properly. Sooner or later, those who disregard the fundamental laws recorded in the very cells of the human body must suffer the consequences of bad health. How many of us damage our health by smoking or overeating, by hurry and competition in our work, by nursing hostility or anger? In one view, diseases of the lungs and other vital organs are random tragedies. The mystics would say no; they are the natural result of violating natural laws.

Though this may sound harsh, the mystics make a

very encouraging comment: if our thinking and acting today shapes our tomorrows, then the future lies to a significant extent in our own hands. The Lord does not sit above us, judging us and decreeing rewards and punishments for our actions. Our actions themselves carry within them the seeds of pleasant or unpleasant results.

This is the principle behind the law of karma. According to this law, whatever situation we find ourselves in today, we have contributed to that situation by all the desires and fears, the acts and aspirations, of our past. If we have lived a wrong life, it is only natural that our health should be poor, that we should have emotional problems, that we should find it difficult to relate to people.

This is not the Lord punishing us. We have created the situation for ourselves. But if we got ourselves into a mess, we can get ourselves out. The surest evidence of the Lord's compassion is how swiftly a deep, heartfelt change in our ways of thinking and acting today can bring a better tomorrow.

This point of view is very liberating. For the present, it admits, we have to bear the burden of the past. We have all committed mistakes and tried wrong methods of living, so there is a certain amount of unpleasant consequences that we have to face today. But by changing our habits, by reminding ourselves that we and others are one, by training ourselves to think more of the needs of the whole and less of our own private desires, we can change our future into one of health, security, joy, love, and wisdom.

In the utmost depths of meditation, when all the distinctions of space and time dissolve, we pass from time into the eternal Now. Therefore the Lord is said to be the ruler of time, past, present, and future. After all, past and future are not real except insofar as we carry them around in the present, in the form of emotionally charged memories, desires, hopes, and fears. Going beyond time means that all these fall away, and with them go a great many personal problems. "This emptying of the memory," says Saint John of the Cross, " . . . is in reality a great good, because it delivers souls from much sorrow, grief, and sadness, besides imperfections and sins."

The Immeasurable

NOT ONLY CAN we not comprehend the Lord, we cannot even comprehend his handiwork. He is *Aprameya*, "that which cannot be measured," cannot be grasped, cannot even be imagined. Mystics compare God to an ocean that cannot be fathomed, but Shankara, the towering mystic of the eighth century who reawakened India to its spiritual heritage, reminds us that even to compare him with something is to limit what is limitless. Words and thought, trying to approach him, turn back frightened at the frontier of what can be conceived.

The Hindu tradition has a genius for conveying these profound truths through deceptively simple stories. Many episodes in the life of the boy Krishna remind us that although he seems like any other boy, playing with his friends and getting into trouble now and then, there is another dimension which is revealed in the twinkling of an eye when the veil of maya, the illusion of separateness, is pulled back for a moment.

One day little Krishna decides to steal freshly made butter from his mother's kitchen and distribute it to his friends. When Yashoda walks in and sees Krishna handing out her butter and yogurt to his gang, including the village monkeys, she decides it is time for drastic measures. Krishna is so lovable that he always manages to sweet-talk himself out of disciplinary action. This time he is not going to get away with it. She is going to tie him up until he promises to behave himself.

Yashoda finds a piece of cord and starts to wrap it around her divine imp. But the ends of the cord will not reach. She gets a longer piece of rope, ties it to the first, and tries again. Still it isn't long enough. And all the time Krishna just sits there, trying his best to look contrite but barely able to suppress a grin.

Yashoda brings yet another rope, this time long enough to tie up a cow. Still Krishna remains free because the rope is not long enough. No rope can ever tie him because he is immeasurable. Finally he takes pity on the long-suffering Yashoda and allows himself to be tied up. The infinite Lord can be tied by love; nothing but devotion can secure him.

Yashoda has tied him to the mortar she was using to churn curds. Krishna, needless to say, is not without resources, and he soon manages to get out of this embarrassing position. He sees two trees growing nearby and drags the mortar between them. Such is his strength that both trees come down with a crash, bringing the whole village out to see what the noise is. As it turns out, two spirits had been imprisoned in these trees, and

Krishna's escape has released them. Praising his compassion, they fly off to the heavens.

Seeing this miracle, Yashoda and all the villagers marvel at the divine nature of the child they had taken for merely human. Then Krishna deludes them with his maya once again, appearing before them as any ordinary child. But Yashoda has forgotten why she ever was angry with him.

Peace

"PEACE" here means not political concord but the profound peace that comes in the deepest stages of meditation, the peace that "passes understanding." When the mind desires no more desires, but rests in the Self, the Upanishads say, that is the state of perfect peace. "As an eagle, weary after soaring in the sky, folds its wings and flies down to rest in its nest, so does the shining Self enter the state of dreamless sleep, where one is freed from all desires." The Upanishads describe our restless lives as the efforts of a bird that flies hither and thither, never finding rest until it settles down in its own nest at last.

These stupendous concepts may sound philosophical, but they have a very practical application. As Pascal exclaimed, "Not the God of philosophers!" Realization of God means "certitude, joy, peace."

After a lot of sustained, systematic effort in meditation, we may finally succeed in breaking through the surface crust of consciousness. What lies below is the unconscious, which has many layers – strata on strata deposited by habits of thinking and acting, little by little, every day of our life. Drilling through these strata in meditation means overcoming limitations, all the obstacles created by self-will: the fierce, driving compulsion to have our own way, get what we want, stamp ourselves separate from the rest of life. The biggest leap in meditation comes when we run headlong and throw ourselves over the rim of all duality to land in the unitive state, where nothing is separate from the Lord. This state is *shanti,* perfect peace.

Giver of Peace

MOST OF US have so little peace in our hearts that we direly need this peace of the Lord's. Even in our most intimate personal relationships, our usual attitude is an exercise in civil law; half the time we are the plaintiff and the other half the defendant. We go about saying "He did this to me" or "She said that to me" or "It's not my fault!"—all simply because we lack detachment and get blindly wrapped up in our own pursuits. Caught in ambition or jealousy, we go about playing the role of Macbeth or Othello, suspicious of everyone around us.

The Buddha's approach is easy to understand. When we get angry with someone, he says, we are punishing ourselves; anger is its own punishment. When we are being jealous or self-willed, we are punishing ourselves; jealousy and self-will are their own punishment. When we act self-willed, we don't need any court to come and sit in judgment on us and mete out a sentence: "Two months in the jug or five hundred dollars fine or both." We ourselves are the judge, the jury, and the executioner.

Take, for example, the person who is angry. The proof of the punishment is in the physical changes that take place. Every time that person becomes angry, his breathing rhythm is thrown off, his heart races, his blood pressure rises, and all the chemicals of stress are dumped into his body. If anger becomes a habit, the body becomes conditioned to these physiological reactions, and chronic health problems can develop over time. It is the same with digestion: the person for whom anger has become a habit is subject to all kinds of digestive problems.

Last, most frightening of all, are the effects of anger on the nervous system and the heart. Whenever I see someone getting angry, what I see with my spiritual eye is one thousandth of a heart attack, one thousandth of a seizure. Medical evidence is beginning to bear this out; it is no exaggeration. And this is just to mention the physical consequences; the damage in strained and broken relationships hardly needs illustration.

Again, far from being pessimistic, this view has positive implications. Because we are the entire court ourselves, we can change the proceedings. We don't have to go on playing plaintiff or defendant; we can take the stand as the internal witness. When we begin to find out who we really are, we see everyone's needs more clearly, including our own. We gain compassion for our own mistakes, and compassion for the mistakes of others as well. Then, though we try to correct our own behavior, we will not criticize our little personal version of Othello or Macbeth, because we understand how our responses to past events shaped the direction of the drama. Childhood, neighbors, school, friends, all were factors in what made our life into what it is today. In the same way, we will not criticize others, because we know how powerful the influences are which lead people to make mistakes.

When we have the detachment to recognize some of the sources of trouble in our own lives, we see clearly that love sometimes means saying no when those around us are about to make a mistake that will bring sorrow to them and others. This kind of tender opposition is one of the biggest challenges of the spiritual life. When we see our partner or our friend or our children making mistakes, most of us are afraid to say anything for fear of stirring up trouble. We tell ourselves, "Well, it's a free country." Our concern is not really with freedom; we are simply afraid of the other person's response. A true friend is one who has the faith and loyalty to put up with a harsh response, and who will continue to oppose resolutely and tenderly.

In the long run, this kind of opposition always leads to greater respect. Our friend may not speak to us for a week or so, but after he has a chance to see things more clearly, he will realize that here is a person who cares more for his best interests than about blame or praise.

My grandmother was fond of repeating something

that it took me many years to understand: "A good friend should be like a mirror." One side of the face, I am told, is supposed to be more attractive than the other. Imagine a mirror that showed us only the more attractive side of our face, the brighter side and not the darker side. We wouldn't call that a mirror at all. A good friend, similarly, should show us both sides of our personality.

Then she would add, "It hurts me if you get sick, or if you are insecure, or if you don't have your own respect." Here again she would have me in a corner. Like most teenagers, I occasionally had to hear my grandmother tell me things like "Ramaswami from the corner house doesn't have a very good opinion of you." I would answer, "What does it matter what Ramaswami thinks?"

"His sister says you and your cousin are not very polite."

"What does it matter what his sister says?"

Then she would say, "What about your own respect? Does it matter what you think of yourself?"

"Oh, yes, Granny."

"Well, then," she would say, "if you want your own respect, you have to earn it. You can brush off Ramaswami and his sister, but you can't brush off your own self."

Everybody's respect can be easily gained except your own. The Self is the most taciturn, the most difficult, the most impossible observer to curry favor with, because he doesn't need anything and doesn't miss a trick. He has seen everything. You can flatter him any number of times; he will turn a deaf ear. You can offer him tantalizing presents; he will turn a blind eye. And even if you have done enough good deeds to impress the whole world, even if you have resisted so many selfish temptations that the local weekly prints your picture with a glowing review, the Self will just wait. "Let us see," he will say. "Let us see if you go on growing, day after day, year after year, or if you get tired and give up."

That is why there is nothing more exhilarating than getting a little pat on the back from within. At the end of a long, hard day, when nothing has gone your way and you have had to struggle just to keep your composure from disappearing down the drain, you will sometimes feel this pat from within and hear the Self whisper, "Well done."

The Eternal

THE SUPREME REALITY has always existed and will always exist. It is this very reality which we find to be our real nature when we break through the belief that we are physical creatures, governed by the limitations of the body, mind, and intellect.

"You were never born," says Sri Krishna in the Bhagavad Gita; "therefore you will never die." You, the real you, is not separate from that which existed before your body came into being, before even the sun was born. How can that which was never created cease to be when your body dies? This is the experiential discovery we make in the great climax of meditation called *samadhi* (*sam* "with," *adhi* "Lord"), when we become united with the Lord of Love who is enshrined in the depths of our consciousness.

NANDA
Happy

AFTER THESE grand ideas, the *Thousand Names* comes up with a touch of humor.

All of us are familiar with affectionate nicknames. When you want to be intimate, you probably don't address your boyfriend as Benedict. You call him Ben or maybe even "Benny, dear," or you use some pet name that conveys all kinds of private nuances. Similarly, after telling us that his name is Mr. Immeasurable, Mr. Incomprehensible, the Lord must have a wisp of a smile playing on his lips when he says, "But you can just call me Nanda, the Happy Kid."

Nanda means the ground and source of all joy. To attain this supreme state of joy, which brings fulfillment of all personal desires, we have to learn to see the Lord in every person we meet. This vision brings a million times more joy than intimate union with any one individual. Yet at the same time, it brings great responsibility too. When you see someone suffering, it is *you* who are suffering. This identification releases the motivation to do everything you can to relieve that suffering. On the one hand, your sorrow is multiplied a million times; but on the other hand, you have the immense joy of relieving others' pain and sharing their burdens, which is the greatest source of joy on earth.

Toward the end of his life, Saint Francis is said to have retired into the wilderness of Mount La Verna, where he devoted himself fervently to solitude and almost ceaseless prayer. He sought two gifts: first, to feel so far as possible the love Christ felt for all creatures; and second, so far as possible, to feel the suffering Christ endured for all, which is what that love entailed. The two go hand in hand. Brother Leo, Francis's sole companion on that awesome retreat, tells us that after thirty days and nights of prayer, just before sunrise, Francis entered a deep state of ecstasy in which his desires were fulfilled. His identification with his Lord was so complete that like Jesus, the "man of sorrows," he shared the agonies and joys of all mankind.

Few of us dare aspire so high, but everyone is searching for a joy that will never leave. To me, the telling aspect of sensory pleasures is not that they are bad for us but that they do not last. Pleasure is a sensation, and sensations last only for a moment. Nothing in the world can make them stay. We may think we want permanent pleasure, but what we thirst for is not a sensation but a state of being in which all desires are fulfilled. That is joy, a dynamic state in which tremendous resources are released from within to help alleviate the sorrow of the world. We have the unanimous testimony of mystics East and West that this state of limitless joy, love, and wisdom is the birthright of every one of us.

The Unitive State

YOGA, which comes from the root *yuj* meaning "to unite," is a word with many meanings. Yoga is both end and means. It is the state of perfect union with the Lord, who is within; it is also the path to this state of spiritual completion.

In this sense there are several different schools of yoga, teaching various disciplines for Self-realization. Preeminent is the ancient system of Indian philosophy called Yoga, best represented by the *Yoga Sutras* of Patanjali, which emphasizes the practice of meditation. What is usually called "yoga" in this country is actually a system of physical exercises intended to prepare the body for meditation.

If *yoga* means union, the word implies that most of us are suffering from a kind of internal disunity. This division in consciousness is the central paradox of the human condition. We respond to what is beautiful, but on the other hand we feel attracted to things that bring ugliness. We admire somebody who is unselfish, but we have powerful urges to be selfish ourselves. We want abiding joy, but we cannot help going after fleeting, frustrating pleasure.

All these are symptoms of a deeper split in our consciousness which tears us apart. And because we are being torn asunder inside, we express our pain in anger, fear, greed, competition, jealousy, and other negative emotions. It is this inner split that yoga heals – not on the surface but at the deepest levels of the unconscious, where most other methods only tinker with the problem on the surface.

Most people have grown up believing that this primordial urge for union can be fulfilled through sex. This is because we live in such a physically oriented civilization. The more physically oriented we are, the more sensate we will be; and the more sensate we become, the more unshakable will be our belief that sex can heal our loneliness and fill the emptiness in our hearts. Many people honestly believe that it is through sex that two lovers can be united, despite what every sensitive person knows: that whatever we may desire from it, basing a relationship on sex will sooner or later tear those two people apart.

Sex is a sensation. Love is a state of being, a lasting relationship which we can slowly make permanent. That is the deepest desire in all of us, to make this state of union permanent. When we are selfless, in those moments when we feel how close we have come to another person, we taste the joy of love. At these times the split in consciousness is narrower, healing and resolving tensions deep within. Meditation and the allied spiritual disciplines – the eight-point program at the end of this book is an example – are together called yoga because they give us a path we can follow to make this union permanent.

It is the desire to prolong these moments of union into a lasting state of consciousness that is caricatured in the attempt to prolong sexual pleasure for two or three minutes more. Much has been written on this subject, and much research has been done in the name of science. There are manuals to show you just what steps to take to enhance your physical relationship – what kind of music to play, what kind of lighting, what scents to put in your bath. It is cleverly done, but it takes all the beauty and all the sanctity out of sexual union. And along with that, it has also taken its fulfillment. This is a caricature of our real desire, which is to attain a loving relationship that will never end.

In this sense, yoga is the divine marriage that takes place between the human soul and our real Self. In everyone this supreme Person is present, whether we call him Krishna or the Christ or call her the Divine Mother. In trying to live in harmony with all, we are moving closer and closer to this marriage with our real Self.

Sri Ramakrishna describes a glorious experience of union with Christ. He had been studying the life of Jesus, whose personality captivated him, and one day in meditation he saw the radiant figure of the Christ coming closer and closer until he walked into Ramakrishna and merged with him. This identification can come to all of us if we dedicate ourselves completely to this supreme goal. When we finally celebrate this divine union, all inner conflicts will be healed, and that terrible chasm in our consciousness will cease to exist. Then we will live in our natural state of love, which is the state of perfect yoga.

PURUSHA

Spirit

PURUSHA literally means "person": the supreme Person who is our real Self and, at the same time, Lord of the whole universe.

By folk etymology, *purusha* is said to mean "he who dwells in the city (*pura*) of the body." Hindu scriptures often refer to the body in this way, as a kind of walled city with nine or eleven gates: the senses and other bodily openings. The Self is the *Isha* of this *pura*, the Inner Ruler that dwells within and governs our activities.

One practical implication of this name is that this body of ours is a kind of temple or shrine. We have an obligation to take care of it and keep it clean, and not fill it up with substances that do it harm. But we should always remember that we are not the body but Purusha, pure spirit. No matter how well we care for it, the body, like all things physical, has to pass away someday. We, the Self, can never die.

This Self is the same in every creature that has life. The Upanishads say of the time of creation:

He made towns with two feet;
He made towns with four feet.
Then the Person entered into those towns.

This simple truth is the basis of vegetarianism.

The Supreme Self

PURUSHA is "person," the Self; *uttama* means "highest." The Lord is the supreme Person, the highest being in the cosmos. There is nothing loftier than union with him; there is nothing beyond union with him. We can reach our highest goal, attain our greatness, find complete fulfillment, by becoming united with this supreme Person who is our real Self.

Here is Meister Eckhart guiding us on how to attain this state of union:

> To get at the core of God at his greatest, one must first get into the core of himself at the least; for no one can know God who has not first known himself. Go to the depths of the soul, the secret place of the Most High, to the roots, to the heights; for all that God can do is focused there.

He Who Has Beautiful Hair

THIS IS ONE of the favorite names of Krishna. In India we are very appreciative of long, luxurious black hair. It is considered a sign of great beauty, especially in my native state of Kerala.

The Upanishads say that the universe has grown out of the Lord as hair grows out of the body. The simile is both simple and profound. The universe is not separate from the Lord, but it is not identical with the Lord either. My hair cannot claim that it is me. But at the same time, can I say that it is entirely not me? As your hair is a part of you, the Upanishads say, you are a part of the Lord. All of us grow from him and draw our lives from his pure being.

The Thief

THIS NAME IS said to derive from the root *hri*, which means "to take" or "to steal." Hari is he who has stolen our hearts. Having created us to roam in the world of separateness and change, the Lord then stole our hearts so that even while wandering we would long to return to him. Because he has kept our heart, we can never find our happiness anywhere else. As Augustine says, "How can I find rest anywhere else when I am made to rest in thee?"

Haré (pronounced *ha-ray*) is the form used when the Lord is called on by this name, as in the ancient Hindu mantram which was my grandmother's:

> *Haré Rama, Haré Rama,*
> *Rama Rama, Haré Haré,*
> *Haré Krishna, Haré Krishna,*
> *Krishna Krishna, Haré Haré.*

This mantram calls on the Lord with three of Vishnu's most familiar names.

KSHAMA
Patience

THIS IS ONE of the most important of the Thousand Names, because it is so practical. My friends often tell me, "You can talk more about patience any time you like. It's something we always need to hear."

Why do we hear so little about patience today? There almost seems a conspiracy in our modern civilization to counsel just the opposite: be impatient, be angry, "look out for number one." But what is life without patience? What use is money if we live in exasperation with those we love, if we cannot stand to live with our own family? What good is it to have your picture on the cover of *Time* if you cannot be patient with yourself? So many songs are written about love; I would like some enterprising songwriter to sing the praises of patience, without which love is impossible.

In Sanskrit we have a beautiful saying, *Kshama virasya bhushanam:* "Patience is the ornament of the strong." What a wonderful idea! Not swords or guns or medals, but patience. We seldom realize what power there is in patience. All the energy consumed in exploding against others, in retaliating, in unkind words, in the anger that brings grief to others and ulcers to ourselves – all that energy can be harnessed as positive, creative power, simply by learning patience.

This is strength that is irresistible. It is the same power that Mahatma Gandhi harnessed in leading India to political independence without firing a shot. If we could exercise this power in our personal relationships, it would transform our lives and make our homes citadels against violence.

One obvious place we can learn patience is with older people and invalids. Grumbling, complaining, and suffering are part of being sick. It is a privilege to serve those who are unwell and to put up cheerfully with an irritable remark. Similarly with older people. It is good to remember that old age will come to all of us, and when your body is not able to function well, the slightest effort can bring pain. At such times it is very difficult to be generous. Spiritual awareness teaches us to serve someone in this condition cheerfully and lovingly: it helps them, and it helps us grow as well.

Another place to learn patience is in taking care of small children. Infants, in particular, have no language except crying. They can't look at their watch and say, "It's half an hour past my mealtime and I'm famished," or take their cereal off the shelf, repeat their mantram, and eat. So they scream. That's their way of attracting attention, and if the response is not prompt, they scream louder and longer. It's not very easy to be patient and cheerful with a screaming baby on your hands; but that is just what makes it the perfect opportunity.

Nighttime, of course, is best of all. In India, where babies sometimes do not have a room of their own, nighttime can really be a problem. The baby will be in one corner of your room, the brother and sister in a second corner, a cousin who has come to the city for a job interview may be on the couch. And in the middle of the night your baby starts crying. Perhaps he has a stomach problem, perhaps he has an earache; maybe he just wants to play. After all, a baby doesn't see the logic of sleeping all night. "Here it is one o'clock and I'm wide awake. Why are all these people sleeping?" He starts expressing the feelings of the moment, and every-body in the house gets upset.

At a time like this, the only way to remain patient is to repeat the mantram or Holy Name and remember the unity which binds everyone in the family into a whole. This is what spiritual living really means. The whole purpose of meditation and other spiritual disci-plines is to strengthen us so that we can deal success-fully with the trials of life, large and small.

A story about Saint Francis of Assisi illustrates the joy this kind of self-mastery can bring. One day, on a jour-ney across the Italian countryside with one of his dear-est disciples, Brother Leo, Francis exclaims: "Brother Leo, even if all the friars were perfect examples of holiness, even if they taught and healed and performed all kinds of miracles, this would still not be perfect joy."

Leo asks eagerly, "What *is* perfect joy?"

Francis, who knew how to make a point and how to tell a tale, replies, "Even if we could understand the birds, and speak with angels, and know all the secrets of nature – even then, Brother Leo, this would still not be perfect joy."

They walk along a little farther, with Francis going on and on like this, until finally Brother Leo gets lovingly exasperated. "Please tell me what perfect joy is!"

And Saint Francis tells him, "If we reach the next town by midnight tonight, cold and hungry and tired, and the gatekeeper tells us that we can't come in, that we are just a couple of ruffians, and he uses all kinds of bad Italian and beats us and drives us out – if we can remain patient and loving through all that, then we shall have perfect joy."

Imagine someone who cannot be disturbed even if you are rude or unkind to him. Imagine someone who moves closer to you when you get angry, instead of running away; someone who keeps showing respect even when you try to strike out and hurt him. Simply being around such people is a joy. Their patience rubs off. Gradually we want to be like them. When we have a selfish impulse, we reject it; we have seen something higher. Once we have an ideal like this to live up to, we try to stretch ourselves a little every day; we see opportunities in every challenge.

When you reach this stage, all boredom goes out of life. There is no time to feel unoccupied; all your waking moments are devoted to realizing who you are – who is the real Person who lives in this body of yours. You find choices everywhere: Shall I live for myself, doing what pleases me even though it may not be very useful, or shall I give my time to helping others and pursuing the goal of life? As patience grows, you develop the capacity to make these choices in everything you do. Then you will find your spiritual growth swift and sure.

Lover of His Devotees

THE LORD LOVES all creatures, but those who love him with all their hearts have an innate power to draw his love in return. As Saint Teresa of Avila says, *Amor saca amor:* "Love draws love."

This is an especially appropriate name for Krishna, who has a particularly warm corner in his heart for ordinary people who live in the world yet try to remember him. These are the Lord's householder or lay devotees. They haven't left the world, as monastic devotees do; they keep their jobs, live right in the middle of family and society, but do their best to base their lives on spiritual values and disciplines like meditation and the repetition of the Holy Name.

In the Hindu scriptures there is a story about a character named Narada, who is not a householder but a sort of immortal monk. Narada likes to travel about from ashram to ashram stirring people up with spiritual gossip: "In this ashram three people attained illumination last week! In that ashram they are meditating around the clock." Narada appears like this in many of our stories, and the consequences are always instructive.

Once, it is said, Narada asked Sri Krishna, "Lord, why do you like these householders so much? They're not very regular in their practice. One moment they resolve to become very spiritual and the next moment they forget all about it."

Sri Krishna pretended to think awhile. "Narada," he said, "I want you to do something for me. Will you take this little oil lamp and carry it around the temple three times? Then I'll answer your question. But don't let the lamp go out."

As soon as Narada took the lamp outside, Krishna called up the winds and said, "Now, blow!" Soon Narada felt hard pressed. The north wind started blowing and the south wind started blowing, and there he was with this little oil lamp he couldn't let go out. But being illumined and immortal, he wasn't completely without resources. He held the lamp close and huddled over it to shield it from the wind, and somehow he managed to get around the temple three times with the flame still flickering. When he finally got back to Krishna, he was a little disheveled but still undaunted. "Well, Lord," he said, "here is the lamp."

Sri Krishna smiled. "Tell me, Narada, while you were going around the temple, how many times did you repeat my name?"

Narada hemmed and hawed. "With all this storm

blowing, the north wind and the south wind ... actually, Lord, I didn't really remember."

"Narada," Lord Krishna said, "these householders have so many problems, what with television, and babies crying, and Madison Avenue to contend with, the wind is blowing against them all the time. If they are able to remember me only a little part of the day, I am very pleased."

Who Makes Love Increase

EVERYONE WANTS to be a great lover. Through the practice of meditation, anyone can learn. All that is required – which, I admit, is terribly difficult – is to transform everything negative in our personality into the positive qualities we admire in great men and women of God like Mahatma Gandhi and Teresa of Avila.

This is not done overnight, and it is not done by painting pictures or writing poems about self-transformation. It is done over a period of years by exercising our will and learning to love others more than we love ourselves, beginning with those who are nearest to us.

Today we talk a great deal about love. It is supposed to be the theme of thousands of movies and songs. But in all these things I find very little that has to do with real love. In the mass media, the usual presentation is that you go to Venice or Paris, look into someone's eyes, and fall in love just as you might fall into a manhole. I can't imagine how such a notion of love got started. Real love is the result of a lot of hard work over a long period of time. It is developed through trust and loyalty and patience, learning not to say a harsh word or even show disrespect when we are provoked.

Over many years this kind of love can grow to such an extent that those you love will know you are incapable of hurting them, whatever lapses they may have. Imagine the security this brings! Your trust and loyalty can go so deep that you never even have a divisive thought.

This applies not only to one relationship but to all. When we have totally forgotten our own pleasure and convenience in seeking the welfare of others, the wall of our separate ego has broken down. When we see others happy, we feel happy; when we see others suffering, we try to help. There is no individual burden of sorrow that we must bear alone.

This is what is meant by seeing the underlying unity of life. It is not an intellectual abstraction but a living experience, in which we see the Lord everywhere, in everyone, all the time.

The Destroyer

THIS NAME IS a stark contrast with the usual image of a loving Lord. The orthodox explanation is that it refers to the apocalypse. The Hindu view of the creation fits well with contemporary cosmology: the universe is said to explode into being, along with space and time, from a state of pure potentiality, and to expand for billions of years. Then it is withdrawn into a state of potentiality again. That which was before the creation of the cosmos and will remain after its dissolution, changeless and unchangeable, is the Lord.

Yet there is also a personal application of this name, which is often misunderstood by scholars: when we have done everything we can to reduce the selfishness and self-will that stand between us and the Lord, it is the Lord himself who finally destroys our sense of a separate, selfish personality, releasing us from separateness into the unitive state. At that time we will see that even in trying to go against our selfish impulses, it is the Lord, the Self, who gives the motivation. The desire to go against selfish desire is one of the surest signs of spiritual progress, and it has to come from a source far deeper than the petty ego from which self-centered desires spring.

One of the best ways to do this, particularly with people we have to rub shoulders with frequently, is to practice patience. Patience, such a quiet skill, can actually dissolve self-will – and like physical endurance, it grows through practice. To speak gently, to act kindly at precisely that moment when we long to lash back, is the surest way of developing patience. When somebody who meditates comes to me with a sad tale of how he has been wronged, I often want to beam and exclaim, "What an opportunity! This is your chance to break through to a deeper level in meditation."

Increasing patience puts an end to many emotional problems, even some that have been victimizing us for years. Surprisingly, it may even put an end to physical problems, particularly those that are aggravated by stress, competitiveness, and compulsive hurry. Of course, we have to observe the basic rules of right living, both physically and emotionally; patience cannot make up for lack of vitamin B-12. But we will be amazed at how good patience makes us feel, and how much better we are able to work with people who used to provoke psychoallergies. The benefits are so compelling that once you see this, you may actually start asking the Lord to provide you with more opportunities to practice patience and make it grow. "I can take it," you hear yourself promising. "Right on the chin." That is the stuff of which budding mystics are made.

When this happens, you begin to see why great mystics speak so gratefully of trials and tribulations. They are not being perverse. Like an athlete who accepts a grueling training regimen because she knows it will stretch her physical capabilities, the mystics accept hardship because they know from experience that trials draw out their best. I think Mahatma Gandhi actually used to feel uneasy when things were going too well for him. He knew – and so did his opponents – that he was at his best when life was raining blows on him. In a similar spirit, a few lines from Teresa of Avila give a great lover's response to times of trial:

> When that tender hunter from paradise
> Released his arrow at me,
> My wounded soul collapsed
> In his loving arms.
> My Beloved has become mine
> And without a doubt I am his at last.
>
> He pierced my heart with his arrow of love
> And made me one with the Lord who made me.
> His is the only love I have,
> And my life is so transformed
> That my Beloved has become mine
> And without a doubt I am his at last.

When life is difficult, it can strengthen us greatly to

remember this image of the "tender hunter" who strikes us, as John of the Cross says, with the "wound that wounds to heal." Giving up selfish habits, going against self-will, learning to forget ourselves by putting others first – all these can hurt a good deal. What Teresa is implying is that if we are not willing to be subjected to this kind of pain, we might as well forget about becoming one with the Lord. So far as I know, there is not a single mystic who does not talk about the difficulty of it, the distress. The Lord can be quite tough. He says, "I am going to put an arrow straight through Teresa's heart, so that it comes out the other side and sticks in that tree. If she can't take it, she can continue to be separate." If we want to be able to love anyone at all, we have to overcome the very human tendencies to blame, manipulate, and turn resentful.

There is pain in this, but after the pain – even mixed with it, when we understand what is taking place in our hearts – there is joy, the exhilaration of freedom. Releasing ourselves from the tyranny of selfish habits means releasing our hearts and minds from bitter hostilities, from jealousies, from burning desires we cannot control. So mystics like Teresa confide to us, "It was a great day when this divine hunter got me in his sights." We read accounts of their lives and we think, "How tragic! They turned their back on so many good things." Yet here is Teresa telling us that those were the happiest moments of her life. For as she fell, wounded, the Lord's loving arms were there to catch her; she fell from separateness into the unitive state.

He Who Is Invoked in the Act of Sacrifice

THIS NAME HIDES a minor mystery. *Vashatkara* means "he who is invoked by the sacred word *vashat*," which is ice cream to Sanskrit scholars. This ancient word is exclaimed in a particular ritual at the moment when an offering to the Lord is poured onto the sacrificial fire.

Shankara, the great mystic of medieval India whose authority is unassailable on spiritual matters, says that *vashat* is simply a mantram, like the sacred syllable *Om*. But it may be given a more practical interpretation, for all of us are expected to make our lives an offering to the Lord, from whom life came. In practical terms, this has very little to do with rituals and formal worship. Making our lives an offering to the Lord means putting others first, living for the welfare of the whole rather than just for ourselves, for the Lord is present in all.

PRABHUTA
Abundant

WHEN YOU TAKE something from infinity, infinity remains. Similarly, you can take all you can hold of the Lord's qualities and there will always be more. The measure of what we can take from him is what we ourselves can carry. If we go to him with a narrow heart, he will not be able to put much love or patience in. But great mystics like Saint Teresa or Mahatma Gandhi, who have emptied themselves of themselves, are not only full of the Lord but are open conduits for his love. They have burst ordinary human limitations; their resources are endless. The more they give, the more they have to give; the more they love, the more they are able to love.

Not only can you not exhaust such people, you find that they have given you so much patience that you too can pass it around a little more. "Here, Marilyn," they say, "let me give you a basketful of patience." "Hey, Rhett, you take two." They go about distributing patience and their reservoir of love remains full. Even ordinary people like us will find that the more we keep on giving such gifts, the more we have to give. We are drawing on the fullness of the Lord, who is right within.

Intellectually, this idea may be difficult to understand. The problem is our idea of the human being. We think we are very limited creatures, very small, good for maybe only fifteen minutes of love or patience before we have to crack. Instead of identifying with our deepest Self, we are identifying with some biochemical-mental organism. I don't spend much time trying to reason with this idea. I just say meditate, repeat your mantram whenever you can, and try it for yourself; see how far you can stretch your patience.

Of course, there will be lapses. But after a while you will see for yourself how comfortable you feel with everybody, how secure you feel wherever you go. You will find that when you have to go into difficult situations, you will do so with a quiet sense of being equal to the challenge. You know you can listen to criticism calmly, keep your temper, and make your point with kindness and humor; and you know that by and large, other people will respond.

These are tremendous discoveries, which give only a hint of the heights to which a human being can rise. Once we see this for ourselves, we will catch the exhilaration of the mystics when they say that because the Lord is our real Self, there is no limit to the height to which we can grow.

KUMUDA

Water Lily

AMONG THESE LOFTY appellations, we also get some familiar names that celebrate the beauty of the Lord, which love of him awakens in our heart.

Some of the most appealing of such names refer to flowers, which make favorite names for girls in India. In central India, where the university draws students from every part of the country, my roll books carried regular garlands of tropical names. *Kumuda*, for example, is a lovely kind of water lily that the poets say blooms at night when the moon comes up. With such romantic associations, you can see why a girl named Kumuda would be faced with great expectations when she showed up as a freshman on a college campus.

The Lord too is called Kumuda, and the application is that just as this beautiful lily waits for the moon to rise, our heart is waiting for the love of the Lord to open it like a bud. When love of him begins to flood our heart, no discourteous word can come out of our mouth, no unkind act sully our hands, no jealous thought arise in our mind. This is when the human personality blossoms into full beauty.

When the lotus blooms, it doesn't need an advertising agency to generate name recognition. No one can keep away. Similarly, when you do your best to put other people first, even if it means ignoring your own private satisfactions, everybody enjoys being around you.

Jasmine

THIS IS ANOTHER name rich in associations. When I was teaching English at a college in central India, I remember, men leaving campus at the end of the day used to stop by the flower stand for garlands of jasmine to take home to the ladies in the family. Half a rupee then would buy a couple of feet of delicate petals with a haunting perfume.

Walking into my classes in those days was like entering a fragrant garden, so many girls had twisted garlands of ivory jasmine in their shining black hair. Some would do their hair in a style you may have seen in the frescoes from the Ajanta caves, with a bun on top, pulled a little to one side, and a garland woven around. Others had a little chignon at the back. But most simply twisted strings of blossoms into their long, thick braids. And even after the flowers had faded and been tossed away, the girls' hair would still be fragrant with the scent of jasmine. Certain boys used to sit at the back of class, sniff audibly, and heave great sighs of appreciation.

Lovely flowers smell sweet, the Buddha says, but they fade, and their fragrance cannot last. The fragrance of goodness abides. When you have been in the presence of someone who has realized the Lord, you will take home with you a little of that person's kindness and patience, a heart at peace, just as the smell of roses remains in a room long after the flowers are gone. Even you and I, when we can forgive unkind words or malicious behavior and not carry agitation in our hearts, will leave a fragrance that others too will carry away.

What is the appeal of calling an expensive perfume My Sin? "My Forgiveness" would be so much more alluring. Instead of Evening in Paris, this is evening in paradise. When you live with someone who can forgive from the depths of his heart, you are living in heaven here on earth.

He Who Wears Garlands of Forest Flowers

KRISHNA IS OFTEN portrayed as a young man with a garland of wild flowers, the delicate blooms of the forest, around his neck. It's not a sophisticated corsage from the florist's shop; everything is natural, naturally beautiful.

Garlands, called *malas,* are very popular in India, and Indian poets have always been fond of the imagery of flowers. Mira, one of the most beloved saints of medieval India, tells Krishna in a song, "I am going to wear you like a flower in my hair, like earrings in my ears, like a garland around my neck, so that I remember you always." That is the purpose of the *Thousand Names.* If we remember who is the source of all beauty, all plants will remind us of the Lord.

Houseplants are everywhere today; people have African violets on their desks at work, ferns on the stereo, fig trees in the living room corner. In some places it is fashionable to tear down a wall or open up a window and attach a miniature greenhouse. Berkeley, where I used to live, had a store called Plant Parenthood. Why not do the same with patience and forgiveness? We can surround ourselves with compassion, open up our lives to good will. All these flourish with just a little care. When you fly off to Iceland on a tour, don't you ask your neighbor to take care of your African violets – spray them, chat with them, pick off the bugs? Some people spend an hour or more a day with this kind of thing. With the same attention, houseplants like love and tenderness will blossom in your life year-round.

Sri Krishna's garland of wildflowers is always fresh from the forest. When you or I receive flowers on a special occasion, we have difficulty keeping them fresh, but Krishna's garland never seems to fade. The Hindu scriptures say that this is a sure giveaway of a divine being. If you ever meet anyone whose corsage or buttonhole bloom never wilts, be alerted: this is no ordinary Joe or Jane!

The Uplifter

THE LORD IS infinitely tender, but we should never forget his toughness. He and he alone has the strength to lift us out of trouble and despair, and ultimately out of the sea of birth and death.

When I go to the beach for a walk, I sometimes see a Coast Guard helicopter flying perilously low, on a mission of mercy to rescue someone in trouble at sea. This is how I picture Krishna. No matter how close we are to drowning in the sea of selfish conditioning, if we can reach into our deeper consciousness through meditation and the Holy Name, the Lord will act as our internal helicopter. His promise is given in the Bhagavad Gita:

> But they for whom I am the goal supreme,
> Who do all things renouncing self for me –
> These will I swiftly rescue from the fragment's cycle
> Of birth and death to fullness of eternal life in me.

When we get in trouble, repeating the name of the Lord can pull us out; but that in itself is not enough. If, in spite of our best efforts, we accidentally fall into waters that are over our head – for example, if we get into a situation where a strong desire can sweep us away – then repeating the Holy Name can release the will we need to get ourselves out. This help comes from a depth beyond our ordinary reach, which is what the great mystics mean when they say the Lord came to their rescue. But after that we are on our own again. The Lord expects us to learn from our mistakes. If we go on jumping in over our heads and then calling out, "Save me!" he will simply reply, "You'd better save yourself. That's the only way you'll learn."

All-knowing

I REMEMBER ONCE seeing a clever British film dedicated to "all those who got away with it." As far as real life is concerned, I don't think anybody gets away with anything. The Lord is within us; what can we hide from him?

Inside each of us, my grandmother used to remind me, is a perpetual Peeping Tom with his eye right to the keyhole of the mind. Every thought is registered. It took me years to be able to swallow this concept, which seemed preposterous to me as a child. Today, realizing that the Lord is not outside but our real Self, I see how remembrance of him can really keep us on our toes.

One of the fascinations about detective novels and spy stories seems to be the idea of tracking people down. After you finish reading one, you may find yourself thinking up ingenious ways of covering your tracks. It might seem simple. But even though there is no hidden camera focusing on you, no long-range mike, no secret agent to bug the olives in your salad, someone inside is tuned in to everything that goes on in your heart.

The Lord does this not to torment us but to protect

us. Doubts, depressions, and pangs of guilt are really an extremely sophisticated alarm system installed in every nerve and cell of our being, warning us when the things we say or do or think run counter to the laws of life. Blaming circumstances or other people in such cases is ignoring the real culprit in the story. When we repeat the mantram we are praying, "Lord, I know I have wrong thoughts. I know I sometimes say or do harmful things. Please help me to turn wrong thoughts into right ones, and to remember that you live in me and in everyone around me."

He Who Never Sleeps

IN INDIA WE have a great festival called Shivaratri, the Night of Shiva, which devotees celebrate by repeating the mantram and worshipping the Lord in various other ways from dusk until dawn. It is like saying, "Lord, you stay awake all year long to keep us out of trouble, so tonight *we* will stay awake, chanting your name throughout the night, so you can get a good night's sleep."

This is a real measure of love, because sleep is one of the human being's favorite pastimes. After a couple of nights without sleep, people can try to tempt you with anything on the face of the earth; you will just yawn and say, "Ask me again after I wake up." You won't want anything except a nap. If Romeo's friends had kept him awake just one more day and night before that fateful glimpse of Juliet, he might have got as far as "It is the east!" and forgotten all about the sun of his delight looking down on him from her window. He might have nodded off instead of climbing up onto that balcony, and saved both of them a good deal of trouble. That is the principle behind the overnight vigil, practiced in all monastic traditions to keep physical passions at bay.

If you can fall asleep in the mantram, however, you do not have to express your love for the Lord by keeping vigil; you can express it while you sleep. "You've been on duty all day long," you assure him. "Now let your name protect me during the night. With it at work in my consciousness, you don't have to be watchful; you can go ahead and get some sleep." The secret is that if we fall asleep in the mantram, it will keep on repeating itself until we wake up – a constant, comforting reminder that will calm the mind, banish conflicts, and leave us refreshed and restored when morning comes.

Whose Face Is Everywhere

IF YOU WANT to see God, the mystics say, you have only to look around you. Everyone's eyes are his eyes; every face reflects his.

This is not an intellectual understanding. When you realize the Lord in your own heart, that is how you will actually see. The English mystic Thomas Traherne has a beautiful passage describing how the faces and figures around him were transfigured by this vision:

> ... young men [seemed] glittering and sparkling angels, and maids strange seraphic pieces of life and beauty! Boys and girls tumbling in the street, and playing, were moving jewels. I knew not that they were born or should die; but all things abided eternally as they were in their proper places. Eternity was manifest in the light of the day, and something infinite behind everything appeared.

LOHIT-AKSHA
Rosy-eyed

Sri Krishna's eyes are considered particularly beautiful, and they are often compared with
the loveliest of flowers, the lotus. When the lotus blooms
early morning, the rays of sunlight pass right through
the translucent red petals, turning each flower into an
exquisite goblet filled with liquid light. When you look
at someone with love, this name reminds us, the melt-
ing light of the Lord will shine through your eyes, filling them with his glow.

According to yoga psychology, there is immense
power in our human passions. As that power is transformed into love, the light released cannot help shining
in our eyes. That serenity, that luminosity, is a kind of
liquid effulgence that comes not from us but from the
Self within.

The Supreme Blessing

THIS WORD *mangala* is an auspicious one in India; it is repeated many times at a wedding. *Mangalam* means blessing, it means joy, it means purity, it means love. In South Indian concerts, the last piece is the *mangalam*: a prayer for the Lord to give his blessing to performers and audience alike.

The Lord is supreme joy and supreme love; he is the supreme blessing our life can receive. In seeking him through meditation and serving him in those around us, repeating his name with devotion and dedication, we are slowly making ourselves ready to receive this great blessing, the precious legacy of unity that is buried deep within us. For our real nature is none other than joy, none other than love.

The Self in All

THE LORD IS present not only in those we like and who like us. He is present equally in those we do not like and who dislike us. He lives in all, and when we attain spiritual awareness we will see him in all, whether they are for us or against us, whether or not they belong to our race, sex, country, or religion.

To begin to see like this, we must learn to overcome our likes and dislikes. It is only natural to like those who like you, and to return dislike with dislike. We need a certain degree of detachment to be able to get along with people who are difficult – detachment not from them but from our own opinions and self-will.

In English the word *detachment* sounds negative; people usually associate it with indifference. Actually it is attachment to ourselves that makes us indifferent to others. What life requires is detachment from ourselves, which opens the door to sympathy, understanding, and compassion.

Detachment is the key to effective action. As long as we are driven by selfish concerns, we can never see a situation clearly, which means that we cannot act appropriately either. People driven by the desire for fame or power, for example, cannot help manipulating those around them. Gradually they lose respect for everyone, including themselves. They end up estranged from those around them, and the little empire they have built up becomes a source of sorrow.

Lack of detachment, however, is not limited to those who are greedy for their own ends. Many good causes have failed because those who supported them lacked the detachment to see when they were defeating the very purpose for which they were working.

To take just one example, some of the peace demonstrations I used to see in Berkeley were not exactly peaceful. I remember once being amazed to see a student forget himself so completely that he was threatening someone with a big sign saying "Peace Now." This is just the kind of mistake all of us make when we get so wrapped up in our own way of thinking that we cannot see anything clearly.

Some time ago, while my wife was in the bank, I decided to stay in the car and read the paper. The door of the car was open, and a dog, rather plebeian, came up and looked at me for a long time to see if I was worth cultivating. He must have decided I was, because he put two paws on my lap and said, "Bow-wow." I said, "Yes, thank you, I am always well." He had quite a nice way about him, so he probably would have understood if I had said instead, "I don't have time to talk to dogs"; I imagine he would have just said, "I feel sorry for you," and walked away. But I can understand the ways of dogs easily, and I started petting him. By this time he was drawing himself more and more into the car until at last more of him was in than out. He was sitting on my lap and we were getting along very well when a lady who was passing by said jocularly, "He's a mutt. He likes everybody."

Mutt or not, I wanted to tell her, that dog was teaching us a lesson. Those who like everybody, even if their opinions or color or social status is different, have tremendous potential. Such people can go far spiritually, because they identify themselves very little with their body, feelings, and opinions. They do not forget that people are people just like them, so they do not put labels on them: "reactionary or radical," "straight or not so straight," "for me or against me." And they never make the mistake of thinking of people as political animals or economic units; for all of us have feelings that can be hurt and needs that should be respected. When you see someone like this, remind yourself that he or she has already some awareness that all of us are one. That is what detachment means.

Without detachment, however, we cannot help being rigid in our attitudes and opinions. Times change, the needs of society change, but those who lack detachment will find it impossible to adjust their views.

Mahatma Gandhi provides the perfect example of

someone who was never afraid to change an opinion. Most people remember Gandhi as the man who led India to independence from British dominion without ever resorting to violence. But in his earlier days he supported the British Empire, and even went so far as to recruit an ambulance corps for the British army in the First World War. When asked about these inconsistencies later, he used to reply simply, "That was how I saw things then." No defensiveness, no apologies. He had learned to identify himself, not with his attitudes or opinions, but with the Self. When we have this kind of detachment, it can save us a great deal of wasted turmoil over opinions we may have held or mistakes we may have committed in the past.

That

IF YOU EVER find yourself in a dilemma over whether to call the Lord "he" or "she," you can always get out of it by saying "That," which is a word without any gender at all. *Tat* is neither he nor she; it simply points.

Gender is a property of the body, which is a very temporary affair. The supreme reality, your real Self and mine, has no sex. It is masculine and feminine together, and at the same time it is beyond both. When we worship God as Father or Mother or Beloved, we are simply wrapping reality in a particular form that speaks to our love and longing. It may not be logically defensible, but logic is not what moves our lives.

In the Upanishads we find the great statement *Tat tvam asi,* "You are that": that subtle essence of all things, that supreme being in the depths of consciousness. Entering these depths in meditation, in fact, is the only way this reality can be known. It cannot be expressed in words. As the Taittiriya Upanishad says, "Words and thoughts turn back, unable to attain That." Words cannot even get close to that door. Thoughts get farther, try to walk through, but then the mind becomes completely still and thoughts disappear.

Sri Ramakrishna used to illustrate this with a marvelous story about a doll made of salt. The doll went to measure the depth of the sea, but as soon as it entered the water it dissolved and became one with the sea. This is what happens in *samadhi,* the final union with the Lord that is the culmination of all spiritual effort. When the senses are stilled, when the mind is still, when the intellect does not waver, that is the supreme state called yoga or samadhi. Then we see the vision of God, the "face behind all faces," and we know beyond doubt that we live in God and that he lives in us.

In that state, the little "I" that we identify with today is no longer there; so the Self can shine forth in full glory. After samadhi, we keep what Ramakrishna called a "ripe I" – ripe like a fruit that barely stays attached to the tree. That trace sense of "I" is necessary for relating to others with love and compassion; without it, the unitive state can be rather impersonal. But the "ripe I" never really believes itself to be separate from the rest of life, so it can do no harm.

AMURTI

Who Has No Form

THIS IS A rather strange-sounding name for a deity, but the supreme reality has no form. In our modern civilization, with its constant emphasis on the physical, it is difficult for us to imagine even for a moment that we are not physical creatures. But our real Self is not material; it can have no shape.

At the same time, we should never forget that the same reality takes various forms in the eyes of its devotees. Mira, our beloved medieval saint and poet, looks at the Godhead and her loving heart sees Krishna; Saint Teresa of Avila looks at the same Godhead and sees Christ. Both see truly, yet no one can ever see the whole truth: God is formless and has taken infinite forms as well; he is above all distinctions of form and formlessness too.

Here is Sri Ramakrishna's reply to the question of whether God has form or not:

> Think of God as a shoreless ocean. Through the cooling influence, as it were, of the devotee's love, the water has frozen at places into blocks of ice. In other words, God assumes various forms for his lovers and reveals himself

to them as a Person. But with the rising of the sun of knowledge, the blocks of ice melt. Then one doesn't feel any more that God is a Person, nor does one see God's forms.

The Immortal Craftsman

THIS IS ONE of the Lord's more obscure names, but it has a good pedigree: it dates back to the Vedas, India's most ancient scriptures, which in their oral form may date back five thousand years. In the Vedas, Tvashta is a sort of divine craftsman who makes all kinds of wonderful things, especially tools, for the gods. He is also a great builder.

Recently I went to attend the housewarming of a good friend of ours, whose unusual new house other friends had helped to build. I felt pleased to say, "Yes, it was Victor who built all those cabinets; Jeff won some kind of award for the design." But imagine if I had tried to maintain that that house was not built by anyone in particular; it just happened. Some tremendous storm must have felled the trees, and by curious accident lightning split them into two-by-fours. Then a great earthquake might have shaken the timbers together into the form of a house. "Powerful coincidence." The house was built not by design but by a wonderful coming together of various forces.

This sounds silly, of course, yet it is not that different

from the language of some scientific accounts of creation. When I hear someone say, "Oh, there is no 'supreme reality'; there is no one responsible for this universe," I feel a little amused. The Lord is the architect, the builder, and the building too – but not some cosmic being outside it all; he designs and builds and guides from within. This point of view is quite tenable on scientific terms, and in fact physics and cosmology today have taken on a tone of awe in the face of the mysteries of creation.

ANAGHA

Free from Sorrow

SANSKRIT OFTEN describes perfection by
saying what a thing is *not,* the way English uses words
like "flawless." This is especially useful when talking
about the supreme reality, which is beyond description.
The Upanishads use the formula *neti, neti,* "not this, not
that," to remind us that anything within mundane experience falls far short of the divine.

Anagha, "without sorrow or evil," is one such name,
negative in form but wholly positive in meaning. Human
experience is often touched by sorrow, but union with
the Lord means direct experience of a state of mind
beyond all personal suffering. This does not mean that
the man or woman who has realized God never knows
pain. To realize God is to see yourself in all creatures,
which means that you feel their sorrows as your own.
But you no longer grieve over any problems of your
own, and beneath everything else there flows through
consciousness a permanent current of joy which sustains you in the face of pain and tragedy.

"A certain amount of pain in life is unavoidable," my
grandmother used to tell me, "but why bring in any that

you can avoid?" Whenever she said things like this, I knew she was talking from personal experience, and I believed her. Yet for a long time I had difficulty putting this faith into practice.

On the physical level it is easy to understand when someone gives us directions in life. If I tell you that you can get to the bank by going down this road and turning right, you wouldn't turn left; nobody would. But when the scriptures say, "Don't take that road; it won't take you to the bank but to bankruptcy," we often can't seem to understand. Pain, sorrow, and suffering are often guideposts on the road of life, reminding us that the road we have chosen is not taking us where we want to go.

All religions tell us not to follow self-will, the seductive road of strictly private satisfaction. But often what we desire covers our eyes and plugs our ears; we cannot understand. Then the suffering that self-will entails can act like a highway warning sign – "Turn Back! Wrong Way" – prompting us back to the road that leads to the end of sorrow.

He Who Nips Wrong Actions in the Bud

DUSHKRITI IS "wrong actions," from the same root as the word *karma*. As the Compassionate Buddha says succinctly, we get in life what we work for. If we ride roughshod over other people's feelings, for example, we are bound to alienate those we live and work with, which means that after a while they are likely to start riding roughshod over us. There is nothing unfair about the law of karma, and no outside agent is required. We reap just what we sow.

Help comes when we ask the Lord – our real Self – from the bottom of our heart, "I am a victim of my own habits; I want to change, but I've been conditioned to act this way all my life. What can I do to save myself from the bad karma I have been accumulating?" The answer the Gita gives is that our selfish conditioning begins to fall away when we learn to put others first and to return sympathy for resentment and love for hatred. Putting others first quickly dissolves the conditioning of selfish habits, even if they have been entrenched for many years. When we can do this, it means we are learning the lesson which our bad karma had to teach. The purpose of karma is not punitive; it is educational. When we forget ourselves completely in love of the Lord, the nexus with karma is cut. That is why Sri Krishna assures us in the Gita:

> Be aware of me always, adore me,
> Make every act an offering to me,
> And you shall come to me. This I promise,
> For you are dear to me.
> Abandon all supports, and look to me alone
> For protection. I will purify you
> Of the sins of the past; do not grieve.

The Purifier

JUST AS SUNLIGHT purifies running water, the name of the Lord purifies the mind. When you drink polluted water, you are liable to develop ailments from dysentery to heavy metal poisoning. People are beginning to wake up to the danger this problem poses to the whole globe, but almost nobody seems to be aware that a polluted mental environment can cause even greater disasters. When we don't take the trouble to purify our own mind – and, I might add, the mental environment of our society – infective agents like anger, hostility, lust, and greed can spread before we realize what is happening.

Thought-infection is passed by the way we act and the way we speak, and nothing spreads it faster than the mass media. Our magazines and movies, our radio and television shows and popular music, are an environment almost as pervasive as the air we breathe, and the attitudes and ideas with which they saturate us do not often add to the quality of life.

Repeating the Holy Name works like one of those sweepers you see floating in swimming pools, moving slowly around with their long tentacles while they suck up leaves and other debris. We are so mechanically oriented that because the mantram doesn't have tubes and a suction motor, we think it cannot be of much use. But the name of the Lord is a miraculously powerful purifier. If you just keep it circulating around and around, it will clean up the muck of the mind even while you sleep.

We should make use of this potent device on every possible opportunity. While you are riding in a car, waiting in a restaurant, washing dishes, or falling asleep, the Holy Name can be busy. When you are angry, afraid, or caught in an emotional crossfire, you can use its purifying power right on the spot. I can tell you from personal experience that even after repeating the mantram for many years, I still find more opportunities for repeating it. With the mantram, you can use every bit and piece of spare time for spiritual growth.

There is no mystery about this purifying power. The mind has to go on thinking, and what the Buddha calls mental impurities – conditioned trains of thought – are just the mind getting caught in the same thought over and over and over. The mantram breaks up these thoughts and absorbs them, restoring consciousness to a state of calm. If you cannot dwell on anger, for example, it cannot last; the thoughts dissipate and disappear without leaving any emotional residue behind.

Anger *is* dwelling on negative thoughts, nothing more.

When we hold a grudge, some part of our mind is repeating over and over a particular incident which infuriated us. We say, "I can't concentrate today," or "I'm having trouble relating to people." The reason is that part of our mind is not there. The Buddha, one of the world's most penetrating psychologists, tells us that whatever we are doing, we should be totally there with a completely one-pointed, wholly integrated mind. When your mind is all in one place, you cannot get frustrated or impatient; you cannot feel restless, inadequate, or afraid.

A fast mind is always divided. So is a mind that is forced to do two or more things at once – as, for example, reading and eating at the same time. And of course the mind is divided when part of it is brooding on the past or future, which happens much more often than we may be aware. Whenever you catch yourself getting speeded up, caught in the past, or doing two things at once, repeat the mantram. That will help you to slow down and do one thing at a time, with all your mind here in the present. This is the capacity of genius, and the secret of being fully, vitally alive.

The Energy of Life

ACCORDING TO THE Upanishads, our real Self is covered by five layers of consciousness called *koshas,* which literally means "sheaths." Identifying ourselves with these sheaths is no more accurate than identifying ourselves with a favorite turtleneck or parka.

The outermost kosha is the body, which can be compared to a heavy overcoat that we might wear on a stormy day. This is a clumsy covering which often gets in our way, but after all, it is difficult to function without it. In this context the body is called *annamaya-kosha,* "the jacket made of food." Very precise, very scientific: that is all the body is.

The other four sheaths, roughly speaking, correspond to what we call in English "the mind." One of these in particular gives the significance of this name of God. Just "inside" the body, so to speak, is the sheath that provides the interface between body and mind. It is called *pranamaya-kosha,* "the jacket made of *prana.*"

Prana is energy in its purest, irreducible form; all the kinds of energy that physicists measure, such as light, are particular expressions of prana. In the body, prana is the energy of life, the substrate of all the kinds of energy that sustain the body and mind.

The body, therefore, can be looked on as a container of vital energy, like one of those oxygen cylinders you see at hospitals. Each of us has a built-in prana cylinder, and it is the level of our prana that largely determines the quality of our daily life. This cylinder generally gets depleted as we grow older, but chronological age is not what counts most. When Gandhi was in his seventies he could work fifteen hours a day every day of the week; he needed only a few hours of sleep. At an age when many people worry about balancing their checkbook, Gandhi was able to attend with clarity and compassion to decisions that changed the lives of millions of people – and of course he never even thought of retiring.

Millions of people begin to lose mental and physical faculties when they grow old, not so much because their vital organs are unable to function but because they have run out of gas – prana. You may have a Porsche in excellent condition, but if you don't have any gas in the tank, it cannot run. Prana is the gas that runs this little car that is the body and its engine, the mind, and one of the most important skills anyone can learn is how not to run out of gas.

Essentially this comes down to conservation. There are many ways to conserve prana, and one of the most effective is by training the senses. The five senses – taste, sight, and so on – can be trained just as puppies can, so that when they feel drawn to something we do not approve, we can simply say "Come back" and they will respond. This is not denying the senses, but making them trustworthy servants.

Take the most basic example: food. Many people today are very nutrition-conscious and want to eat only what will make them healthy and strong. So it is very important to train your sense of taste to enjoy what is good for the body and adds to its prana, its vitality, instead of detracting from it. If your taste buds clamor for heavily salted foods with a lot of fat and sugar, you can actually teach them to like good food instead.

To take my own small experience, I was brought up on a very different kind of cuisine in South India, and I must confess to you that Indian food is not always the best; often it is too highly spiced and not very nutritious. Today I eat the very best food in the world. We have our own garden and greenhouse, and we eat garden-fresh vegetables every day. We use little salt, few spices, oil only sparingly, and no sugar to speak of. This is a complete reversal of my likes and dislikes. I have seen Indian friends shudder involuntarily when I describe what I eat; they cannot believe I am still going strong. I just explain, "I have taught my palate to like what I want it to." Taste lies in the mind. To me, my meals taste better than anything I could get in a gourmet restaurant. I enjoy a fresh salad because I know it is good for my body, and because it is prepared for me with loving care.

Eating the right food, then, plays an important role in building up our prana. So does right exercise. I go to the beach every day for a long walk, and it is not just an austere exercise. I enjoy the music of the sea, the roll of the waves, the seagulls flying overhead and the sandpipers scurrying along the curl of the tide. That is what the Buddha would call "right enjoyment": taking pleasure in activities that bring health to the body and peace to the mind.

All of our senses can be trained. It is not just a matter of right food and right exercise. In the Upanishads there is a beautiful prayer: "May my eyes always see what is good. May my ears always hear what is good. May my mouth always speak what is good." We eat not only with the mouth but with all our senses; they are constantly taking in what lies around them, and what they take in, we become.

Just as the body is made of food, the mind is made of the sense impressions it takes in. And just as there is junk food, there are junk experiences and junk thoughts – attractively packaged, but most debilitating for the mind. Training the senses means that we need to be discriminating about what shows we watch, what music we listen to, what kinds of books and magazines we read, what kind of conversation we listen to. Every day the senses give the mind a ten-course dinner, and we can add to our prana, our health and vitality, by not serving it junk thoughts.

Beyond Thought

A GREAT WESTERN mystical document, *The Cloud of Unknowing*, sums up all that really must be said on this subject when it declares, "By love God can be gotten and holden; by thought, never."

In my book of life, love can be learned by anybody. If someone is not able to love, all I say is, "Come and learn." That is the purpose of meditation.

Learning to love requires denying your self-will often, because love means putting the needs of others in your life before your own personal desires. It is not just that we should remember the needs of our family; love is more than just affection for one or two people. Einstein once wrote that only "by widening our circle of compassion" will we find a way out of the violence, mistrust, and exploitation that we see all around us today.

One of the great ironies of life is the fact that to understand love we have to go, not to men and women of the world, but to those who have risen above the narrow, possessive relationships we take to be normal. Can the Lord play a bigger joke? It is people like Francis of Assisi and Teresa of Avila who can teach us how to be steadfast in love, how to nurture our compassion so that it can enrich the lives of those around us.

Who Has All the Weapons of Battle

THIS NAME IS quite a mouthful, but well worth the effort when understood. When we love the Lord with all our heart, he gives us every weapon we need to fight the war within.

Our enemies in this war, the Bhagavad Gita tells us, are ultimately three: anger, fear, and selfish desire. And the most basic of the three is selfish desire, which stands for all compulsive cravings. This is essentially an expression of self-will, the compulsive drive to get what we want whatever it may cost others. Nothing stands between us and the Lord, the mystics say, except selfish desires and self-will.

Compulsive desires are like a net. We are like fish, Sri Ramakrishna used to say, caught in a net of desire, and our driving need is to escape. Unfortunately, we often feel we *like* nets. Yet every time we yield to a compulsive desire, we tighten the net a little more.

Sometimes, when I try to untie my shoelace, I only succeed in knotting it tighter. The more I pull, the more impossible it gets. That is what we are doing when we give in to a sensory urge or self-centered desire. Meditation is the undoing of knots, and indulgence only ties them tighter.

As a boy, if I gave in to a desire when I should have said no, my grandmother would say quietly, "Have you forgotten what happened the last time? Now you have to go through that all over again." Those words always struck a responsive chord. I didn't want to have to go through the same situation and its consequences over and over and over. I didn't want to tie the knot of desire any tighter than it already was.

As Spinoza would say, most people mistake desires to be decisions. The practice of meditation can enable us to have freedom of choice where desires are concerned. To right desires we yield, but wrong desires we resist, generating power that can enrich the immune system.

RAKSHANA

Protector

LIFE IS NOT given to us for grabbing what we can; it is meant for giving what we can. When we appreciate that this precious human birth has been given to us for making a lasting contribution to the rest of life, we get continuing motivation to keep our mind and body at their best. Nothing can provide a better shield. For some ineluctable reason, life seems to take care of those it cannot afford to lose. Even medically, a growing body of research suggests that living for a purpose greater than oneself probably strengthens the body's healing systems greatly.

AMRITA-ASHA
Who Enjoys the Nectar of Immortality

THE GOLDEN NECTAR that makes the gods immortal is called *amrita* in Sanskrit. This nectar was churned from the cosmic ocean at the beginning of time. But Krishna doesn't keep this ambrosia all to himself; he wants to share it with us.

The Lord has one great personal desire which haunts him day and night: that you and I should rise above our narrow personal conditioning and be united with him eternally. He is perfect and fulfilled, yet here he is pining away for us, and what do we do but keep him waiting.

SRI

Beauty

THE SYLLABLE *sri* is an extraordinarily auspicious one in the Hindu tradition. When we refer to Krishna we say "Sri Krishna"; when we talk about the Bhagavad Gita, we say "Srimad Bhagavad Gita." Those who attain a high level of spiritual awareness often have *Sri* or *Srimati* attached to their name like this, as a mark of reverence and affection. This is the democratic aspect of mysticism: all of us deserve this title if we grow tall enough to claim our spiritual legacy.

It is not possible to capture all the manifold aspects of our innate glory that this one small word implies. Its root sense is to diffuse light. *Sri* essentially means beauty – not merely physical beauty but spiritual effulgence, "the imprisoned splendor," as Browning says, which shines through the physical form of those whose hearts are pure.

In the Gita, *sri* is considered a feminine quality. The supreme reality can be regarded as having two aspects, and in Hindu thought the masculine aspect of God is considered passive, never involved in the world. It is the feminine aspect, the creative power of the Lord, that is worshipped as the Divine Mother. The auspicious, benevolent side of this creative power is often called Sri. She is personified as the radiantly lovely consort of Vishnu, shining with precious jewelry and iridescent silks, the abundant bestower of all that the word *sri* stands for: beauty, prosperity, good fortune, glory, majesty, and protective power.

Growing up in an ancient matrilineal tradition, where women have held land and legal rights for centuries, I absorbed the deeper meaning of this word *sri* very early. My grandmother had lofty standards of what a woman should be, and when a man in our family brought home a bride, Granny would watch her very closely to see her character. It wasn't easy to win praise from her, but two or three times I remember her saying with deep approval, "That girl has *sri* in her face." You couldn't ask for a higher tribute.

Whenever a man and a woman live together in harmony, cooperating with affection instead of competing, they become established in the permanent romantic relationship represented by *sri*. The question of sexual relations is entirely secondary; what all of us seek is spiritual union. In this supreme secret of *sri* we will find the fulfillment of all our desires. So *sri* has another connotation: that which is divine.

Ornament

WHEN WE FOLLOW in the footsteps of the mystics in molding our lives, we add beauty to the world and become an ornament for all. The halo behind the head of the saints is a symbolic depiction of what happens to a person who has lost all selfishness and shines with love for all. It is quite possible for this to happen in our own life. Just as we feel a great thrill on seeing our son or daughter after a long separation, we feel thrilled to see any living creature when we see the Lord within.

One of the phrases that mystifies me today is "the beautiful people." Beautiful people hang out in certain trendy places, drive certain kinds of cars, have certain slightly decadent habits. And, of course, they are young. Those seem to be the primary qualifications. That beauty is limited to a certain age range – say, eighteen to thirty-nine – to say nothing of tying it to the size of one's bank account, is one of the most monstrous superstitions of our times. This is not being beautiful; it is being silly.

Some people today get offended if they can't fool people into thinking that they fit this golden category. If they are forty, they want to look thirty; if their face shows the lines of experience, they may pay thousands of dollars to get the lines erased. This name suggests a very different perspective. If you are forty and have learned something from experience, you are a much greater asset to life than you were when you were a teenager. Your face should show what you have learned; that is what it means to be beautiful at forty.

There is a beauty appropriate to every age, and to try to appropriate the kind of beauty that belongs to a different age is not only unattractive but foolish. "You are wise enough to be fifty-five" should be a thrilling compliment. We can grow in beauty until the last day of our life, and the desire to look on everyone as kith and kin will draw people to us for the beauty of our lives.

Destroyer of Sorrow

WHEN WE ARE inconsiderate to people, even unwittingly, we are adding to their sorrow. When we refuse to go out of our way to help lift another's burden, their burden becomes that much harder to bear. This is being just the opposite of beautiful. The Lord is not likely to lift a finger to help such people if they turn to him for help; he expects us to draw his help by learning to help others.

When this lesson is learned, however, we begin to see that our own sorrow too is being wiped from the slate of life. When we forget our personal profit and pleasure in living for others, personal sorrow too will be destroyed – not only for the moment, but once and for all.

"I will give you a talisman," promises Mahatma Gandhi: "when you are in doubt or when the self becomes too much with you, try the following expedient. Recall the face of the poorest and the most helpless man whom you have seen and ask yourself if the step you are contemplating is going to be of any use to him. Will he be able to gain anything by it? Will it restore him to a control over his own life and destiny?"

KAVI

The Poet

WHOEVER MADE THIS world must be a great artist. That is the only reasonable conclusion one can draw from observing the beauty and unity that pervades creation. Go to a fresh produce stand and look at the deep wine-red of the cherries, the rich shades of the peaches, the glow of apples in autumn or of fresh-picked August corn. For those with eyes to see, the plainest wildflower not only shows the handiwork of the Lord, it shines with his very glory. The Lord has said, "I will live in this flower." It may be for only a few days, as in the lilacs outside our kitchen window, but he is there. Wordsworth reflects on how the ocean's sound may be heard in a seashell and declares,

> Even such a shell the universe itself
> Is to the ear of Faith; and there are times,
> I doubt not, when to you it doth impart
> Authentic tidings of invisible things;
> Of ebb and flow, and ever-enduring power;
> And central peace, subsisting at the heart
> Of endless agitation.

In one of her "revelations of divine love," the simple fourteenth-century English mystic Julian of Norwich describes how the Lord

> showed me a little thing, the quantity of an hazel-nut, in the palm of my hand. . . . I looked thereupon with the eye of my understanding, and thought: What may this be? And it was answered generally thus: It is all that is made. I marveled how it might last, for methought it might suddenly have fallen to naught for littleness. And I was answered in my understanding: It lasteth, and ever shall, for that God loveth it.

It is only because we are so preoccupied with ourselves that we do not see the Lord in the commonplace things around us.

"In this little thing," Dame Julian adds significantly,

> I saw three properties. The first is that God made it, the second that God loveth it, the third that God keepeth it. But what is to me verily the Maker, the Keeper, and the Lover – I cannot tell; for till I am substantially oned to him, I may never have full rest nor very bliss: that is to say, till I be so fastened to him that there is right nought that is made betwixt my God and me.

Those are very wise words. If we wonder at the beauty of the Lord's creation, how much more wonderful must be the divine source of that beauty, who is beauty infinite.

Holder of the Wheel of the Cosmos

IN DEVOTIONAL portraits, Vishnu is often represented as standing casually with one finger of a right hand held up as if pointing to the sky. On the tip of that finger, perfectly balanced, whirls the disk of the cosmos, called *chakra* in Sanskrit. As the gospel song puts it, "He's got the whole world in his hands."

In the *Mahabharata,* Vishnu's disk is referred to by a name that later passed into Buddhism: *dharma-chakra,* the wheel of dharma, the supreme law of existence which holds that all of life is one. Everything in this vast universe of ours is held together in this embrace of unity.

Realizing the divine unity of life brings a state of abiding joy. Most of us have tasted the joy that comes with loving one or two people. That joy is multiplied a million times when we love all around us. But this does not mean we become blind to suffering. As sensitiveness increases, your awareness of others' sorrow cannot help growing more acute. Famine in Africa, a ruinous earthquake in Latin America, war in the Middle East, will not be just headline stories; they will be tragedies happening to *you*, to your own family. The millions of children – thousands of them even in this country, the most affluent on earth – who do not have enough to eat, who will never go to school or get medical care or even lead a reasonably comfortable life, will be always on your mind. But this awareness is not a burden. It releases compassion, creative resources, and a limitless motivation for doing everything you can to help, and in that effort to relieve suffering there is more joy than the world knows.

Despite all the media talk of economic strength today, there are ominous signs that even in our United States the proportion of people living in poverty is rising. Tragically, most are women, children, and the aged, just those whom a civilized society would try to protect. Realizing the unity of life means a living awareness every moment that wherever they may live, these are *our* children, our parents and grandparents.

Most of us would feel ashamed to spend our time and money lavishly on trivial pursuits if someone in our own home did not have enough to eat. The mystics would say, "There are millions in your own home who do not have enough to eat. Every minute a child is dying next door." If you want to do something to help, you can begin by not being wasteful of the resources of the earth – its food, air, water, and soil, its trees and fuels. "There is enough on earth for everybody's need," Gandhi said, "but there is not enough for everybody's greed."

All life is part of us. This deepest of convictions can turn the most ordinary human being into a powerful force for unity.

Wielder of the Mace

IN HIS SECOND hand Vishnu holds a *gada,* a mace or club. This is a not so gentle reminder of the Lord's power, to remind us that he rules us from within. He is the Lawgiver and he is the Law.

Many years ago I referred to this supreme law of life in a talk I gave on meditation to some hard-headed Kaiser Aluminum executives in Oakland. After I finished, one of these men came up and said, "You know, we Americans are scientifically minded, and it goes against the grain when you talk about spiritual 'laws.' These are just beliefs, and we Westerners don't necessarily subscribe to them. Shouldn't you say something vaguer, like 'spiritual principles'?"

I motioned him over to a big plate-glass window where we could look down from the Kaiser building onto Lake Merritt, hundreds of feet below. "Would you like to see something spectacular?" I asked. "I'm going to soar out of this window and take a spin around the lake."

"Don't do it!" he said, grabbing my arm in alarm. "Haven't you heard of the law of gravity?"

"I've heard of it," I agreed, "but I don't subscribe to it, so it has no effect on me. After all, it's not a *Hindu* law."

"Whether you believe in it or not," he retorted, "the law of gravity works."

"Similarly," I said, "whether anyone believes in it or not, the law of unity works. If you live in harmony with it, it will support you. But just as with gravity, if you go against it, you have to expect some painful, predictable consequences."

The fact that all of life is one means that everything is interconnected, from the world of things to the worlds of thought. Everything we do or say or even think has consequences, good or bad, according to whether we have acted in harmony with the rest of life or at odds with it. When we act in such a way that others benefit from it, we ourselves reap some of the benefit, for we are part of the whole. But if we do something at cost to others, we reap some of the costs ourselves as well. Put bluntly, selfish behavior has painful consequences – if not immediately, then in the fullness of time.

In our contemporary scientific climate, however, it is worth stressing that this punishment is not meted out by some external Lawgiver. Vishnu, "the all-pervasive," is within us, and when we suffer the consequences of self-ish behavior – emotional problems, estrangement, alien-ation, ill health – we are punishing ourselves. Without this painful aspect of the unity of life, unfortunately, few of us would grow. It is not much of a compliment to human nature, but most of us do not learn from pleasure; we learn from making mistakes and suffering the consequences.

In fairness, the conditioning of pleasure and personal satisfaction is so strong that without making mistakes and learning from them, I think very few human beings can be expected to understand where selfish desires lead. The tragedy is not our making mistakes, but making mistakes without learning from them. Suffering is a simple guidepost on the road of life, meant to keep us from running into a disastrous end.

All religions teach the same lesson: do not follow self-will; it will only lead to sorrow. When we live largely for ourselves, life itself will ensure that we get increasing insecurity, ill health, and loneliness.

Today, with our psychological orientation, we may want to object, "But that's not fair! We have been conditioned since infancy to try to satisfy personal desires. Do we have to suffer the consequences of unconscious drives over which we have no control?"

Here we see the Lord's infinite compassion. On the one hand, he says, a law is a law. Selfish behavior has to have consequences. We have to understand and accept that, just as when we let go of a ball in midair, we know it has to fall. Yet despite this, we *do* have a choice in how we act; that is what it means to be human. The burden of selfish conditioning, which everyone bears to some measure, begins to fall away when we heed the signposts of suffering and live for others rather than for ourselves. In this way we learn the lesson which suffering has to teach. Once this lesson is learned completely, the Hindu scriptures say, it serves no further purpose. Suffering is an educational tool, a learning device. When we realize the unity of life, personal suffering comes to an end.

Who Carries a Conch

IN HIS THIRD hand Lord Vishnu holds a conch, which is blown at the time of worship in Hindu temples. Its long, drawn-out cry is a rough reminder of the sound *Aum* or *Om,* referred to in the Upanishads as the cosmic sound. This is not a sound heard by the ear but a transcendent experience of the creative power of the Godhead, of which *Om* is only a limited symbol. Christian mystics too have called this creative power the Logos or divine Word. The Rig Veda says, in terms strikingly echoed by the Gospel According to John: "In the beginning was the Creator, with whom was the Word, and the Word was verily the Supreme."

But the conch has another association also: in ancient India it was blown to rally soldiers to battle. The Bhagavad Gita opens on such a scene, when the "field of righteousness" echoes with the trumpeting of war elephants and the wail of huge conchs from the massed forces of good and evil.

This is a perfect metaphor, for as Gandhi says, this battle takes place inside. The battlefield is each individual heart. In every one of us two forces are at work. One flows toward love, selflessness, happiness, and spiritual fulfillment. The other pulls us back toward our evolutionary past: toward anger, violence, lust, greed, and selfishness.

The force for goodness can never be eradicated, the scriptures tell us; it is the underlying reality of life. So this battle is unavoidable as long as there is selfishness in the mind. We may not be aware of it, but the conflict cannot help going on below the conscious level. Nothing can free us from its stress and turmoil except to face our selfishness squarely and put it to an end.

Bearer of the Lotus

THE FOURTH AND last symbol in Vishnu's hands is the lotus. This most beautiful of flowers is the perfect symbol of the feminine aspect of the Lord that we call Lakshmi or Sri. Vishnu and Lakshmi are not two but one, and in most depictions of Vishnu he is accompanied by his consort, "the Lotus Goddess." When Vishnu reclines upon the cosmic serpent Shesha, Lakshmi rests by his side; and when he is born on earth to rescue us, Lakshmi too takes human form to accompany him as his beautiful lady.

There is practical wisdom in these images and stories, for where man and woman live in harmony, the whole family benefits. Man and woman are not made to compete with each other but to complete each other. Vishnu and Lakshmi, the eternal male principle and the eternal female principle, are not really two; they are one and inseparable. This is an urgently practical reminder today, when man and woman are drifting farther and farther apart.

Wherever two people bring out the best in each other, that relationship is blessed by Lakshmi, the goddess of beauty. Beauty will shine from their eyes and in their lives. This is the real secret of beauty, but no one would suspect it from popular culture. Everywhere the message is that beauty is only skin deep and attractiveness a matter of chemistry.

The perfume industry specializes in this kind of propaganda. They come up with such exotic names that I wonder if they take themselves seriously. What is attractive about a name like Obsession? Nothing you can put on your skin can be as alluring as a loving heart and an unselfish mind; these are qualities that entrance everyone. We trust such people and long to spend more time with them. When they go away, as the Buddha says, they leave a fragrance of goodness no one can forget.

Maker & Destroyer of Fear

LAW AND COMPASSION, two sides of the Lord, come together in these two names.

On the one hand the Lord is *Bhayakrit,* "maker of fear." As the Bible says, "Fear of the Lord is the beginning of wisdom." Unkind words, unkind thoughts, and of course unkind actions should bring fear to our hearts because they set in motion the law of karma – "As ye sow, so shall ye reap" – to bring that unkindness back to our own doorstep.

But the Lord is also *Bhayanashana,* "the destroyer of fear." If we give him all our love he will remove our fears, because in such love all selfishness is dissolved.

The Upanishads say pithily, "Those who see all creatures in themselves and themselves in all creatures know no fear." The idea that each of us is separate from the rest is the very source of fear. "When there is no other," the Upanishads ask, "with whom can I be angry? Of whom can I be afraid?"

In South India, where I grew up, two things brought fear to almost every heart: snakes and ghosts. Each village had at least one ghost, and Kerala's lush climate is as pleasant for snakes as it is for less fearsome creatures. Some of these snakes are harmless, but several are so poisonous that death can come in minutes. A rationalist might laugh at the fear of ghosts, but I would venture to say that no one from South India, however well educated, walks about in the countryside without the fear of snakes somewhere at the back of his mind.

This danger is especially real at dusk, for that is the time when snakes like to come out and enjoy the evening, just like everybody else, and in the fading sunlight it is difficult to see. At such times anyone can be excused if he suddenly jumps and cries out in fear to avoid what turns out to be only a stick or vine or piece of rope lying beside the path.

Shankara, who came from my same state of Kerala in South India, drew on such experiences to illustrate the nature of separateness and fear. When a villager sees a snake where there is only a rope, superimposing his ideas of snakeness on what he actually perceives, his fright is very real. His heart pounds and adrenaline courses through his body just as if a living cobra lay across his path. What causes that fear? Not a snake, Shankara implies, but the idea of it in the mind.

In just the same way, we often impose our fears on an innocent world. The more separate we feel from the rest of life, the more threatening it seems. Ironically, if we act threatened, we may provoke an aggressive response that seems to confirm our fears. All this falls away as meditation deepens. Your eyes clear, and you see that what you had been afraid of was a projection of your own state of mind.

Answerer of Prayers

ONE OF THE most frequent incidents in Hindu mythology is for someone to sit down in profound meditation until the Lord appears to grant a boon. This is a vivid way of reminding us that every strong desire is a prayer. When we have a powerful desire that we can't forget, we are meditating on that desire, actually praying for it to be fulfilled. In time, the very depth of that desire will release the deeper resources to bring it within our reach.

There is nothing occult about this; it is simply the dynamics of desire. When someone is haunted by the desire to make money, for example, that desire focuses all his will and drive and attention. The very intensity of that focus will release creative schemes for extracting wealth in ways the rest of us may never see.

The irony, of course, is that getting your wishes granted is not necessarily the way to become happy. I think the Greeks had a saying that when the gods want to punish us, they grant us our desires. The Buddha would feel quite at home with that statement. We need no god to punish or reward us, he would say; the natural consequences of our actions are their own punishment or reward.

Often we do not realize how our pursuit of personal desires affects other people. We think it's only our own concern. In fact, even desires for little things can have far-reaching effects. From a spiritual perspective, the underlying cause of industrial pollution is desire. Our economy turns out immense quantities of things that are neither useful nor beneficial, for the simple reason that there is money in selling them. Such an economy cannot stop when people have enough; it depends on their feeling that they never have enough. Every day, in the fear that normal human desires might be flagging, many thousands of dollars are spent in whipping up desires for things we may never have heard of, things we may not even know what to do with when they are delivered to our door.

The hazards of pollution, I would say, are part of the stiff penalty we have to pay as a society for letting our desires get out of hand – for what the Pope, in a telling phrase, calls "the frenzy of consumerism." And the responsibility belongs not only to the manufacturers. They only make what they can sell. We do the buying. If we do not buy things we don't need, they will not be produced. That will be bad for big businesses, at least initially, but it will be very good for the health of our children.

The technologists' dream is that someday they will find a way to go on increasing industrial production without such annoying side effects as toxic waste. Either they will discover new ways of mass production that are safe and clean, or they will invent new ways of disposing of byproducts that are hazardous – for example, by shooting them into outer space. Both these sound a little like the age-old desire to get what one wants without paying for it. Even if it could be accomplished, I have trouble imagining an economy that goes on growing endlessly through the increasing consumption of goods and services no one needs.

No technological shortcut is likely to solve the problem of pollution, because the source of the problem is not physical. It lies in our way of living, which in turn reflects our ways of thinking: the desires, aspirations, and values on which we act. If toxic wastes are a problem of overproduction, then I would say the real problem is overconsumption – and to reduce overconsumption, the people to look to are not the politicians or business executives but the consumers themselves, people like you and me.

When I go to a shopping mall, I am astounded to see how many people do not come to get something specific that they need; they come to see what is available that they might want. They walk in asking, "Well, tempt me. I've got time on my hands and money in my pocket; what have you got for me to spend it on?" And the stores reply, "How about a watch that plays video games? A bathroom scale that tells your weight in a simulated human voice? A household robot to serve you breakfast in bed? How about a selection of twenty variations on an unnecessary item which you already have?" Instead of feeling insulted by this kind of approach, we respond in such numbers that new malls spring up every year.

Buying things cannot appease desires. It only feeds the habit of desiring, until we are chronically unable to be satisfied with what we have. Eventually we find ourselves in a state of free-floating frustration, always wanting something more, never content with what we get.

Let me make myself clear: I am not advocating austerity or a poverty-level lifestyle. I am pleading for a middle path between austerity and excess – in a word, for an artistic simplicity, where personal desires are few and a reasonable number of things are sufficient for us to live in comfort, happiness, and good health.

This is not merely a matter of keeping physical possessions to a minimum. What is much more important is keeping personal desires to a minimum, and to a reasonable size. In other words, besides the external environment, we live in an internal environment as well. It is vital to clean up our air and water and soil, but it is just as vital to purify our internal environment, because it is our thoughts and desires that will shape our future actions – not only as individuals, but as a society.

Giver of Wealth

JUST AS DIOXIN or vinyl chloride seeps into the soil to pollute water and food, mental toxic wastes like greed, the lust of possession, seep into the mind from our sensory environment and gradually poison our actions. In magazines and newspapers, on television and radio, in popular songs, we are told every day how wonderful life will be when we own certain things or have certain experiences for ourselves.

The desire for wealth is the most obvious kind of greed, and I see it played up everywhere. I think it was G. K. Chesterton who warned that currency is graven images. We haven't lost religion, he says; we have simply substituted money for God. The great banks are cathedrals to money; the stock exchange is a temple. When friends once took me to a brokerage house, the lofty ceilings, hushed tones, and air of reverence made me feel as if I were intruding on a sanctuary. Market quotations flickered across the wall like a continuous prayer, invoking bulls to protect against the bears. When the Dow went up, it lifted worshippers into an exalted state of mind; when it fell, they slipped into depression. In ancient times, devotees inhaled the smoke of burning laurel leaves or drank soma to alter states of consciousness; today we need only a digital display.

The desires of a society are a very important educational influence, more so even than the curricula of its schools. Nobody escapes this influence. It is, perhaps, the primary way in which we raise the next generation. And what are we teaching? To judge from the way we spend our time and money, from what we read and talk about and pay most attention to, an impartial observer from another planet would conclude that the things in life we find most important are pleasure and profit. Few people would come out and say it, and I think few truly desire it, but that is the atmosphere in which our children are growing up.

California, where I live, must be one of the richest states on earth. Around the globe, wherever Hollywood films have gone, it symbolizes plenty. Yet within a few months after the state lottery system was launched, half the people in California had bought tickets. Any elementary schoolchild will tell you that the chances of winning a big prize are less than one in a million. A friend of mine who is a scientist likes to point out that my chances of winning the lottery without a ticket are virtually the same as if I had one. But all over the state people are standing in line for a chance to get rich quick.

My objection to this kind of activity is rather unusual. I don't argue that gambling is sinful, though I do think it is silly. What bothers me is the injection of more toxic wastes – greed – into the mental environment in which we live. I never look at people or events without considering the mental state beneath the surface, and the mental state here is poisonously seductive. With the constant bombardment of the media, you can scarcely go into a store, read a paper or magazine, or turn on the radio or TV for half an hour in California today without having an unctuous voice whisper, "Hello! Wouldn't you like to get a lot of money *free?*"

What we think about constantly, we become; that is the secret of meditation and prayer. Here we are educating people to worship money. When Jesus said long ago, "You cannot worship God and mammon," it was a living warning which we need urgently today, because almost everybody has been caught. It is not for love of money that we should live; it is for love.

Another mental pollutant we might never suspect is a different form of greed: obsession with pleasure. Bumper stickers and T-shirts ask plaintively, "Are We Having Fun Yet?" It seems like such a reasonable demand. We sit by the sidewalk with a little tin can and beg of life, "I don't ask for much. Won't you just drop in a little pleasure for me today, just one thing that I enjoy?" It may not sound very mature, but where is the harm? Doesn't everyone deserve to have fun?

Here let me say quickly that there is nothing wrong in enjoying life's innocent pleasures. Recreation has an important place in spiritual living, as long as it is not at the expense of any creature's welfare – including our own. But again, we should look at the mental state behind those T-shirt slogans, behind the huge surge in revenue to the entertainment, gaming, recreation, and tourist industries. What pollutes the mind is not enjoying life but living for enjoyment, making pleasure a major personal goal. Pleasure pollutes because it focuses us on ourselves. If we had a drug that could extract pleasure and numb us to any pain, which of us would ever grow? Nothing I can imagine could make a person more selfish, less able to deal with the inevitable ups and downs of life and of other people.

I don't think any sensitive person can be satisfied with having fun, no matter how much of it we may cram into our lives. Our need is not for pleasure but for joy – a deep sense of fulfillment that not only never leaves us but actually increases with the passage of time. Fun is living for ourselves; joy comes from living for others, giving our time and love to a purpose greater than ourselves. "This is the true joy in life," George Bernard Shaw proclaims: "the being used for a purpose recognized by yourself as a mighty one; . . . the being a force of Nature instead of a feverish selfish little clod of ailments and grievances complaining that the world will not devote itself to making you happy."

Punishment

LITERALLY THIS NAME means something like "the big stick." Suffering is one way the Lord has of rousing the deeper desire for spiritual growth. It chastens us to turn away from selfish pursuits and find joy.

Often it is only when difficulties look insurmountable that we can tap this motivation to probe deeper in consciousness for hidden resources. Every human being has a kind of trust fund in consciousness, like a safe-deposit vault. To claim your trust fund at a bank, you have to establish your identity. There is the same requirement for gaining access to this limitless trust within: you have to establish your real identity. Unfortunately, this means that the false you, the impostor ego, has to go. If you are going to enter this endless vault and walk out with all you can carry, every trace of selfishness has to be removed.

A friend of mine in the old days of British India used to work for an English bank with branches all over the subcontinent. None of the tellers were allowed to leave the premises at the end of the workday until their accounts balanced to the cent. The branch manager, who was British, lived in a suite on the top floor, so he could afford to be strict. If dinnertime arrived before the books were cleared, he could just go upstairs, have a leisurely meal, and come down again in his own good time to see how work was proceeding. On several occasions my friend did not get home until eight or nine o'clock.

Similarly, I would say, our internal accounts should be balanced every day. Doesn't the Bible tell us, "Let not the sun set on thy wrath"? As much as possible, not only wrath but all the day's emotional residue should be cleared from consciousness before we fall asleep in it, when its poisons will seep into the mind throughout the night and carry over into the next day. I am not saying to avoid agitating situations; learning to face conflict with equanimity is an important part of spiritual growth. But in the evening, the slate should be wiped clean with the mantram and meditation, so you can start the new day with a clear, serene mind.

It is rather ominous for the Lord of Love to be called *Danda*, "the staff of justice," but the name simply reminds us that he makes sure we pay for our wrong actions. It may sound like a dubious name, but with most of us this proves the most effective method of teaching. If we lead a largely selfish life, riding roughshod over people's feelings to get what we want, the Lord must make sure we get increasing insecurity, ill health, and loneliness. That is the only way we are likely to learn sensitivity. On the other hand, when we remember to open our minds to the needs of other people, we get a dose of security, health, and support.

Lord of War

IN HINDU MYTHOLOGY, Skanda was a divine child born to command the forces of light and destroy the forces of violence and evil. In the war within, the Lord is our commander in chief, the supreme strategist who can lead us to freedom from selfish compulsions and sorrow.

The problem is that most of us keep this great commander languishing in a back office far from battle. We don't ask him for orders, and if he ventures to point out that his side hasn't been doing well recently, we listen politely and then carry on as before. Nothing can be done in this great conflict until we let the Lord act as our commanding officer. If you have seen old war movies, you can picture him with his chest covered with ribbons and badges and medals, striding into the general's tent at the eleventh hour to take charge. At last he looks up from the battle map and announces, "Colonel, victory is in sight. We move forward at 0600." We have to do the fighting; the Lord cannot take our place. But if we let him guide us, he assures us of the courage, the wisdom, and the compassion we need to secure victory if we persevere to the end.

The war within can be thought of in two phases. In the first, our major objective is getting our own fighting forces under control. The second phase, the real battle, is waged against self-will, the fierce demand of the ego to fulfill its desires and have its own way whatever the cost. "Fighting forces" here means our vital energy, which is tied up in the countless desires, drives, urges, and anxieties of the ordinary human personality. The purpose of training the senses, which plays a central role in every major spiritual tradition, is to begin to get this riot of energy in order.

Training begins with teaching our senses to obey us instead of allowing ourselves to be dragged around by their demands. Trained senses are necessary for good health and a long, vigorous life, but the issue is much larger. Those who cannot control their senses are not capable of much depth in their love; consequently their love cannot last.

Most of us have never heard of this idea. We accept the axiom that sensory demands have to be indulged; otherwise, sooner or later, there will be trouble. As a result of this belief, our senses clamor for satisfaction freely, making us miserable until we give in. If we tell them to keep quiet because what they crave is harmful, they pay no attention.

Imagine fighting a battle with five junior officers who followed orders only when they felt like it! At the beginning, getting them to obey is such a fight that they seem more like enemies than allies. But the senses can be trained, and well-trained senses make a powerful force for our command.

The Seven-tongued

SOME OF THE most practical of the Thousand Names are vivid reminders of how vital energy leaks out through the senses. *Saptajihva*, "seven tongues" of flame, refers to the seven centers or planes on which Hindu mystics say consciousness can dwell as prana, the creative energy of life. Each of these centers is represented as a little fire along the spinal column, or as a lotus or wheel around a tongue of flame. But they should not be thought of as physical locations; they represent states of consciousness.

The lowest three levels represent the bodily concerns which consume the attention of most human beings: consumption, elimination, and reproduction. Physically these activities actually require very little energy, but because of our emotional entanglement we burn so much of our vitality at these levels that most people live in a chronic energy shortage. The fourth and fifth centers correspond, very roughly, to the mind – the field of emotions – and the faculty of discriminating judgment. The sixth and seventh centers are awakened only on attaining samadhi, Self-realization.

I said that the first campaign in the war within is to train the senses. What this means is learning to free our awareness from compulsive involvement in the lowest three centers of consciousness, where the senses hold sway. When the mind has been elevated to the fourth center, we have scored a great victory. Then senses become faithful allies, and compulsive cravings and urges are left behind.

Until then, however, the senses burn a good deal of the fuel we need for health, vitality, and general well-being. You can imagine your eyes, ears, taste buds, and so on as little ovens. When you go window-shopping, vital energy leaps out of your eyes like twin tongues of fire, reaching out for the objects you desire. When you bathe yourself in sensation under a stereo headset, you can imagine flames coming out your ears. Every sensory indulgence consumes prana.

Of course, these ovens have a legitimate function in daily living. But when we keep stoking their fires with sensory offerings, danger is in store. Attention is flowing out without our approval, which is how compulsions are made. Worse, instead of elevating consciousness, we are locking it in on the lowest levels of human awareness. This is what is happening when we develop a tendency to overeat, or when we sit in front of the television for hours on end.

To Whom Are Offered Seven Kinds of Fuel

THIS IS A reference to a very ancient ritual, in which offerings are poured into a sacrificial fire. The symbolism is that the Lord asks us to bring him our selfish desires and throw them into the all-consuming flames of love for him. Passions, sense cravings, and addictions, all our fear, anger, lust, greed, and self-will, can be fuel for this fire. Whenever we go against these compulsions, we are making a precious offering. The Lord does not benefit from these offerings, but we do. Every offering releases energy and feeds the fire of self-less love. When that fire has consumed every selfish preoccupation in the heart, consciousness is unified in love.

The mystics of all the world's great religions, who have risen above private, possessive attachments, teach us how to feed the fire of love until it flames so high that we do not merely love; we become love itself. One Western mystic has called this "love without an object." We need no particular person to love, and no particular reason: we love as the sun shines, and whoever comes into the orbit of that love receives it. "I love because I love," says Saint Bernard; "I love in order that I may love."

Every time we freely give our time, our energy, and our personal resources to work that benefits others, we are making an offering to the Lord. That is the symbolism of the sacrificial fire. If you want to love, the mystics say, every personal desire, every habit, every private predilection you give up is fuel for love's fire.

When your longing to love becomes ardent, then, you begin looking for ways to defy your selfish conditioning, seeking opportunities for going against your likes and dislikes if those around you will benefit from it. This may look perverse, but it is no different from strapping weights on your wrists and ankles to build up your muscles when you run. Mystics are athletes of the spirit. When we read about people like Thérèse of Lisieux or Mahatma Gandhi going out of their way to do unpleasant things, we should remember they are in training: training for universal love.

There may be no more moving example in the annals of mysticism than young Francis of Assisi, who was never one for halfway measures. Whether he was pursuing pleasure or pursuing God, to know was to act; there was no gap between his understanding and his will.

Shortly before Francis realized that the Lord was calling him, a strange event occurred which prefigured the stature of the mystic stirring in his heart, ready to burst out of the confines of Francis's old personality. He had been fastidious and fun-loving, and though generous to a fault, he had always hidden himself as much as possible from anything unlovely or unclean. Particularly revolting was the sight and even smell of the lepers who occasionally could be seen on the roads around Assisi. On this occasion Francis was returning from a journey when suddenly he was accosted by one of these unfortunate creatures begging alms.

Francis reacted as any of us would have: with an involuntary cry, he leaped back from the disfigured hand and sunken eyes. His tender heart moved him to toss some coins – probably, from what we know of Francis even as a boy, an over-generous amount. But he did so from a distance, and that old, old revulsion turned his face away even as he gave.

As he started to hasten away, however, he seems to have remembered a line of scripture: "Inasmuch as ye did it not to one of these, ye did it not unto me." Before he could have realized what he was doing, in one of those tremendous upheavals of the spirit that marks the greatest mystics, young Francis turned on his heel, ran back to the leper, and kissed him full on the face. And in that instant, his chroniclers tell us, his revulsion turned forever into joy.

Francis, tradition has it, was a small man, but only a great hero can turn suddenly on a powerful compulsion like this and slay it with a stroke. Yet the capacity is latent in us all. The resources are ours; to get access to them, we have only to take orders from the Lord within instead of following the demands of our own ego. "Make me your commander," the Lord tells us, "and I will give you all the weapons you need."

Wielder of the Bow of Horn

So VISHNU IS represented not only with ornaments but with armaments as well. Just as King Arthur had Excalibur, Vishnu has a sword called Nandaka – "that which brings joy" in battle, for the conquest of selfishness and separateness brings joy to us and others.

Vishnu also wields a mighty bow called Sharnga, a symbol of one of the most powerful weapons we can have in the war within: the mantram. I am not speaking rhetorically. When you have repeated the name of the Lord until it becomes part of your consciousness, you can take it like an arrow, fix it to the bow of concentration, and shoot down any wave of anger or compulsive desire with precision.

You must recall how William Tell, having got himself into a dubious situation, managed to hit the apple and not the apple of his eye. Calling on the Lord with all your heart can lead to the same skill in dealing with challenges, for it sends the mantram deep into consciousness to tap unknown resources.

The mantram has supported me through many

grueling ordeals, enabled me to keep my patience and compassion in the face of the fiercest personal attacks. After many years of ardent repetition it has become the staff of my life, a constant support which I know I can trust in any trial.

One of the most effective times to drive the mantram deeper into consciousness is when falling asleep. Like meditation, it can help immensely to clear the ledger of the mind for the following day. When you have learned to fall asleep in the mantram, the agitation and even tragedies of the day cannot enter to destroy the peace of sleep. Not only will the mantram protect you from disturbing dreams, it can bring spiritual dreams that strengthen and inspire you, restore your confidence, and prepare you for the challenges of a new day. At the moment that sleep comes, there is an arrow's entry into deeper consciousness. When the last waking thought is the mantram, it slips deep into your mind, where it goes on working and healing throughout the night.

Will

WHEN WE HEAR about the transforma-
tion of consciousness, we may feel tempted to object,
"You don't know me. You don't know how unpleasant I
can be, how incorrigible I am. If you did, you wouldn't
be so optimistic. I have made many mistakes, and I am
likely to keep on making those mistakes too, because I
don't know how to change. In fact, I don't believe it is
possible for anyone to change."

This is where the testimony of great spiritual figures
down the ages comes in. Again and again they will
assure us that they too have made mistakes, sometimes
worse than any we may have made. They too have
caused trouble to themselves and others. When they tell
us that we can remake our personality, they know it is
possible because they have done it. By drawing on the
power released in meditation, we can gradually remove
all the blemishes of self-centered thought and behavior
that hide our real Self from view. In order to do this,
however, we must put forth a lot of effort, which is the
meaning of the name Kratu.

Some time ago I was watching a woodpecker, a

creature I hadn't seen since I left India. This woodpecker had a red turban, and while I watched he came and alighted on a huge tree. He was quite a small creature, and the trunk of the tree was enormous. If he had been able to understand me I would have gone up to him and said, "What, make a hole in that trunk with your tiny little beak? Impossible. Preposterous!"

But this little woodpecker was not intimidated by the size of the trunk. He did not throw up his legs in despair; he settled onto a limb and went about looking for the right spot to begin operations. It is the same way with transforming consciousness; you have to look for the right spot. In some people it is a particular compulsive craving; in some it is jealousy; in some, blind fury; and in some lucky characters, all three. Each person has to look for that spot where urgent work is most needed.

After his reconnaissance, this intrepid creature chose what seemed to me the most solid, unyielding spot and started pecking away rhythmically. He didn't just give a peck or two and then fly off in search of a worm and come back in half an hour; he went on pecking until he was done. I was amazed at his skill. When he had finished, there was such a large hole that if he had gone on, I have no doubt that the entire tree would have fallen. That is the kind of sustained, enthusiastic effort that is required to transform personality.

Unfortunately, this is far from a pleasant process. For a long, long time in meditation, all we are doing is pecking away at what we want to change in ourselves, and there is not much satisfaction in pecking away. At best it is tedious work, and often it is downright painful. As Meister Eckhart puts it, the pauper has to die before the prince can be born. The problem is that all of us identify ourselves with the pauper – the accumulation of habits and opinions, likes and dislikes, which we have developed over the years – and we are not prepared to let him die. We all say, "This is how I am. This is me, for better or for worse."

Here the mystics reply, "This is *not* you. All these quirks are extraneous." In the language of Sufi mystiism, these are the veils hiding the face of the Beloved. We have mistaken the veils for the face, the layers of conditioning for our real Self. Our whole job in life is to remove these veils, to overcome all the compulsive aspects of our surface personality.

One of the most crucial of weapons in the war within is the human will, which is another aspect of this name Kratu. Everything in life, everything in spiritual growth, comes ultimately to strengthening the will until no setback can stop you, no trial or temptation deflect your course.

One of the difficulties that most of us face is that we know where we want to go in life, but we lack the will to take the steps that will get us there. I saw an interesting illustration of this the other day in a rather unlikely place: an article on one of the most spectacular advances in modern medicine, microsurgery. Surgeons are now able to magnify nerves and other tissues forty or fifty times, work on them with diminutive forceps, scalpels, and the like, and sew everything up with invisible thread when they are done, watching their work not directly but on video screens mounted around the surgical theater. They have accomplished miracles. One teenage girl, a promising flautist, had her hand severed in a tragic accident. She was rushed to the hospital where a specially assembled team of microsurgeons actually managed to reattach her hand. She was discharged within a few months, with every indication that she will be able to continue her musical career.

In us it is often the will that has been severed, cut off from our understanding. This is particularly true in cases of severe addiction, such as to alcohol or drugs. "I don't want to do this," we say, "but I just don't have the willpower." This is not quite true. The will is intact, but it is lying there lifeless. We need a special surgeon to attach it so it can function again.

Unfortunately, no outside specialists are available for this delicate task; we have to do it ourselves. We begin by connecting the will with the tiniest of threads. One way is to say no to some of those innumerable little things that benefit no one: a second piece of pie, a midnight snack, a TV show you are watching just because it is on. If, on top of this, you can cheerfully give that time to others, your will is strengthened doubly. Not only that, it adds to your capacity to love.

I am not much of an admirer of those who develop a strong will just so they can get what they want out of life. The whole purpose of strengthening the will is to deepen your love. This precious human birth has been given to us not to grab from life but to give to it. When you understand that this is what life is for, you get continuing motivation to keep your body and mind at their best, as instruments of selfless service. As this motivation grows, compulsive habits begin to fall away.

Apart from other things, when we overeat or smoke or drink or indulge in drugs, it shows a lack of love. Everybody can respond to this idea. It is lack of love for others that blinds us and allows us to develop fierce physical and mental addictions. It is love that loosens the bonds of addiction and sets us free.

Without this daily effort at strengthening the will, even little desires can become unmanageable. When a desire outstrips the will, it is a compulsion, which means trouble in every corner of life.

SUNDARA
Beautiful

SRI KRISHNA, the perfect incarnation of Vishnu, is represented as a young man with extraordinary physical beauty. He is thoroughly masculine, yet his thick, long, wavy hair, slim limbs, and delicate features make him as beautiful as a girl. There is even a chic air about him, as if the Changeless were always up with the latest fashions.

One of Sri Krishna's hallmarks is a shimmering peacock feather which he wears in his hair. If you have never seen a peacock dancing, you have missed one of the most magnificent displays of color in nature. I suppose peacocks are not common in the United States, but when one of our small children happened to see a peacock dancing by the side of the road, the hues of his tail glinting and changing in the sun, he got so excited just telling me about it that he almost knocked over the dinner table demonstrating.

The peacock feather makes a perfect symbol for spiritual living. It is the worldly life, the selfish life, that is dull and drab; the spiritual life is full of color. But we have been so conditioned by the glitter of physical attractions that we mistake drabness for color and color for drabness. When we live for ourselves, the Gita says, we are living in the night and calling it day. Sri Krishna's feather is a vivid reminder to wake up.

Krishna is modern enough to be wearing earrings, and his choice of styles would qualify for *Vogue*. But these superbly wrought gold circlets have a fascinating message. If you look closely, you see they are not just rings; they are little crocodiles. "Love the Lord with all your heart," the mystics explain, "and he will come like a crocodile to snap up all your selfishness and swallow your self-will."

I remember reading in the papers that this year's Miss Universe has been crowned. As a former English professor I would like to say, "Let's be precise: Miss *Physical* Universe." I would have no objection to that title; the judges have certain specifications which are applicable to physical beauty. But such qualifications have very little to do with real beauty, which abides. I would ask, "May I interview her twenty years later?" In twenty years, you know, going just by physical appearance, Miss Universe might not even get the title of Miss Fifth Avenue. Yet if she is kind, if she is patient, if she can deal lovingly with those who oppose her, I would still count her among the most beautiful women in the world.

The mystics do appreciate physical beauty; I think perhaps no one is more aware of beauty in natural

things than those who have realized God. But the immanent, transfiguring beauty they describe in Sri Krishna
is not physical; it floods the body from inside. By its
very nature, mere physical beauty excites us at first and
then soon cloys; it beckons but quickly satiates. Inner
beauty – of kindness, of goodness, of patience, of selfless love – may not thrill at the outset; but when you
live with someone with these qualities, year after year
you will fall more deeply in love. Every minute that you
are parted, you will miss that person. Every moment the
message of his life will echo in the depths of your consciousness.

The Cowherd Boy

AT THIS STAGE of his life, depicted countless times in poetry, art, theater, and dance, Krishna is the cowherd boy Govinda, growing up hidden from the tyrant Kamsa in the quiet village of Vrindavan. He spends his days helping the other boys to tend the village cows in the forests and meadows around the sacred river Yamuna. He carries a flute, whose haunting melodies draw the love of his playmates as the Lord himself draws the human soul, and around his neck he wears garlands of fresh wildflowers. His waistcloth is of burnished yellow silk decorated with delicate borders, so carefully draped that I can almost imagine him fixing it every morning in front of a full-length mirror the way women drape their saris, making sure that every fold and crease is right.

Around his ankles Krishna wears dulcet ankle bells, the kind you may have seen worn by Indian dancers; for he loves to gather the boys and girls of the village on the banks of the river and dance and play his flute on a full-moon night. Everyone in the village loves to hear the delicate tinkle of those anklets, which signal that Krishna is drawing near.

This is a North Indian touch, whose subtlety I never fully appreciated until I taught at a university which drew students from all parts of India. Then for the first time I saw girls wearing anklets with tiny bells. Those delicate sounds had a powerful effect on their male classmates, which seemed to go far beyond music appreciation. "When you love a girl," one boy in my classes explained, "her anklets sound different from everybody else's. You can tell she is approaching just by the sound." It is the same with Sri Krishna. When you love him with all your heart, the sound of his anklets is the music of the spheres, the universe moving in harmony to the inner ear of those attuned to its unity.

Stealer of Hearts

PICTURE THIS ENCHANTING youth play-
ing on his magic flute in the forest setting where he is
usually painted, his dark skin set off by the green of
thick foliage and the rich blue-black tones of the monsoon clouds, the flowers around his neck lost in the
profusion of wildflowers all around, and you will see
why Sri Krishna is called *Manohara,* "he who steals our
hearts."

Krishna's charm is so irresistible that once upon a
time he even captivated Shiva, the cosmic ascetic who
is a master of self-control. Shiva and Krishna are different faces of the same Lord, but our mythology has never
been intimidated in the slightest by logic or consistency,
and Shiva and Vishnu – or Krishna, his incarnation –
are sometimes brought on stage together to convey a
particular point.

One such occasion was a tug-of-war between the
gods and demons at the dawn of time, when both sides
struggled to seize the nectar of immortality which had
just been churned from the cosmic sea. Krishna, seeing
the demons getting the upper hand, made himself into

a marvelously lovely woman – Mohini, "she who intox-icates with infatuation" – and strolled casually by, her anklets jingling with her gait. The gods, being gods, kept on pulling, but the demons all looked up and immedi-ately forgot what they were doing. They dropped the rope and sauntered off after Mohini into the forest, and of course the gods grabbed the nectar of immortality and have protected it ever since.

But the story doesn't end there. Mohini, leading this motley procession of demons astray through the forest, happened to pass Lord Shiva where he was meditating. Now, Shiva is probably the most austere figure in Hindu mythology, completely self-controlled. He doesn't spend his days tending cows like Sri Krishna; most of the time he remains in profound absorption, oblivious of the out-side world. But Mohini's beauty was so enthralling that even in meditation Lord Shiva finds strange impulses arising in the depths of his consciousness, just as they would have in you and me. He opens his eyes, and when he sees Mohini's alluring form he gets up and starts to follow her. He is just about to throw his arms around her when Mohini turns and whispers, "Hey, take it easy! It's me, Krishna."

That is the appeal of Sri Krishna, who fascinates not only men and women, gods and goddesses, but even the cows he herds every day. When they hear his anklets, these svelte creatures with their lustrous eyes and grace-ful eyelashes become like devoted little girls. Even the calves, the poets say, stop nursing for a moment and turn their heads up to look at Krishna. You have to have seen a calf nursing to appreciate that; every ounce of its attention is fixed greedily on the udder. Even that passionate attachment dissolves in love for Krishna. When he passes by, the very branches of the trees bend down to touch him and drop flowers in his path, and the Yamuna River begins to sing when he comes to its bank to swim. This is the way the whole of nature looks to those whose hearts are filled with love for the Lord.

In the immemorial mystical tradition of Hinduism, many men and women have had visions of this supreme loveliness in the depths of their consciousness when they attained samadhi. They actually see Sri Krishna, not with physical eyes but with the eye of the soul, and they testify with one voice that he is more real than the separate creatures they see around them with their eyes open. They are not describing someone outside. Whether we call him Krishna or Christ, Shiva or Buddha or the Divine Mother, this is the glory and beauty of our real Self, who lives in every heart.

This is the very practical purpose of an incarnation of God: that in loving his outward form, as Saint Bernard says, we may slowly be drawn into complete spiritual union. For a great devotee like Mira, Krishna was a living presence every moment; Teresa of Avila found Jesus the constant companion of her soul. In this tremendous romance of spiritual living, the whole of our consciousness becomes flooded with beauty. All con-flicts cease; all reservations in our love dissolve. It is in this complete unification of our desires that Sri Krishna reveals his beauty to us, in the thoughts, words, and actions of our daily life.

Charioteer

RATHANGAPANI means literally "he who guides the wheel of the chariot with his hands." In ancient India there were no Thunderbirds, only chariots. The Lord is saying, "Why don't you let me be your chauffeur? Just give me the wheel of your life; I'll drive you to love, to wisdom, to health."

A good deal of shopping around in life amounts to no more than looking for this perfect chauffeur. All kinds of dubious characters – wealth, fame, pleasure – will pop up and say, "You called?" Always ask for their license; and even if they have a clean record, give them a stiff test before handing them the car.

When my wife and I were visiting the city of Madras in South India, we once hailed a taxi to take us round to the reserve bank. The drive took us over an hour. Now, I had some vague reminiscences of Madras from my childhood, and I didn't think the bank was that far. So after we arrived and paid the fee, I checked a map. We were about three blocks from where we had started! The driver had been taking us on the grand tour, all around town.

This is what pleasures do. One comes gliding by and

the driver calls out, "Sure, baby! I'll take you right there." We hop in and go round and round and get deposited in the same spot we left off. And the bill! It is only a very rare taxi driver who will take you to your real destination. Sri Krishna tells us, "Find me in your heart, trust me, love me, serve me in everyone, and I'll take you straight to heaven."

Sustainer of Life

THE POWER WITH which we are able to live is the power of the Lord. No physiology, no CAT scanner, no ultrasound exploration can account for the power that makes your hands move, your tongue speak, your eyes see, your mind think. When we become even vaguely aware of the Lord, we understand that it is his power we are using in everything we do. Then we become very responsible, like trustees of a great treasure. Our life is not ours to use as we like; it is a trust we hold for others.

This is why Mahatma Gandhi says: "I believe that if one man gains spiritually the whole world gains with him, and, if one man falls, the whole world falls to that extent. I do not help opponents without at the same time helping myself and my co-workers."

The Lotus Navel

SOME OF THE loveliest of the Thousand Names evoke the lotus, called *padma* or *aravinda* in Sanskrit, as a symbol of beauty and fertility. Vishnu's consort is often called Padma, the Lotus Goddess. And Vishnu is called *Padmanabha*, "the Lotus Navel," *Aravindaksha*, "the Lotus-eyed," and *Padmagarbha*, "the Lotus Womb" – all references to stories from the rich treasury of mythology with which Hindu children grow up.

One of these stories tells how the universe was born when Vishnu awoke from the long sleep he had been enjoying while floating on the gentle waves of the cosmic ocean. He was reclining upon the great serpent Shesha, just awakening at the beginning of the universal dawn, when a lotus stalk began to grow from his navel. If you have seen a lotus, you may know how it is born on the bottom of a quiet pond and sends up a tender white filament that delicately seeks the surface of the pool, there to blossom into a robust and beautiful flower. In the same way, a mysterious tendril sprouted from Vishnu's navel, gently grew, and eventually produced a magnificent lotus, in the midst of which appeared the god Brahma, the personification of the creative power of the Lord.

Now, Brahma didn't know who he was or how he had come to be seated in the middle of a red lotus blossom, so he looked all around to find out what was going on. That is why Brahma is always shown with four faces, looking north, south, east, and west. But he still didn't know where he had come from. He had been looking all around him for the source of the universe, and of course he could not find it; for the secret of life's riddles can never be found outside.

Finally Brahma figured this out – after all, he is a god. Having searched the universe in all four directions and found no answer to his problem, he began to descend through the stalk of the lotus – a mythic way of symbolizing what happens over many years in the practice of meditation, where we go deep within ourselves to explore our own spiritual roots. He retraced his evolution back down the lotus stalk until at last he reached the source. Then he understood that he springs from Lord Vishnu himself, that he rests in the lotus of Vishnu's being.

ARAVINDA-AKSHA
Lotus-eyed

ONE TROPICALLY LUSH spot in my village was the lotus pond near the temple, which was shaded on all sides by stately coconut palms. It was not large, only about the size of a large swimming pool, and at certain times of the year you could hardly see the water because the lotus leaves covered the surface so thickly. These huge leaves are almost as dramatic as the flower. They float gracefully on the water and never get wet, for not even a drop can cling to their lustrous waxy surface. My favorite time to visit that pool was early morning, when the lotuses open their translucent petals to the first rays of the sun and are transformed into cups of light.

This name, one of the most beautiful given to Sri Krishna, compares the Lord's eyes to these delicate, graceful petals full of light. The reason is not just their physical appearance. Their beauty comes from the response they convey, from the depth of compassion he feels for every one of his creatures.

This name can remind us that it is not mascara that makes the eyes beautiful, but tenderness and love.

Anyone with peace and love in the heart cannot help having beautiful eyes. Similarly, those who are angry at heart, whatever smooth words they may employ, their eyes will say plainly: "I don't like you. You're not worth listening to." If you want irresistibly beautiful eyes, learn to put others first; think about their welfare and not about your own needs.

It is not only spiritual figures who deliver this message. Albert Einstein once gave the secret of a beautiful life in four plain sentences. "I am happy," he said, "because I want nothing from anyone. And I do not care for money. Decorations, titles, or distinctions mean nothing to me. I do not crave praise." What he is trying to say is that even the thought of wanting to get something from others has disappeared from his mind. Then the only question is, How much can I give? How much can I serve?

The eyes, it is said, are the windows of the soul. When you look at others with love in your heart, it comforts them, strengthens them, makes them feel secure. That is one reason why we respond so deeply to the eyes of those who are illumined, for they have love for everyone. In the Hindu tradition, it is said that there are three ways of communicating spiritual awareness to others – through words, through touch, or through a look. Ramana Maharshi, a great sage from South India who shed his body only a few decades ago, used to sit on his cot in his ashram while people came from all over India just to look at him. He didn't need to talk much. Even Westerners with many questions to ask found that their questions melted away; the look of sympathy, affection, and love in his eyes nourished everyone who came.

Only a great saint can do this. It isn't something that we can pretend to do, or that we can learn in a course at night school; it has to come from a heart full of love and a mind that is completely still. If we could plug up the million and one leakages of our vital energy and rest our mind in peace whenever we liked, that would be a tremendous blessing. But no one can do this without control over the deeper levels of consciousness.

Yet this is something we can all aspire to. We can gradually gain access to these deeper levels by meditating regularly and repeating the mantram as often as possible. It may take many years, but the time will come when you know that in times of trouble – when you are having difficulties with others, or you feel inadequate, or your thoughts are starting to race out of control – the mantram will come to your aid and steady your mind, which is the first step toward stilling it.

Big-eyed

THE LORD HAS big eyes, "the better to see you with." Don't you have an expression, "You can't get away with it"? Millions of good, educated people think yes, you *can* sometimes get away with it. But the truth is that those big, beautiful eyes are always looking everywhere.

At midnight, for example, when everyone is asleep, we ask ourselves, "Who will know if we slip into the kitchen? Who will see if we climb up to the top shelf where that special jar is hiding and steal into those special chocolate chip cookies?" We take one small handful, and nobody is the wiser. "After all," we say, "what they don't know can't hurt."

Nobody has seen except for old Big Eyes, our real Self.

SAKSHI

The Witness

WHEN I WAS attending my village school, some of us boys – my cousins and a few of our school-mates – would sometimes rob a nearby mango tree. Of course, we were always absolutely sure that nobody would find out. But I don't think the owner of the tree was quite in the dark, and once, rather exasperated, he went to the extent of complaining to the headmaster of our school. The headmaster became terribly angry. He called all the boys in the class together and interrogated us.

"Raman, did you rob the tree?"

"Yes, sir."

"Is that true, Shankaran?"

"No, sir. I did it, sir."

"Krishnan?"

"I'm the one, sir."

One by one, each boy said he had stolen the man-goes. Our headmaster was quite sure who the real cul-prits were, but he couldn't get any evidence. Finally, at his wits' end, he told some of the better students, "You boys should at least give a few hints. Why do you all say that you did it?"

We said, "We are protecting the honor of the school." He had to agree with us, and so we managed to escape.

When I got home, however, my grandmother was waiting. Word gets about quickly in a village, and the first thing she said was, "Son, did you steal those mangoes?"

I kept quiet.

"Were you in the group?"

I still kept quiet.

"Even if none of you tells anybody else," she said, "there was somebody who saw. Someone inside you is watching everything, someone who never misses a thing."

In the depths of consciousness, beneath the surface of our egocentric personality, dwells the Lord, who is our true Self, ever wakeful, eternally alert. This is the implication of the Sanskrit epithet *sakshi,* "the eternal witness." After we have done something selfish, when we hear a little voice inside saying, "Shabby, shabby, shabby," that is the voice of the Lord within. And when we feel warm inside because we have helped someone, it is the Lord who is making us feel warm.

For the most part, however, we are too absorbed in our personal pursuits to heed these internal cues, and so we are always at odds with our true Self. This is the cause of all the insecurity in our hearts. Somewhere deep down we know the person we want to be, the person who really is within us. But we are so conditioned to look for our satisfaction outside that we ignore this Self, who is waiting so patiently to be found.

Once we make this discovery, we are no longer separate individuals. Our life becomes a lasting, positive force which does not end when the body is shed at death. Francis of Assisi and Mahatma Gandhi are such forces, as alive today as they were when they walked the earth in Italy or India. We may not aspire to become a Francis or a Gandhi, but all of us can aspire to become at least a "mini-force" if we set our hearts and minds to it. The same power which changed the would-be troubadour Francis Bernadone into a saint, and the ineffectual lawyer Mohandas Gandhi into a mahatma or "great soul," can enable us, too, to grow to our full height.

Compared to this realization, all the pleasures of life are insignificant. This is the joy we were made for, the joy of coming home to our true Self.

All-seeing

BECAUSE THE LORD is the eternal witness, moving to another town or a warmer climate to solve personal problems is not very practical. The video camera is always there within us. The lights are always illuminating the stage, and the tape is endless; it never misses a thing. So the idea that we can really "get away with it" is preposterous.

This is the ancient law of karma, which Jesus stated succinctly: "As ye sow, so shall ye reap." You may not be able to see the connections of cause and effect that operate in your life, but as spiritual awareness grows you will begin to make out a pattern. When you can view yourself with a fair measure of detachment and compassion, you can watch the myriad little incidents of daily life dovetail into a tightly fitting pattern. Until then we cannot see this pattern, because it would throw us into utter turmoil. In his love, the Lord draws a curtain over karmic connections until we have developed the detachment to deal with them.

Once you begin to see this pattern, however, you will understand why you are in a particular situation. If you find yourself being raked over the coals, you will know that it is because you have done a good share of raking yourself. Twenty years ago in Kansas you may have said certain angry words; now you are here in California listening to the same angry words being said to you. You understand, and the turmoil quiets down; you can calmly take the lesson to heart.

This law of cause and effect is accepted as a fact of life by Hindus and Buddhists, as natural as the law of gravitation. In this law it is not somebody else that makes you suffer; it is you yourself. Nobody can be cruel to you except yourself, and nobody can be kind to you except yourself. When you take this to heart, you will become acutely vigilant about not getting resentful or bitter or cruel, because you will know that no one will suffer from these things more than you.

RUDRA
Bringer of Tears

ANOTHER OF THE Thousand Names associated with karma is *Rudra,* which comes from the root *rud,* "to cry." We associate the Lord with love, so we find it difficult to understand how he can be called "he who makes us cry." But if God is all, he is suffering as well as joy. As Rudra, he personifies the unavoidable fact that most of us learn from our mistakes only because they bring us sorrow. Suffering is not the Lord inflicting punishment on us. Our ignorance in making choices is responsible for most of the sorrow we bring upon ourselves.

A certain amount of suffering in life is not only inescapable but even necessary for growth. It took me a long time to understand this, though my spiritual teacher tried to teach me very early in life. When I made a mistake and suffered for it, she would not be very sympathetic. She didn't gloat over my suffering or withdraw her support of me either; but in wordless ways, she helped me to learn not to make that mistake again. At the time I didn't understand what seemed a strange lack of sympathy. Today I know that if someone has been behaving selfishly, it is much better for that person to suffer the consequences and learn to change than it is to remain blind and fail to grow, which just means letting problems grow instead.

Every day I see the verification of the law of karma. Ill health is often an instance: if we do not take care of our body and maintain our peace of mind, our health is bound to suffer. That is Rudra making us cry. When our breathing is labored, when our digestion is upset, when our equanimity is destroyed, we do cry – and this crying is a signal, a red warning from body and mind, reminding us that something fundamental in our life is wrong. Pain, illness, insecurity, and mental turmoil are all loving signals from the Lord, who is telling us, "It's time you gave yourself a checkup. It is time you learned to change your ways."

Sometimes we manage to delay payment in the operation of karma, but then often it hits us with heavy interest. I prefer the idea of cash karma, where if you make a mistake, you pay for it immediately. However painful this may be for the moment, there is no interest hanging over your head. You give out six dollars worth of inconsiderateness, and on the spot you get six dollars worth in return. The debt is canceled. When you make a mistake, in other words, it is much better to take the consequences on the chin than to try to put them off, for consequences tend to compound, making the karma load bigger and bigger.

When I was growing up, it was considered imprudent in my village to have any kind of debt. No one would borrow unless they absolutely had to; the consequences of debt were just too serious. If you borrowed a small amount and paid it back quickly, the penalty wasn't bad. But there are certain moneylending practices in India whereby the interest on the loan ends up greater than the principal, so that the longer the loan is drawn out, the more you owe. You can borrow a thousand rupees, pay interest every month, and find out after three years that you owe not one thousand rupees but fifteen hundred. Similarly, in the spiritual realm, the weight of unpaid karma can be a tangible liability. When you accumulate karmic debts, therefore, pay them back right away, before the interest builds up. Don't be tempted to reschedule your karmic debt, and don't wait for interest rates to go down; it doesn't happen.

In India we have a peculiar phrase, "to file the yellow paper." It means to declare insolvency, and it is looked upon – especially by creditors – as being less than fully honest. When you go to ask for a loan, the lender always asks you to declare that you have no intentions of filing the yellow paper.

One of the perennial paradoxes of the human condition is that if you want to avoid filing the yellow paper in life, the only way is to give. By giving you can never go bankrupt, because the more you give of yourself, the more you receive. In fact, it is only by giving that you can *avoid* going bankrupt. When you go through life refusing to give, the yellow paper comes and sticks to your forehead.

Most people who are insecure, for example, have difficulty giving of themselves. Insecurity is a warning from the bank within that you are getting low on funds. But such people needn't go on to the point that they become actually bankrupt in love. They can make themselves solvent again, even rich, by learning to give. As Saint Francis de Sales says, we learn to give by trying to give; we learn to give more by giving more. Instead of dwelling on ourselves and asking what we can expect from others, we should start looking for ways to give our time, energy, and resources to causes more important than ourselves.

Full

THE INNER REALITY that we call the Self, who is the supreme Person behind every face, is always full. The Lord lacks nothing; he can never go bankrupt. You may remember Saint Teresa's beautiful prayer:

> Nada te turbe,
> Nada te espante.
> Todo se pasa,
> Dios no se muda.
> La paciencia
> Todo lo alcanza.
> Quien a Dios tiene
> Nada le falta.
> Solo Dios basta.
>
> Let nothing upset you;
> Let nothing frighten you.
> Everything is changing;
> God alone is changeless.
> Patience attains the goal.
> Who has God lacks nothing;
> God alone fills all his needs.

"Who has God lacks nothing." The Lord is ever full,

and he gives freely of his fullness to all who love and seek him. But nothing he gives can diminish his infinite store of love and wisdom.

As long as we feel an emptiness inside, we cannot help living in insecurity; so we cannot help manipulating others in an attempt to fill that emptiness. Wherever there is manipulation, love cannot enter; in fact, when we try to use others to fill our own emptiness, even the little love we had is likely to vanish. To give freely we have to be full, and this kind of fullness comes ultimately from the Lord within.

Many years ago in India my wife and I had an experience which still reminds me of Teresa's phrase, "Who has God lacks nothing." We were spending a few days in Vrindavan, a sacred spot associated with Sri Krishna's childhood. In this sense there are two Krishnas: the eternal Lord, whom we realize in the depths of our own consciousness as our real Self, and a historical figure who was born about three thousand years ago in North India. Faithful Hindus believe that this historical Krishna grew up along the banks of the river Yamuna in an ancient town called Vrindavan, which today is full of beautiful temples and ashrams. Fortunately, this beautiful village has changed very little over the centuries, and it still attracts sincere pilgrims from all over India.

One evening my wife and I stayed on at one of these temples longer than we realized, and when we started for our host's home it was already quite dark. Night falls quickly in the tropics, and there were no street lights in that part of town. We made our way slowly down the crooked village lanes, and after half an hour or so of stumbling and groping, I decided that San Francisco's claim to have the crookedest street in the world is highly exaggerated.

Just when I was ready to confess that I really didn't know where we were going, a young monk appeared out of the shadows and announced that he had been sent by our anxious host to guide us home. He was a quiet man who evidently knew the streets well, and to show how glad we were to see him, I tried to engage him in the kind of spiritual shop talk that aspirants all over India exchange when they meet: where had he learned to meditate, what kind of disciplines did he practice, and so on. But he was so quiet that all my efforts at conversation failed. We walked home in the deep silence of this holy place, where almost no one lives who is not devoted to Krishna.

Our taciturn guide brought us to our door and was about to take his leave. I wanted to give him something to show our gratitude, but all we had with us was some milk sweets we had bought in the bazaar. I tried to place them in his hands, and then I discovered that this man I had thought so tongue-tied could express himself like a poet. "Brother," he said, "I live where Krishna lives. How can I lack anything?"

That young man's answer has been with me ever since.

It is a small but eloquent reminder of how spiritual awareness makes us feel that we are always complete, that we need nothing.

TARA

Who Carries Us Across

TARA IS "he who carries us across" the sea of birth and death. In the traditional invocation to the Bhagavad Gita, this image is invoked in a magnificent verse set against the background of the *Mahabharata*. The forces of darkness are compared to a fierce river; the five Pandava brothers, under the protection of Sri Krishna, are leaders of the forces of light. "In the river of battle," the poet says, "their opponents were great waves, crocodiles, treacherous whirlpools. But over this dread river the Pandavas crossed safely, with Krishna as their ferryman."

Just as there is a ferry line connecting Sausalito on one side of the Golden Gate with San Francisco on the other, Sri Krishna has a ferry going from insecurity to security, from hatred to love, from war to peace, from death to immortality. We are standing in the "river of battle" that is life, threatened on all sides by destructive passions, and Sri Krishna comes by with his little boat and says, "Hop in. I'll take you from this world of sorrow to the other shore of love and joy."

The Buddha too is represented as a boatman, always

asking, "Anyone for the other shore?" The saints and mystics of every great religion can be thought of in this way. They pilot their boats, not for themselves, but for the benefit of people like us who desperately desire to cross the river of life.

The Grandfather

IN MY VILLAGE, nobody referred to me as my mother's son; I was always "Granny's boy." My mother didn't sulk or feel slighted; she felt very proud. Nothing can take the place of a grandparent's experience.

When Dr. Spock was asked how he came to write about raising children, he confided that these were things formerly learned from grandparents; people turn to books now because grandparents are either cut off from their children or have interests of their own which they prefer to pursue. This is an incalculable loss. In my village we had a woman with seven daughters, each of whom had given her grandchildren. Whenever someone in the village had a complicated delivery or a sick child, it was not the doctor or the midwife who was sent for first. It was this grandmother, who had seen every problem under the sun.

With this name Sri Krishna says, "Just call me Grandpa, the grandfather of the cosmos. I brought into existence Brahma the Creator himself." In one of the most daring similes in Hindu mysticism, Brahma is actually called sexual prowess, the creative power which brings about this entire universe. Just as children are brought into existence by the creative power of sex on the physical level, the universe is said to have been born through the union of the divine Father and Mother – the union of Brahman, the formless Godhead, with Shakti, the Lord's creative energy.

This whole cosmos, then, is the offspring of the Lord. When I hear children quarreling in their sandbox, it reminds me of how physicists describe the first three minutes of creation, when all the elements and forms of energy we are familiar with today were born in the incomparable turmoil of the Big Bang. We can picture atoms screaming and colliding, universal forces fighting for their share of the turf, cosmic screams reverberating through the universe so loudly that astrophysicists can still pick out their faint echoes. If you think a few children in a sandbox can make noise, imagine what heavenly hullabaloo there must have been when the universe was being formed. Sri Krishna says, "Call me Grandpa, and treat me with great respect; for I brought all this into being."

YAJNA
Sacrifice

THIS NAME EXPRESSES a central principle of life. For orthodox Hindus the word *yajna* connotes the many rituals that have been part of their religion for thousands of years. These rituals, however, are only external symbols. Their real meaning is the spirit of self-sacrifice. From the earliest times, side by side with these rituals there has run a mystical stream best summarized in the Upanishads, which urges us to go beyond ritual and realize God in our own heart through the practice of meditation. Rituals are not of much help in the deeper stages of meditation, where to realize God we have to go beyond all sensory experience, beyond words, beyond emotions, and eventually even beyond thought.

In the Upanishads, those who perform rituals without awareness of their deeper meaning are compared to "the blind led by the blind." Ritual has a place in worship, but according to the Upanishads it makes a most unsafe boat for crossing the sea of life. There we need the tremendous spiritual disciplines that have been handed down in every great religion. This is an endless sea, where the dangers are so great and the challenges so overpowering it takes powerful disciplines like meditation and repetition of the mantram to deepen our awareness, strengthen the will, and clear our eyes so that they never waver from the goal. All these disciplines are what is signified by yajna.

Yajna, then, is not just sacrifice but self-sacrifice. Mahatma Gandhi, drawing on the Gita, made it clear that yajna is not a ritual sacrifice performed in a temple, but essentially selfless service in daily living: work for the welfare of others that is prompted not by a desire to make money or enhance our reputation, but by a desire to serve.

"Service" here means more than work which is just for our own family or a clique of friends. Equally important, it means working in harmony. Selfless, harmonious effort, the Gita says, contains within itself the seed and secret of success. However hard we work, however dedicated our attitude, it is not we who determine what we achieve; success is contained in the concept of yajna. "Give your best selfless effort in a selfless cause," Sri Krishna says; "then leave the rest to me."

I find ample illustrations of this in the history of our own meditation center, which we began twenty-five years ago in Berkeley. When I was leaving the University of Minnesota, where the Fulbright authorities had first posted me, I found myself packing my bags for California without anybody to look up there or any real idea of where to go. That day somebody gave me a copy of the autobiography of Yogananda Paramahamsa, who came to this country from India earlier in the century and founded a meditation center in California. Immediately I wrote a letter to the Self-Realization Fellowship in Los Angeles, telling them that I would be coming to California very soon. By return mail they sent a gracious letter inviting me to stay at their ashram. It was just like a little piece of India, where I could meditate without explanation or interruption and take long walks in a quiet, beautiful setting overlooking the Pacific.

Soon I was invited to deliver my first lecture in this country, in San Diego. I had expected one or two hundred people at most. About a thousand showed up, so many that I offered to speak again in the evening to accommodate those who could not be seated at the scheduled time. In those days, you know, more than twenty-five years ago, few Americans had been exposed to India's spiritual heritage; so I was immensely encouraged to draw such a large and enthusiastic audience.

After a few weeks in Southern California I came to the University of California at Berkeley, where I felt right at home. I have always been a campus man who enjoys being around students, whether in India or in the United States. But my academic duties at Berkeley were light, and I was terribly eager to start teaching meditation. Every morning I got up wondering, "Where are all these earnest aspirants who must be wanting to learn to meditate?" I was sure they existed, but how was I to find them?

Every morning in those days I used to enjoy a good, long walk to campus. One day I was leaving the house as usual when a bright red Thunderbird convertible pulled up next to me. "Excuse me," a charming black lady said, "but you seem to be new here."

"Yes," I said, "I'm from India."

She was intrigued, and soon I found myself talking about meditation and the work I was so eager to begin.

"Well," she said, "what's keeping you?"

"I haven't got any place where I can teach," I said, "and furthermore, I don't even have any students."

"My home is in Berkeley," she said immediately, "and I'll give you all the facilities you need. I'd like to learn what you have to teach, and I know some friends who I think would like to learn too. Why don't you start this Saturday evening?"

It happened so simply that I didn't have time to think. I went to her home expecting a handful and found a room full of good, eager people, both white and black – I was proud to learn later that this was the first time any of them had been in a gathering where blacks and whites mingled socially. I began the talks with the Katha Upanishad, whose theme is nothing less than the conquest of death. It's not a familiar scripture even in India, but the following Saturday evening everybody had a copy of the Upanishads, some heavily underlined; they had gone out the day after my first talk and bought every copy in Berkeley.

They were so enthusiastic that I introduced meditation right away, half expecting them to excuse themselves and tiptoe out. But everybody stayed on, rising to the challenge of this most demanding of disciplines. Thus what would become the Blue Mountain Center of Meditation began: so naturally, so simply, just because my only desire was for others, to open the treasury of spiritual wisdom which the Upanishads and the Gita contain. We never asked for money. But little by little support began to come, friends began to offer their skills, and – most important for good work – dedicated people came, and stayed.

If we continue to work together harmoniously, I have no doubt that this work will be able to make an original, lasting contribution to the health and welfare of this country – and not only of this country, but through this country to the rest of the world. This is not something any one of us has achieved. It is the Lord who enables selfless work to prosper. If we do our best, the final responsibility is his.

And I think it has only begun. I hope with all my heart that our work will continue to grow, as more and more friends come to offer their time, talent, and resources without strings or reservations. It will be continued by our children and our friends' children, and those childrens' children; for this is how spiritual work grows and bears fruit from generation to generation.

The Auspicious

IN HINDU MYSTICISM, the sacrifice of self to a higher purpose is powerfully illustrated in the image of Shiva as Nataraja, the Lord of the Dance. There is a splendid statue of this image in the great temple at Chidambaram in South India. Shiva, his arms outstretched in a circle of fire, is dancing on the tiny, prostrate figure of a demon called Apasmara, "he who has forgotten." This pitiful creature is our self-will, the selfish, self-centered fragment of ourselves that has forgotten the unity of life. It is writhing in agony, but Shiva, the divine Self that is our real personality, is dancing in a transport of rapture.

Everyone, without exception, finds the reduction of self-will an extremely painful affair. But we can bear the pain if we remember that this demon of self-will is not who we are. As Shankara says in a famous hymn, "I am neither body nor mind nor senses nor intellect. I am pure consciousness and bliss; I am Shiva; I am Shiva!"

Self-will is the only barrier between us and God – that is, between us and security, between us and joy, between us and love. Those whose self-will has been inflated beyond the normal bounds find it extremely difficult to have loving relationships. As a result they find themselves isolated, and feeling isolated, they become hostile. Then they blame others for their hostility, which is really born of their own self-will.

This vicious cycle is the reason why the most effective of all sacrifices is the sacrifice of self-will. If you work every day at diminishing your self-will, you will find your relationships improving rapidly. Usually you will see benefits even in your physical health.

Very, very few people are naturally selfless. Virtually no one starts life with a perfect self-will score. But every one of us can improve our score with sincere effort. How many people work a little every day to get their golf score down! Reducing self-will to zero is the same idea – infinitely harder, but infinitely more rewarding too. And it doesn't require any special equipment. You can practice at home, at work, among friends, wherever you rub shoulders with others.

The family is an ideal setting for this kind of practice. At every turn you get the choice: Shall I put myself first, or shall I put my family first and myself last? It will be painful, but don't give up; go on trying. At the end of the week, take a deep breath and renew your resolution. That is what meditation is for – helping you carry on through next week, next month, next year.

Shiva personifies the power of the Lord to turn even the stiffest of trials to spiritual progress. He is called auspicious because meditation and the mantram can turn even pain, heartbreak, and bereavement into spiritual growth.

Destroyer of Evil

THIS NAME TOO evokes the Lord's austere aspect, typified by the awesome deity Shiva. Though Krishna is usually thought of as being more approachable than the fear-inspiring Shiva, he too will never let us forget that the spiritual life is often a battle, an inner struggle against all that threatens to undo spiritual growth.

No fight on earth is more arduous or demanding than this fight against self-will. When you are feeling battered, it can help immensely to remember that your second in this fight is Krishna. He is just behind you with his cut lemon and his towel and a little bottle of alcohol, and when you get thrown against the ropes he is there to revive and encourage you and push you into the ring again. "Don't lie there and go to sleep! Get back in there and fight."

You object, "I'm tired." All the more reason to fight! No words can convey how difficult this becomes in the latter half of the spiritual journey, when your meditation has taken you into the dark recesses of the unconscious and you can't make headway against the forces you encounter there. You try and try, but nothing you do seems able to take you to a state of deeper awareness. Every day you go on trying, and every evening you go to bed chastened but more determined than ever.

It seems impossible, but one day you are going to succeed. All those who keep on fighting against their self-will, who refuse to give up whatever happens, will win this battle someday. Then they will discover who has been their second, supporting them every step of the way. Here are Gandhi's inspiring words: "I have not the shadow of a doubt that any man or woman can achieve what I have, if he or she would make the same effort and cultivate the same hope and faith."

The Unconquered

HERE THE IMAGERY of sacrifice and of battle comes together. Only when the ego receives the final blow – traditionally thought of as delivered by Shiva – do we become invincible, *aparajita*.

The greatest sacrifice in life is the sacrifice of self-will. It is not too difficult to find people who are ready to give money or time and talent to a worthy cause, and there is merit in such sacrifices when they are offered without strings attached. But the offering the Lord really wants from us is our self-will.

This is not for his sake. The Lord is only thinking of our own well-being. As the Buddha says bluntly, for a self-willed person, suffering will increase like crab-grass. Self-willed people suffer everywhere. They go to the office and have trouble with the boss. They come out and have trouble with the meter reader. They go home and have trouble with their family; they go to the bowling alley and have trouble with the ball. When you reduce your self-will, you reduce your trouble – that is, you deepen your relationships, improve your health, and further your spiritual growth.

Some time ago there was a lot of excitement over the bout between Mohammed Ali and Leon Spinks. A few fellows coming to my talks, gentle chaps whom you would never suspect of having an interest in boxing, were following developments closely. I told them that compared to the fight that self-will puts up, external fights pale into insignificance. After fifteen rounds, you know, Mohammed Ali and Leon Spinks have got to go soak in the tub, have their massage and a good dinner, and perhaps go out on the town. No matter how long, the fight is over. But in the spiritual life, after you have put in a hard day's work, had your evening meditation, and gone to bed, the fight is still on. You may be knocked against the ropes and throw in the towel, but this fight isn't going to end there. If you ask Sri Krishna when it will be over, he will answer, "When you have won."

In other words, none of us has any choice in this fight. Just by being alive, we are in the ring. In the Bhagavad Gita, Krishna shrugs and tells Arjuna, "This is the battle of life. If you say you won't fight, your own nature will push you into it. Your own karma will get you into situations where you can't help but fight." The struggle for self-mastery is not an optional duel, where you participate if you feel like it. It is absolutely obligatory.

Who Brings Sacrifice to Fruition

IN THIS NAME the Lord assumes responsibility for making good work flourish, and for bringing about the spiritual fulfillment of those who seek him in selfless service. Our responsibility is simply to give our best.

As director of an important center of meditation, with many serious aspirants under my guidance, I carry a responsible load every day. If I do not go around with hunched shoulders, it is because I keep this promise of the Lord's in mind and remember that the burden is on his back, not mine. My responsibility is simply to keep myself out of his way and give him my all. I don't bear the burden, no matter how much work I do. In fact, this awareness allows me to do ten times as much fruitful work as I used to be able to do in my old days as a college professor – and I have always been a hard worker.

It is important to understand, however, that this doesn't mean being irresponsible. We have the responsibility to do everything in our power to make things right. We have the responsibility, in other words; it is the burden that is the Lord's. When we have really done our best, we can say with confidence, "I've done all I can. Now I'm going on your word, Krishna. Protect me if I've made a slip." My mother was fond of a song I used to hear often: "I have thrown myself at your feet, Lord, serving everybody around me; please guard me with your love against all harm."

Good Works

EVERYTHING WE DO should be judged by how much it adds to the unity of life. If it conduces to unity, that work is spiritual. This applies to jobs, to recreation, to everything we spend our time on. When our motivation in eating good food and getting regular exercise is to strengthen the body for service, even these mundane acts become spiritual offerings.

On the other hand, brooding on oneself – cravings, resentments, greed, lust, anger, jealousy, and the like – can never produce good works. Not only that, this kind of self-indulgence drains the energy we might draw on for doing something beneficial. Like letting a car idle all night in the parking lot, brooding on ourselves burns up a lot of vital energy without our usually being aware of it.

When we can free ourselves from most of the personal preoccupations that are considered to be inescapable for a human being, immense vitality is released for selfless spiritual work. I like to call this getting a second engine, and it comes from the very depths of meditation. Twenty years from now, perhaps, you will be able to say something very astonishing to your family and friends: "I can do better work now than I could twenty years ago. I can work longer, more creatively, and much more effectively."

With progress in meditation, the second half of life can be much brighter and more joyful than the first, for the simple reason that you will be master of all your faculties. Your judgment will be sound, your willpower strong and resilient, and your relationships deep and lasting, founded on mutual respect.

The Place of Sacrifice

THIS NAME EVOKES another reference to ancient ritual. *Dharmayupa* originally meant the post where an animal was tied until the moment for sacrifice came. This tragic vestige of primitive religion still survives in a few isolated communities in India. Even in my village, in one of the temples there was animal sacrifice on some occasions when I was growing up.

Eternal credit goes to Mahatma Gandhi for putting an end to this. "If you really must follow these rituals to the last dot over the *i*," he told us, "don't sacrifice one of God's living creatures; sacrifice a zucchini." We loved him so deeply that within a few decades, deft appeals like this had swept away undesirable practices thousands of years old.

Before Gandhiji's message reached my village, however, on certain days my grandmother used to send word to me in school to come home by a different route, in order to avoid the temple where this kind of sacrifice was offered. Once or twice I didn't receive the warning in time, and on the way home I saw the place where they had been sacrificing some poultry. It was a terrible sight. I couldn't understand how anyone could do such a thing to propitiate a loving God.

For me, the sacrificial post is the place where the ego is kept tethered, until we can finally sacrifice it at the altar of love. It sounds frightful because it is frightful. Reducing self-will is painful for everybody, but the alternative to this pain is not only a different kind of pain later but increasing paralysis. When we cannot keep our ego on a very short leash, it has a cumulatively crippling effect on the will. And as the will grows weak, judgment goes, so that we begin to see things that are simply not there. This is the final tragedy of self-will. If you could only see into the minds of people with fierce self-will, you would see how distorted events look to them, how disfigured other people appear.

By comparison with this kind of blind and crippled consciousness, reducing self-will is well worth the cost. Setting aside the question of sacrifice, even keeping the ego tied to its post brings swift improvements in daily living. And as the idea of putting others first becomes natural, it is increasingly easy to relate to people and work with them even when they differ from us. Tethering self-will leaves us free to enjoy deep, satisfying personal relationships. What greater reward could we desire?

Liberation

VOLUMES HAVE BEEN written about this word *nirvana,* a simple word that literally means "blowing out" or "extinguishing." The image is of a fire that has gone out, the fire of the superficial, self-centered personality. Only when this small "I" is extinguished can we realize our true nature, which is divine. Only when we cease to identify ourselves with our separate personality can we realize the unity of all life.

Nirvana is usually considered a Buddhist concept, but the word also appears in the Hindu scriptures. In the Bhagavad Gita, Sri Krishna tells Arjuna, "When you constantly control your mind and senses through the practice of meditation and seek the Self within, you will attain nirvana, the state of abiding joy and peace in me."

It was the Compassionate Buddha, however, who took this image of blowing out a flame and made it into one of the most memorable metaphors in the annals of mysticism. Once, it is said, a young disciple full of philosophical questions kept asking the Buddha, "When one attains nirvana, where does that person go?" Generally the Buddha kept silent for such questions, but this time he took a little oil lamp by his side and asked his disciple to blow it out. The boy did as he was asked. Then the Buddha asked, "Where is the flame?"

"It is gone, Blessed One."

"Tell me *where* it has gone," the Buddha insisted. "Don't just say, 'It is gone.'"

Until you attain it, discussions of what nirvana is don't have any application at all. When someone wanted to ask the Buddha about nirvana, he would say in effect, "I shall be happy to discuss it. Just extinguish all your selfish desires; then we can sit under the trees some evening and have a really learned discussion about what nirvana is."

The root *va* can mean "blow" also in the sense of the wind blowing. Imagine the mind to be as a lake, with a high wind constantly blowing over the surface, always keeping this lake choppy and turbulent. Our mind is just like a lake, over which the winds of selfish desire are blowing all the time. If it is not a desire for this, it is a desire for that. If it is not for one big desire, it is for two smaller desires. This fierce wind keeps blowing all the time, and the water of the lake is never at rest.

In the high regions of the Himalayas there is a lake called Manasarovar, "the lake of the mind," which is the goal of many pilgrims. Hindus of great faith bathe here before going on to the great temples of that region. The waters are icy, but such is their faith that they are able to enjoy this cold bath, which to people from the hot plains of India is very cold indeed. The surface of this lake is said to be always calm, beautifully reflecting the snowy peaks nearby.

This is the image of the mind in nirvana – calm, beautiful, holy. When the winds of self-will have ceased to blow and self-will has subsided, we can look at the bottom of the fathomless lake of consciousness and see for ourselves the supreme reality which is our real Self.

According to the Lankavatara Sutra, "Nirvana is where there is no birth, no death; it is seeing into the state of Suchness, absolutely transcending all the categories constructed by the mind; for it is the Buddha's inner consciousness."

The Good Weaver

MANY NAMES OF the Lord begin with the simple syllable *su*, which means "good" in Sanskrit. He is good-looking, his voice is good, his complexion is good, his thoughts are good; you get the idea. But a few of the names beginning with *su* are a little unexpected.

Sutantu, for example, literally means "he who has beautiful threads." The allusion is to a marvelous metaphor in the Upanishads, where the universe is compared to the web that a spider weaves out of itself.

After reading this name for the first time, I actually became interested in spiders. Their unobtrusive activities in hidden corners took on new meaning. I would watch a spider slowly bringing out one silvery, silken thread, then another, then another, until soon there would be a beautiful web. The Sanskrit word for spider, *urnanabhi*, literally means "the creature that brings wool out of its navel" – the finest wool, you know, real Pendleton.

That is just what the Lord has done. On my way to the beach this afternoon, it filled my heart with joy to see so many black-faced woolly lambs frisking about on the hills. I didn't see them just as lambs; I saw the Lord, spinning out from himself millions of creatures as the "wool-spinner" draws out its web.

This morning when I was having breakfast, I looked out our kitchen window and saw that the grass outside was a filigree of silver where hundreds of new cobwebs glistening with dew caught the light of the rising sun. By afternoon they will be gone again. How fleeting life is! Everything in this delicate web of a universe changes from moment to moment.

Every Tuesday, on my way to my regular talks on meditation, I remind myself, "Another week is gone." This is not morbid reflection. It is good to remind ourselves how quickly life passes, for it throws our activities into the sharpest perspective. Every day's first priority is to learn to move closer to the Lord of Love who lives in the depths of our consciousness.

Who Keeps Expanding His Web

IMAGINE IF, through the miracles of genetic engineering, scientists are able to cross a spider with an octopus. Who knows? It's not impossible. They might be able to come up with a tremendous spider. In the Galapagos Islands, a friend once told me, he saw a turtle weighing several hundred pounds. A spider weighing that much might cover the state of California with its web. Extend this to include the cosmos and you get an idea of how Sri Krishna keeps on expanding his web that is our universe.

There is a ubiquitous billboard advertisement that just shows a picture and says "More." Sri Krishna would say, "That's my motto!" If we ask, "More of what, Lord?" he would reply, "Just *more*. More people, more lambs, more sheep, more elephants, more trees, more bees, more stars, more space and time. . . ." That is the theory of the expanding universe. Sri Krishna's web expands and expands for forty or fifty billion years; then it starts contracting again, until everything goes back into the spider and the spider too disappears. Everything comes, then everything goes – except the Lord in his impersonal aspect, waiting to begin the cycle of creation all over again.

Destroyer of Sin

A few days ago a friend wrote to me that she had found a typographical error in the first volume of my *Bhagavad Gita for Daily Living,* published many years ago. Our lives too have "typos," mistakes we have committed – perhaps long ago – whose marks remain today. Every day that passes is a precious opportunity to correct these typos, by drawing on meditation for the will and the inspiration to change our lives. Whenever we do this, as this name implies, the power for change comes from the Lord.

Resentment, as Jesus reminds us, is a very serious typo. The longer it goes uncorrected, the more glaring it becomes. And self-will is a real printer's devil. In this sense, the beautiful Prayer of Saint Francis is a proof-reader's manual for finding and correcting errors. I recommend it to everyone – Christians, non-Christians, even atheists – for meditation because it spells out perfectly how to undo the conditioning of selfishness to which all of us have been subjected:

Lord, make me an instrument of thy peace.
Where there is hatred, let me sow love;
Where there is injury, pardon;
Where there is doubt, faith;
Where there is despair, hope;
Where there is darkness, light;
Where there is sadness, joy.

O divine Master, grant that I may not so much seek
To be consoled as to console,
To be understood as to understand,
To be loved as to love:
For it is in giving that we receive;
It is in pardoning that we are pardoned;
It is in dying to self that we are born to eternal life.

Correcting habits like impatience, unkindness, lack of sympathy, or preoccupation with our own personal pursuits does not require a cataclysmic reformation. It is in little matters that we show impatience or unkindness, and it is in the correction of these little mistakes, as of an "i" not dotted, that spiritual improvement lies. Remember those wise words quoted by Benjamin Franklin: "For want of a nail the shoe was lost; for want of a shoe the horse was lost; for want of a horse the rider was lost." Ben Franklin was a keen observer. He must have seen this borne out often, in everyday matters as well as in the affairs of state.

AMRITA
Immortal

I CAN UNDERSTAND why children and teenagers find it difficult to grasp the transience of life. They live as if things would always be the same and tomorrow would never come. After you have lived through thirty or forty years of life, however, you begin to notice how many people you once knew have passed on. Almost regularly now I get a letter saying that another of my former classmates or my childhood friends is gone.

Most of us do not want to notice this, but after the first volume of our life is closed, it is necessary to notice and reflect, and then to make changes to focus the remainder of our lives. "Time," says Marcus Aurelius, "is a sort of river of passing events, and strong is its current. No sooner is a thing brought to sight than it is swept by and another takes its place, and this too will be swept away." And he adds, almost in the language of the Buddha: "The universe is change; our life is what our thoughts make it."

We cannot put our trust in any changing relationship between bodies, or even in a relationship based on sympathy of mind or intellect. All these shift continuously. The only relationship that is permanent is the relationship between the Self in you and the same Self in others – the spiritual relationship in which we forget ourselves in living for the welfare of all.

In discovering that relationship, we enter immortality here on earth. The body, which is physical, will die; nothing can alter that. But the Self is not physical; it cannot die. When we *know* ourselves to be that Self, know it in the very depths of consciousness awake and asleep, then there is no break in awareness when the body is shed at death. Dying is no more than passing from one room to another.

Here is the song of Kabir on overcoming death:

O friend, hope for Him whilst you live;
Know whilst you live; for in life deliverance abides.
If your bonds be not broken whilst living,
What hope of deliverance in death?
It is but an empty dream that the soul shall have
Union with Him because it has parted from the body.
If He is found now, He is found then;
If not, we do but go to dwell in the City of Death.

Free from Craving

EPICTETUS HAS AN excellent metaphor for teaching detachment, perhaps the most important skill to acquire for living in a world of change. "Remember," he says,

> to behave in life as you would behave at a banquet. When something is being passed around, as it comes to you, stretch out your hand and take a portion of it gently. When it passes on, do not try to hold on to it; when it has not yet come to you, do not reach out for it with your desire but wait until it presents itself. So act toward children, toward spouse, toward office, toward wealth.

Epictetus would have been at home at a Hindu banquet, for we have three unwritten rules.

One is that there is a regular apportionment of space on the piece of banana leaf that serves as a plate. You don't pile things on top of each other. Each delicacy is served in a particular order in its appropriate place.

Second, when something delicious is put in front of you, you don't start in gobbling immediately; you wait until everybody has been served. Children get so impatient that a mother sometimes has to train her little one by slapping his wrist gently; but by the age of five or so all are able to sit patiently waiting until the serving is done and everyone observes a few moments' repetition of the mantram. After that, as Sri Ramakrishna says, conversation stops; the only sounds you hear are of eating and drinking.

The third rule is that when you are done, you have to wait until the last person has finished the last bite before you get up. This unwritten code of banana-plate manners makes even the largest family feast go smoothly.

In personal relationships, Epictetus suggests, we should observe the same kind of restraint. Don't try to cling to people, to hold people to you: everything changes, and if you try to arrest relationships and hold on to others, making them conform to your own needs, you will lose all the magic of life. William Blake says it beautifully:

> He who binds to himself a joy
> Does the wingéd life destroy;
> But he who kisses the joy as it flies
> Lives in eternity's sunrise.

The Supreme Magician

MANY YEARS AGO I took some friends to an excellent magic show. We had seats in the middle of the theater, but young Josh went and stood right near the stage to be able to expose the magician. Not only did he not succeed, but the magician managed to impress Josh even more than the rest of us.

He began by bringing ordinary little creatures out of his top hat – rabbits, hamsters, doves, the usual contents of a magician's hat. Josh was about to yawn when the animals suddenly became bigger and more offbeat: owls, vultures, a couple of overfed poodles. By the time he brought out a full-grown horse, everybody was sitting up and taking proper notice. He threw a large red blanket over the horse, and when he whipped it away the animal was gone. There was consternation all over Josh's face.

That is what the Lord's magic is like. In Sanskrit, the passing show of life – the illusion that we are all separate creatures rather than an indivisible divine whole – is called *maya*, with which our word "magic" may be connected. Out of apparent nothingness the Lord brings you and me and all these innumerable other creatures out upon the stage. Then, all too soon, he sweeps us away. Those with whom we have grown up, gone to school, shared the joys and trials of our adult years, one by one they just go.

It was this vision of the transience of life that burst like a bomb in the Buddha's consciousness. He saw in his imagination his beautiful wife lying dead, he saw his young son walking into death's jaws, and then and there he turned his back on everything else to seek a path that all can follow to discover that we are not the perishable body but pure spirit, the immortal Self.

When the Lord throws the blanket of maya over us, once he lifts it again we are gone – but only so long as we identify ourselves with the body. We don't have to disappear. If we can learn to identify ourselves with the Atman, the Self, then when the blanket is removed we will still be one with the magician himself, the Lord. In the climax of meditation called *samadhi,* when the mind becomes still and self-will is extinguished, we discover that our real Self is the Lord of Love.

Life is so short, and this discovery so urgent and so difficult, that none of us can afford to waste a day in not doing our best to move closer to the goal. Please take advantage of every opportunity to repeat the mantram, to train your senses, to keep on transforming your passions. And please be regular about your meditation. Don't lose a single day; don't waste a moment doing selfish things. All this time can be utilized for discovering the Self and for going beyond death here on this earth.

Whose Work Is Complete

THE LORD IS simply "the one who has done his job." If we love him and give him our best effort, it is the Lord within who enables us to do the job that every human being has come into life to do: to become aware of him. When that is done, the Upanishads say, everything has been done. "When you have known the Self, everything in life is known," because it is this Self that is the essence of all things. To realize the Self is to love all creatures – in fact, to become love itself.

How are we to make this supreme discovery? Saint Thomas Aquinas tells us in a famous passage,

> Three things are necessary for salvation: one, to know what we ought to believe; two, to know what we ought to desire; and three, to know what we ought to do.

The scriptures and mystics of all religions concur on what to believe: that the core of our personality is divine, and that the purpose of life is to discover this divinity for ourselves. What to desire, then, is the Lord himself, which is why mastery of desire has been called the key to Self-realization. Meditation enables us to withdraw our desires from frustrating, foolish channels and redirect them toward the Lord in an overwhelming, overriding flood of longing to be united with him forever.

When this is understood, the third requirement – what we ought to do in life – becomes clear. The implication is unavoidable: until we discover the Self, no matter how successful we may have been by ordinary standards, we have failed in our main job. Making money, collecting pleasures, visiting exotic places, making a name for ourselves – these are not our real job. They only leave us hungrier than we were before, more alienated, more lonely; for deep in our heart is the awareness that anything less than Self-realization will leave the human being unfulfilled.

Lovable

KRISHNA IS AN exceptionally attractive and affectionate Person; but to take it a little further, those who realize their oneness with Krishna, the Self, become lovable too. We naturally want to be with such people; we find it natural to fall in love with them.

"Once you realize the Self," the Upanishads say, "you will never be lonely again." Loneliness is epidemic today; even people with bundles of money and lofty social status get stricken by this virus. Once we realize the Self we don't have to beg, "Josie, please love me. Bernard, please be my friend." When the lotus blooms, Sri Ramakrishna reminds us, it has no need to say "Bees, come to me"; they are already looking for blossoms. Similarly, when you discover the Self you will find that you draw people to you naturally for inspiration, consolation, and strength.

By the same token, we can move closer to the Lord by moving closer to other people. This is not always easy, especially at those times when we feel inclined to hole up inside ourselves. It *is* sometimes difficult, even exasperating, to work with others with different methods and ideas. As we learn to give and take and to pay more attention to the needs of others, however, security comes without our seeking it; we no longer feel isolated in a meaningless world.

These developments reflect a divine paradox: all of us live in the Lord, just as he lives in each of us. The intellect gets baffled by this kind of contradictory language. In the Bhagavad Gita, when Krishna tries to explain, Arjuna raises his eyebrows and looks blank. Sri Krishna tells him gently, "This is the mystery of my being. You cannot understand." No amount of reasoning can make it clearer, but when we test it in our lives, we understand. The proof is that when we live harmoniously with others, it is we who grow spiritually. We do help them, but it is we who move closer to the Lord in our own lives. When we avoid opportunities to work and live with others, we lose this precious opportunity for growth, which can come to us in no other way.

VASU-MANAH

Whose Mind Is Full of Wealth

THE LORD'S WEALTH is his limitless love, the only kind of wealth that grows with the passage of time. It is not subject to fluctuations, like currency or stocks and bonds. The Lord presides over an endless bull market of love.

Saint Augustine gives us practical advice on how to become really wealthy by learning to love God through cultivating these qualities:

> Temperance is love surrendering itself wholly to Him who is its object; courage is love bearing all things gladly for the sake of Him who is its object; justice is love serving only Him who is its object, and therefore rightly seeking; prudence is love making wise distinctions between what hinders and what helps itself.

He Who Attracts

OF ALL THE Thousand Names, the name *Krishna* has come to be etched most deeply on my consciousness. This is due to the blessing of having grown up at my teacher's feet – as I would say, through her grace. I cannot take credit for my devotion to Krishna; she must have planted it in my consciousness early in my childhood.

When you go on repeating the mantram sincerely and systematically, this is the kind of devotion that the Lord helps to generate in your heart. Once it floods your mind completely, it will not leave you even in your sleep; it walks with you and works with you always. In the Hindu tradition we call this *ajapa-japam,* the name of the Lord repeating itself.

One special instruction I would like to give to you is to make use of every spare moment to repeat your mantram. A million opportunities can be discovered during the course of a single day.

One of the biggest opportunities, of course, is at night, when you are falling asleep. There may come a time when you cannot sleep and find it almost impossible to go on repeating the Holy Name hour after hour; the mind gets tired. At such times, what I used to do is ask Sri Krishna in my heart to make it a joy for me to recite his name. As a result, when I repeat his name today it is not a discipline; I do it with all the joy of indiscipline. I have no limits now, no restraints, no sense of when to do it and when not to do it. I do it all the time, which is what going beyond all disciplines means. But you have to struggle with disciplines for a long, long time before this kind of spiritual freedom comes.

Since we are talking about Krishna, let me treat you to one or two of the stories with which virtually every Hindu child grows up. In one great scene from the *Bhagavatam,* which contains the story of Sri Krishna's life, Krishna the teenager goes to the city of Mathura, where a cruel king called Kamsa is bringing untold misery to his people. Kamsa sends a fierce wrestler named Chanura to give the boy a special welcome. Chanura is the heavyweight champion of the ancient world. He just stands there waiting for Krishna, eager to make a pretzel of him; and the people of Mathura, who have heard that the youngster is invincible, gather to see what will happen.

In Indian drama Chanura is usually played by a fellow about six feet four and weighing two hundred and fifty pounds. The stage shakes as he moves. He plants himself in front of Krishna, blocking his path, and in front of these thousands of Krishna's admirers he roars: "I hear you have tamed the serpent Kaliya and conquered every demon sent your way. I would like to see how you fare with me!"

The onlookers tremble for Krishna at this challenge, because the boy is slender and svelte. He has a wasp's waist and perfectly proportioned arms and chest; every part of him is just right. He looks so boyish, so fresh, so tender-hearted. "And look at King Kong over there!" the crowd cries. "His *arms* are the size of Krishna's whole body!"

Krishna steps into the ring, and it is one of the highlights of the *Bhagavatam* when, after the preliminaries are over, he picks up Chanura as if he were a little mouse. I will spare you the details, since I am sure you have witnessed this sort of confrontation on TV. Briefly said, Krishna makes short work of him, and the wicked Kamsa realizes that his days are numbered.

When we love the Lord with all our heart, every scripture promises, this is the strength he gives us – not of body, but of will. Nothing will be able to break us; we will be able to stand up to any challenge and hold our own.

Sri Krishna's mother, it is said, was so devoted to her son that when Krishna was learning to walk, she used to wrap her arms around him so his beautiful body would not be bruised. "What a miracle, Krishna!" exclaims a great mystic poet of Mysore in a song. "You who protect the entire universe, your mother thinks that by falling once you are going to get hurt."

In other relationships, too, Krishna was mischievous about hiding his strength in tenderness. He had an older cousin, Bhima, who is a great favorite with Indian audiences. Bhima is huge and muscular, highly physically-oriented and often forgetful of his strength and size. He is always doing exercises of some sort: if he isn't running he is swimming; if he isn't swimming he is wrestling or practicing with his mace. He is simple, direct, and very loyal, and he has an awful temper. He is also slightly older than Krishna, and according to ancient Hindu custom one should always show respect to one's elders, greeting them by touching their feet. Still, when Krishna shows this kind of reverence to Bhima, it seems a little wrong. *Everyone* touches Sri Krishna's feet, even kings and sages.

"Krishna," someone finally asks, "you are the lord of the whole universe. Why do you touch the feet of this big cousin of yours?"

Sri Krishna replies, "If I don't duck he embraces me, and I get a few broken ribs!"

The word *Krishna* comes from the root *krish*, "to attract." Krishna is he who draws love from everyone, who draws us to him in the hearts of others. Strangely, when we try to draw love out of others, we get into a tug-of-war that may end in pushing them away, for all we are doing is trying to meet our own needs. It is forgetting ourselves in the needs of others that draws their love irresistibly. Again, this is the paradox of maya: try to grab and you will lose; give, and you will hold others' love forever.

SATYA
Truth

GOD IS LOVE, Gandhi used to point out penetratingly, but He is also truth: *satya* means not only "truth" but also "that which is real." One of the oldest prayers in Hinduism says, "Lead me from the unreal to the real": from a lower state of consciousness in which we are acting out our dreams, to the state of truth and joy.

Most of us are convinced that we are already awake, that we are completely responsible for our thoughts. But we don't seem to be able to have the same thought for a very long time. If a beneficial thought comes, we can't make it stay, and many, many thoughts sneak into the mind that we do not approve of at all. Therefore, the Buddha would say, it isn't quite correct to say that we think thoughts; it is more accurate to say that thoughts think us. To be able to say "I think" and mean it, we should be able to have a regular roll call of thoughts and account for every one of them.

Imagine the mind as a kind of theater. When I go to the art museum theater, the attendant checks tickets not once but twice. After the first show she comes around again, and if you don't have your ticket stubs she will ask you, politely but firmly, to leave. We should have the same capacity to check on our thoughts. If an unkind thought is lurking in a dark corner, we should be able to shine our flashlight on it and say, "No ticket? Sorry, you'll have to go."

When a mood or desire overpowers us, we think it is one thought, one state of mind that can't be altered until it has run its course. A dominant passion or obsession seems a solid block in the edifice of our personality. The Buddha would say no. Every mental state is a momentary flash of thought, one after the other, and no two thought-moments are connected. Think of a million separate thoughts, he would say, standing in line to get into the theater of the mind.

In a movie theater, when the projector is running, you see a smooth, continuous flow of action: horses galloping, people jumping on their horses and falling off again, guns firing, stagecoaches being robbed. But stop the projector and you will see that the film is only a slide show. The action seems real merely because the separate frames are moving by so fast. Similarly, in a person whose mind is fast, thought after thought pushes through the turnstile so rapidly that we think it is one solid wave of emotion over which we have no control. Once the first thought pushes through, the rest follow in a heap.

Get hold of the first fellow, the Buddha says. He hasn't got a ticket – in fact, he has a permanent season no-ticket, a very Zen phrase.

In yoga psychology this thought-leader is called a root *samskara,* the source of a whole chain of compulsive thought. Even after you have learned to keep lesser freeloaders out of the mind, a root samskara is terribly difficult to deal with. If you succeed in locating him and demand to see his ticket, he will answer, "Who do you think you are? Let *me* see *your* ticket." And everybody seated around him will explain, "Oh, he's been here a long time. He must belong; how else could he have gotten in?"

In other words, the roots of compulsive thinking – anger, fear, lust, and the like – go deep in the unconscious. To deal with them with authority, you have to reach an even deeper level of consciousness in meditation. If you can get below a samskara, you can be there waiting for him and say, "Sam, where is your ticket?" He will look sheepish and say, "You got me!" Once you can do this, you know with joy that every trait due to negative conditioning can be undone.

Approachable

MOST OF US know how difficult it can be to approach a person in authority. Mussolini, I think, designed a virtual palace for himself, where anybody wanting to see him had to walk down a long, long hall at the end of which Il Duce sat, looking down from a raised throne. By the time frightened supplicants reached this awesome figure, their bones would have turned to water.

The British government in India used similar architectural tricks to intimidate us: long ascents of stone steps to the viceroy's palace, for example, just a little too high and a little too deep to be taken in a stride, while armed guards with splendid uniforms watched from unapproachable heights. Even Gandhi often found it impossible to get an audience with the viceroy of India, and the rest of us felt we were doing well to get a few minutes with a local British official – in our own country.

Gandhi, by contrast – probably the greatest man this century has produced – made himself accessible even to children, and shed every vestige of authority that might set him apart from others. In those days the British Raj was at the zenith of its power, and all its medieval pomp and pageantry was brought out on state occasions to impress millions of its subjects. Gandhi appeared before us in his simple white dhoti and nothing else.

Sri Krishna too, lord of the very universe, encourages us to turn to him whatever our past or present is like. We have only to turn our face and heart to him and he will respond. In India we say that when we take one step toward the Lord, he takes seven steps toward us. But he will watch to see whether we keep on taking steps – and that first step is left to us.

The Shining One

DEVA, LITERALLY "a shining being," is usually translated as "god," and *devi,* the feminine form, as "goddess." Many, many devas and devis are mentioned in the Hindu scriptures, but as one of the oldest of these scriptures, the Rig Veda, says, "Truth is one, though the wise call it by many names." All these deities are simply names for the powers of life, which are expressions of the power of one supreme Lord.

In India it is perfect manners to add the word *Devi* after any woman's name. The significance is that every woman is an embodiment of the Divine Mother. This is a subtle way of reminding us men to treat all women with invariable respect. Never to use harsh language, never to quarrel, never to exploit, never to manipulate: this is the ideal at which all of us should aim.

In my village, when I was a boy, a woman could go out at any time without fear of being molested or even stared at. This reflects a high image of womanhood, that women should not be treated as sex objects, not as inferior or superior, but always with love and respect. If a society preserves this ideal, women live up to it naturally, and the whole culture benefits by their contribution.

Today, it seems, we are playing a kind of game, trying to show respect for women by changing certain offensive words. Bureaucrats talk a good deal about acceptable replacements for words like "serviceman" and "repairman." But it is not a change of words that is required; it is a change of heart. No special term coined by linguists can conceal a condescending mind.

I sympathize with everyone who has problems with the opposite sex; our modern civilization has made these relationships increasingly difficult. But I find it hard to sympathize with those who do not try every day to solve these problems by respecting the opposite sex and learning the art of nonviolent opposition when they find themselves in a situation that needs to be changed. Domination and competition injure both sexes. Man should not dominate woman, nor should woman dominate man; each should help to complete the other. This is the spiritual ideal.

Full of Glory

BHAGAVAN IS USED much the way we use "Lord" in English, generally in reference to a divine incarnation like Sri Krishna or Sri Rama. In the tradition in which my grandmother and I stand, no one refers to a human being as Bhagavan, only to a divine incarnation.

According to one ancient text, the word *bhagavan* should be used only in referring to those who possess six *bhagas* or "splendors." These are the prerequisites for any divine incarnation, and they are rather demanding.

The first is wealth – not in the worldly sense, but in the sense that an incarnation of the Lord has the capacity to give limitlessly. We can see this illustrated abundantly in the lives of Jesus the Christ and the Compassionate Buddha. Our usual idea is that those who aggressively acquire things for themselves, usually at the expense of others, are to be considered rich. In the spiritual sense, however, these same people may be paupers.

The second quality is power. In modern parlance this means physical power – power to dominate, to threaten, to destroy. But this kind of power is short-lived. Spiritual power – the power to help, to serve, to love – outlives any physical power, because it supports life. Love of power can be seen in many human beings, but a divine incarnation is marked by the power of love.

The third quality is dharma, the unity of life. Hatred, violence, unkindness, disloyalty, greed – any act or urge which sets us apart from others in pursuit of our own self-aggrandizement – all violate the central law of existence, that all of us are part of an indivisible whole. Those who are always aware of dharma will do nothing to violate this unity, no matter what the provocation. It is one of the loftiest tests of spiritual awareness.

Fourth comes esteem: not the superficial fame of the celebrity, but profound and lasting respect. A divine incarnation may not be recognized as such by many, but the scriptures say that he will be widely respected for his wisdom and compassion. In the *Mahabharata,* India's ancient epic about the war between the forces of light and the forces of darkness, Sri Krishna is depicted as commanding the respect of both sides, though he makes it clear which cause is just.

The fifth quality may be surprising: beauty. The Lord is infinitely beautiful, with a beauty that is not diminished by time. Physical beauty cloys with familiarity, but the inner beauty which shows itself in the capacity to give and to cherish grows with the passage of time. It transcends the senses, transcends even mind and intellect.

The last quality is absolutely essential. *Jnana* is sometimes translated as knowledge, but its real meaning is not intellectual learning but wisdom in living – a rather rare quality. A divine incarnation must be a complete master of the art of living, which means that he or she must possess continuous awareness of the unity of life and the detachment required to live in harmony with that unity, without any thought of personal gain.

These are the six qualities that must be present for one to be called Bhagavan. They are marks of perfection, and since no human being is likely to be perfect, I think you will see my grandmother's wisdom in never applying the term to anyone but Sri Rama or Sri Krishna.

On the other hand, there is practical significance in these six *bhagas:* these are qualities we should try to cultivate in our own lives if we want to remake ourselves in a higher image. To give rather than grab, to help rather than hinder, to be aware of the unity of life, to depend for our beauty on the qualities of goodness and kindness, to put ourselves last and the whole around us first – this is how we develop these divine qualities which are the natural endowments of Bhagavan, the Lord within.

Destroyer of Good Fortune

PARADOXICALLY, THERE is another Holy Name derived from *bhaga: Bhagaha,* "he who destroys good fortune." In the ancient Vedas, the goddess of good fortune – later worshipped as Sri Krishna's divine consort, his feminine aspect – was called Bhaga; people prayed to her for health, wealth, beauty, and fame. Why then should Krishna, the all-loving Lord, have this terrible name, as if he bestows worldly blessings with one hand and then tears them away with the other?

The answer is that in the Hindu and Buddhist view, we are here on earth for one supreme purpose: to realize the unity of life. And by some quirk of human nature, the vast majority of us begin to think seriously about life only when things are going against us.

My grandmother tried to teach me this painful truth at an early age, and I resisted for many, many years. "No, Granny," I would say, "that can't be true." It didn't faze her. "One day," she said, "you are going to agree with me."

Today, after many years of bitter experience, I say to myself almost every day, "Yes, Granny, you were right.

This is the best way in which we human beings can be educated." It would be wonderful if we could learn from good fortune, but generally it is only when fortune is snatched away that we begin to reflect, to question what we are doing and ask if it is taking us where we really want to go.

Sit back for a moment and reflect with some detachment. It is painful to realize that whatever growth we may have achieved personally came not when the wind was in our favor, not when we were in the best of health, not when our partner used to leave little notes saying "I love you" around the house. It came rather when we were hit by ill health, or deserted by our friends, or estranged from our family, or cast down by the shattering of great hopes. During these agonizing moments we seem to be able to grow, particularly if we want to grow and are eager to learn.

We can look upon the Lord as that force which makes us think for ourselves and learn from our mistakes. It is the same Lord within who enables us to change direction and find health, happiness, love, and wisdom.

Bringer of Joy

THIS NAME IS sure to be met with appreciation. Everyone wants joy. Yet despite Madison Avenue, which promises it from cars, clothes, drinks, drugs, and even soaps, joy is something rare. It is not just elation or euphoria, but an exalted state beyond pleasure and pain in which the mind is still.

If this sounds drab, that is only because we haven't tasted it. When the mind is still, there is no selfish craving to be or have or enjoy something that we lack. We are at peace, lacking nothing, full of love and the desire to give. When we reach that state in meditation where we can deal successfully with our personal hang-ups and harness some of our strong urges for pleasure and self-aggrandizement, we will begin to taste the indescribable joy that is our legacy as human beings.

In the Krishna tradition there is a passionate devotional poem called *Gita Govinda,* "The Song of Krishna," in which every symbol of lovemaking is used to convey the joy that comes when the separate personality loses itself in the divine. Jayadeva, the great Bengali poet, is trying to convey his devotion through symbolism that can be understood by ordinary human beings like us, who find that the keenest physical pleasure they can enjoy is sex.

Mystics do not deny that sex is an intensely pleasurable experience. The question they ask is simply, "How long does it last?" So keen, so enjoyable, and yet so brief – just a few moments of sensation. Our desire is for joy that never ends. Only when our desires have been unified, when all our fierce longings have been welded together, can we attain the state of lasting joy which is called *ananda*.

Child of the Infinite

To UNDERSTAND this name, we have to do some exploring in Hindu mythology.

In ancient India there once lived a loving couple named Aditi and Kashyapa, so devoted to the Lord that when Vishnu chose to be born on earth as Vamana, one of his many incarnations, he chose Aditi and Kashyapa to be his parents.

At that time the earth was oppressed by a king named Mahabali, and the Lord's descent into human life was to put an end to his reign of terror. Later, when it came time to destroy the tyranny of Mahabali, the tiny Vamana would be transformed to cosmic proportions. But at birth he seemed just like any other infant, weighing seven or eight pounds and skilled in keeping his parents awake with his cries at night.

As he grew, too, just like any other boy, he kept getting into trouble – all of which only added to the joy of Aditi and Kashyapa. They were such devoted parents that the little boy, to show his adoration, once asked, "Mom, what gift can I give you?"

Aditi said, "You'd better not ask that, Vam. I wouldn't really like to tell you."

But Vamana continued to ask, and finally he did something no incarnation should ever do: he slipped up and said, "I promise. I'll grant whatever you wish."

"In that case," Aditi replied, "the next time you are born, I want to be your mother then too."

So, eons later, when Vishnu has to come to earth again to reestablish righteousness, he again is born as Aditi's son. But this time Aditi is the princess Devaki, and Vishnu is born as Krishna.

To me, all this seems only reasonable. Wouldn't the Lord want to be born into a familiar home? He knows from past experience that everything there will be just right. He can't afford to take chances with a new mother; the forces of evil threaten him from the moment of birth.

Even for ordinary people like us, it seems logical that a loving relationship in this life might carry over into the next. In my village, where reincarnation is taken for granted, most people believe that if you try to be a good mother or father, you make it possible to pick up that relationship the next time around. My mother would say that there must have been a perfect relationship between me and my spiritual teacher in former lives, for I was literally born into her arms. I could come into that context through her grace only because I had been with her before.

Aditi comes from *a-*, "no," and *diti*, "limit." Aditi is the Divine Mother, and the practical significance of her name is that we should not restrict our love to just one or two people; we should learn to love without limit.

God is the mother of all. We too should look on all children as our own, and share responsibility for them. We are teaching the next generation by our personal example; so we have to ask ourselves constantly, "What effect will my actions have on the children around me?"

Pele, the great Brazilian soccer star, can name his price to any advertiser, but he turns down all offers to endorse cigarettes or alcohol. When asked why, he responded simply, "I love kids." He knows that millions of children around the world, without exaggeration, look up to him and will follow his example.

LAKSHMI
Good Fortune

ONE PART OF the Lord's being is masculine, called Vishnu. But the Lord also has a feminine aspect, and that is called Lakshmi, personified as Vishnu's eternal consort. These are not really two but one.

Lakshmi is the goddess of good fortune and beauty. When the gods churned the cosmic ocean at the beginning of time to distill the nectar of immortality, she arose like Venus from the waters of life and chose Vishnu to be her eternal companion. Her symbol is the lotus, the most beautiful of all flowers; and this lotus is the womb of Vishnu, from which the cosmos is born. When Vishnu comes to earth as Krishna, Lakshmi is born as Rukmini; when he is Rama, she is Sita.

SAHISHNU
Enduring

SAHISHNU IS A beautiful name that reminds us how compassionate the Lord is, for it comes from the root *sah,* "to be patient, to put up with, to endure." Sahishnu is the Lord who bears with us and forgives us our mistakes.

This name encourages us too to be patient and bear up cheerfully when life hands us something that we would rather not have to deal with. To judge by our responses to life's ordinary ups and downs, most of us say, "Give me only things I like. Don't give me anything I dislike; give it to Brian instead."

Even good people, when they have been struck down by illness or misfortune, sometimes ask, "Why did this happen to *me?*" This is a most peculiar question. What we should ask is, "Why should this happen to anybody?" Simply asking this question at a deeper level of awareness brings the patience to bear tragedies without self-pity, releasing the insight and compassion to help others and to grow ourselves.

Pleasant and unpleasant together are the very texture

of life. Only when we give our best whatever comes, good or bad, can we live in freedom.

Who Brings Good from Suffering

Su MEANS GOOD; *tapas* is suffering freely borne for the sake of others and one's own spiritual growth.

When you attain Self-realization and look back upon your life, you will find it most satisfying to see how even your mistakes have played a part. If you hadn't dipped your fingers in hot water when you were eight, so to speak, you would have soaked yourself in much hotter water later on. The purpose of mistakes is to learn not to go on making them. Eventually we *know* – as Gandhi says, "from bitter personal experience" – that pain and pleasure, disappointment and satisfaction, success and failure, cannot be isolated from each other, and that chasing after worldly satisfactions can never bring fulfillment.

Most of us look upon pleasure and pain as two different departments at war with each other. They are really one department, with only one chairperson, and any attempt to isolate what is pleasant and avoid what is unpleasant is doomed to failure.

For this reason, I never ask those who meditate with

me if they are having fun. The only relevant question is, "Are you growing?" It is this forced fragmentization – "Let there be one department for what I like, which I must have, and another department for what I don't like; let it go to others" – which makes us into pygmies. To grow to our full height, we have to learn to bear what we dislike cheerfully. If it benefits others, we can actually learn to enjoy it. Then a good deal that was bitter in life becomes sweet.

Whose Thoughts Are True

WHILE WE ARE on this subject of pleasure and pain, let us consider for a moment the dream world. The Hindu scriptures say that when we dream, various experiences may come; we may go through travails of sorrow or scale the pinnacles of joy. This is characteristic of everyone's dreams. And as far as the nervous system is concerned, many dream experiences are not much different from their waking counterparts. The sensations and physiological responses are the same. I have heard children laughing or crying in their sleep; I have heard older people talking in their dreams. At that time, those sorrows and joys are real.

When we wake up, however, the dream world melts away. We cannot really say it was unreal: after all, we did experience it. The sorrow or happiness were as real as anything in ordinary life. But when we wake up, these feelings evaporate. The dream experiences seem shadowy and distant, and we see that in reality there was no cause for sorrow or pleasure at all.

Similarly, the scriptures continue, when we attain Self-realization, we shall look upon the experiences of our past life, its pleasures and pains, its successes and defeats, exactly as we look upon a dream. When I look back on my early career, in which I made the same kind of silly mistakes and suffered the same kind of blows that everyone makes and suffers in life, I do not feel any regret or pain. It's all a dream. I don't have any animosity against those who hurt me, because I would feel absurd resenting someone from a dream. That is how you will come to look at your previous life: you wake up, and all the burden of the past falls away. It will free you from so much turmoil, release so much energy and vitality, that you will feel you have a new lease on life.

This is true not only of dreaming but of daydreaming. Do you remember Thurber's famous story, "The Secret Life of Walter Mitty"? Everybody has a secret life, you know. We may not always be aware of it in all its details, but most of us have at least our innocent fantasies. Some of my students in India used to get carried away building castles in the air; one of them liked to take a piece of paper, write his name, and then add "MA, PhD, LLD, Oxford, Cambridge." It was an innocent attempt to add weight to an otherwise airy academic career.

I have also known somebody in this country who had a very poor voice, but who, when no one was around, used to go out under a tree and sing as if she were Joan Baez. She would play her guitar and sing exactly in that style. I had to sympathize. Think of the frustrated hopes, the secret dream of standing in the Greek Theatre and singing "We Shall Overcome" while the audience stands teary-eyed and cheers . . .

Dreams and daydreams, of course, are often a kind of escape, an ingenious attempt by one part of the mind to try to compensate for what is lacking in the other part – that is, for the disappointments of everyday life. Dreaming is a safety valve for the frustration that otherwise can rage when certain dear hopes and deep desires are not fulfilled. I find this a very compassionate explanation. In this sense, dreams and daydreams do have a useful role to play when there is no higher outlet for the energy dammed up in a thwarted desire.

My advice, however, is to forget your dreams – don't dwell on them – and never dwell on daydreams or fantasies of what might be. When you do, you are teaching your mind to live in a dream world, where it can cling to private pleasures and retreat from anything unpleasant. Most Walter Mittys have trouble with work and relationships; when a little pebble in the real world blocks their path, they give up and turn to fantasies.

In Indian folklore, the danger of daydreaming is illustrated in the story of a dairy maid who is going to the market to sell her milk, carrying the pot on her head. She is young and beautiful and fond of dancing, and since she isn't repeating her mantram, her mind begins to wander. "When I have sold all of my milk," she thinks, "I shall have two rupees. After a month, if everything goes well, I shall have sixty rupees. Sixty rupees! What could I do with sixty rupees? . . . I could buy a real silk dancing costume; perhaps I would even have enough left over to buy dancing bells for my feet. Then this is how I would dance . . ." She begins to skip, the pot falls from her head and shatters, and instead of sixty rupees she has none for buying a new pot.

Reality

SAT MEANS ABSOLUTE reality: literally, "that which is." The word comes from the root *as,* "to be," which is related to the English verb *is.* One of the most accurate statements we can make about God is simply God *is.*

God alone is real. Shankara defines the real as that which is changeless. Anything that changes, if not precisely unreal, belongs to a lower level of reality.

If we apply this demanding definition to the universe, we have to admit that the earth and sun and even the Milky Way galaxy will pass away someday. As an amateur astronomer, I find it fascinating to reflect on change and reality at this cosmic level. Imagine: a galaxy that is a billion light years away from us can be photographed at an observatory, but that photograph will not be a photograph of the galaxy as it is today; it shows the galaxy as it was a billion years ago. When I see spectacular photographs in books on astronomy, I remind myself that these are photographs of the past. They are, in Shankara's view, photographs of something that is unreal, because it has changed before we could even see it.

If you want to know what reality is, what the universe and you and I are really like, you must look for something changeless. The only real part of us is the part that does not change. The more we can identify with this changeless core of personality, the more "real" we become.

Most of us, I suppose, have known at least one friend on whom we could depend always. We feel they are reliable, and we trust them to stand by us through thick and thin. In a sense, this is recognizing an element of the changeless in such a person.

On the other hand, we know how difficult it is to have relationships with people who vacillate. We never know where they stand. Their personality seems uncertain, unfounded. If we can learn to keep our mind even, to keep our love and loyalty as steady as possible, to that extent we are moving closer to the reality within us – the core of Sat, the supreme reality that is God.

Even if people offend us and we don't feel like being warm toward them, it is in our interest as well as theirs to be as steadfast and loyal as possible. This steadiness of mind will help us to discover the nature of life as it really is.

Sat also means good. That which is good is real; that which is real is good. Gandhi pointed out this connection. Evil, he said, has no reality of its own; it exists only insofar as we support it. If we withdraw our support, evil cannot continue.

This little word *sat* points to a great truth taught in the Hindu scriptures – that you and I are, at our core, good. Our truest nature is good. We have only to remove the covering layers that are hiding this innate goodness. We should think of our original goodness and not dwell on original sin: for the goodness is our real nature; the sin is a temporary stain.

Unreality

IN A DARING moment, the Hindu mystics also call the Lord by an opposite name: *asat,* that which is unreal. This is a paradox that can cause theologians sleepless nights, but I like to look upon it in a purely practical way. In a sense, we all do live in an unreal world, a world that is colored to such an extent by our individual mental conditioning as to become unreal. But it is only when we wake up to a higher level of consciousness that we can realize this. Until then, we must continue to act as if our experiences are real.

It is helpful to remember, however, that just as the experiences of the dreamer and daydreamer are not real, but only constructions imposed by the mind, so the pleasures and pain of this world have no reality apart from the mind. This world is made up of neither pleasure nor pain. These are contributions of our own nervous system, and they depend very much on personal conditioning.

When you reach a certain depth in meditation, you will look back upon some of the occasions when you felt a great deal of pain and see it as a kind of optical illusion. You will not see any reason for the pain, which means that there was no pain in the world outside. You did suffer then, just as in a bad dream, but now that you are awake at that level of consciousness, you can look on the same experience without any overlay of suffering.

In the same way – and even more revolutionary – when you look back on the occasions when you enjoyed a great deal of pleasure, you will wonder why you looked upon it as pleasure. It was only excitement, the nervous system stirred up in a particular way. What you will prize then is not excitement but joy, which wells up when the mind is not agitated by desire or aversion, but lies still.

This is why, in the Gita, Sri Krishna tells Arjuna to bear not only pain but pleasure with an even mind. When you are enjoying something, he says, don't get excited. Put up with it patiently; it will soon be over. We want to object, "That's taking all the joy out of life!" It is just the opposite. We can enjoy, but we should not cling. If we cling to the sensations of excitement, we are teaching the mind to cling to the sensations of pain, which are bound to follow as night follows day.

Pleasure and pain, the Gita says, have nothing to do with us. They are affairs of the body and senses, something that happens when the senses come in contact with objects of sense-perception. The Self, the inner observer, is not involved. When the senses come in contact with objects they enjoy, it is only natural to identify ourselves with the body and senses and attribute that joy to ourselves. But the same is true in pain. When our ego is hurt, it suffers, and the more we identify with the ego, the more we suffer. Only when self-will is low, when we gain detachment from the ego's demands, does sorrow begin to leave our lives once and for all.

This doesn't mean that we become callous or unfeeling. I live in a world without pleasure and pain but full of joy. I grieve greatly at the tragedies I see around me; in fact, I grieve much more today than I ever used to, because I am a million times more sensitive to the suffering of those around me. But even in that sensitivity there is joy, because it releases limitless resources that enable me to help. Our globe faces terrible problems, but with the dedicated assistance of many friends who support this work, I know today that we can make a difference in helping to solve them.

The Supreme Path

GATI, FROM THE root *gam,* "to go," means both "path" and "destination": it is where we are going and that by which we travel. The Lord is the way and the goal.

After attaining Self-realization, great mystics have exclaimed: It was you, Lord, who roused me to seek you. You were my running and the path on which I ran. You were there with your starting gun forcing me to get started. I didn't have my socks on, let alone my running shoes; in fact, I wasn't even out of bed, but you roused me and wouldn't let me sleep in peace. You laid the track; and when it began to get too hard, you laid down soft grass; but when I got used to comfortable turf, began taking it for granted, you spread stones. When my endurance was coming to an end, you gave me a second wind. You arranged the whole race, and in the last quarter you gave me the superhuman strength I needed to throw myself forward and breast the tape. You held the starting gun and it was you holding the tape at the end. I thought it was I who won the prize, but now I realize that everything was done by you.

RAMA

Joy

THE SCRIPTURES SAY that Vishnu has come down to this earth several times to reestablish dharma, righteousness, in times of great evil. These ten incarnations or *avataras* happen to follow the pattern of biological evolution. They are the fish, the tortoise, the boar, the man-lion, Vamana, Parashurama, Rama, and Krishna. The ninth incarnation is said to be the Buddha, and the tenth, yet to come, the scriptures call Kalki.

Rama – the name comes from the root *ram,* "to rejoice" – shares with Krishna the distinction of being the best-loved incarnation of Lord Vishnu. He was born a prince in ancient times in the city of Ayodhya in North India, and his story is known throughout South Asia in the *Ramayana* epic.

Rama is a lovely word in Sanskrit and perhaps the most universal of mantrams. It is repeated alone (Mahatma Gandhi's mantram was *Rama, Rama, Rama*) or with the name *Krishna* added, as in the mantram my grandmother gave to me:

> *Haré Rama, Haré Rama,*
> *Rama Rama, Haré Haré,*

Haré Krishna, Haré Krishna,
Krishna Krishna, Haré Haré.

Rama is the perfect mantram, because it means the joy that knows no end. Pleasure is something that comes and goes. Joy stays with you, increasing with the passage of time.

You may remember my saying earlier that in yoga psychology, the human personality is said to consist of five jackets or sheaths of consciousness. The outermost jacket is the physical body, the sphere of pleasure and pain; the innermost jacket is very rarefied consciousness, described as made out of joy. That is the jacket everyone wants. When you go to Macy's, that is what you are looking for among the designer labels. Everyone asks, "Have you got the jacket of joy?" But the sales clerks have never heard of it.

The great mystics tell us that we don't have to go to a store to buy this jacket; we already have it. But our closet is so full of garments of nylon and polyester that we don't see it. Only when we remove the synthetic clutter of our internal wardrobe do we cry out in ecstasy, "Here it is! Right in my closet all the time."

After this discovery, we live in perpetual joy. This is not a figure of speech. This joy can never leave us – as the Buddha said, it will follow us like a shadow, even into our sleep.

We don't have to leave our family, quit school, leave our job, or go off to a mountain cave to find this joy.

We can find it right in the midst of life. The Upanishads actually calculate that the joy of Self-realization is a million times greater than any happiness we have known before. To their authority I can add the testimony of my own small personal experience.

Bearer of the Bow

THIS NAME IS an epithet of Sri Rama, who is usually shown in sculpture and painting carrying his bow because he is a great archer. His arrows, *Ramabana,* are the mantram. This is a perfect image, because archery and meditation both require keen concentration. In meditation what we are trying to do is bring all our attention together to focus on one single point, the Self. When we love the Lord with all our heart, all our mind, and all our strength, we are consummate archers, victorious on the battlefields of life.

In Hindu mythology it is Rama, not Krishna, who is known as a great warrior, leading his army to victory against the evil king Ravana. Krishna, the gentle cowherd boy, is not usually thought of as a fighter, and although there are many stories of him slaying demons, his overall image is of a peaceable, loving incarnation. Even when his beloved Arjuna faces the apocalyptic battle that is the climax of the *Mahabharata,* Krishna does not take part in the fight but serves as Arjuna's charioteer.

Yet there are times, the poets tell us, when Sri Krishna recalls his former warrior life. Unlike the rest of us, he has free access to the deeper levels of the unconscious, and sometimes scenes from his past lives bubble up to the surface.

In a beautiful poem, the blind mystic Surdas, who lived in medieval India, captures Krishna in such a moment. Yashoda, Krishna's foster mother, is trying to put baby Krishna to sleep, and the poem is a haunting lullaby that describes the scene. Krishna doesn't feel sleepy, so Yashoda begins to lull him with the story of Rama, which is told in Hindu households all over India. She starts just as every other mother starts: "Once upon a time there was a king named Dasharatha who had four sons, and the oldest was called Rama ..."

Krishna's eyes start to close; he is drifting off into the never-never land between waking and dreams. Yashoda tucks him in and begins to tiptoe away. *"Waaaaah!"* Krishna wakes up. Yashoda rushes back, soothes him, and continues, swinging his cradle as she speaks: "Rama had to go to the forest with his beloved wife, Sita, and his brother Lakshmana ..." Krishna's eyes are closing; he is adrift between worlds again. "But in the forest, while Rama and Lakshmana are away, the demon king Ravana comes and carries Sita off in his chariot, and she cries for help with all her heart: 'Rama! *Rama!* ..."

And suddenly baby Krishna sits up wide-awake, his eyes full of fire. "My bow!" he cries. "Lakshmana, bring me my bow!" He is no longer Krishna; he is back in his previous life.

Self-control

MOST OF US acknowledge the virtue of self-control, but to judge by our actions, what we would really like to control is others. If we could just succeed in making those around us do what we want, where is the need to master ourselves?

This is what anger is all about. If Jack gets angry with Alice, what he is saying is: "You're not doing what I want, and I'm going to make you!" If Alice responds in kind, she is saying the same thing. To mediate their quarrel, all I have to say is: "Jack, why don't you try to control yourself? Alice, why don't you work to control *yourself?*" It's that simple.

Not only is it simple, nothing else is very realistic. The only person whose thinking I can control is myself. You can regulate someone else's watch, but you can't regulate anyone's mind except your own. Even that takes a lot of hard work, but if you find your mind getting speeded up – say, in anger – it *is* possible to slow it down to a reasonable pace, and maybe one day even to stop it completely. When you can do that, you will know what joy really means.

Whom We Desire

IN MY NATIVE language, Malayalam, *ishta* also means "friend." So Ishta is a very good name for the Lord. He is a good friend, and the contribution a good friend can make is twofold. A friend should support us in time of trouble, but a real friend will also oppose us when we are causing trouble or about to cause trouble, whether to others or to ourselves.

My grandmother was a perfect friend. On the one hand she was very softhearted, but on the other hand, I have never seen anybody so tough in all my life. In fact, the two toughest people I have ever known are Granny and Gandhiji. She didn't spare her toughness when she was dealing with me, either. She was usually very tender, but sometimes she was strict to the point of seeming harsh. It took many years to understand that this was an important part of her love for me.

In the scriptures, however, *Ishta* means your chosen spiritual ideal, the incarnation of God to whom you feel most deeply drawn. In India the question, "Who is your Ishta?" doesn't mean who is your friend, but who is your favorite incarnation. It might be the Buddha, or Shiva, or Krishna, or the Divine Mother, or Jesus, or Rama, or quite a number of other divine manifestations. The main thing is that the Ishta is the goal of our spiritual desires.

The Sufis say that we should see the Beloved in everyone we love. In all our relationships, though we are aware of the inadequacies at the present, we should never lose sight of the fact that the Beloved is hidden in the hearts of all. This is what enables us to keep faith with people, to trust and support them, and to oppose them tenderly when necessary to keep them from making a serious mistake.

King of Death

YAMA MEANS LITERALLY "the controller," and in Hindu mythology, Yama is the god of death. This is such a fearsome name that in most Hindu homes it is never mentioned. You must have read those Victorian novels where the father says, "I don't want to ever hear his name in this house again," and after that everyone is careful not to mention Uncle Cecil by name. Similarly, people in my village would never talk about Yama directly; they would just say "he" or "it."

But the Lord, out of his deep love for us, will not let us deny the truth of death. He may strike us hard, if necessary, to make us aware that time is our executioner.

My grandmother was a great spiritual teacher, for she planted this awareness in me very early in life. I never forget how quickly time passes. We grow up, go to school, grow old, and life is over before we know it, perhaps before we have begun to understand why we are here. And we sit here without a struggle, when all our energy should be bent to discover how to go beyond death here in this life.

Krishna comes as Yama to remind us that as long as

we identify ourselves with the body, we cannot escape death. Far from being morbid, this reminder is a great gift. It is one of life's greatest blessings to be constantly aware of death, so long as we use that awareness to deepen our meditation and make every day count in our contribution to life.

No gift, the Buddha says, is greater than the gift of helping someone to understand the nature of our existence. Particularly with our children, it is not in giving things that we show love so much as in showing them, through our own dedicated example, that life's highest goal is to break through our identification with the body and discover our identity with the deathless Self.

Every day in my meditation I remember my teacher with all my love and devotion, because it is she who gave me this gift and enabled me to share it with all who are prepared to give their energy and enthusiasm to Self-realization. Every morning when she returned from the Shiva temple she would come to me, put a flower from the morning's worship behind my ear, and bless me with words that still reverberate in my heart: "May you be like Markandeya." Markandeya is a great sage in the Hindu scriptures, who attained immortality at the age of sixteen because of his profound devotion to the Lord.

ANIYAMA

Freedom

THE THOUSAND NAMES is composed in verse form, with a great deal of poetic play of sounds that makes its recitation in Sanskrit very beautiful. In one verse the poet plays with two names from the same root which echo each other in sound and seem opposite in sense. The root is *yam,* "to control." Yama, the previous name, means "controller"; *aniyama* means "free from control, without constraints" – not lacking in discipline (*yama*), but being free from circumstances.

No one appreciates being dictated to by circumstances, pushed about according to stimulus and response. But it took me a long time to understand that to be free from this kind of conditioning requires great self-discipline. Today, however, I never ask the question, "What will tomorrow bring?" I don't mind if conditions are unfavorable or if people are being unkind. Whatever comes, I know I can give my best.

Aniyama means being without expectations, which is a very positive state. It means you can see things clearly and act intelligently for the benefit of all, without ever being at life's mercy.

Kindness

HERE WE HAVE the secret of the spiritual life in just one word. The great medieval mystic Johan Ruysbroeck, when asked how to become perfect, gave the same answer: "Be kind, be kind, be kind." When we remove all unkindness from our deeds, words, thoughts, and feelings, what remains is our natural state of love.

This may sound simple, but it demands many years of sustained effort to eliminate all unkindness from our inner and outer lives. Some would say that this is humanly impossible – that it is beyond human nature to return kindness for unkindness even in our thoughts. Only when we see someone who has attained these heights do we begin to say, "Maybe it is possible, after all." When we come in contact with such a person, we know there is no limit to the human capacity to love.

This is the role of the spiritual teacher, and it carries great responsibility. A spiritual teacher cannot ever afford to give in to anger or impatience. Whatever the provocation, he or she must maintain this never-changing attitude of love and forgiveness. The word *guru* literally means "heavy" – one so heavy that no storm can uproot him, as heavy as a mountain that withstands the hurricane without flinching.

Strength is often equated with the capacity to attack, but to me it means the internal toughness to take whatever life deals out without losing your humanity. It is those who never stoop to retaliation, never demand an eye for an eye, who are truly strong. They have the toughness to be tender, even sweet, while resisting violence with all their heart. By contrast, those who are ready to strike back at the slightest provocation are not strong but fragile. They may espouse a higher view of human nature, but almost anything can break them and make them lash back at those they oppose.

When someone is being sarcastic or cruel to you, the natural response is to retaliate. If you want to be unshakable, you have to train your mind in patience and endurance, the most grueling training that life offers. Life shows no mercy to those who lack this inner strength. Every virtue requires the toughness never to retreat in the face of challenge.

It is a very poor evaluation of human beings to think that impatience and violent reactions are part of human nature. We have to look to people like Mahatma Gandhi, kind under any provocation, to see what human nature is really like. Gandhi's life showed over and over that even a violent person will respond if exposed to someone who, by being always kind, focuses consistently on the highest in our nature.

As meditation deepens and the mantram begins to get established, some interesting developments take place in the mind. Resentments and hostilities that used to torment us will be getting weaker, yet they will still be present. It is a peculiar position. You find a little resentment, a little sympathy – a curious mix.

For example, suppose somebody is rude to you. You don't like the fellow, but you don't dislike him either – a great advance from your previous attitude. You may feel hostile for a moment, but you know that hostility no longer has the power to push you into doing or saying something you will regret. And because you know you are in control, that experience will leave no residue of resentment in your mind. I don't mean you will like that person, not at first – in fact, for five minutes or so you may positively dislike him. But afterward you say to yourself, "Oh, the fellow comes from a broken home, went to a rough school, fell in with the wrong company; that's why he has become like that."

Once you know you can transform negative feelings in this way, you have won a great victory. Even so, you can't expect to sail through the world in complete tranquility. When people criticize you unfairly, you are not expected to say "Thank you." When they denounce you, you're not expected to praise them. Such responses would be unnatural and unrealistic. The spiritual life requires artistry, and often we may have to answer personal attacks with tender but firm opposition. We should never connive at discourtesy or unkindness, for others' sake as well as for our own.

This kind of opposition requires detachment, toughness, and real love. But when these are present, they generally disarm the other person. In time they may even win him over as a friend, which to me is one of the greatest thrills life offers.

The name *Akrura* has devotional overtones for every Hindu. In the *Bhagavatam,* Akrura is famous as a charioteer who served the historic Krishna with single-hearted love, regarding him not as an ordinary mortal but as an incarnation of Vishnu himself. For Vishnu to be called Akrura, then, is a little like Christ being called Francis or Teresa – a beautiful reminder that, as Krishna says in the Gita, "Those who love me with all their heart, they live in me, and I in them."

Many of the best-known stories in India are about the life of Sri Krishna, and they invariably cast a spell of delight and wonder, of mystery and humor. One favorite of mine deals with Akrura when Krishna was still a young man, leading the pastoral life of a cowherd in the little town of Vrindavan. When the time came for him to assume the role for which he was born, Akrura, because he had some awareness of Sri Krishna's real nature, was chosen to drive his chariot to Vrindavan and bring the Lord back with him to assume the throne of Mathura.

The road to Mathura was hot and dusty, and while they were traveling, Akrura became thirsty. After a while they saw a temple near the side of the road. Akrura went inside to look for water, leaving Sri Krishna in the chariot.

Within the temple courtyard was a pond. Akrura knelt down to drink, but there in the water he saw Sri Krishna. Confused, he rushed out to the chariot again. Sure enough, Krishna was still there, waiting patiently in the chariot.

Thinking he must have made some mistake, Akrura went back again for a drink. But there again he saw Krishna, smiling out at him from the water.

Like a bewildered child, Akrura runs back and forth a few more times, unable to believe his eyes. Finally, in all the innocence of his love, he goes to the chariot and asks, "Lord, how is it that you are here and in the water at the same time?"

Sri Krishna, with a twinkle in his eyes, says, "Look around, Akrura." Akrura looks and there is Krishna in the trees, in the sun overhead, in the birds singing, in the very air. Everywhere he looks, there is the shining face and sparkling eyes of the Lord.

Invincible

THIS IS A popular name for boys in India. Every budding sports star likes to be called Ajit, because it means "he who can never be beaten." Unfortunately, however, some of the Ajits I knew in college never made it to the playing field.

To spiritual aspirants, *ajita* stands for the strength of those whose will cannot be broken. One of the magnificent secrets Gandhi gave us is that strength does not come from bone and muscle – "it comes from an indomitable will." This is not the will to get one's own way whatever the cost; that is what mystics call self-will. When self-will is extinguished, what remains is a will that nothing can break – which means that nothing can vanquish you. I remember a famous Oxford scholar, Professor Gilbert Murray, warning the British government to beware of Gandhi because he could not be tempted by personal pleasure, prestige, or power. Such a person can never be bested, because his will can never be broken.

DRIDHA
Resolute

WE ALL KNOW how long first-of-the-year resolutions usually last. That is because our resolve simply does not go deep enough. We mean what we say, but our subconscious mind objects, "I am not a party to this. That vow is a purely intellectual decision, arrived at without consulting me. Don't count on me for support."

In deep meditation, however, you can get your subconscious to sign on the dotted line. Then your resolution becomes unbreakable: what you say, what you think, and how you feel are one. It is said of Mahatma Gandhi that what he thinks, what he does, what he lives, is all the same; so his will could not be broken even by the greatest empire the world has seen.

ADHRITA
Irresolute

BUT IF THE Lord is resolution, he is also just the opposite: Adhrita, "he who is irresolute too." This is his compassion. On the one hand there is the law of karma, which says that if I have led a life of selfish indulgence for many years, it is going to affect my body and my mind and my relationships. This law doesn't spare anybody; the Lord is resolute about his laws. Yet when we learn to love him with all our heart, he becomes irresolute and says, "All right, for you the law of karma no longer applies." Then we are released from the ill effects of past mistakes – but only so long as what we do in the future is guided entirely by love.

The Lawgiver

IN THE RIG VEDA, oldest of the Hindu scriptures, Varuna is the embodiment of purity and order in every sphere of life, from the laws governing the physical universe to the moral order and the laws of righteousness governing the mind and human affairs.

Varuna is also a name for the setting sun. Just as the setting sun seems to collect the rays of light and withdraw them back into itself, Sri Krishna withdraws the entire universe of name and form into himself at the end of one cycle of creation. Similarly, when the mind is completely still in meditation, the universe of name and form, cause and effect, disappears, and our personal karma is dissolved.

Krishna is also called "the son of Varuna," which is not only figurative but has a specific reference to Hindu mythology. Varuna, it is said, had two fascinating sons: Vasishtha and Agastya. Vasishtha was a great sage who became Sri Rama's spiritual teacher. His answers to Sri Rama's questions, illustrated with many stories, comprise one of India's classic manuals of spiritual instruction, the *Yoga Vasishtha*.

Agastya, the other son, was a precocious sage and a rather colorful figure. He was very short, but nothing daunted him; he was always ready for anything. Once, it is said, he drank the ocean dry. To this day, whenever a very short person in India tries to be aggressive, someone is likely to object, "Who do you think you are, Agastya?"

VRIKSHA
The Tree of Life

TREES ARE VITAL for the life of this whole plane. It is not just that they purify the atmosphere, taking in carbon dioxide and giving back oxygen. Today it is clear that the world's great forests have life-supporting effects many thousands of miles away.

When rain forests in South America are razed, for example, by large-scale corporate operations, the monsoons in southern Asia are affected, pouring their rain into the Indian Ocean instead of on croplands along India's east coast. The precipitous destruction of the world's forests may also contribute to the "greenhouse effect": carbon dioxide and other pollutant gases in the atmosphere, by trapping the sun's radiant energy, may be raising the temperature of the earth, threatening consequences like chronic drought in the wheat belt of the Midwest.

Finally, the massive clear-cutting of rain forests destroys whole species of life, with unknown effects on the biological diversity of the planet. Rain forests, as reported in a conference sponsored by the National Academy of Sciences and the Smithsonian Institution, make up only 7 percent of the earth's land surface, yet they are home to more than half the earth's species. According to the prominent biologist Edward O. Wilson, about 40 percent of the rain forests are already destroyed, "and an area about the size of West Virginia is cleared each year."

At stake, among many other things, are perhaps twenty thousand food plants the world may well need to supplement the mere twenty species on which most human beings depend. Other losses might include the desertification of the tropics and crop failures due to a lack of insect pollinators. It simply is impossible to predict what might result from an "extinction crisis" that Professor Wilson believes "poses a threat to civilization second only to nuclear war."

While scientists are spelling out the details, we might reconsider the practicality of an age-old view, held until a few centuries ago in cultures around the world: that the whole of nature is a life-supporting system worthy not just of respect but of worship. This is not primitive thinking, and it is quite compatible with scientific progress – at least, within a framework that takes into consideration the whole planet and its future. The earth is our mother. Its incredible diversity nourishes all creatures, including the human species. It is in our own interests to shape our uses of technology around the welfare of all life.

In biology, interdependence – which Gandhi always stressed in human institutions – is not just an ideal. It is a fact of life, a fact of love. Trees are an illustration that any child can understand. They give us oxygen, fuel, and the restorative solitude of great forests, which attract water and wildlife to replenish barren places; it seems natural to me to find them holy.

In a hot climate like India's, when you have been walking out under the blazing sun, it is a welcome relief to stretch yourself out under the benign branches of a mango or banyan tree. This perfect symbol of refuge and refreshment was caught in English in this version of a haunting Muslim prayer:

> May God be your shade from tree to tree,
> May God be your guide from well to well.
> God grant that beneath the desert stars
> You hear the Prophet's camel bell.

Vriksha also refers to a powerful image from the Upanishads: the Tree of Life, which "has its roots above," in the Infinite, "and its branches here below." This tree is called *ashvattha,* an interesting word for linguists to quarrel over. In the spiritual derivation, it means "that which will not be standing tomorrow." The whole nature of life is given in just one word: "Everything passes; God alone never changes."

There is a story about a mystic who never stayed in one place, but kept wandering all his days. He had an acute way of reminding the rest of us about the transience of life. When he got old, people began to ask him,

"Holy one, you are getting on in years. Why don't you settle down? We'll build you a little house and take care of all your needs."

"I already have a little house," the sage objected, pointing to his body. "Why should I build another one just for twenty or thirty more years?"

All

I REMEMBER A billboard that promised, "You are somebody at everybody's bank." The Lord is everybody in everybody's bank. It is not at all easy to keep in mind, but everyone around us, everyone we meet, is sanctified by the presence of the Lord in the depths of the heart – whether they are aware of it or not, whether they act like it or not.

"Practicing the presence of God," as Brother Lawrence so aptly phrased it, means learning to behave with under-standing and patience *all* the time. It is worth repeating that this does not rule out a dash of loving, nonviolent resistance. I remember how sharply my grandmother would chastise me when I did something that was not in anyone's best interests. At that young age I used to retort, "My friends don't talk to me that way!" Out would come her pointed answer: "I am your friend; that's why I talk to you that way. If they don't, then they are not real friends."

When a person is riding roughshod over others' needs, most of us find it unpleasant to call him on his behavior. We know it will upset him, and that he in turn will do his best to upset us and others; so we take the path of least resistance. "It's a free country," we say; "he can do as he likes." I have heard this argument countless times. "If he is determined to throw himself in the pit, let him fall." It was only after I began to meditate that I really got the point of my teacher's words: if we say we care about other people, we have to care enough to tell them when they are doing something that will bring sorrow to themselves and others.

After I finished my university education, I had the opportunity to meet important figures from many parts of the world. I had admired them through their books and speeches and through their work in many spheres of life – writers, artists, scholars, educators, scientists, and diplomats who for one reason or another had impressed me with what they had done. Yet when I met them, I often couldn't help feeling let down. With my university degrees, it surprised me to see that they knew so little about living compared to my Granny, who didn't know how to read or write. Gradually I began to understand that perhaps it was she, rather than those the world lionized, who was the best source of living wisdom for me. I began to meditate, and only then did the points that she had never tired of making to me as a child, which I had never quite grasped, really come home.

With this one word *sarva,* the scriptures remind us that every person on the face of the earth is entitled to the resources of nature. Every person is entitled to the support of nations which are more advanced, because the Lord lives in all. It is because we do not realize this that we industrialized nations consume the lion's share of the world's resources – for example, an estimated eighty percent of its energy. When we begin to act as if the Lord lives in all, we shall find that there are enough resources on earth to satisfy everyone's needs – including the opportunity for work that needs doing and for the reasonable leisure that all human beings deserve.

Until Gandhi came, I don't think Westerners were even aware that we in Asia and Africa and South America too need access to natural resources for leading a comfortable life. Before then, with few exceptions, even intelligent, well-intentioned observers in the colonial owners took it for granted that we in the rest of the world needed little in the way of resources because we didn't know the right thing to do with them, which was to extract them from the earth and turn them into items that could make money. Obviously it would have been wasteful to let us sit on resources that we weren't going to use, especially since others knew what to do with them. It was almost a moral obligation for the industrialized powers to take what God had given, make good use of it, and sell back to us what they produced. Few considered that we might have a different point of view.

As just one indicator of this benign blindness, I still

get astonished when I pick up a textbook on world drama, say, and find a thousand pages devoted to drama in the West and perhaps three to the East – one for Sanskrit theater, one for Japanese, and one for Chinese, each of which has a tradition at least as old as that of English drama.

This situation is slowly being balanced, but it still sorrows me to see how little awareness there is in the West of the culture and concerns of the rest of the world. Recently I was looking at a multivolume diary covering the years 1945 to 1962, written by a well-known political commentator in London, to see what he had to say about events in India. Gandhi's name didn't even appear in the index.

Such observations explain why I appreciate the work of the historian Arnold Toynbee. "What I am trying to do," he said once, "is to explain to the West that we are only a small minority in the world." With remarks like this, we Asians became ardent fans. On one occasion, when Toynbee spoke in the city of Madras, he drew probably the largest audience of his career.

It was while he was walking about among the ruins of Greece and Crete, Toynbee said, that great questions began to rise in his mind. Why should such monumental civilizations suffer such a torturous decline? That is the question he tried to answer in his exhaustive *Study of History*. The inspiration came to him while he was on the Orient Express, watching those storied Thracian landscapes flee past. In his unconscious, a plan for history was taking shape.

The outcome appeared in twelve volumes, more than three million words, which took him forty years of dedicated work. The book is not just a recording of facts and figures. It is an interpretation of history, and whether we agree with it or not, it is even more thought-provoking today than when it first appeared. Toynbee asks in detail, Why did twenty-six great civilizations fall? And his conclusion: Because they could not change their direction, their way of thinking, to meet the changing challenges of life.

This is a spiritual question, not just an intellectual exercise or a matter of physical resources. Its relevance came out in an arresting sentence in the interview he gave the London *Sunday Observer* on the occasion of his eighty-fifth birthday: "Man's plundering of nature now threatens him with pollution and depletion." What he is hinting at is that ours may become the twenty-seventh civilization to wither. Toynbee, like the great mystics, harbored an abiding faith in the spiritual regeneration of mankind. Yet without this regeneration, he saw almost no chance of our survival as a civilization.

Destroyer of Evil

ORDINARILY THIS IS a name of Shiva, though it appears as a name of Vishnu as well – a reminder that we all worship the same Godhead, whatever name we use.

My ancestral family, incidentally, built two temples near our home, one to Sri Krishna and one to Shiva. This is unusual, for generally people worship one or the other but not both. The big joke among the neighbors was that the Eknath family likes to butter its bread on both sides. "We're taking no chances," we used to reply. "Who knows who will be seated on the throne on Judgment Day?"

Sharva draws an image from archery again: it comes from the word *sharu,* "arrow." The mantram is an arrow we can use to shoot down any negative emotion or selfish desire, and ultimately hit the target of Self-realization.

The Inexhaustible Treasure

AWARENESS OF GOD is a rare kind of treasure: the more you draw on it, the more you will have. This aspect of Self-realization should appeal to high-powered business types. The more patient you are with people, the more patience you will have. The more generous you are today, the more generosity you will have tomorrow. The more love you give, the more loving you become. It's a strange paradox, perhaps the best-kept banking secret in all of life.

Remember those great words of Jesus: "To those who have, more shall be given; from those who lack, even the little they have will be taken away." The principle can be stated in the plainest of terms: if you are selfish, stingy with your love, the scant security you cling to will be battered to pieces by life. But if you give of yourself freely, without any thought of personal reward, your security will grow unshakable; you will always have more to give.

Being

THOUSANDS OF YEARS ago the Upanishads posed a penetrating question: "When life leaves the body, what remains?" The words are so simple that it takes a while for the implications to sink in. This whole complicated mechanism that we call our body and mind is dead equipment when life leaves us. It is like a Porsche whose driver has abandoned it because it ran out of gas, like a house whose owner has forgotten where it is.

Being, this name suggests, is something that the body "contains." As Sri Ramakrishna used to say, just as the sword rests in its scabbard, the arrow in its quiver, so the soul, pure existence, rests in the body-mind-sense-intellect complex.

Ramakrishna liked to compare the layers of this complex to a coconut, which has a smooth outer rind and a fibrous middle layer surrounding the husk and white flesh. The vast majority of us, Ramakrishna said, are like green coconuts, which feel very heavy because the shell, the kernel, and everything inside are stuck together and cannot be separated.

When a coconut is ripe, however, the insides dry a little, and the kernel pulls free from the husk and rattles around. A skillful cook has only to shake a coconut to find out if it is ripe. It will feel light, and you will hear the kernel knocking about inside. Such a coconut can be used to make hundreds of luscious things.

Those who have learned to identify with the Self, Ramakrishna says, are like ripe coconuts: detached. They never once identify themselves with their container, the body. They are not held by anything: no selfish ties, no purely personal urges. They are free.

The Highway of the Free

THIS WORD "free," *mukta,* is related to the word *moksha,* which means freedom or liberation in the spiritual sense. This is the freedom we are really looking for: not the freedom to do as we please whenever we please, but freedom from the limitations of self-centered conditioning that tie us down. These limitations make us into chickens, scratching at the ground to look for a few crumbs of pleasure and profit. We should be like eagles, Saint Teresa of Avila says, soaring in the sky.

The other day in a bookstore I saw an intriguing title: *The Handbook of Knots* – a complete manual for tying all kinds of knots, from useful to decorative, very stylishly produced. I wanted to suggest to the proprietor that my little book *Meditation* would sit perfectly on the same shelf, for meditation is the art of *untying* knots.

In today's tense world, most of us have nights when we go to bed and can't sleep because our shoulder or neck is knotted up. Similarly, there are knots in the mind, and they produce much the same kind of effect but farther-reaching. It is these knots in the mind that make life frustrating and unsatisfying. In meditation we work at loosening these knots and finally untying them altogether, and each one undone means a release of vital energy.

Support

IF YOU CAN reach deep into your consciousness to rest on the Lord, you will have all the support you need to face anything in the world of experience. On the other hand, most of us have little connection with this divine support, so we lack the security necessary to face even one hostile person. Without some awareness that the Self is within us, the same Self in all, it is natural to get agitated, resentful, or afraid.

Mahatma Gandhi says memorably:

> I have been a willing slave to this most exacting Master for more than half a century. His voice has been increasingly audible as the years have rolled by. He has never forsaken me even once in my darkest hour. He has saved me often even against myself and left me not a vestige of independence. The greater the surrender to him, the greater has been my joy.

Lord of the World

HINDU STORIES SOMETIMES like to have a little fun with some of the gods and goddesses in which the Lord is worshipped so devoutly. These stories have a subtle way of showing something of the divine paradox at the bottom of life. How, for example, could Krishna, the divine master of the universe, be born and grow up more or less like any other child, getting in trouble, playing tricks on his mother, and having fun with his chums?

In one of the marvelous stories about baby Krishna, his mother gets anxious because her little one has been eating sand. She grabs him by the hand and pries open his mouth. But when she peers inside, she sees the entire cosmos there within that tiny mouth. Awestruck, she goes into ecstasy. When she finally returns to ordinary consciousness, Sri Krishna draws a veil over her mind again, so that she can still relate to this cosmic child as her son.

This gives a valuable insight as to how to deal with our own children. First, we have to remember to treat them with the utmost love all the time. We have to remember their needs before everybody else's. In many ways children are closer to divinity than we adults are. On the other hand, we need to be practical: while their core is divine, their outer crust need not be so.

The Son of Man

THIS VERY ANCIENT name is a patronymic of the word *nara,* which means "man." So Narayana means, roughly, "son of man," or perhaps "he who is the resting place of man." "Man" here means human being, and this name reminds us that we can find our cure only in him, our rest only in her, if we think of God as the Divine Mother. Narayana is the resting place of all.

The name Narayana in itself is an ancient mantram, and it also appears in the longer mantram *Om Namo Narayanaya,* "Om, I worship Narayana." Narayana is also a rather popular name for boys. It is very, very common in our Hindu tradition to give children a holy name. Millions of boys are called Rama, and millions of girls are called Sita. I even had one cousin who was called Shivaramakrishna. This is a useful custom, for it means that the household is alive with the Holy Name. Even if the younger children are quarreling, it is still "Hey, Rama, you have my toy!" and "You're wrong, Radha, it's mine!"

There is a famous story in our scriptures about a rich merchant whose son's name was Narayana. This proved very fortunate for that merchant, because he was a rather greedy man – in fact, he was so selfishly attached to his wealth that he had very little love left over to give to anything else. Only his son Narayana was important to him, perhaps even more than his money.

As this merchant got older he came to be more and more of a misanthrope, never wanting to see anyone but his accountants, staying all day in his storeroom counting his money. The only exception was Narayana, whom he welcomed at all times.

Finally, while his son was away on a business errand, the old man fell deathly ill. He lay on his deathbed waiting for the end, bitterly resenting the fact that he would soon have to leave behind everything he had so carefully and compulsively hoarded. But most of all he yearned to see his son. And at the very last moment, as death claimed him, he forgot all about his money and his possessions and called out with all his heart, "Narayana! *Narayana!*"

In a moment Yama, the King of Death, appeared to claim the old man's soul. But then something very strange happened: the Lord, Vishnu, also appeared. "What are you doing here?" Yama protested. "You know this man was no saint."

"I know," the Lord agreed, "but I had to come. He called my name with all his heart."

"Don't worry about that," said Yama, relieved. "He wasn't calling *you*. Narayana is his son."

"That doesn't matter. He called my name with devotion with his dying breath, and whoever calls on me like that, I can't refuse."

So the wealthy merchant won on a technicality.

BRAHMAN

The Supreme Godhead

BRAHMAN COMES FROM the root *brih*, "to expand." This is the divine nature of reality, and when I read about the theory of the expanding universe, I get fascinated by the applications it has for understanding the concept of Brahman.

Black holes today have become a conversation piece. Once the vogue was to talk about existentialism; now it is, "Did you know that black holes have negative mass?" or "Have you heard the latest joke about black holes?" One prominent South Indian astrophysicist says that when he was in the hospital, the nurses kept asking him to explain about black holes.

One lesson of the black hole is that matter can be so infinitely concentrated that it vanishes in a "null point," a "singularity" where an immense amount of matter takes up no space at all. The "Big Bang" theory postulates that the universe was born in a kind of cosmic explosion from such a point – literally everything out of nothing. In the language of Hinduism and Buddhism this is mahamaya, the power that brings the universe – matter and energy, time and space – out of "seed form" and keeps it expanding for eons, until someday expansion will cease and the cosmos will gradually collapse into itself again.

This gives a small clue to the nature of Brahman. Brahman cannot be grasped intellectually. The supreme reality cannot be described. All we can do is to concentrate our love and devotion on those great manifestations of Brahman which have appeared in all major religious traditions, such as Sri Krishna, the Compassionate Buddha, and Jesus the Christ.

BRAHMANYA

The Manifestation of Brahman

IN HINDUISM THE Godhead takes human form as an *avatara,* from *ava,* "down," and *tri,* "to come" – a divine incarnation. But this name also refers to the Self that is within all of us. The Upanishads say simply, *Tat tvam asi:* "Thou art That." The supreme reality is our real Self, and when we discover this truth for ourselves, we attain complete fulfillment and abiding joy. As Saint Bernard explains in simple words,

> For my part, I think the chief reason which prompted the invisible God to become visible in the flesh and to hold converse with human beings was to lead physical men and women, who are only able to love physically, to the healthy love of his physical form, and afterwards, little by little, to spiritual love.

Maker of Reality

ONCE, WHEN I was teaching meditation on the Berkeley campus, I went with friends into a coffee house on Telegraph Avenue and as soon as we sat down, the party at the next table launched a highly abstract discussion about levels of reality, about being and becoming. They may have thought that is the kind of talk a meditation teacher likes to hear. Actually, what reality boils down to is respecting all. It is as simple as that.

However, though this may be simple, it is often not clear to us in the million and one details of the day, generally because we are preoccupied with ourselves. When we make somebody wait unnecessarily, we are not showing respect: our actions say clearly, "My time is more important than yours." When we avoid somebody we don't like, we are not showing them respect, even if we think they won't notice. And when we get offended because somebody hasn't taken proper notice of us, we are not showing respect for ourselves.

I have become so sensitive to this matter of respect that it sometimes makes my wife laugh at how far

I go. The other morning I was seated at breakfast and enjoying some muffins prepared painstakingly by Laurel, when I noticed our dog Ganesha sitting outside patiently waiting for a snack. "You finish your muffins," Christine said, "and then take care of him." But I find I am unable to do that. I treat Ganesha exactly as I would treat a young fellow who has dropped in on me: I feel hospitable. I went out and shared a muffin with him, then came back and finished my breakfast in peace. It's not just that it pleases Ganesha; this is something I owe to myself. I would have felt small if I had made him wait for me to finish.

On the other hand, we need artistry and a sense of appropriateness to carry this out; that is why I am stressing the mental state involved – the mind rather than the muffin. For example, I don't invite Ganesha to come sit at the table with us, and I don't go overboard and have nice shirts and trousers made for him either. I have seen dogs dressed in chic fashions, and I am sure the owners thought they were putting their pets first. The dogs themselves probably had different ideas! It is good to respect the Lord in all creatures, but we also need to use our common sense.

This call to respect all life is an inspiration for us to expand our consciousness. When we get caught up in one person, however pleasant and affectionate the relationship may be, our consciousness is narrowed down to just a slit; we have room for that person, but no one else will fit. That is why I appeal to everybody to seek out others' company, to be sociable with everybody, to spend time working and relaxing with other people. If you are meditating sincerely and following all the allied disciplines, consciousness will expand; your respect will grow broader and deeper.

The Creator

THE LAST *a* of this name is long, to distinguish *Brahma* from *Brahman*. Brahman is the attributeless Godhead, of which all the deities in the Hindu pantheon are expressions; Brahma is the Creator in the Hindu trinity, as Vishnu is the Preserver and Shiva the Destroyer.

As far as my knowledge goes, there is no temple for Brahma anywhere in India. This is an interesting comment on the Hindu outlook. The significance of this omission is profound: it means that we haven't exactly come into a higher state of consciousness by being born here on earth.

Most of us seem to believe just the opposite. From the way the world behaves, we seem to believe that human birth represents a great improvement in our state of being – that we have come from a really unsuitable place and have happily found ourselves transferred to a much more advantageous location. No Hindu would agree with this. We feel much more at home with the Christian mystics' assertion: that all of us come from God, and to God we shall return. This interim period is a kind of exile, a wandering in some alien land; until we discover the Lord in our own heart, so that we live in God every moment, we can never feel quite at home with this life on earth.

East and West, there have been many mystics to go to the other extreme, describing life as the "valley of the shadow of death." This is not my point of view, but there is truth in it, and the message spelled out so clearly in Saint Teresa's lines rings in my ears always: "Everything passes; God alone never changes." Just see how soon each week passes, how quickly each weekend comes. And with it, each of us has moved one week closer to the great change called death. This may seem a grim reminder, but it is one that all of us should keep before our eyes always. It gives meaning to every moment, throws everything in life into perspective.

Who Makes Reality Increase

THIS NAME COMES from the root *vardh,* "to increase, to spread." It is a reminder that each of us has the responsibility of spreading love and increasing others' happiness. There was an emperor in ancient India with a similar name, which I like very much: Harshavardhana, "he whose joy lies in increasing the joy of his people."

To me, it is an axiom by now that nobody can win even happiness by inflicting pain on others. No matter how much satisfaction you think you can get by being discourteous to somebody who has wronged you, I assure you it will never happen, because that is the law of karma. If you give joy, you will receive joy; if you inflict pain, you will receive pain. The choice is ours.

When I see people fishing, for example, I cannot understand how anybody can get pleasure out of inflicting pain on those poor creatures. It goes without saying that I feel the same about hunting, whatever justification is offered. "Deer season" to me doesn't mean it is time to kill deer. For me it means a time to show films about deer, to write stories about deer, to make people sensitive to our kinship with these gentle creatures in every possible way. The deer in our ashram are so trustful now that if we come across one grazing, we have to walk around; the creature won't bother to move. I have even thought of carrying a little brush in my pocket to give their fur a brushing. That is my deer season.

The other day, as we were driving over the creek on our way into town, I spotted a turtle having a snooze near the edge of the pavement. People may not see him there, I said to myself, and they might run over him by accident. So I asked the driver to stop while we picked him up and found a safer spot for his siesta.

To live up to the ideal suggested by *Brahmavivardhana,* we have to spread love everywhere through our personal contact with people and creatures. You will come to feel toward every girl or boy exactly as you would toward your own children. This doesn't take away from your love for your children; it means you gain the same love for other children as well. And they all respond to it, too.

VEDA
Wisdom

THE WORD *Veda* comes from the root *vid,* "to know." The Vedas are the most ancient scriptures to come down to us from the ancient seers of India. They are held to be the sacred word of the eternal, breathed forth at the beginning of time to guide the world to its ultimate goal, the return to eternal Being at the end of time.

It is not without a touch of humor that the Lord is called Veda. It is a little like saying Mr. Scripture. The Veda is the scripture that embodies the eternal wisdom, and the Lord is the personification of that wisdom. In India this wisdom flows in an unbroken stream of sacred works: from the Veda into the Upanishads, from the Upanishads into the Bhagavad Gita, and from the Gita out into many, many channels in the works of Vedanta and Yoga and other schools and traditions. In a sense, all this is the Veda: all eternal wisdom that we can verify in our own consciousness in meditation.

Knower of Reality

BRAHMAVID IS "knower of the supreme"; *brahmavidya* is "the supreme education." That is how the Hindu scriptures refer to meditation, where instead of enrolling in the courses of a professor from Harvard, you get the best professor in the world: your own Self. The Self has degrees from every galaxy in the universe, and those who study with him sincerely do not have to produce transcripts or diplomas or references. Their personal example of love and wisdom establishes their credentials, and through these they pass to others their knowledge of the Self.

True education, in other words, is not so much stuffing knowledge in as drawing wisdom out. The Self is the knower of wisdom because he is the source. This is not just theory. The Self is pure intelligence, pure consciousness, the very principle of knowing. The mind and intellect are inert without the Self; they are only his instruments. When these instruments are purified in meditation, concentration becomes as penetrating as a laser, bringing the learning capacity of genius to whatever field you take up. That is why meditation is what William James called "education *par excellence.*"

One of the best definitions of education I have heard comes, I think, from an Oxford don: the main purpose of education is to enable you to know when somebody is talking rot. Even where experts are gathered, I need hardly tell you, wisdom and discrimination are not always abundant. An expert can get caught in his own tiny groove and forget that there is much more to the world all around him. In the rest of life, experts are just like the rest of us. No field is really isolated. The questions that matter in every field are tied to the rest of life, on which we and the experts stand on equal ground.

This name of the Lord is a reminder that every one of us has the same source of wisdom within. In the Gita, Sri Krishna asks, "Who do you think is the real author of the Vedas? Vyasa? I just engaged Vyasa as a brilliant ghost-writer, to put into verse what I inspired in him." Vyasa gets the credit because even in ancient India it was hard to find someone who is a good Sanskrit scholar and can put ideas into meter on the spot. Instead of Sri Krishna sitting in a big executive chair with Vyasa taking shorthand, imagine Sri Krishna seated inside Vyasa, dictating the Vedas in his meditation. That is what inspiration means.

To get this kind of divine inspiration, all we need to do is still the mind, quieten self-will, put the intellect to sleep with a local anesthetic for a while, and ask the senses to go climb a tree. Then we will be able to hear the eternal wisdom that is the Self.

KAMA

Desire

Our real desire in life, as the Bible puts it, is to love the Lord with all our heart, all our mind, all our spirit, and all our strength. The human being's infinite capacity to desire can never be fulfilled by anything less.

Unfortunately, it is equally part of the human condition to believe that we can fulfill our need to love and to be loved by grasping at things and people. When we search outside like this for fulfillment, we misuse our power to love. When we clutch at or cling to anything other than God, we are denying the very possibility of love.

In his *Confessions,* Saint Augustine gives a very different idea of love. This is the same Augustine who in his early life explored the entire gamut of pleasure. He speaks from his own life when he compares spiritual fulfillment to the ordinary pleasures he had enjoyed before:

> Not the beauty of any bodily thing, nor the order of
> the seasons, not the brightness of light that rejoices
> the eye, nor the sweet melodies of all songs, nor the

sweet fragrance of flowers and ointments and spices:
not manna nor honey, not the limbs that carnal love
embraces. None of these things do I love in loving my
God. Yet in a sense I do love light and melody and
fragrance and food and embrace when I love my God –
the light and the voice and the fragrance and the food
and embrace in the soul, when that light shines upon
my soul which no place can contain, and that voice
sounds which no time can take from me; when I breathe
that fragrance which no wind scatters, and eat the food
which is not lessened by eating, and lie in the embrace
which satiety never comes to sunder. This it is that I love
when I love my God.

Our ordinary conception of joy is limited to a few
bits of sensory pleasure, which we hold on to with a
fierce tenacity that enslaves us. But the suspicion that joy
comes from within us brings a new sense of freedom.
No longer compulsively driven by personal desire – for
money or possessions, prestige or pleasure or power –
we begin to exercise choices where we never dreamed
choices could be made.

Destroyer of Selfish Craving

Kama here means any selfish desire. Often the word is translated as sexual desire, but that is a little misleading. Kama is any private pleasure – something that I want to enjoy just for myself, no matter what the cost to others. It can be any compulsive craving – for food, or alcohol, or drugs, or even power or fame. Only when we are free from such compulsions can we know what a thorn in our flesh kama is, and what a blessing it is to be free from all selfish craving.

It is the nature of a compulsion to be almost beyond control. As long as we are in the grip of the desire, it seems we cannot think of anything else until we satisfy it. Overeating is a familiar example. We may know that a hot fudge sundae means calories we don't need, but the desire has a hold on us and we say this is what we want. Not until we have eaten the sundae, after the clamor of the desire quiets down, can we listen to the voice that reminds us we have made a mistake.

The important point here is not that there is anything wrong in eating a sundae, but simply that we do not have the capacity to choose when it is all right and when it isn't. For hot fudge sundae we can all make our own substitutions. Some of these compulsive desires are not too harmful in themselves, but when this inability to exercise our power to choose extends to smoking or drinking or drugs, we begin to cause serious suffering to ourselves and those around us.

One painful compulsion not infrequently occurs in personal relationships, when we clutch at our friends or partner for support. This leads to all kinds of trouble. When we are grasping at another person, the real tragedy is that we cease to see that person. He or she becomes merely an object for propping ourselves up, which is an open invitation to jealousy and finally to a broken relationship. People with this kind of problem simply go from one relationship to another, always grasping and always missing what they are grasping for. Unfortunately, they cannot see what the problem is because they have lost the power to choose.

The major cause of all these kinds of compulsions is obsessive identification with the body. That the sun takes its bath in the sea at night, as many people in my village used to believe, is a very small superstition compared to the superstition that we are the body. It is because we identify ourselves with the body that when a sensory craving comes, we feel we have no choice but to satisfy it. The alternative is to feel frustrated, repressed, and unfulfilled.

It never occurs to us that we might not be our desires.

But as long as we identify ourselves with our desires, we can never be masters of ourselves. And to be masters of ourselves means that we must be able to choose what we desire, choose what we think: which means that for many, many years we will have to say no to a lot of compulsive thoughts and cravings.

When you are trying to resist a harmful desire, one helpful clue is to remember that the real source of that desire is not the body but the mind. Often, for example, I see people in ice cream parlors who are in no need of nourishment. The emptiness they feel inside them is not a physical emptiness, but they interpret it physically because they identify themselves with the body. Similarly, when we smoke we are simply punishing the body for the restlessness of the mind. This is why physical approaches to these problems can never be of much help in overcoming a destructive habit.

Once you can trace a desire to the mind, you get some detachment from it. The desire loses some of its urgency, and when the pressure of desire is relieved, we can remember what we know from previous experience: that most desires are not very long-lasting. An hour ago we may have wanted a hot fudge sundae, but now what we really want is a piece of baklava. In another sixty minutes our all-encompassing desire will be to fly to the Greek islands for some ouzo. So one helpful tip for resisting a desire is simply to put it off. For all its cleverness, the mind is not difficult to trick. If it asks for baklava now, just tell it to wait until you have finished reading this book. By that time, the chances are that you will have forgotten the baklava completely.

For the more adventurous, however, an even better method for fighting compulsions is to do just the opposite of what they demand. When all you want to do is lock yourself in your room and spend the day with a favorite novel, that is the time to go out and be with people, especially in doing something that will benefit others. This is a sure test of spiritual growth. When the desire comes to do your own thing, to bask in something you just love, even if it is something harmless, try throwing yourself into a selfless job with energy and enthusiasm. When you can do that, you are really making progress.

Spiritual Teacher

GURU IS A word that has come into the English language to stay, but I suspect that few know its actual significance. *Guru* literally means "heavy." A guru is a person who is very heavy – so heavy that nothing can unsettle his love or push over her patience, no matter what the storms.

In the modern world, very few can claim this stature. Most of us behave like wisps of straw or scraps of paper that can be blown about by any gust of passion. We seem just to react to what others do. If somebody is angry at us, we feel justified in being angry in return. Not at all. Those who are subject to resentment or hostility or retaliation or revenge are not *guru* but *laghu*, light. They have very little weight. If somebody pushes them, they push right back, a little like mechanical dolls.

I think it was in an old film of Charlie Chaplin's that I saw this portrayed. Charlie is being chased by the police for an offense he hasn't committed. He finds it difficult to escape them, so when he passes a merry-go-round, he pretends to be one of the mechanical creatures. At a certain point, all these dolls with sticks start hitting one another. Charlie does just what he sees them doing, and his timing is perfect. The performance is so convincing that the police mistake him for a machine.

This is what we do when we try to "get even" – which to me has always seemed like getting odd. If someone hits me, it is absurd for me to hit them back like a mechanical toy. If someone is rude, it is absurd for me to be annoyed. Where is the connection?

If getting resentful could solve such problems, I would be all for resentment. But it doesn't solve anything; it only tears us apart. It is very hard to accept this, I agree; that is human nature. Here is where the guru is most helpful. By his steadiness and unflappability, he shows us that we can endure the storms of life without unkindness, and actually flourish on stress.

In India, no one in his right mind covets the role of spiritual teacher. It is a very, very difficult job. Everyone knows how difficult it is to solve problems even in one personal relationship, to move closer when things are going wrong. A spiritual teacher has this kind of complication multiplied many times over. Only a person who is completely established in spiritual awareness can safely play this role, and only if he or she has perfect detachment.

When you realize the unity of life, as I said before, it means that others' grief, others' problems, become your own. It means that there are always problems, there is always grief, for someone who has attained Self-realization: not personal problems, but the burdens of those around you. So the role of guru is not free of pain. But this pain is not borne supinely, for those who realize God also have the capacity to relieve the pain of others. It is in this that joy comes – the kind of joy that no money can buy, no pleasure ever bring.

This name of God reminds us that the real spiritual teacher is in all of us – the Lord, our deepest Self. When we feel attracted to a teacher, we are expected to scrutinize his life closely and see that he embodies the highest ideals that all religions teach. Then, if he does, we should give him all our loyalty and all our love; for it is primarily by focusing our love that a spiritual teacher helps us to unify our consciousness.

The teacher too will be watching us, looking to see if we are capable of wholehearted dedication. If we are, the time will come when the teacher says, "You are my student." Then the bond is sealed. The job of the teacher is to take us to samadhi, when we see that our real teacher has always been the Self within us. And our job is to give him, or her, our very best, without any reservations. A ballet master at the Bolshoi demands no less.

The guru's is the highest form of love, the greatest gift that one human being can give to another. In the Hindu tradition it is the guru who inspires all the students who are devoted to him to flood their hearts with the ecstatic love of God, which brings all temptations to an end, dissolves all conflicts, and heals all divisions in consciousness.

A great Sufi saint once said, "I am He whom I love, and He whom I love is I. We are two spirits, dwelling in the same body. If thou seest me, thou seest him; and if thou seest him, thou seest both." This is why in India we go to our sages – Ramana Maharshi, Mahatma Gandhi, Sri Ramakrishna, Anandamayi Ma – simply to look at them. We are not just seeing them; we are seeing through them to the supreme reality, which reminds us that we have the same reality within us too. When we have difficulties, we go to our teacher. We don't even have to talk; it is enough just to look and draw inspiration.

"Evil cannot overcome an illumined man, because he overcomes evil. Sin cannot burn an illumined woman, because she burns out sin." This is what the Upanishads said about the illumined teacher. That is why going to a God-conscious man or woman helps us to overcome evil in ourselves. Our love is an open door for the teacher's love and wisdom to reach in, dissolving little by little the negative compulsions that have caused so much trouble in the past.

The Holy Name

THE LORD IS always with us in the Holy Name. He *is* the mantram. So when we use the mantram regularly, it becomes a way of calling the Lord collect. We don't need to know all his thousand names. We can just say *Rama, Rama, Rama,* or *Jesus, Jesus, Jesus;* he will get the message.

The Lord has a thousand names, a thousand hands, a thousand faces: that is to say, his names and forms are endless. Robert, Ellen, Rick, Kate, Claudia, and Jim are all names of the Lord, because he is present in everyone. This is not just a philosophical statement, it is very personal and practical. If we see this, we can never lose respect for anyone. More important, we will never lose faith. This is the marvelous result of the universal vision: we never lose our faith that everybody is capable of revealing the Lord within.

The Lord is the name behind all names, the face behind all faces. This is the realization that samadhi brings. The world is full of God. After samadhi we don't see just the external appearance of life. We penetrate deep into life, and with that same penetration we see the Lord in everybody, all the time. As the Upanishads say, some people have two feet, others (like our dog Ganesha) happen to have four feet; but in all of them dwells the same Lord. In this realization of the One, through the One, with the One comes the beginning of endless love.

When we study these names of the Lord, I would like to repeat, we are not just unearthing old Sanskrit words, however beautiful they may be. These are not mere names. They are marvelous concepts which throw light on how to live: long, healthy, secure, joyful lives, not in seclusion but in a world full of problems. When you reflect on these thousand names of the Lord of Love, who is enshrined in the depths of our consciousness, try to apply them in all your activities. Then each Holy Name can help to improve the quality of your daily life.

The Lord is present in all, so everybody's name is his. He is also beyond all, so he has no name at all. But for me his name is Krishna, whom I find the perfect expression of God's love and beauty. In our Hindu scriptures we have a story of how Krishna got his name. Sri Krishna's mother was spending sleepless nights trying to think of suitable names. Finally, she decides to leave the choice up to a great sage, but when the baby is born and she takes him and puts him on the sage's lap, the sage asks, "What name shall I give him who already has a thousand names?" Finally they settle on Krishna.

Until we attain illumination, we need to repeat our

mantram as often and as sincerely as we can. Whatever name we choose – *Krishna, Rama, Jesus, Hail Mary,* or any other sacred formula that has come down to us in the great religious traditions of the world – without constant repetition in the mind, it is not likely to penetrate the depths of the heart. Mira, the great woman saint of medieval India, said that without the Holy Name, living is in vain. You may be eating, you may be drinking, you may be having a good time, you may be making money, but if you don't repeat God's name, you are living in vain. Without the mantram, Mira says, life is like a temple without a lamp, like a night without the moon, like a meal without salt, like a loving wife when the husband is away, like a tree without leaves, like a pool without water. In all these simple ways she expresses the emptiness of a life without God.

When ecstatic love is awakened in the heart, all this emptiness goes out of our life forever. Repeating the Lord's name then becomes a great joy. To use orthodox language, we worship God whenever we repeat his name.

But we also worship him when we use kind language under provocation, or when we give our time and energy freely and cheerfully to causes that benefit the world. We are worshipping when we meditate regularly, or when we control our senses when they want to go after some harmful pleasure. Then our whole life becomes an offering of love. This is the real spiritual life, where, as Sri Ramakrishna says, we make merry in the mansion of God, seeing and serving the Lord in all.

An Eight Point Program

THE FOLLOWING paragraphs present the Eight Point Program for spiritual living which I have found effective in my own life. These steps are elaborated much more fully in my book *Meditation,* which has a full chapter on each step.

1. MEDITATION. First comes the practice of meditation. You begin by devoting half an hour every morning as early as convenient to the practice of meditation. Do not increase this half-hour period, but if you want to meditate more, have half an hour in the evening also.

Have a room in your home for meditation, or a special corner, and keep it as austere as possible. A quiet, cool, well-ventilated room is best. Have pictures of the great spiritual teachers if this appeals to you.

If you want to sit in a straight-back chair, one with arms is best; or sit cross-legged on the carpet. Sit with spinal column erect and eyes gently closed. As concentration deepens you may begin to relax and fall asleep; if so, draw yourself up and move away from your back support so that you can keep the spine, neck, and head in a straight line.

Have an inspirational passage memorized, such as the Prayer of Saint Francis of Assisi, the second or twelfth chapter of the Bhagavad Gita, the Twenty-third Psalm, the first chapter of the Dhammapada of the Buddha, the Beatitudes of the Sermon on the Mount, or a selection from the Upanishads. Go through the words of the passage in your mind as slowly as you can, letting each word drop singly into your consciousness. Do not follow any association of ideas, but keep to the words of the inspirational passage. When distractions come, do not resist them, but try to give more and more attention to the words of the prayer. If you find that your mind has wandered away completely, go back to the first word of the prayer and begin again. Keep adding to your repertoire of inspirational passages from the scriptures of all religions to prevent dryness in meditation.

The secret of meditation is that you become what you meditate on. When you use the second chapter of the Gita in meditation, you are driving the words deeper and deeper into your consciousness, so that one day, perhaps after many years, they will become an integral part of your consciousness.

2. JAPAM. Japam is the silent repetition of the mantram, or Holy Name, in the mind. The popular etymology

of the Sanskrit word *mantra*m is from *manas*, "mind," and *tri*, "to cross over": "that which enables us to cross the tempestuous sea of the mind." Every religion has its mantram. The very name of Jesus is a mantram; so is *Hail Mary,* which calls on the Divine Mother whose children we all are. *Om mani padme hum* is a great Buddhist mantram; *mani* means "jewel" – the Self – and *padme,* "the lotus of the heart." Jews may use the Shema or *Barukh attah Adonai,* "Blessed art thou, O Lord"; Muslims repeat the name of Allah or *Bismillah ir-Rahman ir-Rahim,* "In the name of God, the Merciful, the Compassionate." And one of the oldest, simplest mantrams in India is *Rama,* from the root *ram,* "to rejoice," signifying the source of all joy.

When you are angry, afraid, or anxious, repeat the mantram to still the agitation rising in your mind. Anger and fear are power rising within us, and by the repetition of the Holy Name we can put anger and fear to work, harnessing them for the benefit of ourselves and others rather than allowing them to use us destructively.

At bedtime, repeat the mantram in your mind until you fall asleep. In the morning you will feel refreshed in body and mind.

Whenever you get a moment, while waiting for a bus or while walking, use this time to repeat the mantram. Boredom is a great source of problems to people who do not know what to do with their time. We may smoke, for example, just because we do not know what to do with the odds and ends of time in our day.

The mind is very much like the restless trunk of an elephant. In India elephants often walk in religious processions which wind through the streets of the town on their way to the temple. The trunk of the elephant is a restless thing, always moving, and as the temple elephant is taken through the narrow streets of the bazaar, it is usually tempted by the coconuts, bananas, and other produce displayed in the stalls on either side. As it walks, if the shopkeeper doesn't watch, it picks up a coconut and puts it in its mouth. There is a loud crack, and that is the last of the coconut. Then from the next stall it takes a whole bunch of bananas. It doesn't peel them, but just puts the whole bunch inside, and it's gone. But the wise mahout, the man in charge of the elephants, knows their habits, so as the procession begins he gives the elephant a short bamboo stick to hold in its trunk. The elephant holds the bamboo firmly and walks through the streets without confiscating anyone's property.

This is what we do when we repeat the mantram: we slowly give a mantram-stick to the mind, and instead of wanting to smoke or overeat, it has something to hold on to. Gradually, this makes the mind firm, secure, steadfast, and proof against tension.

3. SLOWING DOWN. Millions in our modern world suffer because they are constantly pushed and hurried. Hurry makes us tense and causes us to make mistakes and do a poor job. The remedy for hurrying is to get up earlier, so that we can begin the day without tension and set a slow, leisurely pace for the day. When we are concentrated and slow we do not make mistakes; we do a much better job, which in the long run is much more economical than hurrying and making mistakes. In order to slow down we may need to eliminate some unnecessary activities from our day.

4. EKAGRATA, "one-pointedness." The practice of meditation is a systematic exercise in concentration, which will finally become a permanent, spontaneous state. It is a great aid to meditation if you practice being one-pointed during your day. Give your complete attention to whatever you are doing; particularly in conversation, give your complete attention to the person with whom you are talking. After much practice, you should be able to make your mind one-pointed, concentrating on whatever task is at hand.

Almost all of us suffer from a mind which is many-pointed, and we are usually not able to bring all our concentration to bear on a given problem or task. For example, background music while eating, while studying, while working, prevents us from being fully aware of what we are eating, studying, or working at. Smoking while watching a movie curtails our capacity to appreciate the movie, because our mind is two-pointed. When we do only one thing at a time, we are healing the divisions in our consciousness, and when we can give our complete attention to another person, he cannot help but respond by giving his complete attention to us.

5. SENSE RESTRAINT. This does not mean sense-negation or sense-denial but training the senses to be obedient servants. We begin to train the senses by exercising discriminating restraint in our choice of movies, television programs, books, and magazines, and by eating nourishing food in temperate quantities rather than things that appeal to our taste but have no nutritional value. It is good to have a light meal in the evening and our heaviest meal at breakfast and to eat plenty of fresh vegetables and fruits. Avoid overcooked, deep-fried, strongly flavored, and heavily spiced foods.

The training of the senses takes a long time, but finally it will enable us to have mastery over our deepest drives, our strongest powers. When the senses are trained, the body becomes healthy, strong, and beautiful.

6. PUTTING OTHERS FIRST. When we go after our own pleasure and profit, dwelling on ourselves and ignoring the needs of those around us, we are constricting our consciousness and stunting our growth.

People who are driven by anger, for example, are usually those who are full of self-will, who cannot put the other person first. Seldom do they have lasting relationships; seldom are they able to live at peace with themselves and with those around them. But those who have little or no self-will are secure and by their calmness and steadfastness they are able to help others who are agitated to become calm. In the home it is often the privilege of such a person to help other members of the family to be more patient, enduring, and forgiving. I place so much emphasis on the family context because it gives us countless opportunities every day for expanding our consciousness by reducing our self-will or separateness. This need not mean following the wishes of the other person always, but when it seems necessary to differ, this must be done tenderly and without the slightest trace of resentment or retaliation.

7. READING THE SCRIPTURES. My suggestion here is to read the scriptures and great mystics of all religions. If you want to know about the mystical tradition, go direct to the great mystics, rather than relying on books about mysticism. This devotional reading can be an inspiration and encouragement on the spiritual path, but even here it is better to read a few books slowly and well than many books quickly. All knowledge is within, and the practice of meditation enables us to draw upon this knowledge. Through carefully selected

spiritual reading we can be inspired by the spiritual awareness of the mystics of all religions and ages.

8. SATSANG, or association with spiritually oriented people. It is of great importance for all of us to draw inspiration from someone who is able to interpret the sacred scriptures and the great mystics in the light of his own personal experience. It is a difficult task to practice meditation for many years, day in and day out, and we all need the support and companionship of people meditating together. This is the great advantage of a spiritual community, or ashram, where those dedicated to the practice of meditation live together with a spiritual teacher. In your own home, it is very good if members of the family can meditate together.

If we want to make the discovery that will fulfill all our desires and establish us in abiding joy, bringing to our life limitless love, wisdom, and beauty, then the mystics have described the path for us to follow. By following these simple rules of right living and practicing meditation regularly, we can learn to fulfill the supreme goal of life, which is to discover experientially that all life is one.

Guide to Sanskrit Pronunciation

Consonants. Consonants are generally pronounced as in English, but there are some differences. Sanskrit has many so-called aspirated consonants, that is, consonants pronounced with a slight *h* sound. For example, the consonant *ph* is pronounced as English *p* followed by an *h* as in haphazard; *bh* is as in a*bh*or. The aspirated consonants are *kh, gh, ch, jh, th, dh, ph, bh.*

> *h* as in *h*ome
> *g* ‘ ‘ gold
> *j* ‘ ‘ june

The other consonants are approximately as in English.

Vowels. Every Sanskrit vowel has two forms, one short and one long. The long form is pronounced twice as long as the short. In the English transliteration the long vowels are marked with a bar (ˉ). The diphthongs – *e, ai, o, au* – are also pronounced twice as long as the short vowels. Thus, in the words *nīla,* "blue," and *gopa,* "cowherd," the first syllable is held twice as long as the second.

a	as in	*u*p
ā	' '	f*a*ther
i	' '	g*i*ve
ī	' '	s*ee*
u	' '	p*u*t
ū	' '	r*u*le
ri	' '	w*ri*tten
e	' '	th*ey*
ai	' '	*ai*sle
o	' '	g*o*
au	' '	c*ow*

THE SPELLING OF SANSKRIT WORDS

To simplify the spelling of Sanskrit words we have used a minimum of diacritical marks, retaining only the long mark (¯) for the long vowels and omitting the other diacritics which are sometimes used in rendering Sanskrit words into English. Some subtleties of Sanskrit pronunciation, such as the difference between retroflex and dental consonants, are therefore lost. The gain in simplicity, however, seems to outweigh this.

Glossary

ajapa-japam The MANTRAM or Holy Name repeating itself in the consciousness of the devotee, without personal effort.

Arjuna A hero of the MAHABHARATA, where he is the beloved disciple and friend of KRISHNA. The BHAGAVAD GITA is Sri Krishna's personal instruction to Arjuna.

avatāra The descent of God to earth; the incarnation of God on earth, as RAMA and KRISHNA are regarded as avatars or incarnations of Vishnu.

Bhagavad Gītā ["The Song of the Lord"] One of the most widely revered of the Hindu scriptures, in which Sri KRISHNA, representing the Lord within, gives spiritual instruction to ARJUNA, a warrior prince who stands for every aspiring human being.

Bhāgavatam An ancient and popular work in Sanskrit verse which narrates the legends of VISHNU'S incarnations, including his appearance as KRISHNA.

Brahman The attributeless Godhead, the supreme reality underlying existence.

Buddha "One who is awake"; the title given to Siddhartha Gautama (ca. 563 – 480 B.C.) after he attained NIRVANA, Self-realization.

dharma The universal law which holds all life together in unity; duty, the highest obligations of one's nature and position.

Eckhart, Johannes (1260–1327)   (Usually "Meister" or "Master" Eckhart) A Dominican mystic and theologian of Germany, one of the loftiest figures in world mysticism.

Francis de Sales, Saint (1567–1622)   A Carmelite priest and mystic who taught that God could be found by ordinary people leading busy lives in the world of business and family.

Francis of Assisi, Saint (1182–1226)   Perhaps the most universally loved of Christian saints. His simplicity, love, and selfless service inspired the creation of three great Franciscan orders in his own time, and continue to inspire aspirants of all backgrounds today.

Gandhi, Mohandas K. (1869–1948)   (Usually "Mahatma Gandhi"; the title *Mahatma* means "great soul.") Revered as the man who led India to freedom through nonviolence and selfless service, Gandhi is also one of the world's most original and practical mystics, whose contributions to politics and economics are acutely relevant today.

Ganesha   The Lord as remover of obstacles, whose elephant head symbolizes immense power. Most Hindu temples have a shrine to him. In mythology he is the child of Shiva and Parvati.

Gītā   BHAGAVAD GITA

guru   A spiritual teacher.

japam   Repetition of the MANTRAM or Holy Name.

John of the Cross, Saint (1542–1591)   A Spanish Carmelite mystic, one of the great figures in world mysticism. He was confessor, disciple, and friend to Saint Teresa of Avila. His spiritual journey is reflected in his books and poems, notably *The Ascent of Mount Carmel, The Dark Night of the Soul,* and *Spiritual Canticle.*

Julian of Norwich (b. 1343, d. after 1413)   An English mystic and Benedictine anchoress whose spiritual experiences, recorded in *Revelations of Divine Love,* are a classic of spiritual literature.

Kabir (c. 1440–1518)   Mystic and poet of India, claimed and revered by both Hindus and Muslims.

karma   (Literally "something done") Action; the results of action; the sum of the consequences of what one has done, said, and thought. The "law of karma" holds that consequences are implicit in every action, as a tree is in a seed, and have to unfold when circumstances are right: "As ye sow, so shall ye reap."

Krishna   An incarnation of VISHNU, who chose to be born on earth to alleviate suffering and reestablish DHARMA, righteousness. In his divine aspect, Krishna is the Lord himself; in his human aspect, he is a young man in Indian antiquity who grew up in seclusion as a cowherd boy, then slew the despotic king Kamsa and assumed his kingdom. In the MAHABHARATA (particularly the BHAGAVAD GITA) he is Arjuna's friend and teacher.

Lankavatāra Sūtra   A Mahayana Buddhist scripture, of special importance in Zen.

Mahābhārata   An epic poem relating the story of the struggle of YUDHISHTHIRA, ARJUNA, and their brothers to gain their usurped kingdom. This vast poem is a treasury of Hindu myth, legend, and spiritual wisdom. Among many other classics, it includes the *Thousand Names of Vishnu* and the BHAGAVAD GITA.

mantram   A Holy Name or sacred phrase; a spiritual formula repeated to concentrate the mind. (See "An Eight Point Program," page 359.)

māyā   The illusion of separateness; appearance, the phenomenal world, as opposed to the changeless reality called BRAHMAN.

meditation   The practice of training the mind to dwell on a single interior focus at will, until the mind becomes completely absorbed in the object of contemplation and is stilled.

Mīrā (1547–1614)   One of India's best-loved mystics and poets, famed for her songs of love and longing for Krishna. She was a princess of Chitore but renounced everything to live a life of devotion in VRINDAVAN.

moksha   Liberation, release from all spiritual and mental fetters; the goal of the spiritual life.

nirvāna   Extinction of self-will, Self-realization, MOKSHA.

Om (or *aum*)   A sacred syllable, the Holy Word signifying BRAHMAN, the impersonal Godhead, in the Hindu scriptures. Often uttered at the beginning and end of invocations and as part of a MANTRAM or Holy Name.

Patanjali (2nd cent. B.C.?)   Author of the *Yoga Sutras,* the most important ancient work on *raja yoga,* the path of meditation. One of the best translations is *How to Know God,* translated by Swami Prabhavananda and Chrisopher Isherwood.

prāna   Breath; vitality, life, vital energy; the undifferentiated energy of which all forms of energy in the universe are expressions.

purusha   "Person"; the Self, the soul, the deathless core of personality.

Rāma   In his divine aspect, the Lord himself, one of the most widely loved forms of God in India; historically, a prince in ancient India whose story is told in the RAMAYANA. He is worshipped as an incarnation of VISHNU, who came to earth to destroy the evil king Ravana.

Rāmakrishna (1836–1886)   A Bengali saint loved all over India, whose universal vision inspired a renaissance of mysticism in India and around the world. Ramakrishna taught, and lived out in his own life, that God can be realized within any of the world's great religions if one seeks with completely unified desire. His teachings to householders can be found in *The Gospel of Sri Ramakrishna,* by "M," a direct disciple.

Ramana Maharshi (1879–1950)   A famous sage of South India, whose lofty stature and nondogmatic method of self-inquiry attracted many Western seekers.

Rāmāyana   An ancient epic popular throughout India, which tells the story of Rama, an incarnation of VISHNU, and his quest for Sita, his beloved wife, who was abducted by the demon king Ravana. Their story and character embody the ideals of Hindu society.

Rāmdās (1884–1963)   A contemporary saint who traveled throughout India practicing and teaching Self-realization through repetition of the Holy Name. His pilgrimages are described in *In Search of God, In the Vision of God,* and *World Is God.*

Rig Veda   The earliest of the VEDAS, the ancient scriptures of India. The oldest of its hymns date back to the second millennium B.C., if not earlier.

sādhana   A body of disciplines which leads to Self-realization.

samādhi   The unitive state, Self-realization; the climax of meditation, in which the barriers between oneself and the Lord disappear.

samskāra   A deep mental impression produced by past

experiences, a compulsive pattern of thought and behavior.

Shankara   A name of Shiva; also a great mystic and philosopher from South India, who inspired a revival of faith in the Hindu scriptures sometime between the sixth and eighth century A.D.

soma   A drink used in ancient Indian rituals; the drink of the gods; also, personified, the deity of that ritual and its effects.

Srī [pronounced "shri"]   Beauty, auspiciousness, etc.; a title of respect; personified, the goddess of beauty and good fortune, VISHNU's consort.

Teresa of Avila, Saint (1515–1582)   One of the best-loved of Catholic saints, a great mystic who combined insight with practicality and a human touch. With Saint John of the Cross, she inspired a renaissance of spirituality in the Carmelite movement that continues today.

Traherne, Thomas (c. 1634–1674)   English mystic poet, best remembered for his *Centuries of Meditations*.

Upanishads   Mystical writings, part of the VEDAS, which record the spiritual discoveries of the sages of ancient India.

Vedas   The scriptures of the Hindus, regarded by the orthodox as direct revelation. The oldest is the RIG VEDA.

Vishnu   God as Preserver, second in the Hindu Trinity, who incarnates himself in every age for the establishment of righteousness or DHARMA. His most widely worshiped incarnations are RAMA and KRISHNA. (See also Introduction)

Vrindāvan   The village where KRISHNA spent his childhood as a cowherd, revered for centuries as a place of pilgrimage.

Yoga Sūtras See under PATANJALI.

Yudhishthira Eldest brother of ARJUNA in the MAHA-BHARATA, respected by all as the soul of righteousness or DHARMA.

Praise for
PATRICIA WILSON

'Full of raw emotion'
SUNDAY POST

'**I was engrossed** and hanging on each and every word. This book will leave a lasting impression . . . [and is] one that I will find myself recommending to everyone I meet'
REA BOOK REVIEWS

'We race to the end with our hearts thumping . . . **Terrific stuff**'
LOVE READING

'A **beautiful, heartbreaking story** of sacrifice and love in the face of evil'
FOR THE LOVE OF BOOKS

'Full of raw emotions, family vendettas, hidden secrets and three very strong women'
THAT THING SHE READS

'The **perfect blend** of fiction with historical fact'
SHAZ'S BOOK BLOG

'Day by day the story unfolds . . . secrets are revealed, feuds revisited and three generations of women reunited'
PEOPLE'S FRIEND

'Beautiful and evocative'
IT TAKES A WOMAN

'I loved it'
ECHOES IN AN EMPTY ROOM

'I absolutely **LOVED, LOVED, LOVED** this book . . . I can't wait to read more from this hugely talented author'
GINGER BOOK GEEK

'A very **dramatic** novel, one you **cannot put down**'
SOUTH WALES ARGUS

'Thoroughly researched and **very well written**'
THAT THING SHE READS

'The author writes in such an **evocative and emotional** style that the reader cannot help but get totally lost in the book'
KIM THE BOOKWORM

'Attention to detail is second to none . . . **I cannot praise this book enough** and just hope that the author writes another book soon'
BOON'S BOOKCASE

Greek Island Escape

ABOUT THE AUTHOR

Patricia Wilson was born in Liverpool. She retired early to Greece, where she now lives in the village of Paradissi in Rhodes. She was first inspired to write when she unearthed a rusted machine gun in her garden – one used in the events that unfolded during World War II on the island of Crete.

www.pmwilson.net
@pmwilson_author

Also by Patricia Wilson:

Island of Secrets
Villa of Secrets
Secrets of Santorini

Patricia Wilson

Greek Island Escape

ZAFFRE

First published in Great Britain in 2020 by
ZAFFRE
80–81 Wimpole St, London W1G 9RE

A CIP catalogue record for this book is
available from the British Library.

ISBN: 978-1-83877-072-3

Also available as an ebook

1 3 5 7 9 10 8 6 4 2

Typeset by IDSUK (Data Connection) Ltd
Printed and bound in Great Britain by Clays Ltd, Elcograf S.p.A.

Zaffre is an imprint of Bonnier Books UK
www.bonnierbooks.co.uk

For my sisters and brothers:
Josephine, Elizabeth, Francis, Anthony,
Mark and Gordon Wilson.
With all my love.

THE DRESS

'To sleep, to dream,' so Shakespeare says.
And so, I drift back to *our* days.
I dream of those romantic places
Each of which my heart embraces.
Remember the songs in our Pláka café
The Acropolis, majestic, across the way.
There, for a better Greece you planned
All I wanted was hearts in the sand.
On Balos beach, writing a song
We sunbathed there, too long.
Too long. Will I marry you
One day, when Greece has
Risen from this decay? I
Cried, joyous, 'Yes I will!'
That moment in my heart still.
You saw me in my lovely dress
Wrapped me in your warm caress
In the taffeta gown, I will curtsy low
Damming tears with ambition to flow
And in every theatre crowd's applause
The only clapping I hear is yours.
I'll find you in my dreams each night
Feel your strong arms. Hold me tight.
To the olive tree or the wishing well
One day I'll bring your child to tell
Of wars fought against oppression
Freedom was your big obsession!
Your kisses soft as evening dew
I recall at dusk, the night anew.
Now the dawn begins to break
How my lonely heart does ache
And ache, to see the fading stars
Remembering all that love, of ours.
That love
Of ours.

Patricia Wilson

PROLOGUE
SOFIA

Crete, present day.

Under a spreading tamarisk tree on Chania beach, I woke in the ghost of my lover's arms. It seemed a beautiful place to be – until reality reminded me of hot, sweet coffee and breakfast. The last wisps of night still cowered beneath the branches. I lay still for a while, smiling, enjoying the silence, enjoying a world at peace.

The promise of a new day surged over the horizon. The sun rising like Aphrodite from the sea, bathing the island in soft light. The sky sifted through blushing pinks, the yellow of warm honey, and then the startling blue of another Mediterranean day.

Sometimes I wonder if this deep appreciation of dawn is a by-product of very old age. Every new morning is a surprise gift. And every night holds the threat of a final farewell.

I pulled myself up from the abandoned sunbed, plaited my long silver hair, then smoothed the dusty black dress that was past its best. The cool sand felt refreshing under my feet, but I cursed old joints that were reluctant to straighten.

I had bathed after dark, away from prying eyes, in the warm Cretan sea. In the light of day, that sparkling turquoise water seemed to go on forever – like my life.

Sometimes my memories have a similar clarity, enabling me to see a long way back, the pebbles of my past glittering in threads of refracted light. I remembered another time, another place – floating on the Aegean as a child, staring at an endless sky and wondering about the nature of eternity. My opulent childhood days filled with colour and laughter, food and friends and family. I wanted for nothing.

Reaching for my shoes, I noticed a peculiar glint and scooped up a handful of sand. The grains slipped through my gnarled fingers, leaving a smooth nugget of sea glass. Something once flawless, now smashed beyond repair. Only a fragment of its former self. The gem rested in my palm – changed beyond recognition, yet still unique and beautiful in its own way.

Was I, too, nothing but a piece of broken glass? A shattered remnant of a perfect life? Sometimes, I wished God would take me, and sometimes I prayed He would give me a little longer to achieve my quest.

On a whim, I slipped the glass into my pocket, then looked up and saw Ioanis spreading his orange nets on the beach.

He settled cross-legged on the sand, his blunt needle and yellow twine shuttling back and forth, replacing lost floats along the fishing net's edge. If I could cast my nets and recapture all those I held close in my heart, I'd embrace them one last time, tell them how much I loved them, and beg their forgiveness . . .

Ioanis shouted the traditional greeting for the first of the month: '*Kalo mina, Yiayá!*'

Good month, Grandmother! Most people call me grandmother because of my great age.

Now, at the outset of spring, his words seemed doubly poignant. Wild flowers bloomed. Sunny days had replaced the pallor of winter with bronzed faces and wider smiles; the prospect of a busy summer added an air of excitement in tavernas and shops.

A swallow dipped and dived over the water's edge, chasing the last of dawn's mosquitoes. It reminded me of another bird,

2

flitting in through the prison bars of a broken window, then returning outdoors, preferring freedom. That was on the day my baby was born – the day I began to crochet.

If it *was* a good month, in the following weeks I might find my child. Just the thought made my tired heart skip.

I pulled the lemon shawl and crochet hook out of my cloth bag and plucked at the silken thread, working quickly despite my arthritic fingers. The shawl was my talisman, started with my first contraction nearly half a century ago. Later that day, with tears still wet on my face and my spirit as broken as the sea glass, I prayed to God that one day I would hold my daughter again, free to explain that *I* was her mother, and tell her that I had never stopped loving her. On that day, I would cast the final knot in my baby blanket.

A new month? I pulled at the last loop, found the end and rewound the ball of silk. Round and round the thread raced as four weeks of delicate shells and flowers unravelled. This month, I told myself. *This month*, I would complete the shawl.

I stared at Ioanis. My daughter must be about the same age as the fisherman now.

Ioanis ambled over to the beach taverna where his wife laid faded gingham cloths over wooden tables. He disappeared into the kitchen, then returned to my side with a bread roll still hot from the oven and a fried mullet on a paper napkin.

'Here, *Yiayá*, get some breakfast. You look starved.' He thrust the food at me. 'It's fresh – I caught it this morning.'

I wished to say 'Thank you!' but of course I could not, so I tapped my belly, nodded gratefully and held out one of my notes written in neat Greek letters.

'I know, *Yiayá*, you can't speak,' Ioanis said sympathetically, before returning to his taverna.

I sat up straight and picked small mouthfuls of food, despite the growling hunger in my stomach. No excuse for bad eating habits. Mama's words of wisdom came back to me. *Always remember, manners tell a lot about a person, Sofia.*

When Ioanis had returned to his restaurant, I feasted on the fresh fish.

*   *   *

I had arrived from Athens, where I lived, on the twelve-hour ferry the morning before. The packed ship transported two thousand tourists, families and students to Crete for the carnival weekend. Surely my daughter would come to watch the parade?

On the great ship, I took the lift to deck four and hurried to the front lounge. Quickly, I spread my belongings across three cushions under a window and laid my tired body down. Fellow passengers, also unable to afford a cabin, searched for a comfortable place to spend the night. Nobody would disturb a sleeping pensioner.

Oh, the luxury of resting on soft upholstery.

Although the voyage took twelve hours, I started my task at once. These days, everything takes longer. When my fellow passengers had settled, I sat up, drew a bundle of narrow strips of paper from my carpet bag, and started writing the same sentence, again and again.

I wrote long into the night, only stopping when cramp gripped my hand and I had to pull my fingers straight. Once or twice tiredness overtook me and I dozed for a while. At one point, the barman placed a cheese pie, coffee and a glass of water in front of me. I held a hand on my heart and silently bowed my thanks.

When everyone slept, I found the public bathroom, took a hot shower and washed my hair. The single braid that hung down my back had never seen a pair of scissors or felt the tender stroke of a man's hand since the most wonderful – and terrible – day of my life.

Sensing the approach of dawn and feeling the excitement of another new day, I reached into my bag, withdrew my crochet hook and yarn, and began to work steadily on my daughter's shawl.

As the light gained strength, passengers stirred. I left my belongings on the seat and passed out the slips of paper. As usual, tourists unable to read Greek thought I was begging. Some handed over a little money; others turned away, trying to ignore me. I didn't mind. The Greek people read my note, then peered at me, crossing themselves. They said kind words and placed a few coins in my hand.

On the bus from Chania's port to the city terminal, I took a seat by the door and passed my notes to everyone who got on.

A young foreign woman asked her companion, 'What does it say? My Greek's not so good yet.'

He read, '"I am Sofia, searching for my daughter, born in Korydallos prison, Athens, 1 November 1972. Can you help me?"'

She glanced at me, then turned to her boyfriend. 'That's so sad. I wonder what happened.'

The boyfriend lowered his voice. 'Seventy-two was one of the darkest times in our history. The junta controlled Greece and thousands went missing. Martial law, torture, executions . . . nobody wants to talk about it.'

'Good grief! That's not so long ago.' From her accent, I figured the girl must be a British student. 'I've got my dad's record collection from the seventies – Elton John, Michael Jackson, Queen. Hard to believe stuff like that was going on here, in Europe, at the same time. It's a bit close to home, don't you think?'

I studied the handsome youth. He bore a resemblance to the man I married, with his shoulder-length dark hair, intense brown eyes with flecks of gold and strong, lean body. I had loved – still loved – him passionately. I touched my throat, longing to explain how brave and noble my husband had been. How he'd suffered for his country and its people, always putting them before himself.

Leaning back in my seat, I closed my eyes, and allowed my imagination to flesh out the bare bones of my memories. Images from my past returned with great joy and great pain.

CHAPTER 1
ZOË

London, present day.

ZOË JOHNSON WOKE ON A damp pillow, clutching at a dream as it slipped away.

Her first thought was: *Megan, where are you?*

She flipped her pillow. The touch of cool cotton against her cheek brought her back to reality. A simple trick to stop the terrible lurch towards soul-destroying thoughts of *what if . . .*

Her throat ached; she was coming down with a bout of acute sadness. The duvet held her in a half nelson, tempting her to submit and stay in bed. She closed her eyes, reminded herself she was due in court later and pulled herself out of bed.

After slipping into her robe and slippers, she headed towards an ordinary day. Two aspirins and a caffeine hit should help improve her mood.

After seven months of worry, her search for her daughter Megan had nowhere to go. In the month after she had run away, leaving nothing but a note behind, Zoë's heart had leaped with every phone ring or door knock – but this had changed recently. Coping, people called it. Coming to terms. But how could they possibly understand a mother's turmoil when she didn't know the whereabouts of her teenage daughter?

Zoë sighed, and tried to dampen the emotions fired up at the sight of the date on her phone.

She recalled the explosion of joy, on a rainy Wednesday morning exactly seventeen years ago, when Megan had drawn her first breath. Each year that followed, Megan had closed her eyes and scrunched her face with the seriousness of a birthday wish. Sixteen birthday cakes. Zoë remembered them all. Teletubbies, Pingu, Peppa Pig . . . They had sliced through colourful fondant together, Zoë's hands over Megan's, the knife big in her child's dimpled fists.

Zoë hugged herself, wishing she had held her daughter more often in the last few years. Knowing that teenagers wanted freedom, not cuddles, she had stood back, her heart bursting with love and pride.

Now she paused in the kitchen, tears itching, Megan's seventeenth birthday filling the day. Another cake, red-and-white-iced L-plates on chocolate fondant, awaited collection at the bakery. Her birthday gift would be driving lessons.

If Megan came home.

She *had* to come home today.

Zoë tried to think of happier things, and cast her mind back to this time last year. The day after Megan's birthday, they'd set off for Crete. It was their last holiday as a family, just weeks before Frank's election campaign. Just months before Megan disappeared.

They'd cycled through traditional villages, enjoyed the company of locals in ethnic *kafenia*, and joined in the Greek dancing. They had planned their vacation to coincide with Greek Easter, as that year it fell within the British school holidays, knowing that Megan would love the local processions, bonfires and fireworks of Crete's greatest four-day festival. Even thirteen-year-old Josh was determined to make the most of the holiday. Walking the Samaria Gorge was something Zoë would never forget.

* * *

At the edge of a dull plateau, the Samaria Gorge started with astonishing suddenness. They were faced by a great cleft opening right before their brand-new hiking boots. Across the way, in spitting distance (as Frank so elegantly put it), rose the gaunt face of Mount Gingilos. Megan picked up a pebble and hurled it at the mountain and Zoë squealed, fearing she would lose her balance and fall into the deep canyon. At 6 a.m. the freezing air had them bellowing steam like angry bulls.

'Come on, let's get going before it gets too hot,' Zoë said, her voice echoing in the stillness, over a thousand metres above sea level.

They gripped the handrails and started down log steps, zigzagging to the base of the gorge. Half an hour later, they drank cold water from a spring and admired the view, then followed a stream that gushed and gurgled through lush vegetation. The air warmed; butterflies and dragonflies chased each other over wild flowers that fringed the brook. Hours later, they stopped to bathe their hot feet in icy water, Megan and Josh splashing each other, children again in the privacy of the canyon. Two of the national park's wardens, hardened hikers, had passed, reminding them to fill in a questionnaire at the end of the trek. Then the four of them were alone.

Zoë needed the loo, and the constant sound of running water didn't help. The guidebook told of a WC in the abandoned village of Samaria, a couple of kilometres ahead, but she couldn't wait.

'Need a wee,' she called to Frank and the kids, the words echoing embarrassingly around her. 'Don't wait, I'll catch you up!'

She scrambled towards the wall of the canyon and noticed a cave almost entirely covered by a pink-flowering oleander bush.

What a blessed relief to hide behind the shrub and relieve herself in relative privacy. With her shorts around her ankles, she glanced into the grotto, and was suddenly startled to see a pair of amber eyes staring back.

My God! Someone's watching me!

'Do you mind looking the other way?'

The culprit was probably an illegal camper who had stayed overnight in the gorge.

The eyes continued to stare. Zoë felt her stomach turn. She had an intense feeling of danger – no, not exactly danger, more like powerful evil.

'Frank!' she yelled. 'Megan! Josh!'

The eyes jerked back into the dark interior. Zoë dragged her shorts up and felt around the ground for her rucksack, never taking her stare from the murky depths of the cave.

This was a mistake.

She snatched hold of a vicious thistle. The thorns drove deep into her palm.

'Ouch!'

The moment she took her eyes away from the cave he rushed out, straight at her.

Zoë fell onto her back and lay there, stunned, like a dead bird in the road. In an instant his thickset body was over her, eyes fierce, breath snorting from his flared nostrils. The largest pair of ribbed horns she had ever seen turned back from his enormous head. They were curled almost into a circle, a metre across. She stared into his blazing old-gold eyes; the rectangular pupils were satanic, and at the same time hypnotic. Hardly breathing, she kept perfectly still. He took another step, his cloven hoofs clacking on the rock. He sniffed the air between them, then made a deliberate nod, as if giving her permission to leave.

Slowly, Zoë reached for her bag, got to her feet and backed away. Once the oleander was between them, she turned and ran along the path like Persephone from Hades. On reaching Frank, she fell, gasping, into his arms.

'Hey, calm down,' he said. 'What's the matter?'

'Did you see a snake, Mum?' asked Megan.

'How big was it?' Josh's eyes widened as he stared back down the track.

Zoë shook her head. 'No, oh my God, no! It was a, I don't know . . . a thing. I don't know what. I've never been so terrified.' She dropped onto a boulder and drank water from a small bottle in her pack.

'Take your time,' Frank said gently. He dished out energy bars and told Megan and Josh to stay close.

A guide, checking the route in preparation for the season's tourists, stopped to ask if Zoë was all right. When she told him what had happened, he stared in the direction of the cave.

'That was a *kri-kri*,' he said. 'You're *very* lucky to have seen one. They're almost extinct. Did you get a picture?'

Zoë wanted to hit him. Trembling, she covered her face with her hands, remembering those hypnotic eyes. A shiver ran through her.

Megan produced a pack of face wipes from her tote. 'Here, Mum, use one of these to freshen up. It'll make you feel better.'

Frank smiled. 'Good thinking, Nurse Megan.'

For a moment they were all taken back to Megan's early years, her little nurse's outfit, and how she loved to stick plasters onto everyone's imagined wounds.

'Stay back! Stay back!' Josh dramatised lifting a halting hand. 'I remember Nurse Megan sticking one of her plasters over my mouth! Probably my earliest memory.' His eyes slid around to

11

glance at his mother, checking his comic performance was having the desired effect. 'You realise my chances of growing a moustache were seriously damaged when that Band-Aid was ripped off? I could sue you for deformation, Nurse Megan. I know a very good lawyer.' He nodded sideways, towards his mother.

Zoë glanced into Frank's face, sharing the memory, instantly calmed. Everyone laughed as they set off again, eventually reaching the village of Samaria, where they stopped for refreshments. After the village, the path levelled and became easier. The high cliff walls closed in, and they were forced to cross the river several times using slippery stepping stones. The kids went on ahead and Zoë and Frank caught them up at the highlight of the trek. The narrowest part of the gorge, where the high walls came so close together they could almost touch both sides.

The view was breathtaking. Cliffs rose straight up to a dizzying height. A wooden walkway kept their boots dry above the gushing river. Despite the astonishing surroundings, every time Zoë closed her eyes, she saw those terrifying black and gold eyes and couldn't help glancing over her shoulder again.

She had nothing to worry about. She was on holiday with her faultless family – her wonderful husband, her clever, caring daughter, her funny, kind son. She had a great job waiting for her back home, a house she loved and a perfect life.

So why did she keep thinking of that creature with its devilish eyes? Why did her mind keep telling her that you could never really tell what was lurking in the dark beyond?

* * *

In the kitchen of their Victorian semi-detached house, Zoë stared at her reflection in the polished steel as water thundered into the kettle. Had they really been the perfect happy family, just twelve months ago?

Josh lumbered into the room – crumpled T-shirt, heavy lids, clutching a bottle of window cleaner.

'Morning, Mum.' He yawned, raked through his curly dark hair and headed for the Nescafé.

'Josh, you haven't been using window cleaner on your spots again? That stuff'll play havoc with your skin.'

He rolled his eyes.

'Seriously! What if it gets into your system, leads to God knows what – cancer of the testicles?'

'Mum!' He threw a *don't embarrass me* squint before turning away to mutter, 'No point in having nuts if I've got a face like a pizza.' He poked his forehead. 'It actually works. I had a zit coming last night and now it's almost gone.'

'Come here. Give your mother a hug.' She pulled him to her and, ignoring his adolescent awkwardness, squeezed hard before letting him go.

Next door's dog yapped in their front garden. Was someone walking up the path? The stab of hope from those early weeks returned fresh and sharp. It could be Megan. It was her birthday. If she was going to come home, then surely today, of all days . . . But she hadn't taken her key. Zoë rushed down the hall, swung the front door open, imagining her daughter in her arms at last.

The postman stared. Zoë guessed her expression was wild. God knows what he thought, her dressing gown open, her cotton nightshirt blown against her body. He took the last two steps forward and offered the post, his arm out, keeping maximum distance.

'Morning,' he said, with practised cheerfulness.

Zoë half smiled, knotted the belt of her robe and took the mail.

'One to sign for,' he said.

The tickets.

She slipped the manila envelope into her pocket before Josh saw it and signed the receipt.

Of course it wasn't Megan. It was never Megan.

With a sigh, she closed the heavy oak door and flicked through the mail. Phone bill, what appeared to be a birthday card addressed to Megan, and an official letter from her mother's solicitor in Crete. She stared at the envelope from Greece, addressed using her full name: *Zoë Eleftheria Johnson*. Probably taxes, death duties or the solicitor's bill, she thought. She didn't want to deal with it, not today. She sat on the bottom stair and opened the birthday card.

It came from Frank's sister, tactless Judy. The card featured a woman in a frilly apron and a Brylcreemed man in a suit kissing her ear. *Don't whisper sweet nothings, just give me chocolates*, said the woman with a speech bubble.

She's seventeen, Judy, not seventy.

Sadness ached in Zoë's chest like a dark bruise. She hugged her knees and muttered, 'Oh, Megan.'

Josh plodded down the stairs, dressed this time.

'Mum, what's the matter? Come on, don't get upset.'

Zoë kept her forehead against her knees and held out the card.

'Oh, sorry. I forgot. Hell, is it today?'

'Yes. Your sister's seventeen.'

'Right, seventeen ... Old enough to take care of herself, Mum. Believe me, she'll be all right. Don't fret so much.' Their eyes met, and he glanced away. 'Honestly, she'll come home when she's ready.' He twitched, lifting one shoulder, the way he always did in an uncomfortable moment. 'When I'm seventeen, I'm going to get a motorbike.'

A motorbike?

Zoë stared into her son's face and saw life through his eyes. He knew everything and confidently put her right, but there was always that hint of rebellion. Josh had given up fretting about Megan because he'd convinced himself she was fine. She touched his soft, stubbly cheek and considered her own stupidity, side-stepping what she had to concentrate on what was missing.

'The trouble is, you still think of us as kids. Look at me, I'm an adult already.'

Zoë turned away to hide her smile.

'Okay, so you're upset,' he said. 'Let's do something about it instead of moping. Take the day off today and start a fresh search.'

When did he grow up?

'Love to, but you've got school and I've got Youth Court.'

'It's Friday – mostly sports and music – and you don't do court today, you shop. *Friday*, Mum.'

'I know.' Zoë followed him back into the kitchen. 'But Pritchard has appendicitis. I'm taking his cases today. What about tomorrow, Josh?'

His eyes clouded. 'My weekend with Dad. We're go-karting.'

Zoë sighed. Josh lived for his weekends with Frank. His father was apparently more fun than his mother.

'Next weekend?' she asked.

'Yeah, let's make a day of it. Check the Sally Army, do a fresh blog, Facebook, Twitter, AMBER Alert.' He unplugged his phone charger and headed for the front door. 'Make a list on WhatsApp – divide and conquer,' he called from halfway down the hall.

The front door closed.

The phone rang, she picked up. 'Zoë Johnson.'

'Hi, Zoë – we still on for lunch?'

'Hi, Trisha. Lunch – I wish! I'm standing in for Pritchard. What about tomorrow?'

'Sure, cool. You all right? You sound sniffly.'

'Megan's birthday's today – could've done with company.'

After a beat, 'Okay. This evening? A few drinks and a natter.'

'I'm not sure. Megan might call. She just might . . .'

'Zoë, come on, daft girl. You've got call forwarding, Josh can stay home. I'll pick you up at seven. No arguments. Be ready.'

Trisha hung up, blocking any chance of an excuse.

Zoë allowed herself a smile. It was something, to have friends who cared. Then the sinking feeling came back. She returned to her bedroom and prepared for work, feeling strangely out of kilter in her grey court suit on a Friday.

* * *

Zoë sat in a side office, studying Pritchard's case files. The room smelled of bleach, polish and old paper. One strip light flickered and even the grubby corners of the sky-blue vinyl floor were polished to a high gloss, reminding her of Crete again. In her darkest hours, memories of those holidays dragged her back from recent bouts of depression.

She trawled through the files. First up: car theft, vandalism and possession of marijuana. After the break: more of the same. One of the defendants was a seventeen-year-old girl.

Zoë's mind spooled towards Megan. The terrible thought she usually managed to block penetrated her sadness. *What if she's dead?* What if somebody had hurt her? What if her last words were 'Mum! Help me!' and Zoë didn't, couldn't, wasn't there? The first thing the police had asked her and Frank after

16

Megan's disappearance was if they were surprised she had run away. Why hadn't she known Megan was unhappy? Why hadn't she spent more time with her daughter instead of working to help others in need?

Zoë sighed, and tried to concentrate on the prosecution files.

Donald Wilkins from the Youth Justice Board stuck his head into the room. Despite Zoë's melancholy, she smiled. Don, with his short red-brown hair and neat beard on his oval face, always reminded her of a coconut.

'Quick, let's run away together,' he said in a stage whisper, his Welsh accent giving the words a lyrical edge. 'Let me carry you off to my exotic isle and feed you ambrosia.'

'It's a close call, Don, but court duty just pips rice pudding on the Isle of Dogs.'

He grinned and came into the room, his voice becoming serious.

'Thanks for standing in today. Poor Pritchard's been in agony for days. We've got the usual cases – apart from case four, who's refusing to speak. Pritchard set up a meeting between the defendant and the victim last week.'

'How did it go?'

'Ah, you know, same old, same old. The kid's at loggerheads with the world. The old girl has a broken arm, still in plaster. The accused grabbed her handbag on pension day, outside the post office.' He sat on the desk and folded his arms. 'The pensioner tried to clobber the girl with her stick and lost her balance.'

Zoë glanced at the file. 'Bon Bluebird. Not her real name, I presume?'

'She says so.' Don shrugged. 'Been sleeping rough for six months. Needle tracks up her arm, but she says she's not using now.'

* * *

The magistrates filed into court and dealt with the first three cases before breaktime. Bon Bluebird was next, and Zoë's mind was all over the place. The young woman was the same age as Megan, had been on the streets for six months. Was it ridiculous to hope?

'Madam!'

'Sorry, miles away.'

The clerk had called for their return and Zoë's coffee cup was still full, but almost cold, in her hand. She left the drink, and tried to control her breathing as they filed into court.

* * *

In the bar that evening, Zoë was still thinking about Bon Bluebird, wondering how she would cope with three months in the remand centre, when Trisha broke her thoughts.

'It's no good going over it, Zoë. So this Bon Bluebird wasn't Megan . . . but you didn't really think it would be, did you?' Her voice was gentle, her eyes sympathetic. 'I mean, come on, what're the odds?'

'I know. Stupid me, clutching at straws like that.'

The barman slid their drinks forward: for Trisha, a small glass of tequila set on a little plate with a salt cellar and a lemon wedge; for Zoë, half a Guinness, robust and comforting.

'She might be on the other side of the world . . .' Trisha said, before her eyes widened. 'Sorry, thoughtless thing to say.'

Zoë pressed her fingertips on the bar top. 'It's just a gut feeling she's somewhere close, Trisha.' Angry at nothing and eager for the alcohol, she lifted her drink. 'Anyway, happy seventeenth, Megan. Come home soon, darling.'

They chinked glasses.

18

After making an impression on the malty, liquorice-y stout, Zoë locked onto Trisha's eyes, hunting for the truth when she asked, 'How are things with you?'

'Ah . . .' Trisha frowned and glanced away. A tightly coiled sprig of hair escaped her fat ponytail, and she tucked it behind her ear, her perfect skin smooth and rich as polished chocolate. Five years younger than Zoë, Trisha had an unbelievable IQ and the kindest heart – yet when it came to love, she always fell for the bastards. 'He's buggered off back to his wife. End of story.'

She dashed salt onto the back of her thumb, licked it, knocked back the tequila and sucked the lemon wedge.

Zoë blew her cheeks out. 'Miserable pair, aren't we?'

'How's it with you?' Trisha asked, her smile still in place but sadness hanging onto the corners.

Zoë hesitated. They'd gone through this a hundred times. 'Was it my fault, Trisha? Can I do anything else to find Megan?'

'Oh, sweetie . . . Come on, let's have another drink.'

She nodded at the barman, her scarlet fingernail drawing a line above the two glasses.

'I *hate* myself for wallowing in this self-pity. I mean, it's my job to keep the family together and I failed. I feel as if Megan's taken *my* life away with her.'

'And you resent it, and then you feel guilty?'

Zoë nodded, then downed the last of her Guinness.

'What we need is a holiday!' Trisha grinned. 'Come on, let's make a plan. You used to drive me crazy going on about Crete. Let's go and find the terrifying old goat you told me about. Give him what for.'

Zoë closed her eyes and the memory of that last Cretan holiday came rushing back, Frank's comforting arms around her shoulders after she'd seen the *kri-kri*.

Two weeks had passed since she'd received the divorce petition from Frank. Somehow, she never believed it would happen – but who could blame him? Not her, not after everything she had put him through these last seven months.

Frank was wedded to his career, and sometimes it was a relief not to have him around, even after their twenty years together. He was an MP with ambition, and his social life was exhausting. Frank needed a Stepford Wife: a sexy, undemanding robot, great cook and entertainer, athletic in bed and full make-up 24/7. Zoë had done her best, but never quite fitted the bill.

There were times when she loved him with an intensity that defied description. Even now, any small thing could light that spark. She recalled moments when they were so happy, always in each other's arms. Frank was clever, driven, funny, *fun* – and they made a great team. Ironically, it was this very support for each other, as they ascended their respective career ladders, that had led to the collapse of their marriage. With Zoë at his side, Frank became a respected MP, a fighter for the return of family values. The last thing he needed was a marriage breakdown after the next election. Better to get it over with now and enter the race in a stable relationship.

As far as Zoë's ambition was concerned, she had risen through the ranks in the law firm that she had joined after university, much to her mother's delight. The offer of a senior partnership, the very week before Megan's disappearance, had been the highlight of her career.

Without her mother, Anna, managing the household and two demanding teenagers, these achievements would not have been possible.

Since their last holiday, the Johnson family had spent little time together. Then Megan ran away, leaving only a short note that said she needed space to find her own way. The fact that her family life, her marriage itself, was seriously flawed, had been the biggest shock of Zoë's life.

CHAPTER 2
SOFIA

Crete, present day.

I FELT A HAND ON MY SHOULDER.

'Come on, *Yiayá*,' the elderly bus driver said. 'We're at the bus station, end of the line.'

I blinked and got to my feet. The driver cupped my elbow and helped me down the bus steps. He dipped into his pocket, then placed a couple of euros in my hand. I thumped myself in the chest and lowered my eyes humbly.

'Get yourself a coffee. God keep you,' he said. 'Stay safe, *Yiayá*.'

I ambled to the small café next to the ticket office and bought a bottle of water, then found a seat in the shade and rested my weary body. Was it really a year since I was last in Crete? It seemed less, and now perhaps I would never come again. The journey took too much out of me. Nobody would miss me. Yet, even as I resigned myself to these facts, I still hoped to hold my daughter one more time, before I passed away.

Everywhere seemed busy, everyone rushing. Many school and university students were making use of the bus station's free Wi-Fi; their thumbs worked furiously on smartphones.

This generation – they have no notion of who I was, or how many people once threw flowers at my feet. They have never heard the roar of the applause, felt the adoration, seen the standing ovations in my honour. To them, I am nothing more than an old woman.

A family at a nearby café was clearly celebrating one of their children's name days. The father beckoned a balloon seller. His child picked a helium-filled foil Pokémon from the brightly coloured selection that hovered like a parachute over the seller's head.

I noticed several children clutched balloons and toys, while adults carried boxes of cakes or chocolates.

'*Yiasou* Thalasa! Big year to you!' somebody cried. Then I realised it was Saint Thalasa's day. Such a beautiful name: *thalasa*, the sea. Every Thalasa and Thalasos in Greece, young or old, was rejoicing in the same way that other countries celebrated birthdays. 'Congratulations! Big year!' strangers called to those marking the day. Everyone was smiling, happy in the spring sunshine.

A young girl in her party dress twirled with her arms out. The skirt billowed to make a pool of shadow beneath her. She swayed dizzily, just like I had on the day my life changed forever. The moment came back with such clarity that I hugged myself, feeling the strong arms of a theatre usher, Big Yiannis, around me. The tragedy of that long-past Christmas Eve came spinning back and, with it, the things my husband had told me so many years later. Secrets that had broken my heart – and yet shaped my life.

CHAPTER 3
SOFIA & MARKOS

Sofia, Syntagma Theatre, Athens, 1944.

FOR MAMA'S PERFORMANCE, I WORE my emerald-green taffeta dress she had made for my tenth birthday, with its full net petticoat. I knew every song Mama would sing that evening. Keeping out of her way in the corner of the theatre dressing room, I watched her apply lipstick as vibrant as a poppy in spring. Mama wore her brunette hair rolled up and back in the latest style, made popular by women working in the munitions factories. It was safer to have long curls pinned away from the cogs and wheels of machinery. My mother said her new hairstyle was a way of supporting those workers. She used a pencil to define her dark eyebrows, then added a beauty spot above her jawline.

'How do I look, Sofia?' she asked, turning her head left and right.

'Oh, Mama, you're perfect as always,' I whispered.

And she was. The darling of the soldiers, Alexa Bambaki, my wonderful mother, was about to perform a collection of Christmas carols and popular songs before visiting British dignitaries. The Christmas concert was a significant occasion for her. She hoped the event would lead to venues all over Europe now that the war was ending.

The day before, after my piano lesson, I had strolled across Athens with my parents and two older brothers. We passed the Acropolis, then climbed through the pine trees and gardens until we reached the top of Mount Lycabettus, the highest point of the city. I had never been up there before. Since the war began it had been out of bounds, and before that I was too young for the steep path. The walk had two purposes: to calm Mama before her big performance, and to reach the chapel of Saint George to celebrate the name day of my oldest brother, Ignatius. Pavlos, two years older than me, had his name day on 29 June, the day when all the Pavloses in Greece handed out cakes to their friends and anyone who wished them 'A big year!'

We had honoured the feast day differently this year. Terrible food shortages in Athens had led to people huddled on steps, dying of starvation. One morning I'd ventured onto our balcony at daybreak and, looking down, I saw the open wagon that collected the poor souls who had perished in the night – skeletons in rags that had fallen, starving, in the street. They were tossed into the truck like rubbish, faces gaunt and stretched. I had cried long and hard, and from that day Papa said I was not allowed on the balcony until after breakfast.

Only the wealthy could keep food on their table.

On Pavlos's name day, Mama, always an angel of kindness, had baked trays and trays of bread rolls. We sprinkled them with olive oil, salt and wild oregano, and handed them out to the unfortunates in the street. One wizened man in rags had begged for another bun, telling Mama that his four children were starving. His sunken eyes stared at the bread as Mama gave him four rolls. She had tears in her eyes as we watched him hurry away, muttering his blessings and thanks.

On the walk up Lycabettus, I had kept pace with Mama, proud when folk looked our way. People said 'Good afternoon,' as we passed, and we nodded and smiled and said 'Good afternoon,' in return.

When we reached the steps leading up to the summit of Mount Lycabettus, it was easy to forget that we were still in the city. The greenery, lush and vibrant, soaked the air with a fresh perfume, and I realised that in a few weeks the cyclamen would break through with their delicate upside-down flowers.

'Look, Sofia, narcissi!' Mama cried, pointing at clumps of grey-green straplike leaves. 'They'll flower in a few weeks, then we'll come back and pick them.'

Narcissi were my favourite bloom. Every year, we went out together on a Sunday afternoon and picked the flowers. I loved how the spicy gardenia perfume filled the rooms of our house.

At the summit of Mount Lycabettus, the sky appeared so clean and blue I felt I could reach up and touch it. I dashed to the low-retaining wall and looked over the top.

'I can see to the end of the world!' I cried, pointing out over the Parthenon, the city and the distant sea's horizon. 'Isn't that the most amazing view, Papa? Look at the ships. Do you think the sailors can see us?' I jumped up and down, waving my cotton handkerchief, imagining the men looking up from their ships and waving back.

Windows in the city buildings below glinted gold, reflecting the setting sun. Two soldiers appeared on the summit and marched until they came to a halt below the flagpole. One played his bugle as the other lowered the Greek flag. Papa stood to attention, and my brothers and I lined up beside him and did the same.

Athens had suffered terrible bloodshed only weeks before. On the third of December, in Syntagma Square, the city's police and the British army had opened fire on peacefully demonstrating students, killing them in what Papa called 'an unholy bloodbath'.

'This is an important concert after the tragedy, Sofia,' Mama said, taking in the view. 'My first song will be for the poor mothers who lost their children – and just before Christmas, too. So much for the season of peace and goodwill.' She sighed. 'Thank God your brothers were too young to take part in the protest. Swear to me you'll never get involved in politics, child. Keep out of it like me and your papa. It's the only way to stay safe.'

'Yes, Mama,' I promised.

* * *

Sitting in the corner of Mama's dressing room, I thought how lucky we were not to be starving or shot at, and to have beautiful clothes and a fine house. I watched Mama slip into her new gown, black taffeta with a sweetheart neckline. The tight-fitting dress flounced into a mermaid skirt that swished along the floor when she walked. I helped zip her in, then watched her don delicate lace gloves that reached the tops of her arms.

I had never seen anyone look as lovely as my mother did that night.

'Are you all right, Sofia? Do you have a clean handkerchief? I can't have you sniffing in the theatre.'

I patted the pocket of my skirt and nodded. 'I'm so *proud* of you, Mama. You're the most beautiful woman in the world. When I grow up, I want to be just like you.'

'I don't usually wear black, do I? Bright colours stand out nicely for the audience, but I thought black was appropriate after the massacre.'

I smoothed the full skirt of my dress. 'Do you think I'll ever own such an amazing frock?'

Mama's laughter was tense, tinkling, nervous as always before she went on stage. Although I couldn't speak English, I had practised the new words with her, ready to sing to the British dignitaries in the front row. Now we recited the refrain together, ending with '. . . *My love, you are life's sweetest songs*'.

Mama raised her hands towards me as she ended the song, then we both laughed. I loved my mama so much sometimes it hurt my heart. I told her this once and she smiled and took me into her arms.

'True love can be very painful, Sofia,' she had said. 'One day you'll find out for yourself. But life without love is nothing.'

A knock sounded on the door.

'One minute!'

The tension returned to Mama's eyes. She would calm down soon. Her nerves always disappeared the moment she walked on stage to the sound of applause. Tonight, I would be clapping louder than anyone.

She straightened the bow in my hair. 'I must go now. Run to your seat, Sofia. Your father and brothers are in the middle of the second row. Hurry!'

As I rushed through the door, she called, 'Sofia!' I turned. 'I'm *very* proud of you, too,' she said, her head to one side, a soft smile on her ruby-red lips and a sparkle in her eyes.

My mother's loving words, forever in my ears.

* * *

Markos, Athens, 1944.

Six young men, members of the communist-led resistance movement, EAM, the National Liberation Front, huddled at the end of a long alley behind the theatre.

'Markos Papas, we're proud of you,' said their leader, Sotiris, as he placed his hand on the fourteen-year-old boy's shoulder. 'Today, you're our hero! Now, hold your hands above your head and turn slowly.'

Markos, the youngest and smallest of them, had the most difficult task to perform. He raised his arms and turned, while two comrades fed out a roll of fuse wire. The coil steadily wrapped around his waist. Markos's heart hammered violently in his ears.

The youths froze as the stage door flew open. A pretty girl with a heart-shaped face, wearing a bow in her hair and an emerald-green dress, emerged. The door closed quickly behind her, trapping the hem of her skirt. She banged her fist on the door. It opened and a beautiful woman appeared, wearing the most amazing black dress. The woman bent and kissed the girl on the cheek before returning inside. The girl ran down the alley towards the theatre front, without appearing to notice them.

Markos and his comrades sighed with relief.

'You know what to do, Markos?' Sotiris said. 'Pull yourself along on your elbows – there's no room to crawl. Every half a metre, roll over to unwind the wire around your waist. We'll fix this end to the grid. When you get to the explosives, fix the blasting cap as we've shown you, then return. Be careful not to snag the fuse.' He took off his neckerchief and passed it over. 'Tie this over your face – it's putrid as hell in there.'

Markos nodded, unable to speak for the trembling that seemed to rise from his bony knees. Someone tied the cloth over his mouth and nose. Sotiris fixed a miner's torch onto his head. A metal grid on the pavement was lifted and Markos stared down into the narrow, stinking sewer pipe a metre below.

'Good luck,' their leader said. 'Don't fail us now.'

Markos glanced at the stage door, remembering the young girl, glad she would not be in the theatre. This concert was for the hateful warlords, not the place for innocent children.

* * *

Sofia, Athens, 1944.

I raced down the backstreet and around into the foyer, almost tripping up the marble steps. After getting my hem trapped in the stage door, I was worried I would miss Mama's opening number, and couldn't bear that thought. This was the most precious day of my life and I could hardly breathe for excitement.

'Wait!' Big Yiannis, the chief usher, caught hold of my arm. 'You can't go in, Sofia. The lights have gone down, you know the rules.' He reached into his pocket and gave me a barley sugar. He always had a sweet for me, and usually a smile as well. This time he seemed tense.

'But my mama – I *have* to watch her sing, Mr Yianni. I have a seat with my family at the front.'

'Sorry, child, you'll have to sit this one out. Wait for the interval, and then you can go in.' His attention was caught by a cavalcade of black cars, each with a little flag fluttering from the bonnet. As the vehicles drew up outside, Big Yiannis straightened and smoothed his green-and-gold uniform. Looking round at me, he tapped his cheek and laughed. 'You've got—'

Before he could say more, a commanding voice at the entrance distracted him.

'They're here!' the concierge cried.

Theatre staff hurriedly formed a line near the door, and Big Yiannis glanced over his shoulder.

'Scoot! Get out of sight, Sofia!'

I didn't need telling twice and ducked through to the auditorium. I would be in trouble with Big Yiannis later, but I couldn't miss Mama's big moment.

My plan to dash down the steps to the second row was scuppered when I found another usher blocking the aisle. As he started to turn, I dropped to my knees and crawled along the narrow gap behind the last seats.

A lot of coughing and whispering was going on, and several men clacked their *komboloi*. I wanted to tell them all to shut up and still their worry beads. Soon, Mama would come on stage, and she ought to have silence. Wedged in my dark corner, I prayed nobody would notice me.

A fire door near the orchestra pit opened, and silence fell. A shaft of light silhouetted the line of uniformed men as they entered. The audience rose to their feet as the orchestra struck up the British and then the Greek national anthems. I longed for that moment when the curtain rose. As soon as Mama appeared and everyone was focused on the stage, I would sneak down to my empty seat between Papa, Ignatius and Pavlos. I tried to pick them out in the audience, but then the door closed, and we were thrown into darkness.

* * *

Markos, Athens, 1944.

Helped by his comrades, Markos lowered himself into the cement sewer pipe. He hesitated, afraid. Unable to bend at the

31

waist because of the fuse wires, he struggled to manoeuvre into a horizontal position.

Then they replaced the manhole cover and he was plunged into darkness.

His hands and knees sank into the sludge. The pipe was less than a metre in diameter, lined with lumpy moss. It touched his shoulders, creeping against his skin. A shudder ran through him. The rancid dankness stank like nothing on earth.

He waited for his comrades to tie the end of the fuse wire to the grid. Two clangs, metal against metal, told him it was done. His destination lay fifty metres away, directly under the first row of theatre seats. A ton of dynamite had been accumulated there over the past months, awaiting Markos and the detonation caps.

Light filtered down through the drain holes. Ahead, there was impenetrable darkness. He switched on his torch.

Brown slurry filled a third of the tunnel. Straining to keep his head above water, he moved onwards. The top of his head scraped along the dank detritus that clung to the overhead curve. A pair of tiny red eyes flashed in the torchlight, then they were gone.

Markos crawled forward, fighting the grey grip of claustrophobia. He was in the bowels of Athens – the hellhole of the city. Slimy blobs were touching his bare arms and slinking past in the black fluid. The eerie sounds, ghostly whispers – then nothing but rushing water somewhere far away – made him tremble with fear and revulsion.

A metre further on, and the air changed. Stagnant fumes burned his throat. Now he had to straighten, lie in the quagmire and roll over, careful to keep his face out of the slurry. Trapped, with panic rising, he reminded himself why he was doing this.

Markos remembered it only too well. His pride, to labour beside his father, shearing the sheep in a field just outside the city. They worked as a team. Papa pulled a ewe from the fold, sheared the belly, crotch and legs, and then passed it to Markos. The back was easier to clip, with less chance of a bad kick to his body, or an accidental snip through the sheep's skin.

And then the foreman, pointing at the sky, shouted to Papa. 'Spyridon, look!'

They both heard the plane, and looked up in time to see a British bomber drop its payload of bombs over the Athens suburbs. An area rumoured to be a communist enclave. An area packed with innocent families going about their daily lives, including his mother, his three sisters, and his newborn brother who hadn't yet received his name.

They both stared in shock as dust mushrooms bloomed upwards after each explosion.

'Isabella!' Papa screamed.

He dropped the shears and sheep and ran full pelt towards home. By the time Markos caught up, his father was already tossing slabs of mortar aside as if they were paper. Their house, their home, reduced to nothing but rubble.

'Isabella! Isabella!' he cried.

Only five-year-old Marina showed any sign of life. She had been playing with her dolls under the table, as she so often did. Her little body hung limply, yet as Papa lifted her, she blinked at him and smiled. Then she was gone.

Markos forced himself to remember Papa's tears. They ran into his beard the next day as he swung the *skapáni*, bringing it hard down into the earth with a cry of anguish, venting his anger and grief to dig the family grave.

Together, they had carried Mama's body into the centre of the rectangular dig. How tenderly Papa had unbuttoned the front of her dress. He placed his dead, unnamed baby at her

breast while muttering holy words between sobs. Then he strad-
dled Mama's body and fell to his knees. He moved his face over
hers to meet her lifeless gaze. Smoothing her thick, dark hair,
he whispered, 'I'll always love you, Isabella,' his voice heavy and
choked. Then he closed Mama's eyes.

Markos had cried too. He could almost hear his mother's
whispered reply. *I love you too, Spyridon.* He longed to feel her
arms around him again.

'Pass me little Kiki,' Papa whispered. He spread Mama's arms
wide, the way she often did to gather her children.

Markos lifted his two-year-old sister. She lay silent in her
eternal sleep, featherweight, limp against his chest. He kissed
her forehead, his grief heavier than he'd ever thought possible.
He handed her over, and Papa placed her to rest, curled towards
Mama's heart, her head lying on her mother's shoulder. Then
Markos helped his father lay five-year-old Marina on Mama's
arm, next to her sister. He turned her head to face her mother
and placed her little rag doll in her hand.

Poppy was eight years old, the double of her mother but
with the determination of her father. She wanted to fly aero-
planes when she grew up. Everyone laughed and said she never
would.

How right they were.

He imagined her now, flying on angel's wings, looking down
on him with a smile.

See, Markos, I told you I would fly . . .

'Fly . . .' he whispered into her ear, unable to say more.

Poppy wasn't heavy, but Markos's tears had unmanned him.
He struggled, distressed and ashamed that he couldn't carry his
dead sister to her resting place.

'I'm sorry, Papa, sorry . . .'

Markos's father climbed out of the grave, took Poppy from him and laid her on the grass. He pulled Markos to his chest and held him tightly. Neither spoke; their grief racked both of them with shuddering sobs.

Finally, they managed to lay Poppy on Mama's other arm.

Papa rested two coins on Isabella's eyes for the ferryman.

'Safe journey, my darling wife, darling mother of my children,' he whispered.

Together, they shook out Mama's best embroidered bed sheet and placed it over their cold, dead family. Markos opened the sack of myrtle branches he had collected that morning and spread them over the sheet. With each shovel of earth, the sweet scent of crushed herbage rose on the air.

* * *

In the narrow tunnel, Markos mourned the innocent lives destroyed by Churchill's bastard plot. The British leader was determined to restore the loathed Greek monarch, George II, to power. Like Churchill, King George hated the communists and despised their ideals.

Churchill had forgotten how Markos's older brother and his comrades had fought and died for the British during the war in Greece and Albania. Some were still fighting, facing death to support the Allies. And the British leader repaid them by bombing the homes of their families while they were away.

The tables were about to turn. He thought about the British warlords, sitting in their comfortable theatre seats above his head.

Markos felt the tug of wire and rolled in the stinking muck to release another loop from around his waist. He slid along with renewed fervour until he came to the explosives. They filled half the tunnel. His heart thumped and his head reeled from the putrid air in such a confined space. After wriggling out of the last metres of fuse wire, he pulled the negative and positive wires apart, attached a detonation cap to each, then stuck them deep into the dynamite putty. His task almost completed, he had to return to the alley without snagging the wire and pulling the caps out of the explosives.

Before he started his long crawl back, he crossed himself.

This is for you, Mama. For my baby brother, for little Kiki, for Marina, and for Poppy flying on her angel's wings.

* * *

Sofia, Athens, 1944.

The auditorium fell silent as the curtain went up. I was expecting Mama, but instead a compère stepped forward and made a long and tiresome speech, welcoming the British dignitaries. Crouched in the cramped space, my legs tingled. I longed to stretch out, to move, but the usher remained at the top of the aisle, blocking my chance to creep down to Papa and the boys. Finally, the master of ceremonies ended his monologue. The spotlight died. I held my breath.

In the darkness, the orchestra struck up with a few bars of Mahler's Third Symphony. The gentle notes drifted through the theatre.

Then came the moment I had waited for.

The spotlight blazed down again, a cone of light, centre-front of the pitchblack stage. Mama stepped into that circle and my heart soared. Applause thundered. I rested on my haunches and clapped so hard my palms burned. Mama, in her wonderful dress, appeared to bow to the foreigners, but I knew the curtsy was intended for my father and brothers behind them. Then she bowed to the audience, who clapped even harder. She acknowledged the conductor. He lifted his baton. Silence fell.

The orchestra played the introduction to Mama's latest refrain, and my skin tingled. I took a breath and mouthed the words as she sang them.

Mother, you are life's sweet song,
Without you, it's hard to be strong.
But you live in my heart
Even though we're apart,
So, I'll sing for you life's sweetest songs.

My child, you were life's sweet song,
Though you were not with me for long.
I glimpse your empty chair,
Through tears, see you there,
Lullabies are now your sweetest songs.

Oh, lover, you are life's sweet song,
I'll see you again before long.
Angels, wings give you flight,
Every star-spangled night.
My love, you are life's sweetest songs.

Mama sang that long last note, and I felt tears on my cheeks. I pressed my back to the wall and stood, no longer caring if they threw me out. A second spotlight played over the spectators as some people rose from their seats, applauding. Mama raised her eyes from my father's row and glanced over the auditorium. At the back, I waved my white hankie high above my head. Mama held her hands in my direction. She had seen me! Her final word of the refrain, '*songs* . . .' went on and on as she gazed at me.

Then the audience were standing, blocking my view. Applause thundered. The lights went up a little to show the audience's appreciation, and I imagined Mama's joy, her deep bows and her wide smile.

Grinning and crying at the same time, I ducked back down behind the seats and knuckled my eyes. The barley sugar Big Yiannis had given me fell from my pocket and rolled under the seat. I flattened myself to reach for it.

And then—

CHAPTER 4
MEGAN

Manchester, present day.

'HELL, EMILY, IT'S THE RAINIEST day ever!'

Megan stared at the reflections of red-brick Edwardian buildings in the wet pavement. Manchester alternated between being magical and morbid, and Megan missed home.

She had hardly known Emily a week, but they quickly became friends and the aching loneliness of homelessness had eased a little. If only she could go back to her family . . . but she had caused too much trouble already. She could imagine the headlines – it would all come out. What if someone had taken photos and was just waiting for the right moment to sell them to the press? Her parents' careers would be over. She could see the headlines: *The underage daughter of prominent MP involved in scandalous sex party and drug abuse.*

Mum and Dad would never forgive her. Better if she just disappeared. Let them get on with their busy schedules and dynamic careers.

She thought of Josh guiltily. He must miss her. She missed him.

Megan held a plastic bag over her head and jogged after Emily.

'Manchester must be the wettest place on earth, and I'm bloody starving!' she cried.

'There's a hot dog stand round the next corner,' Emily called over her shoulder. 'Pete's Dogs.'

Megan saw the white van, overtook Emily and raced towards it as the shutter lowered over the counter.

'Stop, stop!'

The side rolled halfway up and a broad man in a grease-spattered overall said, 'Watcha, girls. I'm shuttin' shop.'

'We're so hungry,' Megan pleaded. 'Have you got anything left? Scraps, anything at all? Please.'

A cigarette hung from the corner of his mouth. 'Why don't you come inside and get warm, girls?'

'Fuck off,' Emily said, and then staggered sideways with the force of Megan's punch against her arm.

'Please, mister, we're starved,' Megan pleaded, widening her eyes.

'Yeah, don't suppose you've any money either?'

They shook their heads.

'Dirty beggars, get yourselves some work, why don't you?' He took a plastic bag and tipped the contents of his heated tray into it, threw a couple of buns on top and held it out. 'I don't want to see you girls round here again, right?'

Emily snatched the bag. 'Ta!'

They dodged bins and rubbish down a narrow alley, Megan following close behind Emily.

'In here,' Emily said, with her shoulder against a graffiti-covered door. 'Help me push it open.'

Inside, the building was dark and quiet as death.

'Wait – leave the door open while I find my light.' Emily scrabbled in her rucksack and yanked out a pocket torch and a six-inch knife.

A police siren drifted in from the street. Emily shone the torch, and Megan recognised the place as an abandoned office.

Partition walls had gone. Rubbish, empty bottles and rotting office furniture littered the floor.

At the back of the space, Emily illuminated a crumbling staircase.

'Is anyone here?' she yelled. 'I've got a knife!' Her voice echoed.

'Seems we're alone,' Megan whispered. 'Let's shut the door. It's great to be out of the rain.'

It was odd that their friendship had started with an argument over a pitch outside Debenhams and ended in a double act. Megan juggled while Emily rapped and mimicked her idol, LP. Emily also had a whistle that hit the notes and turned heads. They took advantage of the fact that they looked so alike – both skinny with a great mop of dark curls. They almost looked like twins.

Megan had made more money busking with Emily than she had for weeks before, and after they'd split their profits, they decided to try and perform together every Friday and Saturday afternoon.

The door dragged, seeming heavier than it was. The top hinge hung loose. They shoved together and then pushed an old desk against it.

Megan rubbed the wet sleeves of her denim jacket and nodded at a drum half full of burned rubbish. 'Look at that. Let's light a fire.'

Emily shook her head. 'The ground floor's not safe. I've dossed here before. Pissheads and druggies use it at night. Let's get to the top floor. There's a mattress there.'

The torch beam turned orange, barely lighting the way.

Emily swore. 'Bloody batteries! Only put them in yesterday. Just shows you can't trust nothin' these days. We'll nick a new pack tomorrow.'

They picked their way up the dilapidated stairway to the third floor. The torch died as they reached the top of the stairs, but they managed to find the room by the light of a street lamp through the grimy windows.

'Quick, let's shut the door.'

The room was littered with ripped-out fittings. A mouldering mattress lay in the corner on the bare floorboards. Crumpled at the foot rested a ragged duvet.

'Let's get the food inside us,' Emily said, as she pushed the door closed and jammed half a dozen abandoned fluorescent light fittings against it. 'We're safe here if we're quiet. If you need to squeeze ya lemon, go in the far corner, okay?'

Megan frowned, then laughed. 'Okay. Never heard it called that before!'

'There's a bathroom on the next floor down. We can use it in the morning.' Emily pulled the food bag open. 'Four dogs, two buns and a pile of onions – I should have nicked his mustard.'

'Ha! He wanted to give you more than his mustard,' Megan said, pulling off her damp jacket. She hadn't felt so good in ages. It was great to share with a friend. To *have* a friend. They sat beside each other, shoulder to shoulder on the mattress, and ate everything.

Grease from the fried onions ran down Megan's arm. She licked it off and sighed.

'God, that was good. Now I'm thirsty.'

'Tough,' Emily said. 'There's water in the bathroom, but best not go there now.'

'You mean the tramps might get us?'

'It's not the dossers, it's the pimps. They come like rats in the night, searching for the likes of us. Before you know it, they'll have you drugged up and sucking dick.'

Megan recoiled, and glanced at Emily. 'That's why I left London.'

Emily's eyes widened. 'What? You had a pimp?'

Megan heard the shock in her friend's voice and for a moment enjoyed it.

'No, not really. I was with this guy, Simon. I stayed at his flat and everything, but he was an arse. Started usin'. He brought this bloke round one night, tried to get me to snort stuff. Things got nasty. Anyway, I don't want to talk about it.'

'Well, stick with me and you'll survive. How long you been juggling then?'

'Six months. Started while I was living with Simon.'

'I got some balls, too. Shacked up with this guy who dealt in this and that, a bit fishy, but he always had loads of dosh. He got a consignment of juggling balls from China, so I helped myself to a set and scarpered. Never got the hang of it though.'

'You got them now? It's just a knack – I'll teach you.'

'Cool!' Emily pulled the knife out of her bag and fingered the point, then produced a set of three juggling balls. 'How much did you get today?'

'Fifteen quid, outside Deansgate Station,' Megan said. 'Took the entire day. It's much better in London. I could get nearly double that in a couple of hours.' She pulled her own juggling balls from the long pocket of her camo trousers. 'Look, first you have to get used to the rhythm of throw and catch. Here we go. Do what I do.' She threw a ball in the air and caught it, again and again. Emily did the same with hers – and then dropped it. The room was too dark to see it among the rubbish.

'Don't fret, I'll find it in the morning,' Emily said. 'Fifteen quid's good.'

She slid the knife under the edge of the mattress, and yanked the duvet over them.

'I'm saving to go to Greece,' Megan said. 'I'll be going any day now. Just waiting for the ticket prices to drop. My gran's from there. What about you, how much d'you get?'

'Six quid altogether, rapping in the doorway next to Boots, but I spent three on a McDonald's. Where's your nan live then?'

'She was a refugee from Athens when my mum was a kid, but she was actually born in Crete.'

Emily's face blanked.

'It's a Greek island. My brother told me she went back there just after I left home. We went there on holiday lots of times when I was little – I'd kick up a right fuss when we had to leave for home.' Megan smiled, remembering how it became the family joke. Then she shook her head. No point thinking about her parents now. 'Granny Anna's amazing. You ever been to Greece?'

Emily shook her head.

'It's just pure magic. I love it.'

'What makes it so special?'

Megan thought for a moment. 'Oh, I don't know. Look, remember when you were a kid and you had a doll's house?'

Emily stared, but said nothing.

'You know, you move things around and imagine you're inside, living there, and you have this great feeling of control, like with juggling. When you look out, you don't see the bedroom carpet, you see groves of beautiful lemon trees, colourful butterflies and birds, and everything is zippadee-doo-dah. Well, that's Crete – magical. You feel anything's possible, and my Granny Anna is a hundred per cent fairy godmother.' She paused for a moment, and realised she was grinning. She loved her grandmother so much. 'She has a little stone cottage in a fishing village. I don't think she's ever bought a packet of biscuits from a supermarket. She bakes every day and the house always has that lovely honey-herby smell.' She laughed. 'I'll tell you something mad. She's not just this cute old lady – she's sort of sexy, too. I was at a bus stop with her once and I saw this old geezer wink at her, and she stuck her chest out and grinned. I mean! She's got plastic teeth and everything . . . unbelievable! She's like the queen of our family. I'm going to go there and live with her for a bit. She's cool – she won't tell my parents if I ask her not to.' She paused, knowing that was a hope rather than a certainty. 'What about you?'

'I'm from Albania, like me mam. Illegal. My dad was from London, but they never got married. You're not illegal then?'

'No, got a passport and everything.' Megan patted her tote. 'Just need to get some more money together for Crete. I have to pay my way, you know. My gran's not rich and I don't want to bum off her. I've got most of it. When I get there, I'll basically be a travel rep. I hear they're always looking for them through the summer. But my passion's to perform. Like it's in my blood, you know? Anyway, they have this really cool Mardi Gras there, in the next few weeks. I'm desperate to juggle in the carnival.'

'Wow, that *is* cool! You got any other family?'

'My brother, Josh, and Mum and Dad.'

'What're they like?'

'Awful. No, sorry, that's not true. My brother's all right, kinda cool actually. But Mum and Dad, they . . . well, I hardly saw them, even when I was living at home. They're important people, always trying to make things better for others, that's all. Me and Josh have them to ourselves for one week a year – when we all go to Crete. I mean, it's not such a bad thing – we always had Granny Anna. But I found out something, something bad, really bad, about my dad. I was at this party that I shouldn't have been at, and he was there too. I couldn't believe my eyes – and he saw me! Anyway, I only intended to stay away until it'd all blown over, but then I found out Granny Anna had gone back to Crete, so I started saving to go out there. Just to take care of her for a bit, and talk things over. And perform in the carnival, of course. What about you?'

Emily shrugged. 'Me mam's dead. After she died, I found Dad, but he had a girlfriend who got up the duff. I bet they're married by now. She kept bossing me. Dad always took her side – said I was nothing but trouble. I never want to see them again. We're better off on our own, aren't we?' She curled up with her back to Megan. 'What you doing in Manchester if you're from London, then?'

'Putting as much distance as I can between me and the druggy boyfriend.'

Silent for a moment, Megan thought of her parents and Josh. 'You ever wonder what your family are doing now, Emily? If they remember you, like?'

Emily sniffed, but didn't reply. She must have fallen asleep.

With the wall against her back, Megan curled her limbs against Emily, savouring the heat from her body. They could be sisters – they looked enough alike. Megan had always fancied having a sister to share things with. It might have been easier to talk to a sister about everything than it had been with Josh or her parents. Perhaps if she'd had someone to talk to, things would have turned out differently.

She dismissed the thought. In the distance, tyres squealed on the wet road, a car horn blasted, another police siren, and then she heard the thrum of helicopter blades.

Later, Megan heard voices rising through the floorboards. She remembered the light fittings against the door and the knife beneath the mattress, and calmed herself. Feeling safe with Emily's body against her, she drifted off to sleep.

*   *   *

The sound of heavy traffic woke her. Daylight streamed through the window, illuminating dust motes in the air. Commuters at rush hour meant money to be earned at the traffic lights. She pulled herself up. Emily had gone, probably downstairs to the bathroom. Megan reached for her bag. It was gone, too.

No, no, no!

Megan unzipped the thigh pocket of her camo trousers, pulled out her juggling balls and her Ziploc bag. The money was still there: all her savings. But her duffel bag, her passport, the photo of her mum, dad and Josh had vanished. All her personal possessions were gone.

She had put so much effort into getting that passport, walking all the way to Salford Keys only to find the interview office closed for urgent renovations, and all appointments moved to Portland Street for the month. Now she would have to return to Portland Street, report it stolen and go through the whole rigmarole again. *Bloody hell!* The woman who interviewed her had been sympathetic, especially when Megan told her why she desperately needed a passport.

'My grandmother practically brought me up. My parents are professional people – they both work all the hours. I hardly see them. Well, now Granny Anna's gone back to Crete and I'm worried about her. She wasn't well and, you know, she's quite old. I could look after her while she gets better.'

47

The passport woman had said that was highly commendable, and she'd do all she could to help. Nevertheless, Megan didn't want to repeat the process. She probably needed her birth certificate, also in the stolen bag. She hoped the passport woman would remember her.

Her head itched, something tickled inside her bra and she felt the filth of a week in the same clothes. The skanky mattress probably ran with fleas. Centrepoint, a charity for homeless young people, was a two-mile walk. Nevertheless, she needed to clean up before returning to the passport office, and Centrepoint had hot showers and free food.

Perhaps they would help with her birth certificate and passport stuff. Then she could go to Poundland – a clean pair of knickers and a nylon backpack would cost two quid. She'd soon make enough money to get to Crete if it stayed dry.

Megan stared at the indent in the grimy mattress. She thought she'd found a friend, a sister. Her shoulders dropped: she was a fool. No one had ever really been her friend, her ally. No one except Granny Anna, who had always had time for her, always loved her, who would love her still.

Megan knew she should have spoken to her grandmother before she ran away. Sometimes Granny Anna could sort things out – but the day she'd decided to talk about her problems, her grandmother hadn't been feeling too well. Megan found her clutching her belly and rocking back and forth, pain etched on her face.

Granny Anna claimed it was just a tummy bug and asked Megan not to go worrying her mother, who was snowed under with her new promotion. Although Granny Anna was fiercely proud of her daughter's achievements, she was also Megan's number one ally.

There was Josh, too. He'd always stuck by her, in his way. She had phoned him not long after leaving home. In truth, she missed him.

'Swear you won't tell that I called, Josh?'

'Megs, get real, I'm not a child. 'Course I won't tell.'

She believed him. 'I'm not going back to school. Mum and Dad can't make me be what *they* want.'

'Is that why you left? Just because you don't want to go back to school? That's a bit mad. You should discuss it with them, Megs. Tell them you want to study performing arts.'

'I've tried. They don't want to listen. Anyway, they're always busy. I was going to ask Granny Anna to speak to them, but she wasn't well. Is she better now?'

'Granny Anna's gone back to Crete to stay with her sister for a bit. She told me she wouldn't be surprised if you turned up there, considering how nuts you were about the place. Christ, Megs, I can't believe you ran away over school. Mum's been frantic. The police were here.'

'The police? Shit! To tell the truth, there was other stuff, too. Dad caught me at a party and – God, it couldn't have been worse. There were drugs and booze, and ... anyway, I don't want to talk about it. There's this guy, Simon. He's so cool. I love him to death. He's teaching me to drive, and his mate's got this great band. They're turning pro, and they're going to let me have a go at singing with them, one of these days. Imagine! It's like a dream come true. I'll bet Mum and Dad have hardly missed me.' She had paused, waiting, but he didn't contradict her. 'They can both get on with their boring careers without me to worry about.' Her voice was bitter. 'Anyway, I'd better go. Food to cook.'

'You, cook? Ha! Call again, Megs. Don't be a stranger.'

She laughed at his grown-up words, but once Megan had ended the call, she realised how much she missed him.

They had always fought like cat and dog, until the day Megan came out of the school gym and saw a couple of bullies having a go at her brother. They had Josh against the back wall, trying to rob his lunch card.

'Oi! That's my brother!' she'd yelled, whacking ferociously with her hockey stick. After, she'd lain awake at night worrying that they'd get her back.

Megan thought about calling him now, but it was seven o'clock in the morning. Besides, she had to be careful. She didn't want to call him when Mum or Dad were around. But it had been months since they'd spoken. She missed him, and she wanted to ask how Granny Anna was.

She didn't know why her grandmother had returned to Crete, and the thought made her a little sad. Granny Anna and Mum were so close – they did nearly everything together. Maybe she could persuade Granny Anna to come back home, and they'd get on a plane together and walk up to her parents' door, and . . .

Megan shook her head. She couldn't face her parents again, not after that night, the night before she left.

Megan remembered the lies she'd told her mother. 'It's just a sleepover, Mum, so we can study together for the end-of-terms.' But it wasn't that at all. The party was an adult affair in a huge house, and the host's son, a sixth-former Megan didn't know, had been allowed to have his friends around and use the pool house in the grounds.

She'd snuck over the lawn to take a peek through the French windows, shocked to see adults behave in such a way. Too much drink and drugs, and one or two couples were actually groping each other, without a worry about who saw them.

And then she had seen her dad, that glamorous young woman all over him. She barely remembered what had happened after that. She'd drunk even more than before, smoked pot by the pool. And later her dad had seen her, too – drunk, stoned and half-naked in the pool. She had seen his expression, heard him shout her name. She had wanted to die of shame.

No, she couldn't face her father after that. And she couldn't face her mother, knowing what she knew. If Mum knew Dad was having an affair, then God, who knew what might happen! No: she needed her grandmother's help to put things right.

Megan had loved her holidays in Crete. One day she would watch *Mama Mia* on her own telly, there, on the island. Or on a tablet. Yes, she'd have a tablet again, and a smartphone. She'd get a job as a holiday rep through the summer, perform her music and juggle in bars every night and swim in the sea every morning. In the winter, she would hike and write plays, and one day her mother would email her and say she loved her and missed her, and ask her to come home.

Do you ever wonder where I am, Mum?

CHAPTER 5
SOFIA & MARKOS

Sofia, Athens, 1944.

AT THE BACK OF THE theatre, I slowly regained consciousness. Sounds were sharp, yet muffled, as if behind closed doors. The high-pitched screeching hurt my ears, but the human screams were more terrifying. Inside my head the noise felt like a hot wire being pulled through my brain. I tried to put my hands over my ears, but I couldn't move. I had a flashback, an image of a lost second. Hurled into chaos, pinned down by a dead weight of adults. My first thought: I'd been discovered in the back of the auditorium and pounced on by angry theatregoers who'd paid high prices for their seats. Had they punched and kicked me unconscious? The weight on top of me made it difficult to breathe – and then acrid smoke caught in my throat.

A disturbing sensation grew in my body, like those seconds before a numb limb gets pins and needles. Bristling, electrifying, but more intense.

The stench of burning wool, hair and flesh made my eyes water. The ear-piercing sound seemed to fade, but perhaps I had simply adjusted to it. The rising 'whooo' of the air-raid siren gained velocity. Alarm bells clanged through the Athens streets. I imagined emergency vehicles racing across Syntagma Square.

Where were they going? How could I hear these things from inside the soundproof theatre? What had happened?

A thought half formed in my mind. A bomb. There must have been a bomb.

Under the crush of people, I tried to shout for help but couldn't draw enough air into my lungs. Each breath tore at my throat.

'Help! Help me!'

I was pressed against the marble floor. Something hard dug into the palm of my hand. The barley sugar. I tried to wriggle free but my head banged against solid wall and I realised I was jammed into the corner where I had hidden. Nothing made sense.

'Please! Can you move, please!' I whispered to the people that weighed me down. 'You're crushing me.' I pushed with all my strength, gasping for air. There was a shifting. Someone moaned: a man, his voice soft, guttural, with the bubbling sound of wetness.

'Sorry, I have to get to my father, please let me go!'

There was a sliding movement and suddenly I could see the dusk sky above.

Bodies slid around me as I pushed and shoved my way out of the heap. Someone whimpered.

'Help! Papa!' I cried.

As my eyes adjusted, I stared around in disbelief. The stage area and the front half of the theatre was a giant smoking hole in the ground. There were limbs, grotesque faces; people lay scattered, limp over wreckage. Everything spun and tilted. White dust rose like steam. The only wall still standing was the one against which I had hidden. It leaned at an angle that defied gravity. Rows of upended seats were tangled around my corner, and plaster and people were scattered about.

'Help!' With each shout, the pain in my head exploded.

Then there were shadows leaping, black devils cast by a fierce flashlight.

'Sofia! Is that you?' a man cried. The light came my way, blinding me. Big Yiannis, chief usher, his uniform almost white with plaster dust. 'There's a child here, alive!' he yelled over his shoulder, as he rushed towards me.

I straightened, stupefied, glancing back at the heap of bodies. They were too still. Warm limbs, soft and relaxed.

'Sofia, get out of there. The wall's about to come down!' Big Yiannis scrambled under twisted rows of seats. 'Sofia, move! Come towards me, quickly!' His eyes bulged, fear on his face, a gaping gash on his forehead.

Pale sand sprinkled down, then lumps of plaster. My legs were paralysed. I stared at him as he faded in the fog of dust. Something hit me on the head and pain raced down my spine. Lights flashed behind my eyes and I was falling, fading into oblivion.

I felt myself swept up by strong arms. We stumbled, bumping into solid matter, snagged on metal, lunging forward over soft, shifting debris, bodies, masonry. An ear-splitting noise cracked the night open, and the back wall collapsed, covering the people that had buried me. The theatregoers that had saved my life. I thought about the woman's cries, the man's groan.

Then we were sitting on the pavement outside, in Syntagma Square. Yiannis clutched me, his chest jerking in great sobs.

'Oh God, oh God!' he cried, patting me all over. 'Are you all right? Where does it hurt?'

I tried to make sense of the chaos. People in white tin helmets were coming from the wrecked building with stretchers. Bodies were lined up on the road.

'Are you all right, Sofia?' Big Yiannis asked. 'You've got blood on your cheek.'

I pressed my hand against my face. It didn't hurt, and when I looked at my palm, there was a red lipstick imprint of Mama's kiss. *Oh, Mama!* I curled my fingers and held onto that kiss as tightly as I could, as the truth of the day dawned on me.

'It's Mama's lipstick,' I sobbed.

'Ah, yes, I remember,' Big Yiannis said. 'You had it on your cheek earlier.' He buried his face in his hands. 'My wife was in there. Your father got her a free ticket...'

* * *

Markos, Athens, 1944.

Minutes earlier, in the alley behind the theatre, one of Markos's comrades had poured a bucket of water over him in an attempt to wash away the stinking *ka-ka*.

'Leave it! Run!' Sotiris cried, lifting the T-plunger on the detonation box.

In a moment, Markos and Sotiris were beside each other, racing like hell along the cobbles, then flying through the air. No one had expected such a blast. Everything changed into slow motion and Markos knew tonight would be etched into his brain for the rest of his days.

Glancing back, he saw the cast-iron sewer cover lift and hurtle towards them. Sotiris stumbled, the spinning manhole cover smashing into him.

The blast threw Markos flat and pushed him forward in a skid on his belly. Cobbles ripped the front of his vest to shreds, then grated the skin from his bony ribcage. Masonry flew over him and his prostrate comrades. Chunks of brick and plaster rained down. The air filled with black smoke, then fine white dust that billowed towards the darkening sky.

In the first moment, he heard nothing but the deafening explosion, followed by a roar as the building came down. He tried to stand and reach Sotiris, who lay across the alley, but his balance had gone. Before he was halfway to his feet, he staggered sideways and fell to the ground again. Terrible pain thundered through his head, and the ringing in his ears deafened him.

Trying to ignore the pain from his own bloodied torso, Markos crawled to his leader. The manhole cover lay embedded below Sotiris's ribs, almost cutting him in half. A pool of blood paled in the blanket of dust. Sotiris opened his eyes wide, stared in horror at Markos, and tried to speak. Blood flowed from his mouth and, with a splutter and a shudder, his life ended.

Markos stared at his lost friend, and the world began to fade around him.

* * *

The day after Markos had buried his mother, three sisters and the newborn, he needed to be alone. His heart was so heavy he couldn't speak to his father. He pulled on his jacket and walked three kilometres into the centre of town. His favourite church, the Sainted Mother, stood on Erminou Street. He likened the building to an old man – rounded and stooped, chipped at the corners, a grandfather of churches. Bullet holes spattered the stucco and red brick, but over the door, glinting in the late-afternoon sunlight, was the most beautiful golden mosaic of the Blessed Mother and Child he had ever seen. He closed his eyes, thinking of his own dead mother and the nameless baby at her breast.

Once again, he cursed the armed forces. Finding the church door locked, he kicked it harder and harder as his rage rose up and destroyed his senses.

'*Malaka! Malaka! Malaka!*' he yelled, swearing and thumping his clenched fists against the portal. Tears ran down his face. 'Damn you to hell, God! Damn you to hell and back!'

God wasn't listening, but the *papas* and a policeman were. They grabbed him by the shoulders and yanked him away from the door.

'Hey! Do you want to be locked up for the night?' the policeman said, twisting Markos's arm up his back. 'What do you think you're doing?'

Such was Markos's rage that he hardly felt the pain in his shoulder. He swung his foot as hard as he could at the policeman's knee and instantly found himself free. The priest made a grab for his hair, but Markos ducked under his arm and ran for the side streets.

'Oi!' a voice called from a half-open door. 'Hide in here.'

Markos saw a youth in a ragged striped shirt. He hesitated, then ducked into the building. The door was slammed shut and bolted. He found himself in a shady, high-walled courtyard with four other youths and two girls.

'What's going on?' he asked, staring around.

'I ask the questions around here,' the one in the striped shirt said. 'Why were they chasing you?' The other lads joined their leader, blocking Markos's escape.

He glanced at the surrounding wall, doubting he could scale the height before they grabbed his ankles. 'I guess I got a little heavy-handed with the church door.'

'And why was that?'

Suddenly weary, Markos noticed a bale of clover next to an empty rabbit hutch. He sat down slowly, his back against the courtyard wall.

'Because I wanted to light a candle for Mama, my three sisters and my baby brother. I buried them yesterday.' He turned his head, fighting his emotions. 'Who are you, anyway?'

'We're from the orphanage. They kick you out when you're sixteen.'

'And the house?'

'Jews. I doubt they'll be back any time soon.'

'Why did you help me?'

'I have my eye out for a good runner, someone small.'

'I'm not small!'

'You're smaller than us, my friend. I'm Sotiris.' He reached out and shook Markos's hand. 'If it's revenge you want, you can join us.'

'I'm Markos,' he returned. 'What do you mean, join you? Who are you, part of the Barefoot Brigade?' He had heard of this highly organised bunch of boys. The Barefoot Brigade had stolen from the Axis, informers and black-marketeers, and given their booty to the needy, often saving the lives of the starving.

'Not exactly. We are, what you might call, their older brothers. We do as much damage to our dictators and oppressors as possible.' He stared at Markos for a moment. 'You can run, and I saw your courage, kicking the policeman like that. We need you. Will you join us, brother?'

Markos stared at the scruffy group and thought of his dear mother buried under the earth. The idea of belonging drew him. He felt so lonely, without Mama and his siblings, and now Papa was angry all the time, throwing things, yelling at Markos. He almost wished he had been in the house with his mother when the bomb dropped.

Perhaps if he helped to commit some great act of revenge, his father would be proud of him and forgive him for being the only survivor.

'What do you want me to do?'

'Not so fast. First you will take the oath at midnight, at the start of a new day in Athens. Now eat, meet the others and get some rest. There's rusk, herbs and water inside.'

* * *

At midnight, Sotiris and the other youths crept back to the church of the Sainted Mother. Two kept watch as Sotiris picked the lock, then they slipped inside and closed the door. Each crossed himself three times, then hurried to an icon of Saint George slaying the dragon.

'Kiss the saint, place one hand on the icon and the other on your heart,' Sotiris whispered. Markos did as instructed. 'Now, repeat after me – "I swear with my life to keep the secrets of our group, and obey orders without question".'

Markos repeated the oath.

Sotiris continued. "'I swear to fight for the freedom of Athens from the clutches of the Allies, the Axis and the royalists. I swear to fight for the liberty of Greece, free to be ruled *by* the People, *for* the People".'

Markos thought the pledge so simple. He had to stop himself shouting the words. *The People* of Athens would not have bombed his home, killed his family, as the British had done. *The People* of Greece would not have cut off the city's food supplies, as the Germans had. He recalled the begging skeletons on street corners, and the morning wagon piled high with those who had succumbed to starvation and perished in the night – some of the 300,000 innocent Athenians who had died on the city's streets.

At last Markos had a cause, a purpose, and he resolved to obey orders and fight the dragons that oppressed his Greek countrymen – those heartless warmongers who kept thousands of bellies craving for food, and those cowards that dropped their bombs from planes to kill mothers and nameless babies.

At midnight on that fateful day, Markos Papas became a freedom fighter for the Communist Party.

* * *

Sofia, Athens, 1944.

On the pavement outside the theatre ruins, I stared at the imprint of my mother's kiss. My other hand was bunched into a fist, and when I opened it, I saw the barley sugar. I offered it to Big Yiannis. With a shake of his head, he reached into his pocket and pulled out another one. In unison, we pulled on the ends of the wax paper, unwrapped them, popped them into our mouths.

After a few minutes, Big Yiannis said, 'Stay here.' He glanced over his shoulder at the smouldering theatre and got to his feet. 'I'll be back, child. Don't move.'

Stunned and confused, I found myself overcome by tremors. There was an awful wailing going on, but I couldn't tell where it was coming from. 'There, there,' someone said, through the ringing in my ears. They placed a blanket around my shoulders and asked if I could stand. When I tried to thank them, I realised it was me making the dreadful racket.

What had happened? Where were Mama, Papa and my brothers? I stared at the chaos; the line of bodies on the road grew ever longer. People were running, shouting about a bomb. The air-raid siren still wailed.

Big Yiannis returned, his face streaked with dust and tears. 'My wife!' he cried. 'I can't even remember what she was wearing . . . and now she's gone!' He turned his big face to the sky as if searching for her.

I wanted to comfort him, but I couldn't speak. Rescuers were emerging from the dust and rubble, and I told myself Mama and Papa would appear at any moment. 'We were looking for you,' they would say, hugging me. The ringing in my ears would stop, and we would walk home together and drink cocoa before bed. We always had cocoa on very special occasions.

Time dragged by, and my shivering calmed. Big Yiannis ambled away again. I tugged the blanket around me. After a while, a new thought struck me and I got to my feet. Mama and Papa would have gone home, of course. When they couldn't find me, they'd have gone home to see if I was there.

Big Yiannis returned. 'Where are you going, Sofia?'

'I have to go home, Mr Yianni. My parents will fret if I'm not there.'

'Sit here, child. Someone from the orphanage will come for you.'

The orphanage? That terrible place where children with no mother or father were kept? No, no. That wasn't right. My family must have missed me in the confusion and returned home. I had to join them. They'd be expecting me. They'd be worried.

A line of men passed lumps of masonry from the theatre to a lorry that had trundled over debris in the street. The man at the start of the chain shouted, 'Doctor, here! We've got a woman – she's alive.'

But what if they weren't at home?

My head filled with terrible thoughts. Screaming 'Mama! Papa!', I raced along the line of rescue workers. Poor Mama, her dress would be ruined.

Someone swooped me up and handed me to a man wearing a Red Cross helmet.

'Now, now. You can't go in there, little girl. Don't fret, we'll look after you.'

He carried me to a covered wagon and placed me on one of the two benches inside. I recognised some of the staff from the foyer. The concierge held a wad against his face, blood trickling down his arm. One of the ushers wore a bandage around his head, covering his eyes. The woman who sold tickets had both her arms in splints.

'Did you see my mama?' I asked the concierge. 'Did you see her?'

He exchanged a glance with the ticket seller and made a shake of his head. My tears broke free. I searched for my hankie but it had gone, so I used my fingertips to brush them away. Someone thrust the tailgate up and bolted it. The engine started with a shudder. I peered out of the back and saw Big Yiannis standing alone in the crowd. His head hung down, shoulders hunched. The big man appeared utterly defeated.

'Mr Yianni, please!'

He lifted his head and peered from under heavy brows.

'Mr Yianni, it's me – Sofia! Please! Don't let them take me! Please!'

The wagon started creeping forward. I jumped onto the bench, put one foot on the top of the tailgate, and leaped.

Mr Yianni caught me, staggering backwards. I clung to his neck.

'Don't let them take me to the orphanage, please!'

62

I felt his chest shudder against me.

'Oh, Sofia, you should go with them. What can I do?'

'Take me home, Mr Yianni, please. My parents – they'll be there, they'll come.'

We stood for a moment, surrounded by mayhem. He rocked me from side to side.

'Do you have a key?'

At last, there was hope. I nodded, remembering the emergency key buried under the bougainvillea. I would go home, and tonight would be undone. Mama would be there, Papa, my brothers. Everything would be all right.

CHAPTER 6
ZOË

London, present day.

ZOË TURNED HER PHONE OFF and worked through the morning's court files: one car theft; two shoplifting offences; threatening behaviour in possession of a knife; and one second offence for prostitution. She thought about the coming weekend. She and Josh were going to restart their search for Megan.

Her son was the steady one of the family. Not artistic or excitable like Megan, he simply buckled down and got on with his work. Zoë was looking forward to spending Saturday afternoon with him, even though it meant eating in a burger bar.

Staring at her hands, she noticed the pale band of skin on her ring finger, strangely bloodless after twenty years in the dark. That wide gold wedding ring lay buried in her purse. *Rest in peace, old friend.* Memories of the day she and Frank bought it came back, and she smiled. It hadn't been all bad. Later, the symbol of never-ending love would be in a jeweller's window, and the love it represented would be living in a flat ten miles away.

It seemed impossible that they were breaking up, after twenty years together, but they both agreed that life had become impossible. All they had done since Megan left was snipe at each other. Zoë had found she was constantly testing how far she could push Frank. He, on the other hand, had only talked about work, barely listening to her worries about their daughter.

Zoë stared at the offender's file again. A sixteen-year-old prostitute. Dealing with youth prostitution was difficult. Vulnerable kids with complex emotional problems. She saw the need in their eyes, the hopelessness disguised as anger.

Megan was only one year older than this girl. She frowned, wondered . . .

Somebody knocked on the door.

'Come in!'

Don stuck his head around the door. 'Morning, Zoë, can I have a word?'

Zoë stood up. 'Sure, come in.'

His usual smile was absent as he came round the desk and placed a hand on her shoulder.

'Sit down, Zoë.' He bit his lip, the beard bristling below his mouth. 'Take a breath.'

Zoë felt the blood drain from her face. She stared into his eyes, fear building.

'What is it? Is it . . . ? It's Megan . . . ?'

Don nodded, then shook his head, clearly emotional.

'Christ, tell me!' The question surfaced. 'She's alive, Don? She *is*, isn't she?'

He nodded, and a smile came to his lips.

Although anguished, her body felt numb.

'Where is she?'

'She's all right, Zoë. Take it easy.'

Countless days and nights of dread were lifted from her in seconds.

'Where is she? I have to go to her. I have to tell Josh – has anyone told Josh?'

'No. We've just received a call from the Met. Yours and Frank's phones were turned off, and you must have given my office number as a work contact.'

Six whole months of hope and bottled feelings overwhelmed Zoë.

'She *is* alive, Don. Tell me again! Tell me I'm not dreaming.'

'She's alive.' He sat on the edge of her desk. 'I've postponed court for an hour and called Pritchard in. There's a rail strike, so Janis has booked you a flight to Manchester. You'll be there in a couple of hours.'

'Manchester? What's Megan doing up north? You're sure it's Megan? It's been so long. I couldn't take it if . . .'

'She's been remanded for shoplifting. Don't worry, she's safe. Not talking – but she's safe. It's definitely her. They found her passport and birth certificate in her bag.'

*   *   *

Don drove Zoë to Heathrow from the court. She called Frank on the way, but his secretary answered.

'I'm sorry, Mrs Johnson, he's in a meeting. Can I give him a message?'

Damn. 'It's important – I need to speak to him now.'

'I'm sorry.'

Zoë balled her fist, trying to contain her frustration. She needed him. If she couldn't have his arms around her – and God knew she could do with the strength of him at her side at that moment – then at least she should be able to tell him this news herself. She drew in a breath, hating the barrier of his job that so often came between them.

'Tell him they've found his daughter,' she said into the phone, and then ended the call. A harsh thing to do, perhaps, but their children were more important than any job. She should always be the exception to his 'no interruptions' rule.

Zoë felt ashamed when she remembered what he was working on: reuniting refugee kids with their parents.

'There're thousands of them,' he'd told her last week, when they met at Josh's parents' evening. 'They're stressed and frightened, and their parents are frantic to find them and get them back. You can't imagine what they're going through.'

'Of course I know what they're going through,' she'd snapped back. 'Have you forgotten our own daughter already?'

'God, no! Don't twist things around, Zoë. We're privileged, and have everyone on our side looking for Megan. Those people have nobody to fight for them.'

Now she wanted to thump him, or put her arms around him. Her emotions had gone haywire since the day Megan disappeared. The months after she ran away had been unbearable. The relentless loneliness she felt in her search had led to depression, pills to help her sleep and far too much to drink. Since Frank left, afraid of her own actions, Zoë had refused to have alcohol in the house.

The truth was, she wanted Frank so badly – and yet whenever he was near, he became the target for her anger and frustration. She could hear herself sniping at him, not satisfied until he retaliated and some small incident turned into a blazing row. Life had been unbearable for them both, and poor Josh had spent most of his home life locked in his bedroom, gaming.

Zoë was utterly destroyed when Frank finally announced it would be better for everyone if he moved out for a while, three months ago. She didn't want him to go, couldn't stand to lose someone else that she loved – and yet she couldn't say it. Her outrage and fear of what might have happened to Megan always got in the way.

She called Trisha, who offered to drop everything and go up north with her – but the plane left at noon, Trisha wouldn't make it across the city and besides, Zoë wanted to be alone. Trisha said she understood and agreed to collect Josh from school and then take him to Frank's. Call waiting beeped.

'Sorry, got to go, Trisha.'

'Hello, darling,' Frank said.

Zoë's heart tumbled over at the sound of this old endearment.

'They've found her, Frank. She's alive ...' A sob escaped before she could stop it. 'She's in Manchester. I'm nearly at the airport, on my way up north.'

'I know, Don texted me. I can be there this evening. Would you like me to come?'

Be nice, be nice! Zoë told herself. Of course she wanted him to come!

'Look, you're busy and, who knows, we'll probably be on our way back later today. I'll call you as soon as I understand the situation. I can't tell you how relieved I am.'

'Me too,' he said quietly. 'It's the most amazing news.' After a moment of silence, he murmured, 'It's been hell, hasn't it?'

* * *

In Heathrow's departure lounge, Zoë stared into a gift shop window. What do you buy a seventeen-year-old whom you haven't seen for months? She placed one hand over the other and pressed them against her chest, imagining the weight of Megan's body as she hugged her.

Nothing in the shops seemed suitable, but then she spotted an elegant page-a-day diary. Megan loved writing, and from her poems and songs, Zoë recognised her talent. The diary would be perfect for her jottings, so she bought it along with a stupidly expensive pen. While the assistant gift-wrapped them, Zoë imagined Megan recording the great times that awaited her once she returned home. They would shop together, eat at McDonald's and talk, talk, talk. But Megan was practically an adult now – Zoë swapped McDonald's for a grown-up lunch in a wine bar. The thought made her incredibly happy.

Of course, there was much they had to discuss. Why had Megan run away? In her work as a youth magistrate, Zoë had heard many reasons from the kids themselves. Almost every instance could be worked through and resolved, and not one was worthy of the trauma inflicted on those who loved the runaway. They could sort out their differences, of that she felt confident.

Her mobile rang as she walked towards the gate. Uplifted and eager, she saw Don's name on the screen.

'Zoë, there's no easy way to say this so I won't fanny about. It might not be Megan.'

Zoë stopped dead. She couldn't speak. She'd bought a diary. It was full of blank pages. The news was like a whiteboard filled with questions, wiped clean in a second. She stood in the scentless, clinical airport with people rushing around her. Noises echoed. A baby cried and its tired keening mirrored Zoë's despair.

'They took her fingerprints,' Don continued. 'They don't match Megan's. The girl's being questioned but refuses to talk.'

Zoë recalled the day Megan disappeared. The police had taken a cola can from Megan's room to get prints. She had insisted. The officer in charge said Megan was likely to return within forty-eight hours. She had left a note saying she was leaving, and had taken some clothes, so she was probably just staying with a friend. Zoë had urged them to treat her disappearance more seriously.

A chill rushed through Zoë. If the girl had *found* the bag, then her dreams of finding her daughter could turn into her worst nightmare.

'Zoë, speak to me,' Don said.

She snapped back, 'I'm going anyway, Don. The girl had Megan's bag, so she's probably seen her.' There was a silent moment as they both considered the alternative. 'Cancel my court cases. I'll stay in Manchester for a few days. I *know* she's alive, Don. Call it gut instinct, but for the first time, I feel I'm really close to finding her. You can't imagine what it's been like, adrift, wondering, imagining the worst. I know it's still possible that' – she swallowed hard – 'well, you know my fears, but somehow, I feel confident Megan is out there and I'm close to finding her.'

'I *can* imagine the hell you've been going through, Zoë. Is there anything I can do?'

She spoke her thoughts as they rushed into her head. 'You said Megan had a passport. Her last one expired before she ran away, so she must have had an interview at the issuing office. I need that information – will you find out as much as you can?'

She thought about the pictures on the website which Josh helped put together, wishing she had copies of them with her to hand out.

'Don, when Megan applied for a passport, she must have had a recent photo. A duplicate would be invaluable, and I wonder who signed the back?' Megan might have changed drastically in the last few months. What if she were to walk past her own daughter in the street without noticing? Surely that wasn't possible. But she wished she had a recent photo. 'Can you call the issuing office, pull a few strings? I'll find her, Don, I will.'

'That's the attitude. I'll do everything I can, and get back to you soon. Phone if you need anything else. Any time, okay?'

'They're calling last passengers. I've got to go. Will you tell Josh what's happened? I'll call him this evening.'

On the plane, Zoë took out her notebook and made a to-do list. Her thoughts returned to the passport. She pulled hers from her handbag and flicked through the pages. Zoë Eleftheria Johnson. The woman in the photograph appeared much younger than the one staring at it. Well groomed, with carefully applied make-up on a line-free face. Today, Zoë could be mistaken for her mother, age-wise. As far as looks were concerned, she must have taken after her father, whom she barely remembered. Zoë's mother, Anna, had been a short, fine-boned woman with an aristocratic look. Although Zoë was slim, she was curvaceous and tall.

The last time Zoë used her passport came to mind: when she returned from her mother's funeral. A hollow of sadness expanded inside her. She had not found the space to grieve, and that in itself was heartbreaking. Her mother had been a saint, and deserved her daughter's sadness and sense of loss. Now, Zoë wished she had spent more time with Mama. An enormous need to tell her she was sorry had nowhere to go. Zoë's mother knew she had cancer but kept it to herself, so that all Zoë's energy could go into searching for Megan.

She unclasped her seat belt and stared out of the aeroplane window. Her mother was from Crete, where she had met and married Zoë's father. She didn't know much about her parents' past; Mama never wanted to talk about it, always said it was too painful. All Zoë knew was that her father was a soldier who died in Greece in 1975, and Mama had brought Zoë to England as she approached school age.

Zoë had been devastated when Mama announced she was returning to Crete, barely a month after Megan disappeared.

'You'll be better off with me out of the way,' she had said. 'It will give you more time to concentrate on looking for Megan. Besides, I'd like to spend a little time with my sister. We're not getting any younger, you know.'

'Please don't go, Mama!' Zoë had begged.

'It's something I have to do. You'll be fine, Zoë. Megan will come back soon – she's only been gone a few weeks. The novelty will wear off and she'll realise she's better off here, trust me. I'll see you all when you come to Crete on holiday.'

'But you can't just walk out on us. We need you so much.' Zoë wasn't just being selfish; she wanted her mother to know how much they all appreciated her. Neither Frank nor Zoë could have progressed in their careers the way they had without the rock that was her mother at home, taking care of the kids. 'I know I haven't been the nicest person to live with lately, Mama, and I'm truly sorry. It's just the stress. I can't seem to hold it in some-times. Please don't tell me I've driven you away too.'

'No, my darling, of course you haven't. I'm going to miss you all terribly, but perhaps you need a little more time alone with Frank, too. I'd have to be blind not to see that you're both strug-gling, but I know you still love each other. He's a good man, Zoë. I hate to hear you two fighting after so many happy years together.'

'But how will I manage without you?'

'That's the trouble – you've never had to. My fault entirely. I've always given you everything you wanted, but I can't help you now. You'll be fine. You just have to work this out for yourself. And trust me, I'm confident Megan will come back.' She took Zoë's hand, peering at her daughter, and as she did, Zoë saw the gentle smile on her lips, but also the deepest sadness in her eyes. 'Sometimes, it's a mother's job to step back, let their children grow to reach their full potential. Even push them out of the nest when the time is right. It's the nature of things.'

'We need you,' Zoë had repeated.

'I know. But there are people who need you, too. It's not because I don't love you. You'll never understand how much I do. We never love our parents as much as they love us,' she said softly. 'One day, you'll understand. Like I said, I'll see you when you come over on holiday.'

And now Zoë understood the secret behind her mother's departure: Anna knew she was dying. She had wanted to be buried in her homeland, and hadn't wanted to give trouble to those she would leave behind. If only Zoë had known. Resting her head against the plane's window, she cried silently.

The man next to her left his seat and, a minute later, a flight attendant offered her a cup of water. She smiled ashamedly, tears still wet on her face.

* * *

Outside the arrivals lobby, a tall man waved a sheet of card, her name written in broad black marker. He wore a green tweed jacket and pale yellow turtleneck.

'Colin Dylan . . . Colin,' he said, offering a hand with long spindly fingers. 'Court liaison officer. Your colleague, Donald Wilkins, was in touch. How was the journey, Mrs Johnson?'

She caught a whiff of spearmint with garlic undertones. 'Zoë, please. The flight was fine. Good of you to meet me.'

Although desperate to interrogate him, she decided to wait until they were clear of airport traffic. They joined cars and minibuses in a rush to flee the terminal. Minutes later, on the M56, they hogged the middle lane, heading for the city through a sudden shower.

'You're positive she's not my daughter, Colin?'

The wipers counted her heartbeats before he turned them off.

'Yes, we're sure. The young lady refuses to give her name. Security cameras caught her stealing, then she threatened the store detective with a knife. It's a serious offence.'

A knife . . . Zoë yanked the seat belt away from her neck.

'The police took her prints.' He shook his head. 'No comparison. The girl bears a strong resemblance to the passport photo, though. Had us all fooled for a while.'

'And she won't say why she has Megan's things?'

'No, but you might have more luck. We're going straight there. You can talk to her.'

Zoë pulled the notebook from her pocket and scribbled a list of questions to ask this girl, wondering how stubborn she was and how difficult it would be to get her to talk. If she had met Megan, if she knew her, then just maybe she could give Zoë the information she needed.

They turned left into the city of Manchester and Zoë leaned against the car door with the momentum. Her life revolved around London. She believed it was the best city in the world, that nowhere could compare to the capital. But with the first glimpse of Manchester, her preconceived ideas faltered.

They passed over a quaint canal bridge, and up ahead, an unusual building grabbed her attention. The angular structure seemed sci-fi in the early dusk light. The construction was an irregular tower of glass cubes protruding from the sides with no visible means of support, like a filing cabinet with the drawers pulled open to various degrees. What appeared to be a flat steel spine rose through the centre of the structure. Light and shade shifted as they approached, and Zoë found herself mesmerised by the complexity of the architecture.

'What is that?' she asked Colin.

He smiled. 'That, my dear lady, is the Civil Justice Centre. Largest court complex in the UK – forty-seven courtrooms, seventy-five consultation rooms, and all the amenities to go with them.'

Zoë forgave him for addressing her as *my dear lady*. 'I'm impressed. Is that where we're going?'

He nodded.

They stopped at traffic lights. On the opposite corner, with her back to them, a skinny girl juggled with white clubs that appeared too big for her small hands. Clearly talented, she threw the skittles high, then dropped one. As she bent to pick it up, the black bowler fell from her head. She rolled it along her arm, flicked it into the air, then caught it. All part of the act, Zoë realised. After a sweeping bow, the girl ran along the line of cars with the hat held out. Zoë found herself smiling as they pulled away.

Her focus returned in the lift as it rose through the central spine of the building. The girl in custody had probably stolen Megan's bag. Her defences would be up. A difficult situation awaited, and everything depended on the right tactics.

Colin led her to his office, where a child psychologist joined them. She talked condescendingly for twenty minutes on how to handle the offender, and Zoë's nails dug into her palm. She did know how to deal with troubled youngsters; it was part of her job as a youth court magistrate. In this case, they all wanted the same thing: to discover the identity of the young woman and learn where Megan was.

'Right, are you ready, Zoë?' Colin finally said.

Zoë nodded and followed him to the interview room.

The girl sat at a table in the centre of a square office. Waiflike beneath a mop of tangled dark hair, she didn't look up. She thrust her chin forward, her forehead puckered in a frown as she stared at the tabletop. The large woman beside her wore a square, badly fitting grey suit. Beneath her red-blonde hair she had kind-looking eyes, and Zoë could see that she was probably very well suited to this line of work. She offered a hand for shaking.

Colin introduced her as June Tree, the juvenile's appointed solicitor. He gave Zoë an encouraging nod and then left the room. Zoë pulled her chair to the side of the table so as not to sit opposite the girl. The detainee lifted her head slightly, her glance not reaching anyone's face.

'Listen, I'm not here to make trouble for you,' Zoë said softly. 'I know you don't want to be here and that it might be scary, but please understand I'm desperate to find my daughter, Megan.'

The girl ignored her.

'I haven't seen Megan for seven months now, and for every one of those days, I've been out of my mind with worry. Can you imagine?' The words that she thought so often, but never dared say, tumbled out. 'I've feared the worst every single day. Feared she's dead and buried on some wasteland. Terrified I'll never find her or hear from her again. Can you imagine the hope and the dread that comes with every phone ring or knock at the door?' As Zoë said these words, she wondered if they were true of this girl's family, too. Where had she come from? Who was she?

The girl did not move, and the room became almost tangibly silent. A pain grew in the back of Zoë's throat and spread, making her neck stiff. Almost overcome by emotion, Zoë paused to let the words sink in. She suspected the girl sitting in front of her didn't feel as tough as she was acting.

The girl shrugged, and frustration crept in, briefly eclipsing Zoë's misery. Zoë steeled herself, knowing that anger would get her nowhere here. Drawing all her strength and experience from questioning people in court, she continued.

'Listen, I understand you don't want this aggravation. I don't care if you stole Megan's bag, or if you found it, or if she left it with you. Please – I just want to know if you've seen her recently!' The words were louder than she intended, then a cursed sob escaped her.

The girl's eyes narrowed, hateful. 'Yeah, right. Nobody's interested in me. Well, guess what? I don't give a shit about your daughter, and she doesn't give a flying fuck about you either.'

'That's enough,' the solicitor said. 'Mind your language. It's in your best interests to co-operate. We're both here to help you.'

'So, you *have* seen her?' Zoë's scalp tingled.

'I'm not sayin' nothin'. It's my right.' The girl reconsidered for a moment. 'I found the bag. I was going to give it back to her.'

She found it? What did that mean? For a moment Zoë lost her concentration. Every word mattered in a situation like this. She had to be professional and bottle her emotion.

'Can you tell me where you found it?' she asked.

The girl picked at chipped black polish on her bitten thumbnail.

'You must know Megan. Otherwise how could you give it back? How could you know what she thinks of me?'

Startled for a moment, the girl lifted her head. Her eyes reached Zoë's. She saw anger, stubbornness and, sparking like static somewhere in the back of her eyes, she saw fear. The girl rolled her lips and bit down.

Zoë turned a pleading glance to the woman in grey, who said, 'Mrs Johnson, you've had a long journey, how about a coffee?'

Realising the solicitor was using it as an excuse to leave the room, Zoë said, 'Thank you. No milk, no sugar.'

'Okay, I'll be ten minutes.' She turned to the girl. 'I'll bring you a Coke. I'm locking you in, so behave.'

The girl glared. The solicitor frowned, left, and a key turned in the lock.

They sat in silence for a moment before Zoë softened her voice and tried a new tack.

'Look, I'm not trying to trick you, or trap you, I'm just searching for my daughter. If I sound a bit brittle, it's because I'm exhausted. I've just come all the way up from London to talk to you. You're my only hope. Will you at least tell me your name?'

The girl remained silent.

'I wish you'd understand that I'm on your side. In fact, I can help you. Have they told you that I'm a youth magistrate?'

Her head snapped up.

'Not from here,' Zoë said. 'I work in London, but I can put in a good word for you.'

The girl glared about the room, fixing on nothing.

'You do understand the gravity of the offence?' Zoë said. 'Threatening behaviour with a serious weapon, obstruction and theft. If you help me, I can help you.'

'Get lost. You'll just get what you want and go,' she snapped. 'That's what always happens. I'm not stupid.'

'You have my word. Now, please, tell me about Megan.'

Bolder now, she stared at Zoë. 'How'll you help me then? What can you do?'

With a sinking feeling, Zoë knew she was about to do something that went against her principles – buy information. She leaned forward and placed her hand over the girl's, who pulled away. Then she asked, gently, 'What do you want me to do?'

CHAPTER 7
SOFIA

Athens, 1944.

'I HAVE TO GO AND take care of my wife,' Big Yiannis said, lowering his eyes. 'Will you be all right on your own, Sofia? Get something to eat, then off to bed. I'll come back in the morning. Don't go out, will you?'

'No, I promise, Mr Yianni. Anyway, they'll probably be back soon. I have to wait for them.'

He got down on his knees, so our faces were level.

'Sofia, your parents aren't coming home,' he said. 'You have to understand – they were at the very *heart* of the explosion. Almost everyone in the theatre died, your family and my wife included. You and me – we were lucky to escape. I went outside for a cigarette, and you, under the seat at the back, searching for your sweet. The angels were looking out for us both.'

Time seemed to stand still. I couldn't process his words, they didn't make sense. How could an explosion have a *heart*? If it had a heart, it wouldn't have killed my family. And my heart, it was in bits, shattered beyond repair. And my mama and papa, where were their hearts? Not in Heaven. Surely not. Heaven could wait. I needed them now. My parents couldn't be dead . . . not my brothers, and Mama and Papa. People like that, they lived forever. Mama was always saying 'I live for my children'. Let her live for me, now.

Please, God, send them back. Give me one of your miracles. I'm begging you with everything I have.

I tried not to cry, but the tears came anyway.

Big Yiannis pulled me to his chest and I sobbed.

'There, there,' he whispered. 'It happened so fast, child, they wouldn't have felt a thing. One minute they were in the theatre, full of happiness, the next moment they were in Heaven.' He breathed deeply. 'And my wife's there with them, too, thanking your father for the free ticket.'

I pulled away and focused on his eyes. They were wet and shining below his furrowed brow.

'Sofia, they wouldn't want to see you in the orphanage. Tomorrow I'll try to find someone to take you in.'

* * *

When Big Yiannis had gone, I went upstairs onto the front balcony and peered up and down the street. My family *had* to be out there somewhere, looking for me, with their hearts safely in their chests. Perhaps they were in hospital. I wanted to go out and search for them, but the orphanage people might get me. Anyway, I knew I should stay home and wait.

'Is Big Yiannis right?' I whispered to the night air. 'Are you in Heaven?'

Our square stone captain's house, with its pale blue shutters and doors, had always felt solid and safe to me. Indestructible. Now, I felt intimidated by the high, empty rooms.

Hit by a stab of hunger, I searched through the larder and found six jars of spoon-sweet. Mama bought the rolled-up orange peel in syrup from local women who needed the money. Charity with pride, she called it. None of us really liked it, and when it took up

81

too much space in the pantry, Mama gave the stock to our priest, who would distribute it among the starving.

I ate an entire jar, feeling a little sick after. Sadder than I had ever been, I changed into my flannelette nightgown and hung my beloved but dusty dress on a hanger. In bed, the house seemed silent at first, but then noises I had never noticed before snuck up on me. Footsteps, creaking doors, the Bogeyman. Afraid and alone, I pulled the eiderdown over my head and fell into an exhausted sleep.

* * *

The next days were a blur. Big Yiannis called in each morning. Although he forced a smile, it did little to hide his pain and grief.

He checked the food in the larder and took three jars of spoon-sweet.

'I'll swap them for something, Sofia. You can't live on this stuff – you'll end up with the sugar sickness.'

'Have some yourself, Mr Yianni. It's very nice, but I ate a whole jar last night. I don't think I'll ever eat it again.'

Sometimes, I was afraid by myself in the big house. The strange noises and shadows made me jump. Every day I half believed they might come home. Perhaps they'd been injured, were in hospital, waiting to get better.

Big Yiannis called every day. He gave me reading and writing to do, checked I had clean clothes and brought food. There was no Christmas, no gifts or church. I missed it all that year. I learned new things instead, like lighting the fire, boiling the eggs that Big Yiannis brought, and washing the dishes and my clothes.

After the Christmas and New Year holidays, I returned to school and was told to stay back after lessons. The teacher asked me where I was living.

'I'm at home, miss.'

'But who's looking after you, Sofia?'

When I told her Big Yiannis was taking care of me until my family returned, she seemed surprised.

'But your mother, your family, they were—'

'They're in hospital, miss,' I said, before she could go on. 'They'll come home soon.'

She slumped in her chair, her mouth turned down. Then she told me to wait, left the room and returned with the headmaster.

That night I slept in the orphanage. Everything I took for granted was changing. Everyone I knew was leaving me. I cried myself to sleep on the lumpy flock mattress. Other children cried too, although I learned later that their tears were not for their parents, but simply because they were hungry.

CHAPTER 8
SOFIA

Crete, present day.

MY HEAD JERKED FORWARD, waking me. For a moment, I wondered where I was, and then remembered my trip to Crete for the carnival. I sat in Chania's bus station, looking back on my life, recalling with such dreadful clarity that terrible time when the theatre exploded.

Memories of joy and pain come back in equal measure these days. At eighty-five, my time on earth is drawing to a close.

Would I shortly meet God in Heaven? It was such a wonderful idea that my family were still waiting for me in some invisible place, and it had given me great comfort when I had needed it most. But being realistic, was this likely? And who was this God anyway? And what or where was Heaven? *I* did not want to live on forever in Heaven. I wanted to live on in my daughter's heart, as my mother had lived on in mine.

With that thought came the terrible yet uplifting truth. More than anything, I wanted my daughter to *know* me. The reason I had to find my child was to tell her I had never stopped loving her – and to say goodbye, because only then would I be free. Free to live, and free to die in peace.

I pulled the baby shawl out of my bag and started to crochet.

CHAPTER 9
ZOË

Manchester, present day.

'GO ON, TELL ME WHAT you want,' Zoë said to the girl who had been caught with Megan's bag.

The girl stared out of the office window. Her shoulders lifted and dropped.

'Can you get me out of this place?'

'That's impossible if you refuse to give your name.'

'And if I do, what's gonna happen?' she mumbled.

'First, tell me if you know Megan, if you've seen her.'

They had reached a stand-off. The girl chewed her thumbnail, then bobbed her head once.

Zoë fought to keep her voice level. 'Prove it. Tell me something Megan said.'

'She's got a brother, Josh. She hates you, but she hates her dad more. She ran away because she found out something bad about him. Something really bad. And he found out something bad about her, too, and after that she didn't want to see any of you lot again.'

Zoë frowned. Something bad. Something bad about Frank. What did all this mean? If Megan had found something out, something about her dad, or if he'd known something about her, if they'd had some kind of row . . . This didn't make any sense. Surely Frank would have told her about something like this, something that might have explained why Megan had run away? They were supposed to be a team. They were supposed to trust each other.

Using all her restraint, she said, 'Excuse me a moment,' to the girl and went over to the door. She needed to get away, to compose herself, to make sense of what the girl had said.

One thing above all stuck in her mind. She'd known Josh's name. That meant she must have known Megan.

She knocked on the door, heard the key turn, and then found herself in the corridor facing Colin.

'I just need a moment to think,' she explained.

He nodded and stepped into the room.

After a few moments, the solicitor approached from down the hall with a tray of paper cups and a can of Coke.

'Are you all right?'

Zoë gave a small nod. 'It just got a bit much. I needed a little space.' She sighed. 'It's been a difficult day. I was so sure we'd finally found Megan.'

Zoë felt sick with tension. Concentrating on the progress, she reminded herself that Megan was alive, that Megan had met the girl she had just spoken to, and that Megan had acquired a passport. That alone proved her daughter was taking care of herself. They'd also found a family photograph in Megan's bag, which meant Megan still thought fondly of them all, and contradicted the girl's statement.

'I need more time with the girl,' Zoë said suddenly. 'Will you give me another twenty minutes alone with her?'

June Tree paused.

'Please, June,' Zoë said, changing tack, fine-tuning her 'meek and mild' channel like her mother with an old 1950s radio, aiming for the right spot. 'It's been months of worry and prayers and tears and, finally, there's some hope. This is the closest I've come to finding Megan. Don't take it from me. I *will* tell you everything she says, and I'd be so grateful.'

The corridor was empty except for the two of them, and a few tense seconds hung in the air.

Then June said, 'Okay, against my better judgement – another twenty minutes, but no more. I've got another client waiting.'

'Thank you. I understand the pressure you're under – been there myself.' Their eyes met. Zoë touched her arm. 'It's a thankless job, but it's worth it.' June nodded. Zoë followed her across the corridor.

Back in the room, Colin sat with his arms folded. A form and a pen lay before the girl.

June nodded at Colin, then spoke to the girl. 'You've got twenty minutes to help Mrs Johnson. Make the most of it.'

The moment they closed the door, Zoë sat at the table, pulled the form towards her and lifted the pen.

'At least tell me your first name. I can't help if you don't exist, and we haven't much time.'

Sullen, the girl stared at Zoë's hand.

'Come on,' Zoë said. 'If I don't give them something, they won't let me help you. Just tell me your name. What harm can it do?'

'Emily.'

Zoë nodded encouragingly as she wrote on the form. 'Emily what?' She kept her eyes lowered.

'It's your turn,' Emily said. 'What're you going to give me?'

'What do you want?'

'Money. I've got none.'

'Wasn't there any in the bag?'

Emily shook her head. A pink braid slid from between her dark curls and hung across her cheek.

'So, Megan had no money?'

'Oh, she had tons of fucking money,' Emily said. 'Almost all she needed.'

So, she had definitely seen Megan! Zoë told herself not to get carried away. She had to concentrate on the girl.

'Needed for what?'

'The money for a plane ticket to get to her granny in Crete.' Emily chewed her lip. 'It wasn't in her bag though, was it?'

She's planning to stay with her granny in Crete?

'Megan's grandmother died two months ago.'

Emily's mouth fell open. 'Oh . . . she doesn't know. That's dead sad. She said her granny was ace. The best friend she ever had.'

Zoë's heart squeezed with sadness. She pulled a twenty from her purse. 'That'll cover a lot of answers, so talk. Where did Megan get the money?'

She placed the cash on the table in front of Emily, who snatched it up, stuffed it into her bra and shrugged again.

Zoë recalled the teenage prostitute case from that morning's court. Keeping her voice level, she asked, 'Was she soliciting, Emily? You can tell me. I simply want to find Megan and help her.'

Emily blinked. 'No, she never! She got the money juggling on the streets.'

The girl at the lights!

Zoë's concentration slipped. Her dream of finding Megan seemed imminent and the anticipation overwhelmed her. Had she seen her without realising it? Surely not? She would recognise her own daughter. She had to believe that.

'Describe her. Please.'

A crooked smile flickered across Emily's lips before her guarded look returned.

'Megan's skinny with dark curly hair, same as mine. She wears camouflage pants and, when she juggles, a red velvet jacket. She has an eyebrow stud.'

'How long have you known her?'

'A week,' Emily said.

'If I get you out of here, do you promise to take me around the places where Megan juggles?' Zoë sensed this was a mistake – but nothing else presented itself.

Emily nodded rapidly. 'Swear down!'

'Let's fill the form in and see what we can do.'

They battled over the form until Colin and June returned.

Zoë had: Emily X, no fixed abode. On the next three lines, it read: no previous offences, a date of birth making her seventeen, born in Manchester.

'Let's hope it's enough, Emily,' Zoë said, before handing the form to Colin.

She was still thinking over what Emily had said. What if Megan really had found something out about Frank, something bad? Perhaps he'd got himself into a messy situation at work, or perhaps there was another woman. After all, his secretary had taken Zoë's place at functions on many occasions. And she always seemed slightly hostile when Zoë called her husband. Surely that couldn't have been why Megan left. Surely she'd have spoken to them, like the adult she nearly was. There had to be something else.

Startled by the silence of the room, she realised they had stopped talking. June, Colin and Emily stared at her.

'Sorry, I missed that,' she said, unaware of what had been said. 'Look, would it be possible to have Emily released into my custody?'

June appeared shocked. She and Colin exchanged glances, and then left the room to discuss the situation.

'They ain't going to let me go 'cos they're sure I'll scarper,' Emily said. 'They're not stupid.'

'And will you?' Zoë asked. 'If I get you released into my care, am I just making trouble for myself? Because, let me tell you, if you run, I would be in the most awful trouble. I'd lose my bail money and could lose my job. That means I'd end up losing my house. I have a son to consider. On top of that, I wouldn't have money to keep searching for Megan. I could be prosecuted for perverting the course of justice, and so on.'

Zoë was making it up as she went along, but soon realised she wasn't far off the mark. Fraught with fear and hope, she tried to get a grip on reality. The girl would almost certainly try running once she was free.

Emily chewed her lip. 'What's gonna happen? I'm scared. I don't wanna be locked up.' Her tears rose and she blinked at Zoë, her eyes pleading.

'They'll hold you on remand tonight. It's too late for an emergency hearing. I'll try and sort something for tomorrow morning. Make sure you understand. If you cause me any trouble, Emily, or abscond, the police *will* find you and they'll lock you up for a long time.' Zoë studied her face and gave her a moment to consider. 'You're guilty of a serious offence. I'm your only way out. If I can get a hearing tomorrow morning, and I stand bail, then you *must* help me find Megan. Think about it. I'll do everything I can for you – I've given you my word. The rest is up to you.'

Her phone buzzed in her pocket. She pulled it out to answer and recognised Trisha's number. She moved over to the window and briefly updated her friend. Trisha was silent for a minute.

'Don't believe her,' she said. 'I'll bet she's a hard-faced little liar who's adept at getting around people.'

'I'm too exhausted to concentrate, Trisha. I'd feel better if Josh was with you, or you stayed at our house while I'm here. It would be one less thing to worry about.'

Her phone beeped. Low battery.

'Josh is at Frank's,' Trisha said. 'He'll be fine. Why don't you phone him in the morning? Decide what to do when you've slept.'

'My battery's packing up. I'll buy a charger and call you later.' She ended the call.

Zoë glanced at Emily. Could this girl really lead her to Megan?

Emily read her face. 'God's truth, I won't run. Just get me out of here, will you? We'll find Megan. I know where she goes. I'm your best chance.'

Zoë longed to be alone with the girl, on neutral ground, and find out everything she knew about Megan. She knew perfectly well that she wouldn't get any more information out of Emily while they were in the court building.

When June and Colin returned and took Emily to an overnight holding cell, the girl broke into tears. Zoë watched solemnly, sad that society hadn't taken better care of this child. Then her tension returned. She was so close to finding Megan, yet still she had no idea where her daughter was at that moment. Or, in fact, the real reason why she had run away in the first place. She tried to write a to-do list in her mind to calm herself. Her next task was to find a bed for the night.

* * *

Zoë bought a phone charger, found a small hotel and booked in for two nights.

After a restless sleep, she woke, disorientated until the events of the previous day came back. She showered, and dressed hurriedly in yesterday's clothes, eager to return to the Civil Justice Centre. After a quick breakfast, she headed for the courts.

Noon had come and gone before she emerged into the dull day with Emily at her side.

The girl glanced around furtively.

'Don't run,' Zoë said. 'I can help you. It can't be easy, surviving on the streets alone – I can't imagine how lonely it must be, too.' She knew this was not the time to be soft. She had to set boundaries and insist on them being adhered to. A firm but kind hand was needed. 'Before we go any further, I wanted to tell you what opportunities are open to you at the moment.' Emily stared at her, confused. 'There's the Runaway Youth Program in Manchester.'

'I won't run away, swear down.' Her face was pale with grey circles under the eyes.

Zoë smiled. 'Sorry, I didn't make myself clear. The RYP is to help set you up in a proper job, with a permanent roof over your head. A fresh start. You just scrape inside the age limit to qualify, so it's something to think about. I can probably get you enrolled.'

Emily's eyes widened. 'You'd really help me?'

Zoë nodded. 'First, let's get some food inside us, buy a change of clothes and find Megan.'

Now that finding Megan was a real possibility, Zoë was impatient to get going. When they got to the burger place, she had to remind herself that another hour made little difference.

Emily attacked a Big Mac Meal. 'This is totally perfect,' she said to the bun. 'Totally.'

'Tell me again, as accurately as you can – what did Megan say about me and her dad?'

Emily froze, the burger inches from her mouth. A slice of gherkin, streaked in ketchup, slithered out of the bun and plopped onto the table. She took a bite of the burger and chewed for a moment before answering.

'Megan said she was at this party, and she found out something bad about her dad. I guess he was there. And that he found out something bad about her, or saw her . . . I don't know. I guess they had a fight or something, a really big one.'

'What do you mean? What's this bad thing he's supposed to have done?'

'Supposed?' The girl scowled. 'See, Mrs Johnson, you've already decided it's Megan in the wrong, not him. Sounds just like my dad, always taking his girlfriend's side. Then you wonder why she ran away.' She took another bite and glared at Zoë across the table.

It took a moment for Zoë to take in Emily's words. She knew she'd get nowhere if she didn't dampen Emily's animosity.

'Look, can we try to get on, Emily? I'm trying to help you as well as find my daughter.' She softened her voice. 'Come on, call me Zoë, won't you?'

'Right, so we're big mates now?' Emily scoffed.

'Why are you so angry with me? I'm not trying to be your mate, but I *am* trying to help,' Zoë said. 'We can be civil to each other, can't we?'

'I guess.' She pointed at Zoë's unopened burger box and stood. 'You goin' to eat that?'

Zoë shook her head. 'No, take it if you want.'

Emily stashed the food in her bag and stepped away from the table.

'Just give me a minute, will you?' Zoë's tone said it wasn't a request. 'Let's start again. What did she tell you?'

Emily sighed and dropped back into her seat, indecision flickering across her face.

'I'm not making trouble, Emily. Can't you see I need to understand? Megan's disappearance has always been a mystery. She took some of her clothes and left a note saying she was leaving, that we weren't to try and find her. And that was all. I had no idea that she was unhappy, or in trouble of any sort.'

Emily shrugged. 'I can only tell you what she told me. That she found out something bad about her dad and then she left.'

'And you don't know anything else?'

Emily shook her head. 'Shall we go then?' she asked suddenly.

Zoë glanced at her watch. Josh would be on his lunch break at school.

'I'll just give my son a call.'

'Can I use the bog? It's upstairs,' Emily said. 'I won't run, I swear.'

Zoë nodded, forced a smile, and felt for her phone as she watched Emily go up to the next floor.

Josh picked up.

'Josh, hi! How are you?' She tried to inject cheer into her voice.

'Hi, Mum, fine, how's things? Have you found Megan?' He sounded far away.

'Not yet, but she's here and we're close. Listen, Josh, you understand you can tell me anything, don't you? It doesn't matter how bad something is, I'll always be on your side.'

'For God's sake, Mum. Leave it out.'

'Okay. I just wanted you to know. What's going on over there?'

'I'm back home and Trisha's staying at ours till you're back. Everything's cool. Trisha let me have my mates over to revise. Where's my football kit?'

'In the washing machine. Put it back in after practice, will you?'

'Sure. When're you home?'

'Tomorrow, or the day after. I'm not sure – as soon as I've found Megan. She's taken up juggling for a living.'

He laughed into the phone. 'Cool! I told you she was okay. See you. Bye.'

'Bye. Love you.'

She heard him *tut* before ending the call.

Zoë was still gazing at the stairs when Emily reappeared.

'Right, let's get going,' she said, eager to get out of the high heels and tailored suit. Zoë wanted Megan to see her as approachable, not as a court magistrate.

Half an hour later, rushed and flushed, they came out of Asda. Zoë wore jeans, a sweatshirt and flat shoes. Emily had new trainers, leggings and two baggy T-shirts, black over pink. Thank God for credit cards.

'You look nice,' Zoë said.

Emily blinked, jutted her jaw and turned away. Still, her attitude had changed a little in the store. She soaked up attention.

Zoë's phone rang. It was Don.

'Just a quick one, Zoë. Megan has an appointment at the passport office at 1.45 today. I've told them you're coming. Westminster House, Portland Street. Good luck.'

A moment later, Zoë hung up, breathless with anticipation.

'Emily, quick, I know where Megan is!' She grabbed the girl's hand and dragged her across the pavement. 'We need a taxi to Portland Street.'

They stood at the kerb, peering up and down the street like a couple of meerkats.

Emily shoved her fingers into her mouth, produced a deafening whistle, then stuck her arm in the air. Several cars honked as a black cab U-turned and weaved to the kerb.

There was a spark of magic in the moment, and Zoë laughed.

'The passport office, Westminster House, quick as you can,' Zoë said to the driver.

'You should laugh more often,' Emily said inside the cab. 'It makes you tons younger – not half as scary.'

'Cheeky madam,' Zoë said, straight-faced but with humour in her voice. In a few minutes she would hold Megan in her arms. In a heart-wrenching moment, she remembered her own mother, holding her limp, cold hand on the day of her death.

She paid the cabbie, adding a hefty tip before clutching the door handle, ready to leap out the moment they stopped. With the cabbie's sudden halt, she lost her grip and hurtled back in the seat.

She and Emily raced towards the rectangular glass-and-cement building. It had started raining again. Their new shoes slapped on the wet pavement. Zoë had half an eye on Emily. She might turn and run at any moment and, if she did, God knew what Zoë would do.

CHAPTER 10
SOFIA

Athens, 1945.

THE ORPHANAGE WAS OVERCROWDED. Every day I thought about running away, but the outside doors were locked and the windows nailed down. Although I knew that my family had been killed in the theatre, the longer I stayed in the dreadful orphanage, the more I convinced myself there was a slight chance that somebody might have survived the explosion. Every night, I gave my imagination free rein and dreamed of home: the larder shelf full of delicious food; the kitchen's comforting aroma of freshly baked bread; Mama at the Singer, starting a new dress for my eleventh birthday. These fantasies helped to soften the harsh reality of institutional life.

In the dormitory, a lot of children cried for their mama, or *Yiayá*, at night. They were the darkest times for us all. We were three to a bed, one girl older than me, one younger. I clung to the edge of the mattress so that I didn't slip into the dip in the centre. I wanted to be alone with my misery and my visions of home. The older girl tried to cuddle me but I elbowed her away. The only arms I wanted were my mother's. The younger one, about five years old, had just arrived and she clung to me as she cried herself to sleep. I lay there, wondering what would become of us all. Every night, as the smell of mildew and urine rose from the mattress, I promised myself I would not be there much longer. I would find a way out.

As the days passed, the conviction that my parents were out there somewhere crumbled. Had the orphanage taken away my childish desire for play, and replaced it with logic, or was I simply growing up and learning to reason? Mama and Papa would never allow me to stay in such an awful place. So, the seed of acceptance that I was an orphan had set root in the dark of night. But still, in the light of each new day, I rose with fresh hope that a miracle had happened and they were at home, unaware that I had survived. There was such chaos on that disastrous day, I told myself it was possible . . . just possible.

* * *

I had been at the orphanage for several weeks when I had to share my bed with a new arrival, a little girl called Sugar. She had lived with her grandmother who had recently died. I never found out what happened to her parents. Sugar cried a lot. On the second night, I could stand no more tears. In desperation, although I knew it was forbidden, I snuck out of the dormitory to find some food or a toy to give her. I remembered a threadbare teddy she'd clung to through the day and hoped to find it in the day room.

Every stair creaked, and the door into the day room groaned as I opened it. I stopped and listened, but the house was silent. Moonlight shone through the bare window, illuminating the toy box.

My mission was not so simple. Every one of the battered toys had its own peculiar noise as I shifted it. Tinkle. Scrape. Wheeze! At last I laid my hands on the teddy – but just as I slid it clear, the light came on, blinding me.

'What do you think you are doing?' Matron cried.

At first, I couldn't speak. She looked so fierce in her night-gown and her hair tied in rags.

'I . . . I was just getting the teddy for Sugar. She's crying, Matron,' I stammered.

'Get back into bed this instant!'

I raced upstairs and found Sugar already asleep.

* * *

On the way to the dining room the following evening, I heard someone banging on the front door. A teacher, also heading for the dining room, reached under a book on a shelf above the staff coat hooks and withdrew a key. Then she opened the door to receive a parcel.

Finally, I knew where they kept the key. Now I could make a plan to escape.

I continued to the dining room, where we lined up with our chipped enamel plates in hand. After being served a scoop of pasta with herbs, we returned to our benches and sat with our arms folded, waiting for the command to start eating. Mrs Orpheus, our head mistress, entered the hall.

'Pay attention, girls!' she boomed. 'We have strict rules here, and I must remind you that anyone caught breaking those rules will be severely punished!'

I was still thinking about the key, hardly listening. How could I reach it? I was small, and there wasn't even a chair in the hall. My stomach growled loudly, breaking my thoughts. I wished Mrs Orpheus would hurry up – we were all starving! I stared at my plate; the wet shine had already faded and the pasta looked dull, cold and glutinous.

A fly was buzzing over the plates. We had to keep our arms folded until the gong to eat sounded, but everyone's eyes were fixed on the insect. I slid my hand from under my armpit, ready to flick it away. *Shoo!* I blew at it, then regretted it immediately. I was only making my food colder.

Mrs Orpheus droned on. 'After an incident last night, I am forced to make an example. This is what happens when someone breaks the rules. Sofia Bambaki, come to the front.'

Me?

All eyes left the fly and turned my way. My cheeks burned. What about the pasta? I was starving. And the fly might land on it . . .

I got up and went to Mrs Orpheus. When I saw the cane in her hand, my knees trembled.

'Climb on the bench so that everyone can watch you receive your punishment.'

Punishment?

She stood behind me, lifted my skirt and gave me three stinging swipes across the backs of my thighs. I don't know if it was the shock, or the pain, or the shame that made me cry out. I had never been hit before. I reached down and covered the backs of my legs.

'Hold your arms out!' Mrs Orpheus said, whacking the backs of my hands.

When I did, I received another blow. Tears were rolling down my face as I stumbled from the bench.

'No supper for you. Return to your room. And remember, rules are meant to be kept!'

I ran out of the dining room into the hall, towards the stairs – and then stopped.

The key was still in the door lock! The teacher had forgotten to put it back. My heart thumped so hard it was all I could hear.

I stepped slowly towards the door, turned the key and dragged it open.

Then I ran away from that orphanage, that place of pain and hunger and misery, as quickly as my burning legs would carry me.

* * *

I didn't know how many months had passed since the explosion, but a clump of narcissus that I could see from the orphanage window had blossomed and died. I had stared at them – closed my eyes and inhaled the imagined perfume, remembering Lycabettus. Now, all that remained were a few yellow leaves lying limp on the earth. They would rise up and bloom again one day, and so would I.

As I raced along empty streets, everything seemed possible. I was free. I could almost believe that the last few months, every day since the explosion, had been nothing but a terrible nightmare. I could almost imagine that my family were waiting for me at the old house, Mama, Papa, Ignatius and Pavlos. I would burst through the door and we would be reunited. We would drink cocoa and everyone would be happy.

These thoughts tumbled around in my mind as I hurried from the port of Piraeus towards Athens and my home. Darkness had fallen now, and the city was a frightening place at night. Although our house was ten kilometres from the orphanage, once the spotlights on the Parthenon, above the Acropolis, went out, I became confused and nearly lost my way.

I heard distant gunshots, which made me wonder if the war had started up again. Then a dog with a long bony face and protruding ribs leaped off a doorstep and ran at me. Terrified,

I thought it was going to bite me, eat me, and I ran as fast as my legs would go. I guess it was only guarding its territory, because it didn't chase me and returned to the door. Still, I was shaken. I wondered if it was half crazed, waiting for an owner that might never return.

Papa once told me of a dog that sat on its master's grave, attacking anyone who came near, until eventually it starved to death.

It was probably around midnight when I approached Syntagma Square. It became clear the city was host to two types of people at this time of night. The rich, eating and drinking and dancing to music that drifted into the streets; and the poor, ragged, starving unfortunates, huddled in doorways and behind bins.

When I entered our street, I saw that lights were on in our big house, and stopped. What if, all along, they had been here, waiting for me? What if I had been wrong to give up hope? My whole family, alive and well! I was in tears and almost at the door when it opened and a group of soldiers tumbled out. They were laughing, perhaps a little drunk. I stopped short, confused.

One of them grabbed my arm and held on tightly.

'What are you doing out at this time of night, little girl?' he asked. 'Are you a spy?'

The words were mocking, and his friends laughed again. Although he spoke Greek, I recognised a foreign accent.

Unable to speak, I shook my head.

His grip became tighter. 'Tell me! What are you doing here?' he yelled.

'I was going home, sir.' I pointed at the front door. 'This is my house.'

'Where have you come from?'

I panicked. If I said 'the orphanage', they would send me back there for sure.

'My aunty, sir. She's sick and I've been looking after her. I need my clothes.'

'Where are your parents?'

I hung my head and mumbled, 'They were in the theatre when it exploded.'

The soldier's grip loosened and, if I'd been quick, I could have run away – but how could I? Behind that door was my old home, where I'd spent so many happy years. Everything I knew, everything Mama and Papa owned, all of those memories . . .

The soldier shook his head and gave a sobering look to his companions.

'Come inside, child,' he said. 'What's your name?'

'Sofia.' I followed him into the house. The moment I stepped through the door I was overwhelmed and dismayed. 'Mama!' I shouted as loudly as I could, almost without knowing what I was saying. 'Mama! Papa!'

Although I was in our house, my *home* had disappeared. Kitbags lined the hall. As I ran from room to room, I saw that our furniture had gone, replaced by as many beds as would fit inside. Even the pictures and photographs had disappeared from the walls. At that moment I knew with a horrible certainty that I could not go back. My family were gone. My home was gone.

Between the front salon and the kitchen there was a store-room, where I saw an official-looking sign on the door in English. The soldier pulled me towards it, and straightened the front of his uniform, throwing his shoulders back before he knocked. I had a feeling there was someone of authority inside. They would send me back to the orphanage.

I ducked under the soldier's arm and bolted out of the front door.

Behind me, I could hear them shouting.

'*Ela! Ela!* Come back!'

I ran across Syntagma Square as fast as I could, then around the parliament building, where lights blazed down, making dark shadows under the bushes next door. I squeezed through the railings and escaped into the royal park. What should I do? Where could I go? I reached the marble monument of Lord Byron, sat on the step at the bottom of the plinth and stared out at the darkness.

Why had I been left behind, all alone? I should have died with my parents. If I had made it to my seat, I would be in Heaven with them now . . .

And yet I knew my parents would want me to be safe, want me to live. I stared up at the stars.

Mama, please don't let anything bad happen to me this night.

I was so tired that I could not even sit up. The backs of my legs still burned and when I slid my hands over them, I felt four long, hard welts where the cane had swiped me. I stretched out on the stone, gaining some relief from the cold marble. Before long, I closed my eyes. Pressing myself into the hard angle of the steps under the statue, I tried to imagine what Heaven was like.

The next thing, I jumped when someone shook my shoulder. Sunlight made me squint.

'What are you doing here?' a boy asked. 'You'll get into trouble.'

I rubbed my eyes. 'I had nowhere to go. Who are you?'

'Markos Papas.' He had a loaf under his arm, broke a sizeable chunk off and held it out. 'You want some breakfast?'

Hunger dragged at my ribs, not having had a scrap to eat since the bread and thin soup we were given for lunch the day before.

'Please take a seat,' I said politely, knowing it was rude to start eating while someone stood. He grinned and sat next to me. I took the bread, longing to stuff it into my mouth, yet trying to mind my manners.

'May I share it with you?' I said.

His grin widened. 'No, just eat it. You look starved.'

He appeared to be a few years older than me. Fourteen or fifteen, perhaps. Around the age of my brother, Ignatius. Markos wore his school clothes, though I noticed his shirt needed an iron, and although his shoes were polished, his socks were baggy and concertinaed down to his ankles.

'I'm Sofia Bambaki. How do you do?'

I shook hands with him, trying to retain my decorum as Mama would have wished, but the bread was screaming my name. I broke a piece off and started eating. Oh, the taste of that freshly baked loaf! It was delicious. I told him how I'd escaped from the orphanage after they had beaten me, and that there were soldiers in our house. Then I almost cried.

A boy, about eight years old, dashed out of the bushes and stood before Markos, his brown eyes wide, staring at the loaf. Markos broke the remains in two and held one half out.

'Take it!' he ordered.

The boy stuffed a chunk into his mouth as he raced back into the bushes.

'I've got to go to school,' Markos said, still looking over at the bushes. 'Why were you in the orphanage?'

I shrugged. 'My family all died.' It was so hard to say I stopped and stared at the ground.

'Mine too,' he said, and gazed at the earth in front of his feet. 'Apart from my father. The British dropped a bomb on our house.'

'Mine were in the theatre when it blew up.'

'In the theatre ...' He frowned and chewed his lip for a moment, then thrust the rest of the bread at me. 'There's a soup kitchen in 28th Street. Get there before two o'clock or you won't get anything. Take care, I'll see you around,' he said.

I watched him hurry out of the park. There was something about him – I didn't know what, but as I watched him leaving, I knew I wanted him to turn around and come back.

'You take care yourself, Markos Papas!' I cried.

He looked over his shoulder and winked, then he was gone.

I was still staring after him, grinning like an ape, when a rustling in the bushes drew my attention. A thin girl, a little younger than myself, came towards me. Dressed in rags and clutching a skinny baby with big, vacant eyes, she stared at the bread. At that moment, my mother filled my heart. I felt all the pain Mama had experienced when she tried to help the starving people of Athens.

'Please,' the girl whispered desperately, opening her mouth.

I broke off a bite-size piece of bread and put it into her mouth. She chewed frantically then, like a mother bird, transferred it to the baby's mouth. I almost wept.

I pushed it into her hand. 'Here, take the bread.'

She threw a worried glance at the bushes and I wondered how many more starving children hid there. She hurried around the back of Lord Byron, where she continued to feed the frail infant, rapidly losing its grip on life.

CHAPTER 11
ZOË

Manchester, present day.

THE PASSPORT OFFICE PROVED A huge disappointment. Megan didn't show.

Rain pelted down outside. They loitered in the lobby for an hour, Zoë's spirits as damp as the weather. When the rain drizzled to a halt, she and Emily couldn't find a taxi, and ended up jogging from station to mall, looking for Megan. Zoë's heart leaped at the sight of the girl she had seen juggling the white clubs at Deansgate traffic lights, when she first arrived in Manchester. But on closer inspection, it clearly wasn't Megan. She checked the time and realised school was out, so she phoned Josh, but he didn't answer.

They peered at traffic lights, trotted down underpasses, checked the bus and coach stations. Exhausted and disappointed, they jumped onto a bus to Centrepoint, in Oldham Street.

'Where can she be, Emily? Megan can't have simply disappeared again. We're so close.' Zoë sighed. 'You'd have to be a mother yourself to understand how dreadful this all is.'

'I nearly had a kid once,' Emily said. 'I was pregnant.' Then a startled expression flashed across her face. 'I, hum, shit . . . Forget it.' Her eyes darted in all directions as if afraid someone had overheard. 'Anyway, it was ages ago.'

She threw a penetrating glance at Zoë, and in that instant, with Emily's hard exterior gone, Zoë saw a vulnerable young girl.

'What happened?' she asked, keeping her voice soft.

'My dad's girlfriend made me get rid of it.' She shrugged. 'I was still using, see. Little bugger would have been an addict even before it was born. Best thing to do. No big deal. Dad's girlfriend was pregnant too. They were getting married.' She hesitated, her eyes flicking up to Zoë's again. 'She didn't want me competing for my dad's attention, did she? And I'd have made her a granny, for fuck's sake.' She screwed her mouth around to one side. 'Best thing really. I mean, take a look. I wouldn't be much of a mother, would I? I ran away just after.'

'Have you seen them since?'

She shook her head.

'So you have a father, a stepmother and at least one little half-sister or brother?'

Emily's head jerked up. She blinked and frowned as if she hadn't thought about that before.

'Have you considered paying them another visit?' Zoë said. 'They've had time to settle down. People do change.'

She frowned again and glared at Zoë, chin thrust forward, shield up – but Zoë saw a chink in her armour.

'Why would they want to see me? They'd rather I was out of their way.'

'We all make mistakes, Emily – parents, teachers, probation officers, even magistrates. Your dad might be missing you. Maybe he worries about you every day, wonders where you are, like me with Megan.'

'And maybe he doesn't,' Emily said.

She had a point. 'You'll never know if you don't give them a chance.'

'Megan must be totally fuckin' mad,' the girl muttered.

'What makes you say that?'

'She thinks you don't care about her at all – but you do. If you were my mum . . .'

She lowered her eyes, grabbed her left hand in her right and gnawed on a fingernail.

Zoë held back an urge to move Emily's hand away.

'After they'd nabbed me and took the bag,' Emily said quietly, 'they called me Megan because we look alike. It gave me this mad idea – well, if *you* thought I was Megan, I could . . . Stupid plan, wasn't it?' Her eyes flicked to Zoë's before she turned away. 'Do you really think my dad would . . . ? Nah, it'd never happen.'

'I'll tell you something, Emily. When you grow up, you grow away from your parents and gain your independence. But parents grow towards their children all their lives. A parent's love continues to grow, even when their kids are independent and grown up. You can't imagine that right now, but one day you'll understand.'

Emily stared at her, then huffed and glugged her Coke.

'Give over, will you? I said I'd help you find Megan, not put myself up for therapy.'

'Right, okay, none of my business.'

They had no luck at Centrepoint. Afterwards, Zoë's shoulders slumped under the weight of disappointment. She stood on the pavement, lost for a moment, weary from all the emotion, and wondering how Josh was coping.

Emily softened her voice as she joined her. 'Do you want to see where we slept the night before I got nicked? But first, we need to grab a torch and batteries. It's too dark in there.' She bit her lip.

'Okay, where's the nearest shop?'

Fifteen minutes later, they were on their way again. Zoë held the torch and Emily held a three-pack of gum, which Zoë hoped would stop the nail-biting.

Emily led the way. Desperate to see where Megan had slept only forty-eight hours earlier, Zoë broke into a jog, almost tripping over rubbish in a dirty alley in her haste.

'Don't get your hopes up,' Emily panted, struggling to keep up. 'It's just a scabby dosshouse.'

Still, a ridiculous thought overwhelmed Zoë. She wanted to place her hand on the spot where her child had slept, sense the warmth of her body, breathe the same air. They ran into another alley, near a hot dog van, and together they shifted a heavily vandalised door.

They tumbled inside the building. In the dark, Zoë fumbled to turn on the torch, a big orange thing with a handle on top. She shone it around and gasped as the beam bounced over appalling detritus. She had never seen anything so disgusting.

There was a terrible stench – then something moved in the far corner and she turned the light that way. At first, Zoë thought it was a heap of rags and empty bottles, but the bundle turned over to face the wall, muttering obscenities. It was a man. An empty wine bottle rolled off his chest and clattered onto the concrete.

'It's okay,' Emily whispered. 'He's Pissed George. Harmless. Follow me. We're going up the steps at the back.'

'Here, Emily, you take the torch and lead the way,' Zoë said.

The girl gave her a crooked smile. 'All right.'

There was a new tone in her voice. Despite Zoë's obsession with Megan, or perhaps because of it, she realised she was becoming fond of this wild kid.

They reached the floor where Megan and Emily had slept.

'Please, Emily, re-enact everything that happened in this room?'

Emily shrugged. 'Sure, but I don't see how it'll help.'

'Just humour me.'

By the time Emily was stealing Megan's bag, Zoë was fighting an inner battle against tears. She sat on the filthy windowsill and stared around the room. In all her years as a lawyer and a youth magistrate, she had come across so many kids who had slept rough, but the reality had never penetrated her middle-class world. Now it hit her like a ton of bricks. What could make any child live like this? How could society allow it? Even Pissed George was some mother's son.

Zoë grieved for them all – and for her own shame and her regretted ignorance.

'. . . so I just grabbed the bag and ran,' Emily said. 'Honest to God, I'm really, really sorry I scaved her stuff. I wouldn't do it again, swear down I wouldn't.'

Zoë had an urge to hug her, but she simply nodded. 'I believe you. Do you think she'll sleep here tonight?'

'By herself?' Emily shook her head. 'No way. Why? You're not going to stay here overnight, are you? It's not safe after dark, Zoë.' She shone the torch over the filthy mattress. 'No, she'll probably sleep at a shelter if she can.'

'I have an idea. Give me your gum, Emily.' The girl reached into her pocket. 'No, the one you're chewing.'

Zoë pulled out her notebook and started writing.

* * *

Back in the hotel room, Zoë logged on to AMBER Alert EU.

'I'm just going to check on the missing kids website. Won't be a minute, then we'll have something to eat.' Emily pulled a chair close and watched, then grinned when Zoë said, 'Three cases closed.'

'Great!'

The optimism of youth, Zoë thought, hoping Emily was right. She opened the first case.

A nine-year-old girl was found dead on . . . She read through all three cases. Bad news. She glanced round at Emily, who gaped at the screen.

'Christ,' she muttered.

'Every day, more of the same. Look, here's another one, just up.'

UPDATE – The Czech Child Alert that had been issued in the early morning of Wednesday 8 April 2015 has been cancelled. The 10-year-old boy from Brno, Czech Republic, has been found safe and unharmed. The boy was missing from 7 April. Thank you all for being on the lookout.

'There are some happy endings,' said Zoë softly.

She logged off, and looked around the hotel room.

'That's your bed, Emily. You take the first shower while I call my son. Think about what you want to eat. It's getting late and I want an early start tomorrow.'

'There's a chippy round the corner. I could go while you phone.'

'I'm not stupid,' Zoë said.

Emily shrugged, disappointed. She stared at the floor, then at Zoë.

'I won't run, I swear. I, well . . . I've had lots of chances to scarper and I'm still here, aren't I? You can trust me. Honest.'

Zoë stared into the girl's eyes and thought she glimpsed something new. That need to be trusted – but should she trust her? There was no rule book guidance for the situation. She just had to make up her mind. She took a twenty-pound note from her purse, hesitated, and then shoved it into Emily's hand. Was she lowering the boundaries too soon?

'Fish, chips and peas for me, and whatever you want.'

Emily's eyes widened and the crooked smile appeared for a second. She made one swift nod.

'Let me down, Emily, and I'll make your life hell, I swear.'

'You don't have to threaten me,' she said quietly.

Zoë watched her leaving. Before the door closed, she called, 'Don't be long!'

CHAPTER 12
SOFIA

Athens, 1945.

BEHIND THE CHURCH, I STOOD in line at the soup kitchen. Like everyone else, I didn't care if the food was tasty or nourishing, so long as it staved off the belly cramps for a while. The youngest children were crying, and the rest of us looked as miserable as we felt, eyes dulled by malnutrition, hair thin and matted. We no longer played or laughed, but wore serious expressions and stood still, only moving when we had to, conserving our energy like old men.

Desperately hungry, I gripped my tin and spoon against myself, but the cauldron was scraped clean before I reached the front of the queue.

Hunger was a beast in my belly, biting chunks out of my insides, howling and clawing its way up to my throat. Apart from a throbbing pain, my head was empty, spinning, so light it almost lifted my feet off the ground. My legs felt hollow too and I trembled as I tried to walk. *Sit down*, I told myself, *save your energy*. There was a restaurant nearby in Saint Cathryn Street. I knew they kept the food scraps for their chickens, but perhaps *something* edible would be thrown out.

A smooth pebble near my feet caught my eye. Could I fool my stomach for half an hour? I rubbed it on my skirt and popped it into my mouth. Instantly, the memory of Big Yannis's barley sugar filled my mind. Oh, that sweet, syrupy taste. Saliva rushed into my mouth and I licked my dry, cracked lips.

Oh, let me die now, while I'm happy and free of pain.

But too quickly reality returned. My mouth dried and the barley sugar went back to a useless pebble. I walked slowly, arms hanging limp, head bowed, until I reached a taverna with EL GRECO's painted in gold and white over the entrance. The door opened and the tantalising smell of baking wafted into the street. A kitchen woman stepped out and tipped a bucket of waste into the bin. The moment she returned inside, I raced over and scrabbled in the rubbish for food.

There was nothing but used wax paper!

Tears of desperation pricked my eyes – and then, a flash of snow white caught my attention. Icing sugar and flakes of baklava were stuck to the paper! Clutching the crumpled baking sheets in my arms, I backed into the next doorway and licked furiously at the cake remains. I ripped a damp patch out of one sticky sheet, crumpled it and stuffed it into my mouth, chewing and sucking to retrieve every last speck of delicious sweetness out of the paper. Fixated on what was in my mouth, it was a moment before I sensed a new scent in the air. Fresh, yeasty bread. I looked up to see the baker across the street filling the wooden shelf outside his shop with round brown loaves.

The baker had a flat, straight back and a protruding round front, reminding me of a tortoise we called Apollo that my brother once owned. But the baker stood upright and seemed to wear his shell on the front. Like the tortoise, his face had a slow, sleepy look to it.

The first of the morning's shoppers were out on the street, and various food stores were opening, bringing their goods onto the pavement. Outside the dairy a woman called, 'Milk, cheese, yoghurt – fresh today!' At the butcher's shop, a man in a red striped apron came out and yelled even louder, 'Belly pork, sausage, sheep's innards, calves' hooves, marrowbones!'

My brain was singing and my mouth watered.

In a manic frenzy for food, my eyes returned to the bakery. I blew the ball of paper out of my mouth and crouched like an animal. The baker emptied his wicker basket onto a plank set on two tea chests outside his shop. He returned inside to refill it. My heart clanged like the church bell. Now was my chance! Even if he saw me steal the bread, he would never be able to catch me. I leaped to my feet, ran across the road and grabbed a loaf.

I would have escaped if the grocer, a tall, strong man, a few doors before the corner, hadn't seen me and stuck his broom out. I went flying. Cursing, he grabbed my hair and lifted me off my feet.

'Dirty little thief!' he yelled and slapped me hard on the face.

I didn't know if it was his palm, or the shame of stealing, that burned my face so fiercely. Crying, I wriggled and kicked while keeping that bread clutched to my chest.

'Please, I'm starving, I'm starving!' I sobbed.

He drew his hand back to slap me again, but the baker reappeared and shouted, 'Stop! She's just a child. Bring her here.'

The greengrocer complied, holding me out at arm's length but keeping a grip on my hair. He plonked me in front of the baker and stood facing us with his other fist on his hip. All eyes were on me. It was then I spotted Markos, the boy from the park. He came up behind the grocer. Markos met my eyes, placed a finger over his lips, then scooped up a large watermelon from outside the grocer's shop. He stealthily returned the way he had come and disappeared around the corner.

The action seemed to energise me, as if we were a team. My face still stung, and tears ran down my cheeks, but I felt a kind of glory that I'd helped to stave off someone else's hunger.

All this happened in a matter of seconds. Then the grocer turned me around to face the baker.

'I'm sorry, sir, truly sorry – but I haven't eaten for two days. I couldn't help it, honestly. I've never stolen anything in my life before. I don't know what came over me.'

'Where are your parents, child?' he asked.

'My family were in the theatre when it blew up, sir.' With that, fresh tears rose. 'Please, I'm so terribly hungry, but I'll give it back if you want.' I could not take my eyes off the loaf as I held it out.

He took it off me and said, 'Go around the back of the shop and wait until I come out.' He turned to the grocer. 'Let her go, Tasso.'

'Are you mad? She'll just run off and steal from somebody else! You'll never see her again.'

'We'll see, won't we?' He narrowed his eyes and stared at me. 'Go on then, round to the back door. I've got things to do here!'

I didn't need telling twice. The moment the grocer let go of my hair, I raced to the end of the street, around the corner and into the back alley. Markos was there, a knife in his fist, hacking into the watermelon and giving pieces to other children who gathered around him. They all looked ragged, and shrank into an adjoining entry as I approached.

'Here, get some of this, quick!' Markos said, thrusting a chunk of melon my way.

I almost fainted with joy, shoved the fruit into my mouth and gobbled it down, pips, skin and all.

'Where are you going?' Markos asked me.

'I have to wait outside the baker's back door.'

'Senseless girl! Why? Run while you can.'

I shook my head. 'I can't. I promised.'

The boy rolled his eyes, but before he could say anything, a door opened further down the alley and the baker stepped out. The boys scattered faster than cockroaches when the light's turned on. The baker lifted an arm, wide and muscular from a lifetime of kneading dough. He beckoned me.

'You, girl! Get in here!'

I felt a spark of fear. What if he was one of those bad men who hurt little girls? I'd heard warnings about these people but didn't understand what the danger was, or how you could tell if he was a baddie or a goodie. Like a meek fool, I went over and stood before him. Perhaps he would cane me like Matron. Just thinking about it made me tremble.

The baker snapped his head sideways, indicating that I should go into the back of the shop. I glanced through the doorway, but the room beyond appeared so gloomy I could not make anything out.

'Hurry up, child! I've work to do.'

Cautiously, I stepped inside.

He followed me, then threw the high bolt on the door.

'What's your name?'

'Sofia Bambaki, sir.'

'Bambaki?' He pulled his chin in and frowned.

'Yes, sir. My mother was Alexa Bambaki, the singer.' I stared at the floor, trying to control my emotions. 'She was singing when . . .' My tears rose again, '. . . when it happened, and I . . . I miss her, sir, every day, and I tried to go home but there are soldiers living in our house, and I don't know what to do!' My woes tumbled out. 'And my brothers and Papa were in the front of the theatre and Big Yiannis says they are all in Heaven now, and . . .'

'Shush now,' he said. Putting a finger under my chin, he lifted my face and studied it for a moment. 'Right, Sofia Bambaki.

There's a bucket and lye soap in the sink. Take *all* your clothes off and wash yourself properly, hair included. I don't want fleas in here! Put your clothes in the bucket of water when you're done and leave the soap on top. Then put these on and come into the shop.' He handed me a drying cloth. 'Tie it like a nappy, for drawers.' He reached for a shirt hanging on the wall. 'And put this over. Roll the sleeves up. Think you can manage?'

I nodded and whispered, 'Thank you.'

When he had gone, and my eyes had adjusted to the dim light, I studied my surroundings.

Sacks of flour were piled against one wall, and above them, blocks of yeast, bags of sugar and salt and various trays. Opposite was a pair of scales set on a wooden kneading table the width of the wall, above which hung a row of icons, the faces all staring at me forlornly. A brick oven and wood store filled the outside wall, and opposite that, backing on to the shop, was a deep sink, and hooks that held items of clothing and aprons. In the centre of the room stood a giant mixing bowl with a paddle mechanism in the centre and a great wooden turning handle on the side.

I didn't want to take my clothes off, even though they itched and stank. Still, the baker seemed kindly in a stern, do-as-you're-told sort of way. So I lifted the bucket out of the sink and stood on it. I put my face under the tap and slaked my thirst. Feeling vulnerable, I took all my clothes off and climbed into the big white sink.

I soon forgot my embarrassment in the joy of washing months of grime away. I soaped and soaped, the sting of lye cleansing me to the bone. Afterwards, I wrung my wet hair and dressed in the nappy and shirt. After putting my clothes to soak, I went through the curtain that divided the bakery and the shop.

The room was empty, but I heard the baker's booming voice call outside, 'Bread! Fresh bread!'

The loaf I had attempted to steal lay on the counter. I could grab it and run, but something inside me, stronger than the acid hunger that corroded my innards, told me I couldn't continue this daily fight against starvation on my own. I touched the bread with the tips of my fingers, leaned in and sniffed it. For a moment, I stood on the edge of my future, deciding what to do.

Then I turned my back on the loaf and went to stand at the shop door. In the street, a queue of adults stood in line. Each put a coin in his hand and took a loaf. One old woman tried to buy two.

'No, Mother. Only one loaf. There are not enough for everyone as it is.'

He glanced over me. 'That's better,' he said. 'Now, go back inside, cut that bread into four, and return to me when you've eaten a quarter.'

Bewildered, I stared at him, then spun around, raced into the shop and grabbed the stolen loaf.

The first taste of fresh, crusty bread after the mouldy crusts I'd lived on was pure heaven.

Why was the baker being so kind? I was confused, and a little afraid, but I had no choice but to trust him.

Before half an hour passed, the baker had sold out and came back inside.

'You will call me Mr Zacharia, Sofia,' he told me. 'Now get the broom and clean up outside the shop.'

I did it as quickly and thoroughly as I could.

By midday, all the rusks and pastries were sold. I had cleaned the floor, wiped the shelves and made him a cup of coffee, which he said was the worst he'd ever tasted. He gave me the remains of the stolen loaf, threw a stack of flour sacks under the counter and told me to sleep there. We would start work again at 1 a.m.

I woke from a deep sleep, disorientated and afraid when the shop light went on.

'Come on, you little ragamuffin, get yourself onto your feet, we've work to do,' he ordered.

I jumped up. 'Yes, sir!'

'Go and scrub your hands up to your elbows.'

I smoothed down the crumpled shirt and rolled the sleeves up again. After following him into the back, I drank lots of cold water and finished off the small piece of loaf saved for breakfast.

I was exhausted by midday. I had learned how to turn the mixing bowl while he hefted a sack of flour, buckets of warm water and yeast into it. My arms were on fire by the time the dough was ready to knead. Mr Zacharia pulled off chunks of dough, threw them on the scale and made sure they were exactly half a kilo.

'I can do that, sir,' I said, thinking it was easy. I dived into the bowl and grabbed a sizeable lump of dough, but it seemed to come alive and stick to my hands and arms. The more I tried to pull it off and make it into a round chunk, the more glutinous it got until I was tangled up to my elbows in a terrible mess of stringy, sticky dough. To make it worse, I needed to *pee-pee* so badly I was doing the knock-kneed desperate dance.

Mr Zacharia roared with laughter. 'What's the matter with you, girl?' he boomed.

'I need the closet, sir. I drank too much water.'

He helped me out of the elastic dough, his eyes twinkling.

'Go on then, girl. I don't want *pee-pee* on my floor!'

When I returned, he said I should wash my hands and arms, then dip them up to my elbows in a flour bag, so the bread

121

wouldn't stick to me. Slowly but surely, I learned to do as he showed me. Later that day, one of his customers brought a bag of clothes. I rummaged through them, excited at first, but then disappointed to realise they were boy's things. Nevertheless, the trousers, shirts, socks and underwear fitted, and I no longer had to wear the cursed nappy.

* * *

'Your mother was a wonderful singer, Sofia,' Mr Zacharia said one morning.

I threw a lump of dough onto the scale, pleased to see it was exactly half a kilo.

'I know. It's not fair.'

'Don't you sing? I'll bet your mother always thought you would.'

I considered his words for a moment. Mama had taught me scales, and we often practiced together.

'I haven't wanted to sing since that day, Mr Zacharia. It makes me too sad. Her last song was in English. She said it was very special, but I'm not sure what it was about. I learned the melody with her, but not the meaning. All I know is the last word means "songs".' I closed my eyes as I remembered that terrible moment. 'I was standing up at the back of the theatre waving my hankie. She reached out her arms to me and sang that last word and that was when it happened.' I sighed and cut off another chunk of dough.

Mr Zacharia kneaded two loaves at a time, pushing with the heel of his hand, then pulling it over with his fingers. His biceps bulged rhythmically as he plodded through the work. I was reminded of the tortoise Apollo again, and wondered if Mr Zacharia ever walked around the garden eating lettuce.

'Let me hear it then,' he said without looking up. 'I'll translate it into Greek for you.'

For a horrible moment, I couldn't remember the start. I stared at Mr Zacharia as panic built in my chest. I couldn't let Mama down; she might be watching me, might be disappointed in me. My tears were rising. I pressed my fingers into the dough ball and closed my eyes to try and recall the song. There she was, in my mind: my Mama, as if she had been waiting since that day, in her beautiful black gown and red lipstick, stepping into the cone of light on the stage. All the love she had for me seemed to wash through my body.

I sang the first few lines and Mr Zacharia translated them. I felt as though my mother was talking to me. After swallowing hard, I continued, and so did he. My tears brimmed and spilled over, but in hardly more than a whisper, I struggled on to the end of the song:

Angels, wings give you flight,
Every star-spangled night.
My love, you are life's sweetest songs.

*   *   *

After midnight, when Mr Zacharia let himself back into the shop, he called me.

'Sofia, come out here for a moment.'

Sleepy-eyed, I scrambled off my flour-sack bed and hurried to the shop doorway. As I stepped onto the pavement, he pointed to the Acropolis that rose over the city. In the night sky, lighting the pillars of the Parthenon with a yellow glow, was the largest full moon I had ever seen.

Φτερά Αγγέλων σας δίνουν πτήση – Angels, wings give you flight.

Κάθε νύχτα με αστέρι – Every star-spangled night.

Αγάπη Μου, είσαι τα πιο γλυκά τραγούδια της ζωής. – My love, you are life's sweetest songs.

I sang softly, raising my arms towards the moon, tears rolling down my face.

CHAPTER 13
MEGAN

Manchester, present day.

MEGAN HURRIED THROUGH THE CITY towards the passport office. Queuing for a shower at Centrepoint had made her late for the appointment. She turned into Portland Street, breathless, the perspiration on her face cold in the breeze. She ran around the corner to the front of the building, came to a halt and backtracked.

Emily raced across the pavement – and behind her, was her mother! They disappeared into the passport office.

What was Emily doing with her mum? First, she'd robbed her and now this. Why was her mother in Manchester? What were they doing at the passport office? Were they looking for her? She ducked back and peered around the corner of the building, her cheek pressed against the cold grey cement.

Spots of rain fell from a thunderous sky. Megan wanted to stay and watch for her mother coming out of the building. If she followed them, perhaps she would work out what was going on. She'd bet Emily would nick her mother's handbag at the first opportunity.

Megan *had* to keep her passport interview. Joyce at Centrepoint had gone to a lot of trouble to get it. Now what was she supposed to do? A small part of her ached for her mother, but she shoved that pain aside. She couldn't face a confrontation until she understood the situation. She hurried across the road to shelter under the Tourist Information Centre's overhang.

Megan watched the passport building for nearly an hour. They still hadn't emerged. Rain splattered the pavement.

'You waiting for somebody, love?'

Megan saw a dowdy middle-aged woman halfway out of the Information Centre.

'Come inside, before you get soaked,' the woman said.

Megan wondered what she wanted. Everybody wanted something. Still, she was cold, hungry and wet, so she stepped inside the empty, glass-walled office.

'I'm making a cuppa,' the woman said. 'Want one?'

Megan nodded, stood by the window and stared across the road. A procession of buses blocked her view. Perhaps she had missed them.

The woman brought a mug of tea and a packet of ginger biscuits around the counter.

'Here, help yourself.'

She put the biscuits on a small table of brochures at the corner of the window.

'Thanks,' said Megan, reaching for a biscuit, still gazing at the building across the road.

'Boyfriend, is it?'

'Mind . . .' Megan stopped herself from a rebuff. 'No, it's my mum.'

'Ah, I see.'

How could she 'see', Megan thought. She glanced at the woman, who had come to sit near the window.

'You don't recognise me, do you? I'm Pam. I volunteer at Centrepoint. I've seen you in there, haven't I?'

Megan blinked at her. 'I . . . Sorry . . .' Then she wondered what she was apologising for. 'It's my mum . . .' she said again, jerking her head in the direction of Westminster House.

Pam smiled, though her eyes were sad. 'It's a difficult step. I understand. But it will only get harder, love.' She smiled softly. 'You'll walk towards her when you're ready. When you find the courage.'

Megan sighed, thinking she was in for a lecture.

But the woman dropped the subject and chatted instead about her kids, and how worried she was about one of her boys who'd sagged school and was giving her trouble.

'He's in with a bad lot,' she said. 'Thinks we don't care. It breaks my heart. He says he hates me, but I'm at my wits' end.'

Megan's eyes swivelled back to the building – and then, quite suddenly, they were there. Her mother and Emily stood in the entrance. She gasped, slapped her hand over her mouth. Mum and Emily side by side. She squinted with a pang of jealousy. Emily was in *her* place.

Her mother seemed older, tired. Megan watched her peer up and down the street. Emily came to the kerb and whistled a taxi, but they were all occupied. They started to walk away. Megan wondered if she should follow them or go and see the passport woman.

'Thanks for the tea,' she said to Pam. 'Got to go.'

'Wait!' Pam called as Megan yanked the door open. 'Take the biscuits.' She held them out.

Megan hesitated, snatched the packet and faltered again.

'Listen to him . . . your son,' she said to Pam. 'Really listen.'

Their eyes met.

Pam nodded. 'I will. Thanks. Good luck. Don't lose her again, love.'

Megan bolted through the door and trotted up the damp street, careful to keep out of sight.

She ate the entire packet of biscuits as she followed her mother and Emily across the city, around all Megan's juggling haunts. She lost them when they boarded a city bus, a number 71. It went past Centrepoint.

That was it then. They really were looking for her. Emily was helping her mum to find her, which meant – well, it meant her mother wanted her. It meant her mother missed her.

Except, Megan didn't want to be found. She didn't want the trouble, didn't want to go back and face the truth.

She sighed, lost in her thoughts for a moment.

What would happen, after all, if she ran up to her mum now? Would she be furious? Push her away and yell at her the way she did at Dad sometimes? She shouldn't have lied to her mother. She should have stayed away from drugs, from cigarettes, from booze. Maybe stayed away from Simon, too. What she'd done was unforgivable. Having a daughter like Megan could ruin her mum's career, and her dad's. Mum might be forced to make an example of her daughter, or else lose her job as a lawyer and magistrate.

And then there was Dad. What would she do if her mum asked her why she'd run away? She'd have to tell her about Dad, about that party, about the woman with her arms around him.

No, she couldn't do it. Best to play safe, stick to the original plan. She would go to Crete, find Granny Anna, tell her everything and take it from there. Her grandmother would help Megan decide what she should do.

At least she had a chance to juggle at the station while her mum and Emily were out of the way. Commuters going home often had spare change, and besides, Megan *needed* to juggle.

* * *

Two hours later, with an extra tenner in her pocket and the rush hour over, Megan realised she was starving. She headed for the nearest chip shop, remembering the family tradition of a chip shop takeaway for supper every Friday. They each had their favourite. Granny Anna, fishcakes and mushy peas. Mum, the whole chippy dinner. Dad, chips, sausage and curry sauce. Josh, hot dog. Megan, burger and chip bap. They would put the kitchen TV on, and all try to answer questions in their favourite quiz programme while they ate, her mum frowning when Megan and Josh overdosed on the ketchup. The blue dolphin salt-shaker that said I ♥ CRETE. She stopped in her tracks, wilting with sadness for those lost Fridays. Would it, could it, ever be the same again? Was her regular chair, to the right of her mum's, empty at the kitchen table, or had they moved it away? How she wished Granny Anna hadn't gone back to Greece, because at that moment, more than anything, Megan longed to go home.

She knuckled her eyes, stood at the kerb waiting to cross and glanced over at the chip shop. Then she had to blink hard. Was that Emily? Coming out of the chip shop? With a bulging bag of takeaway?

The green man flashed, giving her anger permission to cross the road. She ran up behind Emily, grabbed her hair and yanked it back.

'You thieving bitch!' she yelled. 'What're you doing with my mother?'

Emily staggered backwards. 'Stop, let go. Ow! I'll tell you, I will!'

Megan kept hold of her hair. 'Go on then, you liar, you thief! Where's my bag?'

'The police have it,' Emily said, her eyes slits as Megan tugged on her hair. 'I got caught pinching the batteries. You're hurting me!'

'Shit! You mean they've got my passport, too?' For a moment her anger turned to despair.

'I'm sorry, all right? I shouldn't have scaved your stuff, but there's no way I'd have gotten a passport, and I just thought, you know, your . . .' Emily trailed off. 'Your mum's frantic about you.'

'How can I believe anything you tell me? I was your friend – I thought you were mine. You let me down badly, Emily. Really cut me up.' Still, Megan loosened her grip.

In a flash, Emily spun around and pushed Megan so hard in the chest she stumbled backwards and hit the pavement.

Emily raced around the corner.

Megan pulled herself to her feet. Pain shot up her leg. Just what she needed, a twisted ankle. Furious and frustrated, she limped to the corner.

'I could kill you, Emily!' she yelled while hopping on one foot. She leaned against a shop window and glared as Emily sprinted down the road, the chip shop bag swinging from her fist. Just before she reached the far corner, she disappeared into an alley.

Megan tried her foot again. 'Ahh, damn!'

She limped along, pain in every step. Halfway to the alley, she heard a vehicle backfire. With a screech of wheels, a black car ragged it out of the same backstreet that Emily had gone into. The vehicle almost knocked down a couple of elderly pedestrians that were ambling towards her, and the old man rushed into the alley. The woman watched him for a moment, then turned to face the road, waved her hands over her head and yelled, 'Police! Police! Somebody, call the police!'

Megan recognised trouble when she saw it. She about-turned and limped away as quickly as she could. Emily must have been caught nicking something again, and would be running in the other direction . . . Well, there was no point getting involved. *Run away from trouble* was Megan's number one rule.

She jogged into the park, wondering where on earth she should sleep tonight. She couldn't go to a shelter if her mum was looking for her and besides, she wanted to save her money. She thought of the place where they had slept two nights ago – if she returned to the dosshouse, she might catch Emily there and at least find a way to get her passport back. But first, she needed a torch.

* * *

At the pound shop, a woman with a bunch of keys stood at the door.

'We're closing, love.'

'Please, just a torch, I'll be quick. I really need it.'

'Hurry up then.' The woman blocked the shopper behind Megan.

Megan thought about the building as she raced up the shop aisle. She snatched a packet of baby wipes, a torch and, spotting a hammer with a packet of two-inch nails taped to the handle on the same shelf, she grabbed that too.

'I hope you're not a burglar,' the checkout woman said, and laughed.

Megan shook her head rapidly, paid her three pounds and asked the shop assistant to swap her loose change for a five-pound note.

'No problem, love,' the woman said.

Megan hurried for food, from Pete's Dogs, before sleeping in the abandoned office. One of her rules was not to spend more than half her daily earnings, so she had two pounds left for a meal. Before she left the shop, she slipped the five-pound note into her Ziploc bag which, in turn, she zipped into the leg pocket of her camouflage trousers.

At the hot dog van, a smart guy wearing a dark suit and a Burberry scarf was in conversation with Pete. Megan approached the opposite end of the counter.

'Can I have two pounds' worth of hot dog please, mister? It's all I've got.' She held out the coin.

'You're back, are you?' Pete said. 'Where's your friend tonight?'

Megan lifted and dropped her shoulders.

'No idea.' She felt the two men's eyes on her and shivered.

'Throw a Coke and a Mars in with it, Pete,' the smart one said. 'The kid looks starved.'

'Thanks.'

Megan glanced in his direction but didn't meet his eyes. Then she snatched up the food bag and ran down the alley towards the building.

CHAPTER 14
SOFIA

Athens, 1950.

I GREW UP IN THE baker's care. He was like a father to me and I became very fond of him. Our lives were hard, with little more than work and sleep, yet they were happy days. He taught me everything there was to know about different grades of flour, the intoxicating smell of fresh yeast and its proving time, and the best baking temperature for a fine crust. By the time I was fifteen, I'd developed a skill for decorating pastries with nuts and icing, and even sat at his elbow, watching, while he did the accounts.

While the bakery would never make Mr Zacharia rich, the business was steady and reliable, unlike our country. Since the end of the World War II, there had been little improvement in Athens. Civil war raged between the government and the communist parties who, it was rumoured, were shipped out to several prison islands and often never heard of again.

One Saturday afternoon, when my fingers were as white and puckered as damp filo pastry after all the washing-up, Mr Zacharia gave me five drachmas and a dish of leftover buns. The money would buy a desperately needed pair of shoes – I'd been walking on cardboard and oilcloth for weeks. Hopefully there would be enough left for a pair of nylons and a suspender belt. Like any sixteen-year-old, I longed to dress like a woman.

The buns were favourites of mine, with chopped olives in the dough and a sprinkle of salty cheese toasted on the top. My mouth watered just looking at them.

'Make sure you bring the bowl back tomorrow, Sofia. And make sure you're here at one o'clock. We've all the Easter bread to bake tonight!'

I set out to my next job, cleaning El Greco's taverna across the road before it opened for the evening. They paid me by providing a room in an old house nearby. The cook always left me something on a plate in the taverna's kitchen, but I was so hungry at that moment my ribs hurt. I hurried into a side alley to eat one of the rolls before going any further. I should have looked where I was going, but I could hardly take my eyes off the food. In the dingy side street, I leaned my tired back against the wall and, with the bowl in the crook of one arm, I fed myself a roll.

The sudden yank on my shoulder sent the crockery crashing to the ground.

'Oh my God, Mr Zacharia's dish!' I cried, swinging around to face the two ruffians whom I hadn't noticed come out of a door to the side of me. 'He'll kill me! I'll lose my job!'

Before I could bend to gather the pieces, the two men lifted me off my feet and bustled me into the apartment building.

'Help! Help!' I screamed, terrified of what they had in mind, kicking and struggling with all my might. They bundled me along a corridor and shoved me into a room.

'Stand still!' one of the rogues growled, and then delivered a swift slap to my cheek.

I tasted blood in my mouth and realised I had bitten the inside of my cheek. No one had struck me for years. I was so shocked, I could not speak and I trembled in terror. Then anger overtook me, and, without hesitating to think of the consequences, I bunched my fist and aimed for the blackguard's nose. Pain exploded in my hand and shot up my arm. The other thug grabbed my hair, so I jerked my elbow back and hit something solid. He yelped. I might have got away if the first man, blood streaming down his face, hadn't responded with a right hook to my jaw.

As the world rushed away, I caught sight of an elegant and bejewelled woman draped on a chaise longue, watching the proceedings.

*   *   *

When I regained consciousness, I found myself in a small room with a bed, a chair and a wardrobe. My first thought was to check my woman parts to make sure I hadn't been violated while I was unconscious. Everything seemed normal. The only pain was in my face where I'd been struck.

I had to escape wherever I was and get back home. I scrambled to my feet and tugged at the locked door, fear, determination and panic going off inside me. I ran to the window, but found it barred too.

'Let me out!' I yelled, hammering on the door.

After a minute of shouting and banging, the woman I'd seen before came into the room.

'Step back and sit on the bed,' she said.

I tried to dash past her but instantly realised she wasn't alone. The brute who had hit me was beside her. He lifted me and threw me on the bed, then stepped back to guard the door.

'I am Magdalena,' the woman said. 'The madam of this house.'

Her face had the uniform colour of thick pancake and her eyes were rimmed with blackened lashes. She wore long sparkling earrings, and so much perfume it overwhelmed me. Her evening dress made me wonder how long I had been unconscious.

Then her words sunk in. *Madam?* I had heard of these women. They supplied girls for the rich and the not-so-rich. Girls for unmentionable activities.

'Madam, I hope you don't think I'm a *poutana*!' I cried, balking as I said the awful word for prostitute.

'Of course not. I can see by your clothes you are a girl of class,' she said mockingly, her eyes travelling down the simple smock a charitable customer of Mr Zacharia's had given me.

'I *am* a girl of class, Madam, and I'll thank you to tell your thugs to treat me with respect and allow me to continue home!' I said, with all the bravery I could muster.

'Ha! Are you a virgin?'

Shocked, I stared at her for a moment before I replied, 'That's none of your business!'

'You're wrong, doll, it's exactly my business. If you are, then there's five hundred drachmas for you if you please one of my gentlemen friends.'

Stunned by such an unthinkable amount of money, and by the irreparable cost, I hesitated – then quickly recovered myself.

'Madam, I am daughter to the famous singer Alexa Bambaki. I don't need your money, and I will thank you not to suggest such a thing.'

Her jaw dropped. 'Alexa Bambaki? Then you really are a treasure! Can you sing like your mother, doll?'

'I practise with her every day.'

'Ha!' she said again. 'Alexa Bambaki's dead, blown to bits in the theatre. You're a liar!'

Her words wounded me, but then my spirit rose and I raised my voice in anger.

'My mother lives on in my heart!' I thumped myself in the chest. I was not a child anymore. The years since my family's death had taught me to be strong. 'And she'll be looking down on you in disgust, right now, Madam, for abusing her daughter this way. Be sure to understand, you will die a very horrible death if she sees you treating me with less than the greatest respect!'

For a second, her face warped. She glanced at the ceiling, the pink rouge on her cheeks changing into bright red blotches.

She crossed herself, then kissed her fingertips.

'Show me, then! Let me hear you sing. I've been thinking of providing entertainment other than the basics I offer.'

'I will not! I've just finished work. I'm tired. This is not the condition in which to sing. The voice is a fragile thing. Let me go home and sleep, and tomorrow I'll return and sing for you if the wages you offer are fair and you guarantee your thugs will not lay a finger on me.'

Her eyes narrowed. 'You won't come back! I'm not stupid. You'll have to sleep here.'

'I am the daughter of Alexa Bambaki, and if I say I will come back, then I will.'

She folded her arms under her bosom and shook her shoulders.

'Madam, I work at the bakery for Mr Zacharia. You can always find me there.'

Her eyes narrowed and she stared at me for a moment. 'What does he pay you?'

I panicked, wondering if I should lie. 'Fifty drachmas a week,' I said, grossly exaggerating.

She rubbed her fingers over her mouth as she thought, then frowned at her red fingertips.

'Mm, all right then. If you're good enough, I'll think about it. But you had better come back or I'll send these two after you.'

My jaw throbbed and hurt so much I felt my eyes close. I must be late for the taverna. I could lose my job, and my room, if it wasn't cleaned before opening time. I nodded once, and then Magdalena nodded for her thug to move aside.

I hurried back into the street, passing a man with his collar up and trilby down on my way out.

* * *

With only forty-five minutes to opening time, I flew around El Greco's, first with a broom, then a mop. In the kitchen, I groaned at the stack of plates and pans, but the warm soapy water helped to loosen my bruised knuckles. Thirty minutes later, the owner and staff arrived.

'I'm a bit behind,' I explained. 'Sorry, it won't happen again.' I pointed at my red and swollen jaw. 'I was attacked on my way here.'

I winced when the boss lifted my chin. 'Who did this to you?' he asked, aghast. 'We should call the police!'

'A couple of ruffians. I'd rather not make trouble. I have to get the cleaning finished before we open.'

He shook his head, sighing, but left the kitchen to let me get on with the job.

As I scrubbed the pans, my mind was elsewhere.

What would I sing for Madam Magdalena? Did I really want the job? What about Mr Zacharia? How would he manage without me?

'Go home and get some sleep, Sofia,' the boss said, as I dried the last pan. 'And mind you don't get yourself into any more trouble!'

I didn't need telling twice. I picked up the plate of giant beans that the cook had left and shovelled them into my mouth. I had to be back at the bakery in six hours' time.

* * *

My little room contained hardly more than a bed and table. I poured some water into a bowl, soaked a cloth and held it to my throbbing jaw. Too tired to do anything, I lay on the bed, exhaustion making my limbs heavy and my head light.

It seemed I had only just closed my eyes when a hammering on the door woke me.

'Sofia! Sofia!' Mr Zacharia boomed.

I struggled off the bed, unbolted the door and snapped the light on.

'Oh, God! What time is it?'

'It's 1.30. Get down to the bakery! We've got the Easter bread to bake before dawn!' he yelled, clearly angry. Then he stopped and stared at me. 'What the hell happened to you?'

'A couple of ruffians got me.' I put my hand to my face. It hurt and I could feel it was swollen. 'And before you ask, no, I don't have time for the police. I don't have time to sleep, or eat, or wash. I'm exhausted, Mr Zacharia.'

He glanced around the room. 'You work seven days a week for this room? You must be mad!'

'What am I supposed to do? I couldn't go on sleeping in the shop, could I?' Weary to my bones, I sighed. 'Come on, let's get the Easter bread going.'

While we walked towards the bakery, I told him everything that had happened since I had left him at midday. In the back of the shop, Mr Zacharia was silent until I was hacking off half-kilos of dough for him to knead.

'Right, I've made a decision,' he said, standing straight and rolling his shoulders like a prize fighter. 'I'm coming with you to see this Madam Magdalena. You can take the job on a month's trial, so long as it only involves singing. If it doesn't work out, you're back with me, right?'

'But how will you manage for a month without help?'

'That's not your problem. Now, how much did you say I paid you?'

The rest of my face reddened to match my jaw. 'Fifty drachmas a week . . .'

He blinked at me. 'Good thinking,' he said, after a moment. 'And as I provide your clothing . . .'

I stared at him, then his face broke into a wide grin and we both laughed, me wincing and holding my jaw.

CHAPTER 15
ZOË

Manchester, present day.

WHERE THE HELL WAS EMILY?

The girl had been gone for twenty minutes. Zoë paced the room.

Twenty-five minutes ... A car backfired outside and made her jump. There was a screech of tyres. She tried to see down to the road, but the street behind the hotel was too narrow.

Thirty minutes ... She put her coat on. The chipshop queue couldn't be that long.

Shit!

Emily wasn't coming back. What a fool she'd been!

What should she do? She had to act before the urge to fudge things kicked in; she had to face the consequences of her unprofessionalism. Phone Colin. No, phone Don first, tell him what had happened. Don always knew what to do. She was ashamed that she had fallen for Emily's 'trust me' face. As Zoë punched the phone buttons, she was furious.

'Don, she's done a runner.'

'What?'

'I got custody of the kid that stole Megan's bag and now she's scarpered. Tell me what to do, *please.*'

'When did it happen?'

'Just now – well, less than an hour ago.'

'Call the police, do it right away. I'll call you back in thirty minutes. Don't wait, just do it, Zoë.'

Zoë was never great in a crisis. She liked to be prepared, to write lists, to have a plan. It was a relief to be told what to do. She dialled 999, asked for the police, then told them what had happened. Glaring at the hotel room door as she spoke, Zoë still held onto the hope that Emily would return with a plausible explanation. The police told her to go to the station. She called a taxi.

* * *

The nightmare intensified over the next hour. At the police station, Zoë filled in details on a form under the sting of DI Fenwick's disapproving eyes.

When she'd finished, she turned it around and slid it towards him.

'Unusual names, Zoë and Eleftheria,' he said, glancing at the top line.

'My mother was Greek. They mean "life" and "freedom".'

The door opened and a young officer popped his head into the room.

'Sir, you're wanted down the hall. It's urgent.'

Fenwick flicked a glance to Zoë's feet.

'Wait here,' he said, the contempt clear on his scrubbed, tired face. He picked up the forms and left.

An hour passed, and Zoë began to wonder if they had forgotten about her. She should be out there, scouring the city for Megan, hoping to come across Emily in the process. They must sleep somewhere. Would Megan go back to the shelter, or to the building Emily had shown her? Zoë sensed she was close. In a short while, perhaps only hours, they might be reunited, picking up where they'd left off. This time Zoë resolved to be a better mother, more aware of her daughter's needs and troubles. She would talk to her, really talk to her, find out if there was any truth in what Emily had said, if Megan had found out something about Frank she didn't want her to know.

Finally, Zoë decided to go to the desk and find out what was happening. Just as she stood up, the door opened. Fenwick held a vending machine cup, his face drawn and angry. She wondered how many hours he had worked that day and a spark of sympathy went out to him. Fenwick glared at her before he spoke. He had a sheet of paper in his hand and a woman PC behind him.

'Sit down,' he said. 'They've found her.'

Zoë sat down, relief flooding in. 'Oh, thank goodness. I'm so sorry for the trouble I've put you through.'

Fenwick showed no pleasure, or acceptance of her apology. His face was set like stone as he handed her the cup and sat opposite. The policewoman stood by the door, never taking her eyes off Zoë.

'I brought you a coffee,' Fenwick said. 'Would you rather have tea?'

He fumbled in his pocket and produced two sachets of sugar and a plastic spoon. He blew a ball of fluff off the spoon before placing it on the table.

'Thanks, coffee's fine. I'll get out of your hair.' Then Zoë realised he had no hair and bit her lip. 'I need to check Centrepoint for Megan tonight.'

'It's not that simple,' Fenwick grumbled.

Zoë's body slumped with fatigue. 'Go on, what's Emily done this time?' she asked.

Fenwick stared at the window and tugged his lip.

'I regret to inform you . . .' he said, and then rubbed his fingers up and down the bridge of his nose.

'What?'

He exhaled noisily, his hand still covering most of his face.

'Unfortunately, the young woman was the victim of a fatal attack.'

'Fatal attack . . . ?' Zoë stood up. What was he saying? Had she misunderstood?

Fenwick dropped his hand and met her eyes. 'Your description, the clothes and her fingerprints – they fit the victim.'

'Victim? You mean she's dead?' She shook her head. Emily . . . dead; the news seemed impossible. The room was silent. The cup slipped through her fingers, spilling the contents over the floor.

'She was with me less than two hours ago. Why would anyone kill her? I trusted her. She was proud to be trusted. I saw it in her eyes. She went for chips. Chips . . . and she's . . .' Zoë shook her head.

'Take it easy,' Fenwick said, his voice softer. 'I want you to go over your statement again. Then we want a fresh statement with everything you remember from the moment you arrived in Manchester. The sooner you do it, the more you'll recall.'

Zoë told him everything, her breathing hard, her head whirring. She still couldn't believe it. The last few days seemed unreal, as if they belonged to somebody else.

Fenwick left with the statement and Zoë sat alone with her thoughts. What should she do? Who could she talk to? The door opened and Colin came in.

'This is a mess, isn't it, Mrs Johnson?' His voice was formal, accusing.

'The poor kid. I still can't grasp it. We must find out who and why – and also find my daughter – she can't have disappeared again. If Emily was in danger, then Megan's in danger too!'

144

'I think it's better if you leave everything to the authorities, don't you?' he said, walking to the window and staring out. 'If we hadn't released this Emily into your custody, she would be safely locked up in the remand centre right now and we wouldn't have a murder to deal with. A young woman's lost her life. We've got a lot of explaining to do, because, in some way, we're all responsible.'

Zoë understood the truth when she heard it. 'You're right. It's awful.'

Colin didn't answer; his face was expressionless.

'How did it happen?' Zoë asked. 'They won't tell me anything.'

'According to a witness, there was an argument going on, then a struggle. A gun went off. The hospital say it was instant – she wouldn't have known a thing. The shooter scarpered.'

Overcome by sadness, Zoë thought of Emily, limp as a rag doll in her new clothes.

'Why? It doesn't make sense. She wasn't into drugs or anything. She was trying to keep out of trouble.'

'We don't have a theory yet. It could be an abduction gone wrong, or drug-related, or someone she'd crossed on the streets before. We've got tyre marks and shoe marks from the alley. Forensics are at the scene and the police are checking wreckers' yards and chop shops right now. There's a slim chance that's where they'll dispose of the vehicle for a few bob. More probably, they'll torch it or drive it into the Ship Canal.'

'What about my daughter? Is there any news?'

'She slept at Centrepoint last night,' Colin said. 'That's the last anyone's seen of her. A volunteer at the centre made the appointment for Megan with the passport office but, as you saw, she didn't turn up.'

Centrepoint was going to be Zoë's first port of call when she got out of the police station.

'Where did it happen, Emily's ... murder?' She found the word difficult.

'In the alleyway behind your hotel,' Colin said. 'They found fish and chips, along with your change, in a carrier. The car ran over it.'

Zoë put her head in her hands. 'She'd got the food. I thought she'd just run off when she didn't come back.'

She remembered Emily's crooked smile as she left the hotel room, the car's backfire and screech of tyres. She had stood at the window, doubting Emily, fearing for her own reputation.

'I heard the shot.' Suddenly cold, Zoë shivered and hugged herself. 'Colin, I need to add to my statement.'

He left the room. The WPC didn't move.

Another hour passed before Zoë was out of there, and it was 3 a.m. before she found herself back in the hotel room. Although desperate to go to the Centrepoint shelter and see if Megan had returned, Zoë could not. She found herself battling with tears and trembling with exhaustion. The police were checking anyway, and it was unlikely that anyone would go to the shelter with a patrol car parked outside.

She kicked off her shoes, lay on the bed and recalled the last twenty-four hours. Poor Emily, on the brink of adulthood, yet full of childish vulnerability. Zoë had been right to trust her – she saw it was a big moment in the girl's life – but she was wrong to let Emily out of her protection. If they had gone to the chip shop together, Emily might still be alive.

The terrifying question surfaced: was Megan in the same danger?

Zoë needed to talk to Frank. If she hadn't driven him from home with her obsession, her unwillingness to think of anything but Megan, she would be calling him right now, telling him her worst fears and searching for a solution.

Her mind wouldn't rest. *Where are you, Megan?* Still fully clothed, she pulled the duvet over her body, curled her knees towards her chest and hugged herself to sleep.

CHAPTER 16
SOFIA

Athens, 1952.

DESPITE OUR UNFORTUNATE START, I enjoyed singing for Madam Magdalena. As the months passed, she became fond of me too. She protected me from the more lecherous of her clients, and always praised my singing. Since my arrival, things had changed dramatically at the bordello. I worked from six in the evening until two in the morning, singing and playing the piano. The gentlemen waited in the lavishly furnished ground floor with its burgundy and gold flock wallpaper, chandeliers and chintz drapes. Madam's women entertained them for half an hour or so in private rooms on the second and third floors.

One evening, just after my eighteenth birthday, Madam led me into the salon, and sat down between a loud and pompous major I recognised and a smartly dressed stranger. Another four men occupied the ornately carved armchairs around the piano in the high-ceilinged reception room. I acknowledged them all with a nod and a smile.

'Madam! You look as enchanting as ever,' the major said to Magdalena. 'I swear you grow younger each day.'

The old siren placed a hand over the ropes of pearls that hung around her neck, covering her uplifted cleavage.

'Why, thank you, sir. We have a special treat for you this evening. Sofia has a new gown and a new song for us.'

'I hope it's not one of those damn-awful *rebetika* songs about the rebels,' the major said, raising his voice in my direction. 'They should be shot, the lot of them. Damned communists!'

I smiled, shook my head and curtsied in my satin, rose-printed dress.

The major continued, full of self-importance. 'Now we've joined NATO, that should be an end to them all! It's time we had a stronger leader to sort out the mess this country's in!'

The stranger's eyes scrutinised my body to such an extent I wanted to snap my fingers at him. I hoped he wasn't going to give me trouble.

'Can you sing like Maria Callas?' he asked, catching my eye. He seemed as startled by the sudden question as I was, and touched his cravat. It was then I noticed his tiepin, a tiny locket, clearly a piece of woman's jewellery in the shape of a simple gold heart.

'I can sing anything you like, sir,' I replied boldly.

'Callas is performing here in town, in August. A fine singer. Beautiful, too. I saw her at La Scala. Magnificent!'

The major clapped his hand down on Madam's thigh and gave it a fierce squeeze.

'General Eisenhower arrives in the city tomorrow. Be prepared for a few of his aides patronising your fine establishment, Magdalena.' He turned to me. 'Now come on, young woman, let's have a song out of you.'

I bowed, sat at the piano and fluttered my eyelashes at him while I performed a soldier's love song.

A light came on over the door and flickered twice, telling Madam that two of the girls upstairs were ready for their next client. Magdalena whispered into the major's ear and he left the room; then she turned to the stranger and informed him he could go upstairs too.

'I am quite content to stay here and listen to this beautiful girl all evening, Madam. Someone else can go upstairs.' He turned to me. 'Can you sing popular music, the sort young people are dancing to, girlie?'

'Certainly, sir.'

As I sang, I entertained myself, imagining I was on the stage performing to a huge audience. The smart stranger with the gold locket kept a straight face all evening, not showing any pleasure – but he never took his eyes off me. When I had finished work, the man approached and requested that I join him for a bite of supper at El Greco's.

I still cleaned the restaurant in order to keep my small apartment round the corner. The idea of walking into the establishment as a patron, wearing the glamorous, close-fitting dress Madam Magdalena had provided, amused me greatly. But I did not want to invite trouble. Many men had offered to take me out and I always refused.

'I regret I cannot accompany you, sir. I'm a singer, not one of Madam Magdalena's companions,' I replied.

'I am not interested in your body, young lady,' he said, with a snort. 'It's your voice that fascinates me. Madam Magdalena tells me you're the daughter of Alexa Bambaki – is that true?'

Reminded of my mother, I nodded sadly.

'Then join me – I have a proposition for you.'

I hesitated and looked at him suspiciously.

He sighed and held up his hands in dismay. 'Allow me to introduce myself. I am Spyridon Papas, booking manager and agent for the stars.'

'Spyridon Papas!' I tried not to stare, but then I realised my mouth hung open and snapped it shut.

'I'm looking for a new singer to make records and perform, but if you're not interested . . .' He stood and moved towards the door.

A jolt of excitement raced through me. I glanced around the room. All eyes were on him, then me.

'Wait!' After a calming breath, I continued. 'I'd be honoured to join you, sir. If you could give me a moment to change?'

'Come as you are. We're going to El Greco's – it's very near.'

My heart was tap-dancing. I looked at Madam Magdalena and, although her pencilled eyebrows were higher than usual, she gave me a nod.

* * *

As we walked into El Greco's, I resisted the urge to run to the kitchen and tell the cook why I was there, and who I was with. Seven years had passed since they took me on as a frightened little girl wearing boy's clothes. They had put a roof over my head and, along with Mr Zacharia, kept food in my belly. I owed them a lot, and wanted them to see what they had helped me achieve.

In the restaurant, Mr Papas pulled out a chair and indicated for me to sit. He ordered food without asking what I liked, which meant one of two things. Either he had suffered extreme hardship in the past, like me, in which case anything would be a feast. Or, he was arrogant and expected me to eat whatever he ordered. I decided to reserve my judgement and listen to what he had to say.

Mr Papas was talking about his plans: to find a new singer, make records and perform at specially organised concerts

151

all over Greece. I heard the restaurant door open and close behind me and wondered if it was someone who knew me as the restaurant's cleaner, or the baker's assistant. The urge to stand and say 'Just look at *me*!' was difficult to resist.

'I need some money, Papa,' the voice behind me said. 'Can you give me something off next month's allowance?'

Mr Papas looked up and spoke over my head. 'Enough! I'm not handing over more money for you to give away, son. You can't save the world!' Then his voice softened. 'Come and eat with us – I'm in the middle of a contract.'

The speaker came around the table and sat, his enigmatic dark eyes barely glancing my way. I hardly recognised the wild and handsome man, with his black beret and his shoulder-length hair, though I felt sure I had seen him somewhere before.

'Good evening,' he said in my direction, before returning his attention to Mr Papas. 'So be it, Papa, but instead of eating with you, I'll drink water, and you can give me the cost of this meal. My friends are starving. If I don't get milk to them, I'm afraid the baby will die before sunrise.'

Mr Papas huffed. 'Look at you! You've turned into a champion of the poor and needy!'

I watched Mr Papas's face. Clearly, he was having a conscience battle, startled, sad, determined, annoyed – all these things fluttered across his face. His hand came up and he touched the heart tiepin, his eyes staring into space for a second.

'Please, Papa.'

'Damn it, Markos, you always manage to wangle money out of me. I'm not a charity!' He pulled his wallet out and passed a couple of notes to his son. 'Don't ask me again this month. I'm trying to build a business here.'

That was it. I remembered the name. Markos Papas, the boy with the bread in the park.

Markos grinned. 'I love you,' he said mischievously to his father, before giving me a fleeting nod and heading for the door.

As soon as his back was turned, Mr Papas touched the locket again and smiled proudly. But when Markos swung round and returned to our table, his father replaced the grin with a stern face.

'Not another penny!' he said.

But Markos turned to me and his eyes narrowed. 'Don't I know you?'

It was my turn to smile. 'It was a long time ago. I was a starving child who slept in the park. You gave me some bread. I've never forgotten your kindness.'

'Miss Sofia works for Madam Magdalena,' Mr Papas said brusquely.

Markos glanced at his father, then at me, and I swear he blushed.

'Oh! I see. Nice to meet you again. Goodbye.'

He turned abruptly and left the taverna. Mr Papas roared with laughter.

My face burned. Markos had guessed I was a *working girl*. I couldn't sit there and allow him to think that.

'Excuse me. I'll be back in a moment, Mr Papas.'

I leaped up and hurried into the street.

'Hello, Markos!' I called after him.

He glanced over his shoulder, then stopped. My close-fitting dress was not made for walking. I stumbled and clutched a lamp post to stop myself falling over. He turned, put his hands on his hips and laughed.

'Do you mind! That's a bit rude, don't you think?'

'Well, you're wearing a ridiculous dress!' he said, grinning still. 'But I guess in your profession—'

I interrupted. 'How dare you? I'm a singer, not a . . . I mean I don't . . . I've never . . .'

Lost for words, I swung round and returned to the taverna as quickly as my narrow skirt would allow. I could hear his laughter behind me.

*　*　*

I didn't know much about politics, and nor was I interested. I kept the promise I'd made to Mama, minutes before she was killed, and stayed away from all things political. They said the civil war was over, that Greece was now under the thumb of America because the USA had given vast amounts of money towards our recovery from the war. The central party, EPEK, had inadequate influence over parliament, and at the last election the government were defeated.

The political situation confused me. I think it confused everyone. Feelings ran high not only between neighbours, but also in the hearts of families, too. My country seemed to have returned to a 'communists versus capitalists' conflict once again, only now America had everyone's arms up their backs. One thing I did understand, from Markos's conversation with Spyridon tonight – father and son supported opposite sides of the political spectrum.

*　*　*

At 3 a.m., I got out of bed and drank some cold water. Sleeping with a full stomach was not something I was accustomed to.

On top of that, I couldn't believe the proposal Mr Papas had put my way. What an opportunity! He wanted me to cut a record. Me . . . a record! And even more exciting, the great Maria Callas had a concert scheduled this autumn, in town, and he was going to try and get me a spot at the start. Just imagining the great singer and her enormous audience thrilled me.

I could not stop thinking about my mother. She would have been as great a celebrity as Callas if she had lived. As I climbed back into bed, I decided that my mother *was* alive, inside me, in my heart, and that I would make her proud.

* * *

Mr Papas told me I could work one more week singing at Madam Magdalena's while she found my replacement, and the same with my cleaning job at El Greco's. Then he would find me a new apartment in the city, and hire a piano teacher to coach me.

'You are destined for stardom, my girl! I've heard a whisper that Callas is not taking any more bookings in Europe. She's going back to America after her next concert here. Athens needs a new star, and I intend to make sure you fit the bill.'

My thoughts went back to Markos. His laughter had infuriated me, but why should I care what he thought? Next time I was in his company, I would simply ignore him.

CHAPTER 17
MEGAN

Manchester, present day.

ONCE INSIDE THE BUILDING, MEGAN turned on the torch.

'Is anyone here? I've got a knife!' she yelled.

She wished she did have a knife – not that she had the guts to hurt anybody. After picking up a length of broken wood near the oil drum, she ventured up the stairs.

She found the filthy bathroom on the second floor. The place was covered in graffiti, mostly giant dicks and women's bits. The toilet was blocked and shit-splattered, and there were shitty finger streaks down the wall next to it. She decided to just hold it.

On the third landing she opened the door cautiously, stepped inside and closed it quickly behind her. Then she nailed the length of wood across the door with the hammer, bashing her thumb a couple of times and swearing in the dim light. She propped the redundant light fittings against the door, stood back and considered her security system reasonably well done.

The mattress appeared even more disgusting than before. Just being in the same room as it made her itch. The stink of the bathroom still cloyed in her nostrils. Despite the morning's shower at Centrepoint, Megan felt filthy. Using the baby wipes, she cleaned her face, ears, neck and hands until half the pack of wipes had gone. Then, feeling better, she sat on the mattress and realised how hungry she was.

The hot dog tasted great, smothered in extra mustard and ketchup. She ate noisily with her mouth open – a rebel and loving it – for transient moment. Stuffed full and feeling warm inside, she decided to save the Mars for breakfast. She popped the Coke can, threw her head back and drank. *Brilliant!*

As she drank, she spotted a piece of paper stuck to the dusty window. The dim streetlight shone through it and, even from the mattress, she could make out handwriting.

If someone had left a note, that meant they were expecting another person to come and read it. That could be bad. She should get out of there, leave the building. Perhaps her security system wasn't exactly fantastic. When she'd finished her drink, she would chance Centrepoint, or ask around the doorways where the Sally Army shelter was. Darkness had already fallen outside, so she had better hurry.

As Megan got to her feet, she heard voices drift up from downstairs. She glanced at the door, and jumped when somebody rattled it. Her skin shrank. She leaped back and stared at the shaking fluorescent light fittings, then snatched up the note, ready to slide it under the door. If they got what they'd come for, perhaps they'd go away.

She stared down at it in disbelief, shocked to see MEGAN written across the top of the paper.

Somebody thumped on the door before she could read further. She stuffed the paper into her pocket and slung her bag onto her back, ready to run. With the hammer clenched in her fists, she backed into the corner, standing on the skanky mattress.

Then the banging stopped. Whoever was at the door seemed to have gone. Megan's heart was beating hard. She waited a few moments and then, on her toes, crept towards the door.

It was probably Emily. Emily must have left the note, must have been the one who'd come back and tried to get in. Maybe she had come to say sorry and straighten things out, and bring her bag back.

157

'Emily, is that you?' Megan whispered. She wouldn't want to shout her name, wouldn't want the tramps to know who she was.

She listened hard, but no sound came from the door. Whoever it was had gone. She let out a long, slow breath.

The voices rising through the floorboards were louder, raucous, as if a fight was taking place on the ground floor. It didn't sound like Emily. She stood in front of the door, deciding whether to go down or not, when . . .

WHAM!

'Jesus Christ!' Megan gasped.

The strip of pallet flew off the door frame and hit her. Some of the light fittings clattered to the floor, but three of them had jammed into the door panel, keeping it closed.

WHAM!

Megan squealed and threw herself against the light fittings, keeping them in place.

'Go away! I've got a knife!' she yelled. 'I'm calling the police!'

If only she had a phone.

She pressed her ear against the door and heard men's voices, clipped words that she couldn't make out.

'Hello! Emergency, police! I'm being attacked in an abandoned building, third floor, in the alley behind Pete's Dogs, the hot dog stand. Come quickly!'

The voices faded as the men moved away. What should she do? Why had she gone up there? She was trapped. What a stupid plan.

She had no idea what would happen if she went downstairs. Perhaps the harsh voices below were just quarrelsome drunks. But it might be worse – pimps on the prowl, just as Emily had said. How many guys were there? What if they grabbed her when she tried to leave the building?

She thought of the state of the bathroom, and imagined their snagging, rough hands on her, black splintered fingernails gouging her skin . . . prodding her, groping, holding her down. She whimpered.

Trembling, she pressed into the corner of the room. What if she crept down the steps and then made a run for it . . . ? But the door was too heavy. She wouldn't be able to shift it fast enough by herself. They'd get her, be all over her like rats. She daren't go down. She daren't move.

Megan had never experienced anything like this before. She'd only been on the streets for three months, since she left Simon, and she'd tried to spend as many nights as possible in the shelters. The only times she slept in deserted buildings like this were when she had somebody else with her. She had spent the night on the street a few times, too, but at least on the street you could run.

Megan froze in the corner of the room, crouched on the mattress with the hammer in front of her and her bag still on her back. She stayed quite still, until the shakes stopped and her legs were going numb. She had no idea how long she'd been waiting. It might have been an hour by the time she straightened and rubbed the backs of her legs while the pins and needles raged and then faded.

The voices below had quietened. If she dragged the mattress to the door, nobody would be able to get inside the room. She didn't want to shift the mattress and disturb whatever lived beneath it – cockroaches, woodlice, mice. She shuddered and went over to the window, rolling her feet over the floorboards, holding her breath.

After pulling her sleeve over her hand, she rubbed a space in the grime on the glass. The window was low, a single sheet of glass one metre wide and one and a half high. The sill, illuminated by the street light, was only two feet from the floor. She noticed a cleaner patch where someone had recently sat. Three floors to the alley below, but she saw no way down.

As Megan peered out, she saw a couple of men leaving the building. One of them turned and looked up at the window for a moment. What if he was a pimp? Emily's words came back to her: *Drugged up and sucking dick.* They would never make her to do that.

She'd rather die.

As quietly as possible, she stood the rest of the light fittings against the door. She gripped the hammer and the plank, which still had the nails sticking out of it. Back in the corner of the room, alone and afraid, she hunkered down and waited for dawn. She should have run to her mother when she'd had the chance. Now a long night stretched ahead.

Sometime later, her head lolled, jerking her awake. She wondered how long she'd slept. A few moments, or a few hours? The building was quiet as death. Megan listened for the traffic: just the occasional passing car. It must be the early hours.

As she rolled over, something crinkled in her back pocket, and she remembered the note. After rubbing the sleep from her eyes, she turned on the torch to read it.

Dear Megan,

Emily told me you sleep here sometimes. I'm at the Cherry Tree Hotel. Please get in touch. I've been searching for you ever since you left home. Emily told me some things about why you left. I am so sorry. I'll help you, I promise. I love you more than you could ever know, Megan. Don't run away from me. Remember, I love you very much. Mum

XXX

Megan gulped. *Mum!* Her mother had been up there, seen where she slept. Her face heated with shame. She remembered clean sheets, her comfy bed, clothes washed and ironed and hung in her wardrobe. Her mother's Sunday dinners, always chicken, the best meal in the world, the kitchen bursting with delicious smells. Fighting Josh for the last roast potato, pulling the wishbone, laughing. Teasing Josh, loving the hero worship in his eyes when she exaggerated about some tale from school. No matter what had gone on through the week, Sunday dinner marked a new beginning.

Was it true? Did her mum really love her, really care about her? Could she ever go back to a life of rules and standards and pressure? Could she ever face her parents again? She didn't know.

She would stay until first light, go and find her mother, then decide whether to speak to her or not.

She slipped the bag off her back, found the juggling balls, replaced her backpack and hunkered into the corner again. Juggling cleared her head, helped her think. The soft leather red, yellow, green and blue quarters cooled Megan's hands and calmed her. The three balls curved rhythmically before her eyes, comforting, steady as a heartbeat. Scoop, throw, scoop, throw. Up and over, like life itself.

Megan would get herself on an up curve again. She needed to try harder, not feel sorry for herself. She would tell her mum the truth about her dad and that woman, tell her how unhappy she'd been, that she didn't want to go to university, that she wanted to study performing arts. Then one day soon, she could be on that Greek island with Granny Anna, in the sun, with a proper job, and she could perform in the tavernas and theatres like she'd always dreamed of.

She would leave at dawn, when the tramps on the ground floor would be too drunk or passed out to be a threat. The drug dealers would be gone and the pimps also. She kept on juggling. Scoop, throw. Up and over . . .

Megan listened hard. Nothing.

Moonlight filtered through the window. Then she caught the acrid smell of smoke.

With a surge of panic, she remembered the oil drum of rubbish on the ground floor. The odour thickened. Vagrants could have set fire to the building. She jumped up, shoved the hammer up her sleeve and the juggling balls in her bag. She tugged at the light fittings and tossed them to one side, making no effort to be quiet. Her mouth dried, eyes watered, adrenaline pumping as the aluminium brackets clattered to the floor.

She turned on the torch and saw plumes of smoke drifting up through the floorboards. She had to get out of there fast.

Her mind raced. The stairs were cement, but how big was the fire? She was on the third floor. What if she had to run through flames? Was there time to douse herself in that awful bathroom? She cleared her exit, yanked the door open and raced down the smoke-filled stairway.

Spurred on by terror, Megan careered down steps she could hardly see, afraid of tripping. The big door was open a little way, but it was darker down there and the smoke thicker.

A pile of rubbish blazed in the back corner. No sign of the tramps. She hurtled over rubbish, a broken chair, rags and bottles and sprinted towards the doorway and the street. Then she remembered Pissed George, whom Emily had pointed out the other night. Was he still in there? She couldn't leave somebody to die!

She crouched and shone the torch in an arc around the floor. The smoke was less dense near the ground. Green and red light

162

glinted from a nest of wine bottles. Something exploded with a crack, an aerosol or bottle. Flames leaped higher and then ran like water across the floor towards her.

And then she saw a figure, crumpled on the ground.

She pulled her sleeve down and held it over her mouth. Bending low and blinking furiously to clear her eyes, she dashed towards the tramp. Heat seared her face as she got closer to the flames, but it was the dense smoke she found most difficult to deal with. Her eyes and nose streamed. Pissed George seemed to be unconscious. She dropped the torch, grabbed his bony ankles and started to drag him over the twenty-metre obstacle course, towards the door.

Megan could hardly see, hardly breathe. Another leap of flames lit the smoke orange for a second. She pulled the neck of her sweatshirt over her mouth and nose. Closing her eyes as she lunged backwards, she managed to haul him further away from the fire. Her heels caught something solid. She stumbled and landed on her bottom. Turning quickly, she got to her feet, gripped the tramp's ankles either side of her waist and, bending double, dragged him like a cart behind her.

Distant sirens grew louder and wailed in from the street. She didn't know how she would get the unconscious tramp out of the doorway. With three metres to go, and her strength exhausted, Megan cried for help as she ploughed on.

Then the door opened and two firemen with blinding searchlights rushed towards her.

'All right, love, we've got him,' one of them said, holding something over her mouth that made breathing easier. 'Anyone else in here?'

She shook her head. She was being guided out into the street. In the cool night air, she fell to her knees, sobbing, unable to

163

speak. Someone placed a blanket over her shoulders and a bottle of water in her hand.

At the end of the alley, red, yellow and blue lights oscillated. Two uniformed men rushed towards them with a stretcher. George, still unconscious, had a mask placed over his face and was carried away. The next hours were a blur. Shaking and shocked, Megan allowed herself to fall under the control of the authorities.

*　*　*

She was taken to the local hospital and checked for smoke inhalation. While she was there, a policeman came and took her statement, and then she had a visit from social services.

Some time later, Megan found herself at the Salvation Army centre. She finally relaxed under a hot shower with shampoo suds running down her body. Tired and weak after a sleepless night and all that had happened, she thought about Pissed George. He could have died. *She* could have died. If she didn't get her life in order, what would become of her?

Megan felt herself at a turning point. She had saved a life, done something good for once. Despite the circumstances, she knew her parents would be proud.

The Salvation Army towel was old but freshly laundered. It smelled of bleach, school swimming practice, her mum's bathroom. She scrubbed the clean cotton against her body while forcing her mind back to happier times. The Sally Ann had given her a grey jogging suit and offered to bin her filthy clothes, but Megan wanted to wash them.

What if she got a job? What if she managed to become a real performer, or a stagehand at a theatre? Could she possibly impress her parents?

But then, she doubted anyone would give her a proper job. She hadn't even finished school.

Megan loved performing. Even juggling in the street brought her a great deal of satisfaction. The sound of applause excited her. The performance itself meant more than the money spectators threw. The ability to capture and hold an audience, even if it was only a mother and child shopping in the mall, thrilled her.

She washed her camo trousers, the soapy water making the ends of her fingers white and wrinkled. She stared at them. If she had a soul, that was how it felt right then – anaemic, puckered and lifeless. She hung her clothes over a line in the drying cupboard and went into the women's dorm.

Desperate for sleep, she stared at the twenty plastic-covered mattresses that lay on the floor. More than half were taken already. She looked at the ticket she'd been given; hers was number eleven. Someone snored softly. Megan used her bag as a pillow, lay down and closed her eyes. That had been the worst night of her life, and she wanted to put it right out of her head.

She relaxed her tense body and stretched out, taking herself away from the trauma, to another time and place. She thought of her last holiday in Crete, with Mum, Dad, Josh and Granny Anna.

* * *

'This is totally amazing, the best holiday ever,' she had whispered.

Stretched out on white sand with the warm sun on her face, her body relaxed after a swim in the crystal water. Balos Bay had to be the most beautiful place on earth.

After walking the Samaria Gorge, they were all exhausted. Aching thighs and tight calves meant the planned bicycle ride for the next day was cancelled. A unanimous decision.

'Swimwear and T-shirts,' Dad had ordered. 'You're going on a magical mystery tour that starts with a boat trip.' He turned to Mum, bobbed his eyebrows and muttered, 'Time to put on that new bikini.'

'I'll have to pack the Factor 50, it's going to be a hot one,' she replied with a wink.

The comment went over Josh's head, but Megan had grinned. She'd loved it when her parents were sassy with each other.

Dad drove them to Kissamos and they had breakfast with Granny Anna and Great-aunt Calliopi, then boarded a slinky modern trip boat in Kissamos harbour. They sailed out along the promontory to the far west of Crete, stopping at noon in a secluded bay for a barbecue buffet. Josh leaped off the boat, swimming to the rocky shore. Mum took pictures, always one eye on Josh. Dad drank beer with the skipper and talked about British tourist figures and Greece's next elections. Megan threw bread into the water and watched silver fish leap about in a tumultuous squabble for food.

They set off again and rounded the tip of the peninsula. Then, suddenly, there were dolphins. The powerful creatures dipped and dived under the prow. Mum was almost in tears with joy. Dad grinned, proud to have suggested such a great outing. Megan had hung over the bow as it cut through the water, the dolphins tearing back and forth in the wake. She made eye contact with one and felt it had looked right into her, understanding her completely in a fraction of a second.

They headed to a small island, not far from shore. The stark tower of rock rose from deep blue water.

'Gramvousa, a Venetian stronghold!' the skipper cried. 'Climb to the top, my friends. Nearly a hundred metres of sheer cliffs rise from the sea to the fortress walls. Magnificent!

Enjoy! We're here for two hours, then we go to swim in Balos lagoon.'

Megan and Josh set out for the summit, while Mum and Dad lounged in a deep rock pool on the shore that was so salty they were forced to float.

Later, they all returned to the boat for a short sail into Balos Bay.

The sea was so clear and flat that the boats seemed to be floating in mid-air. The sand was white and fine as powder, and the air as still and warm as the water. They all waded across the bay to the fez-shaped atoll and relaxed for a couple of hours. Someone had drawn huge hearts in the pristine sand, and fringed them with white pebbles. The peace of the place made it feel almost sacred.

CHAPTER 18
SOFIA

Athens, 1953.

SPYRIDON KEPT HIS WORD. By Easter I really was a star.

Greece was in turmoil, practically in the grip of civil war once again, and a terrible earthquake raised the island of Kefalonia sixty centimetres from the sea, leaving many dead and a hundred thousand people homeless. People used music as an escape from these political and natural disasters. Protest songs were in great demand, and I kept a book dedicated to writing new refrains whenever the mood took me.

Spyridon and Markos could not be together for five minutes without arguing about politics. Nevertheless, they were unique individuals and I had come to love them both: Spyridon, for being a steady manager, and Markos with his fiery sense of justice, which had quickly captured my heart.

We saw each other every day when he was home and, before long, Markos declared his love for me. We were walking under the Acropolis, past the ancient theatre of Dionysus. Without warning, he whisked me behind the crumbling façade and pressed his lips to mine.

'One day, when this war of oppression is over, I'm going to marry you, Sofia,' he whispered into my ear. 'I love you. Promise you'll wait for me. Tell me there'll never be anyone else.'

I could hardly speak for the joy in my heart. 'On my life, there will never be anyone else but you for me, Markos.'

He took my hand and pulled me across the street. 'Come, we must make a vow to the ancient gods of Olympus.'

There, in the heart of Athens, we came to an ancient well in a small area of abandoned excavation.

'Throw in a coin and swear,' he said, rummaging in his own pocket. 'We'll do it together, so our coins hit the water at the same time – always together through the long drop that is our lives.'

He took my breath away.

'You're so romantic, Markos.'

Our hands were side by side. We counted to three, then Markos simply dropped his coin and it went straight down to the water; I, in my eagerness, gave mine a little throw. It hit a small ledge on the way down, rolled for a moment, and teetered for what seemed like an eternity. We stared at it, holding our breath, willing my coin to be with his at the bottom of the well. Both of us sensed this was some kind of omen.

Eventually it fell, joining the other.

'United forever,' he whispered.

'In the end,' I replied.

*   *   *

Markos had been away for two months. He was due to return from Crete, where his work involved a citrus-fruit-planting co-operative in Fodele, birthplace of El Greco, the artist. The Communist Party, of which Markos was a member, ran a scheme to help poor farmers who got next to nothing for their olive crops.

When he put his heart and soul into an organisation that improved people's lives, he became so animated. Energised by the knowledge that someone else's life had been enriched, he would smile quietly, eyes sparkling. His happiness and selflessness filled my heart. When he was away, waiting for his return was pure agony.

Often, I found myself wandering around my apartment, daydreaming. In my bed at night, I dreamed of his body against mine and wondered what it would be like to make love – but I was determined not to give myself entirely until we were married. In those days, such a thing would be unthinkable – though there were times when we thought about little else.

We both knew Spyridon would not approve of our love for each other, so we kept it hidden from him. He drummed it into me that I was to appear unobtainable to my fans.

'No fraternising with the opposite sex, Sofia. That way they will want you all the more. Each one of your fans believes you belong to them alone, and we're not going to disillusion them with a boyfriend on the scene.'

My big regret was that I didn't see Markos often enough. Sometimes he was away for weeks, and when he returned, he wouldn't talk about his activities. One afternoon, he fell asleep in my apartment and had a terrible nightmare, crying out mumbled, half-formed words. His distress frightened me and I had to wake him.

'You were having a bad dream. It sounded terrifying. Please, my darling, tell me about it.'

He stared for a moment, confused, and then finally shook his head. 'It's nothing.'

'It didn't sound like nothing.'

'Look, Sofia, it's better you don't know everything about me. Sometimes, bad things are done for the greater good.' He frowned. 'Life's a confusion of regrets.'

'What do you mean? You did something you wish you hadn't?'

'Sometimes there's no choice. There's always the bigger issue . . . and I'm not infallible. Things go wrong, and the people we are trying to help become worse off. Life's a mess.' He stroked my hair. 'Listen, Sofia, I may have to go away for a while. Don't forget me, will you?' He kissed me tenderly. 'When I come back . . . I have plans. Just promise you'll wait for me?'

'Of course I'll wait for you. I made a vow – remember the wishing well? But, Markos, what's making you so sad?'

He was silent for a minute, then he said, 'There is something I must tell you – it's difficult, but important. You have to understand that I want the world to be a better place by the time I have my own children.' He cupped my chin and peered into my eyes. 'My little brother hadn't even received a name when I helped my father bury him.'

He pinched the bridge of his nose and my heart shattered as I realised he couldn't say any more. That was the nearest I got to understanding anything from his past. Markos Papas, communist, *Andartes*, mostly kept himself to himself and refused to talk about his activities or his history, only the vision he had for the future.

'Hand on my heart, Markos. I'll be here when you return.'

* * *

On Clean Monday, the day after Carnival and the first day of Lent, everyone in Athens went out with their families to fly kites. I had a concert on Filopappos Hill, across the city from the Acropolis. On that beautiful spring day, families were enjoying being together for the celebration. While singing, I stared past

171

the Parthenon to the summit of Mount Lycabettus, remembering that last stroll across the city with my family, the day before my mother's concert.

Lost in that happy memory, it was a while before I realised Markos had appeared in front of the stage. He grinned and my heart lifted. I sang the rest of the song for him alone.

During the interval, I hurried off the stage.

'You're back,' I said, as he took my hand and we walked side by side to my private section of the refreshment tent.

'It looks that way.'

'I missed you.'

'Marry me?'

Songbirds, flowers and sparkling happiness.

'We've been through all this, Markos. I can't marry you until you have a job that will support me and our children.'

I longed to fall into his arms, but any public display of affection was off limits, according to Spyridon's rules. He would even berate me for holding hands in public. In the privacy of the tent, I fell into Markos's arms and he asked me again.

'Marry me, Sofia. I swear I'll get a steady job. There's an opening at the university, in agricultural studies. Perfect for me. I have the qualifications, and I feel sure I'd be appointed if I applied.'

'Markos, I love you, I really do, but when I first met you, I was in rags – dying of starvation – on the verge of giving up on life itself. I had nothing. No clothes, no food, no family, no home. The only things I owned were the fleas in my hair and the hunger in my belly. Now, life is good. I have enough to eat, enough to live. I'm not giving this up until I am sure you can take care of a family. Get that job. Show me a secure future where we can bring up our children without worrying about money or your safety, then ask me again.'

Although hoping desperately that I was wrong, I doubted Markos would take the job. There were too many mortals to save. Deep down, though I loved him for his good intentions, I did find it hard. I wanted him all to myself.

* * *

I knew Markos was heavily involved with the communists, trying to improve the lives of the underprivileged and attempting to build a better world. He was clever enough and confident enough to have been in parliament, fighting for the rights of the poor and needy, replacing those power-hungry leaders who had forgotten *who* they represented. Behind the scenes, the civil war was gaining momentum again, and tearing our country apart. Markos would disappear for days, and when he returned, exhausted and battle-scarred, he brought with him more stories of corruption and injustice.

On the opposite side of the political equation was his father. Spyridon had nothing but scorn for those who didn't support the government.

I had saved all the money I could, but that was not enough to secure my future, let alone that of a family. If Markos and I were to marry and have children, I needed him to take an equal share in that responsibility.

Spyridon Papas was a fearless entrepreneur, a capitalist who lived for the challenge of becoming famous and improving his financial status. A gold-digger, according to Markos. Spyridon hadn't always been like that. There was a time when Spyridon had been a communist, too. He had wanted more for the poor – a minimum wage, healthcare and equality. But the tragic loss of his beloved wife, Isabella, and the rest of their children, had been too much to sacrifice for his ideals. He blamed himself and his beliefs for their deaths. So he abandoned all those communist principles and turned his attention towards financial gain.

'It's money that puts food in bellies, hard cash that builds houses!' he would yell at Markos when their discussions became heated.

Over dinner one night, I listened to Spyridon as he explained to his son.

'Look, I know you think I'm greedy and extravagant, but you should try to understand my point of view. I dine in a nice restaurant when you think I should eat boiled beans at home because others are hungry, and so you think that I'm being excessive?'

Markos nodded at his father.

'But listen here. Because I eat in that restaurant, three people have a regular job in the kitchen, a wage to take home each week. The restaurant owner makes a profit, half of which he may use to buy new chairs. The carpenter gets a job, and the woman who sews the cushions.'

Markos frowned.

'On top of that, when he has time – which is not often – the restaurateur goes out himself and spends his money on wine, food, a nicer car . . . even girls. Everyone makes a profit from his "good fortune", which is better described as endless hard work. That money goes on to improve the economy, in an upwards spiral, and everyone benefits directly or indirectly.'

'Papa, I see your point,' Markos replied, being the diplomat. 'But you can't let people die on the street while the money-makers flourish. There must be a balance and help given to those that need it.'

'Yes, right – but then everything is held up, and there are too many that are content to stay where they are and live off the state. They're the ones who need to be encouraged to find a way to earn a living.'

'And you don't think that attitude is encouraging people to turn to crime?'

*   *   *

The concert on Filopappos Hill was a great success. Although I was on and off the stage for six hours, through the afternoon and evening, I didn't get paid.

'It's just a little extra work,' Spyridon told me. 'A promotional exercise, Sofia, to push your records.'

The next morning, exhausted after two hours bent over the bath with soapsuds up to my elbows, I lugged the laundry out onto the balcony. On the third floor across the way, a thin woman with whom I shared a clothes line, but didn't know, pulled in the last of her bedding. She nodded to the sky, crossed herself, then pointed down to the street below.

Two men were loading old man Jacob onto a cart, his starved body nothing but bones in rags. My heart wept. Jacob spent the night on the prowl, searching for cats or dogs to feed his family. Competition had been fierce and now the city was all but cleared of its abandoned pets.

I had kept last night's potato peelings for him and wondered where his family lived. Were they as emaciated as their dead father? I hurriedly gathered the scraps onto a sheet of wax paper and took them down to the street, leaving them in clear view on the step. From dark alleys, I felt the stare of sunken eyes in wizened faces. Even before I had closed the door, I heard the slap of running feet.

Athens had become a living tragedy once again, and I thanked God I was not among the starving this time.

'Markos, can't we do something to help those poor people?' I asked later.

'Yes,' he replied. 'Ask my father for more money. He's making a fortune out of you. *Malaka!*'

'I owe him a lot, Markos. He took me on. He's made me a star.'

'You don't owe him anything! How can you be selling thousands upon thousands of records and not even earn enough to live on? Something's not right, is it? You're being taken advantage of.'

'There are a lot of people worse off than me,' I said. 'And plenty of other artists waiting to step into my shoes. The words "fame" and "fortune" don't necessarily go together, so I have to be grateful for what I've got.'

'Just because you're talented and love your job, it doesn't mean you should be paid a pittance compared to your agent and record producer. Besides the fact that you're being ripped off, how many people could eat well tonight if my father drove a Fiat instead of a Jaguar? Don't you see? All people are equal. They deserve the same money for the same hours' work. That's what I'm fighting for, Sofia – equality. What we have here is exploitation to feed the greed of the elite. It's not right!' Markos sighed, and shook his head. 'Anyway, I haven't come here to talk politics. Let's go down to the *kafenio* tonight. My friends are waiting to meet you.'

'I can't. Your father's taking me to meet a new record producer this evening.'

'Then leave the laundry and come to the beach with me now.' He took me around the waist and pulled me against his body. 'You make me crazy, Sofia. I love you so much.'

*   *   *

An hour later, we stepped off the bus near a small sandy cove, outside the port of Piraeus. As we walked onto the sand, he

176

pulled me against him again. I laughed, pushing him away, despite my own eagerness.

'Behave, Markos! You know I'm not giving in until we're married. I'm not that sort of girl.'

'Then marry me, Sofia. Be my wife. Marry me and make babies with me. You're the only woman I want, for now and always.' He took me into his arms again. 'Say yes, and make me the happiest man in Athens.'

I looked at him, hesitant. Of course I loved him – but I knew the sort of life I wanted.

'Oh, Markos . . . yes! Yes, yes, yes! I love you so much.' I stepped back from him. 'But first, like I said, you must get that job.'

*   *   *

On a stage two days later, just before midnight, I sang the final song of my performance. My latest record was already a great hit and life seemed almost perfect. Despite the long show, the applause raced through my veins, thrilling every part of me. Elated, though my head buzzed and my throat ached, I bowed, waved at the audience and left the stage.

Spiro took me by the shoulders and turned me around.

'Go back on – they're demanding an encore.'

'But Spiro, I'm exhausted. My throat hurts. I'm losing my voice!'

'Nonsense. Get on that stage and sing your latest again. Give it all you've got.'

The audience went wild when I returned. How I loved the sound of their applause. After the refrain, Spiro came on stage and presented me with a bouquet of red flowers. He kissed my hand and then stepped back, clapping, as I finally walked into the wings.

'Marvellous!' he cried in the dressing room. 'Remove the make-up and gargle with some salt water, then olive oil – and get some sleep. We're catching the 6 a.m. ferry to Crete. You've got three concerts there. Chania, Rethymnon, and Heraklion. Just wait until you see your new dress!'

Almost paralysed with exhaustion, I dropped into a chair.

'Spiro, I'm so tired. Could you give me a few days off at some point?'

'Yes, of course, of course – but not now. We're on a roll and we can't afford to lose momentum. Keep the crowds wanting more, then give it to them before they choose somebody else to idolise!'

'I'd like to spend some time with Markos,' I blurted. 'He's going after a job at the new university.'

Spiro blinked at me. 'Markos, a steady job?' He shook his head solemnly. 'I'm sorry to say it, Sofia, but he'll never settle down. He's had so many opportunities, but he's always on a mission to save the world.'

CHAPTER 19
ZOË

Manchester, present day.

ZOË WOKE AFTER A RESTLESS NIGHT. Her first thought: it was Josh's birthday tomorrow. She should go back to London and return to Manchester later. She had two children; she couldn't neglect her son in her desperate search to find her daughter.

Then she remembered the tickets for Silverstone, still in her dressing gown pocket. Josh loved Formula 1, and the tickets had cost a fortune. She hoped Frank had remembered the three of them were going together – a family day, for Josh's sake.

Not that they would ever be a family without Megan.

Zoë packed her things into a carrier bag and went down to breakfast, knowing a confrontation with Frank loomed. She had to find out if Frank knew more than she did about why Megan had run away. She sighed. The eggs on toast lost their appeal and she shoved them to one side.

After paying the hotel bill, Zoë decided to check the abandoned office block before she left Manchester, hoping Megan had found the note. The sky, a sheet of dark grey, threatened rain again, and the thought of going into the derelict building alone made her nervous. Would she find the right street? Zoë marched past a newsagent and saw a picture of Emily on a newspaper front taped to the window.

MURDERED TEENAGER

She entered the cluttered shop and grabbed a paper, scrolling down the print as she stood in a queue at the counter.

'Seventy-five pence, please,' the assistant said.

She handed over a pound. 'I'm looking for a hot dog stand. I think it's called Dave's, maybe? Pete's? A big white van.'

'Pete's Dogs, third on the right,' the shopkeeper said, jerking her head at the door.

Zoë rolled the newspaper, shoved it into her bulging carrier and went down the street. A police car overtook her and turned into a side road a couple of streets ahead.

Megan!

She broke into a clumsy jog, the carrier bag thumping her thigh until the handle snapped and her things tumbled onto the wet pavement. She stuffed everything back into the bag, gathered it into her chest and rushed on. Three police cars were parked behind Pete's Dogs, blocking the way to the abandoned building. Zoë approached them, her heart racing. One of the officers, a policewoman, stopped her when she tried to get closer.

'I'm looking for my daughter!' she cried. 'What's happened?'

'There's been a fire. You can't go any closer. It's a crime scene.'

'Please! Tell me what happened.' Zoë asked again. 'Was anyone inside?'

'A teenage girl and an elderly man.'

Zoë whimpered. 'What happened?'

The policewoman must have recognised the horror on Zoë's face because she added, 'The kid's okay. She saved the old man's life. You say you're looking for your daughter? Give me your name and your daughter's name and I'll see if we can help.'

An officer's voice distracted the policewoman and she let go of Zoë's arm.

'Mrs Johnson!' DI Fenwick called. He looked as though he hadn't slept. 'What are you doing here?'

'I left a note for Megan, up there, yesterday.' She nodded towards the upper window. 'I came to see if she'd taken it.'

'What made you do that?'

'Emily brought me here and said she and Megan had slept there a few nights ago, so I wrote Megan a note and stuck it on the window with Emily's chewing gum, in case she came back.'

'So, let me get this straight. You were here yesterday, with a girl that was later shot. You were expecting your daughter to come here last night. Now the building, where you stuck a note to your missing daughter with the dead girl's gum, may have been the subject of an arson attack. Is that right?'

Zoë cringed and nodded. It was all such a mess. Two men in white coveralls carried their forensic cases into the building, and Zoë turned to Fenwick.

'You'll probably find my fingerprints up there,' Zoë said. 'On the glass.'

She remembered the dirt on her fingertips and the desire to wash her hands.

Fenwick sighed. 'Sit in the police car. You'll have to come back to the station for questioning, make another statement and have your prints taken so that we can eliminate them. You should have told us all this yesterday, and now I'm wondering why you didn't.'

'I thought it wasn't important. And with the shock of Emily being . . . I forgot.'

Another car came to a halt alongside. Again, two men got out, pulled on white coveralls, gloves, shoe covers and masks, and hefted a heavy-looking case between them. Police officers ran blue and white tape across the alley.

An hour passed before DI Fenwick returned to the car.

'What was on the note?' he said over his shoulder.

'I can't remember exactly. I told her I loved her, and wrote down the name of my hotel, and my mobile number in case she'd forgotten it.' She took a breath. 'Was it still there, the note?'

'We haven't found it. I don't suppose you know what shoes your daughter wore, or her size?'

'She was a size five, but I haven't seen her for six months, so she might have grown.'

'We found a ball. Looks like a juggling ball. Could it have been your daughter's?'

'Megan was busking, juggling at the train stations and traffic lights. Didn't I say so in my statement? That's why I asked for Emily to be released into my care. We were looking for her.'

'Right. Well, your daughter was checked over at the hospital this morning and released.' Zoë felt her shoulders drop. 'She made a statement to the local branch, but now there's been a development and we have further questions. We'll check the building for your prints. There were a number of wipes, the sort my wife uses to remove her make-up. We might get lucky and find a DNA sample to confirm she was up there. I'll need a sample from you. There is always the bizarre chance that this is not the same Megan Johnson. Weirder things have happened, and I have to follow procedure.'

Zoë prayed Megan would stay in Manchester long enough to be found.

She got out of the police car and followed DI Fenwick into the station. A woman police officer took her fingerprints and a cheek swab. Then, she filled in form after form before DI Fenwick joined her again.

182

He sat down heavily, elbows on her table, chin resting on her fists.

'Was your daughter using drugs, or had she ever used illegal substances before? Do you know?'

'No, she would never do that!' Then Zoë frowned; she hadn't seen Megan for seven months. 'At least, I don't think so . . . Whatever makes you ask such a thing?'

Fenwick stared at her. 'Because the juggling ball we found was stuffed with diamorphine.'

'Diamorphine . . . ? You mean heroin?'

'Exactly, 120g of white powder. That would be 360g of pure heroin in a set of balls. By the time it's cut, we're looking at a street value of something in the region of twenty thousand pounds.'

Zoë stared at him. 'Do you think these drugs were behind Emily's death?'

He shrugged. 'We can't know yet, but the girls' similarity, and the fact that Emily was with you, may have led to an identity mix-up.'

'But that means Megan's in danger.' Zoë swallowed hard. 'We have to find her.'

'Yes, we do, and sooner rather than later.'

Zoë understood what he meant by 'later'.

*   *   *

Zoë was torn between her children. Josh deserved more from her, and she had to go back to London in time for his birthday. Megan was in danger, but the police were on the case, and she trusted the law. With a heavy heart, she walked back to the train station, searching the underpasses and traffic lights for buskers along the way, but there was no sign of her daughter.

At Piccadilly Station, she bought a ticket to London, took a seat at a café and ordered a club sandwich. She watched the commuters, hoping to catch a glimpse of Megan.

Numbed by the events of the week, she stared through the crowd as she sipped an Americano. The rush of people, leaden acoustics and lack of sleep dulled her senses. Zoë's mind fogged, and she found herself remembering Crete and her mother's last days.

Then it hit her. What had made Megan think her grandmother was in Crete? Granny Anna didn't move back there until after Megan had disappeared. As far as Megan would know, Zoë's mother was still living with them in London. The idea that Zoë's own mother and Megan had been in contact, while Zoë herself was distraught, was too awful to contemplate. Besides, if they had been in touch, Megan would have known that her Granny Anna had died, or at least noticed when the contact stopped. She dismissed the thought.

Perhaps Frank had told Megan about her grandmother? If he really had known more about why she'd left than he had ever said, then maybe they'd been in touch since . . . Or there was Josh. Had Megan been in contact with her brother? They'd always wound each other up, but Zoë knew they were close really. Josh was still a kid; he could have been persuaded not to tell anyone that Megan had called. And how many times had Josh told her he was completely certain Megan was fine, and that she'd come home when she was ready?

*　*　*

The train was packed due to the disrupted service. They had pulled out of Crewe when Zoë decided, birthday or not, she had to talk to Josh straight away. If he'd been in touch with

184

Megan . . . She glanced around the carriage and that saw most of the commuters were working or playing on their smartphones. As she reached for hers, it rang.

'Mrs Johnson?'

'Yes, who is this?'

'The receptionist at the Cherry Tree. I hope you don't mind me calling. I got your phone number from the check-in details. I thought you would want to know – your daughter came here looking for you just now. I told her you were coming back on Monday.'

'She came in? Megan's looking for me? Oh, this is so important, thank you. I'm coming straight back. Can you keep my room, please?' A train announcement drowned the receptionist's reply. Frustrated, Zoë's heart raced. 'If she comes back, please keep her there. Tell her I'm on my way. Tell her I love her!'

'Sure, I will. The police were here this morning. They're looking for her too. I'm about to call them but I wanted to let you know first.'

'Please, call them immediately. Thank you so much.'

Zoë ended the call, breathing hard. She would get off at the next stop and go straight back. Megan was looking for her, Megan.

Desperate to tell someone, she phoned Trisha and explained what had happened.

'I wanted to get back for Josh's birthday tomorrow, Trisha. I'm on the train now, but I have to go back to the hotel. Megan's looking for me. I'm afraid for her. I don't think she has any idea of the danger she's in. I'll phone Josh and explain why I'll not get back for his birthday. He's going to be hurt, Trisha, but Megan's in real danger and I'm desperate to get her back home.'

'Poor you! Sounds like hell's spinning over there.'

'It is. Look, I've got Josh tickets for Silverstone, Formula 1, tomorrow. He doesn't know, and now I'm pretty sure I'm not going to make it. Will you go in my place? The tickets cost a fortune. Frank's going but there are three tickets.'

She didn't have to say she didn't want Frank's secretary to have her ticket. Trisha would understand that.

'Formula 1, sure. I'd love to go, sweetie!'

'Thanks. You're a real friend – I don't know how I'll ever repay you for all this. You'll find the tickets in the pocket of my pink dressing gown, on the back of the bedroom door. I'll call Frank to remind him.'

'Okay, that's cool. Don't worry about anything. Would you like me to phone Frank?'

'Oh, yes, if you don't mind. He's useless at remembering these things.'

Zoë didn't want to speak to Frank. Not yet. If Frank knew why Megan had left, and Josh had been in contact with her . . . Had all her family been lying to her?

'You there, Zoë?'

'Sorry, Trisha. I'll be back as soon as I can. I'm getting off at the next station. Speak soon.'

'Let's hope it's with Megan. Best of luck!'

Zoë ended the call. Her fellow passengers were staring. As she gathered her things ready to disembark, her phone rang again.

'This is DI Fenwick.'

CHAPTER 20
SOFIA

Athens, 1954.

MARKOS WAS AWAY AGAIN. I hadn't seen or heard from him for three months. Spyridon was anxious, too, though he never said it. We were in El Greco's having supper one evening when I told him how concerned I was.

'There's no point in worrying, Sofia. He'll turn up when he's ready.'

'How can he expect me to marry him if I never know where he is?'

Spiro's head jerked up. 'He's asked you to marry him?'

I nodded. 'He didn't tell you?'

'Look, Sofia, you're twenty years old with a career to think of. Next year, I plan to take you to London, Amsterdam and Paris. You can't give up all this to get married. The next thing you know, you'll be having babies and your career will be over. There's time for those things later.'

'But you don't understand, Spiro. He loves me, and I *want* to marry him.'

'Ha! So he loves you so much he doesn't bother to let you know where he is, or when he's coming home? He gets up to all kinds of stuff you don't know about.'

'You're wrong – he tells me everything. I know he's made some mistakes, but it's all for the greater good. You know very well he's trying to make Greece a better place for everyone, you and me and him and our children.'

Spyridon glared at my belly, horrified. 'You're not . . .' His fists bunched either side of his plate.

'No, of course I'm not.'

His shoulders dropped. 'Thank God – now's not the time to start a family. And I still don't know how you can forgive him so easily for destroying your family! I know I'll never forgive Churchill for what happened to mine!' He got up so suddenly his chair toppled. 'I'm ashamed of some of the things Markos does . . . but what's a father supposed to do? I know he believes what he's doing is right, but he's my son, and he's all I've got left.'

What was he talking about? I had never seen him so emotional. I stared at him, unable to grasp what he had said. He righted his chair and sat down again, but his fists remained bunched as he glared at the tabletop.

A horrible sense of foreboding rushed through me.

'What do you mean, "destroying my family"?'

Spyridon's eyes clouded before he turned away. His thoughts were elsewhere.

'Spyridon, explain what you mean!'

He appeared startled. 'Nothing. Forget it. I'm worried about him, too. You know that. But he cares about nothing but the cause! Underneath it all, he's just crazy for revenge. Don't fool yourself into thinking he will devote his life to you. Marry Markos, and all you'll have to keep you company is worry. That, and children you can't afford to feed.'

'Don't try and sidetrack me. Tell me what you meant.' My panic was rising. 'If you don't . . . if you don't, I'm out of here and you'll never see me again!'

His eyes widened. 'Don't be ridiculous! Just forget what I said.'

I stood. 'Tell me now, or I swear I'm gone!'

188

Fear flashed across Spyridon's face. 'Stop it, Sofia. You need me as much as I need you, and you know it.'

I rushed out of the taverna, regretting every step – but what else could I do? His words kept going around in my head. *I still don't know how you can forgive him so easily for destroying your family.* I tried to sleep, but it was impossible. After midnight, I pulled on a dress, walked to the bakery and knocked on the back door.

'Need any help?' I asked, when Mr Zacharia opened up. 'I can still cut a mean halfkilo.'

He smiled and let me in.

I scrubbed and floured up to my elbows and we worked in silence until the bread was ready for the oven. While I cleaned the mixer, Mr Zacharia reached for a dusty bottle on the top shelf and poured two small glasses of raki. He plonked himself on the upturned bucket and held his hand towards the only chair.

'*Yammas!*' he said, when I'd taken the seat. He banged his glass on the kneading table and waited for me to reciprocate.

'Tell me what's wrong,' he said.

'I couldn't sleep.'

'So I see.'

'I heard something terrible about Markos – I can't believe it – I don't know what to think, what to do. I know he's done bad things for the cause before, but . . . Oh, Mr Zacharia. He proposed, and I said yes . . . but now, I'm all mixed up.'

'Do you love him?'

I nodded.

'Then perhaps, if it's something from his past, you might be better off not knowing, Sofia. People change, especially when they're in love. Or, why don't you wait and ask Markos when he returns?'

'Because if he really was involved, if . . . if Spyridon meant what I thought he meant, I can never forgive him. But I love him with all my heart!'

Mr Zacharia looked solemnly across at me.

'It's four o'clock in the morning, Sofia. Go home and get some sleep. You'll see things more clearly at sunrise.'

* * *

At midday, Spyridon came knocking on my apartment door. I opened it but blocked his way.

'I meant what I said! I'm not working for you anymore. I'm going back to sing for Madam Magdalena unless you tell me what you meant, Spyridon.'

'You've got a contract! You can't just walk away.'

'Watch me! You can sue me, but I've got nothing, so I'll just end up in prison and you still won't have a singer.'

'Look, Sofia, let me in and I'll explain.' He glanced left and right. 'I can't talk here in the corridor. You never know who's listening.'

Perhaps Mr Zacharia was right; I should speak to Markos first. But I couldn't go on wondering, and I had no idea when I'd next see him. I let Spyridon in.

'Put your hand on your heart and swear you'll go on working for me if I tell you, Sofia. I've invested everything I have on your career, hiring concert halls, booking flights, paying for advertisements, and so on. You've no idea of the costs involved.'

'I swear. Now, explain.'

He pulled a chair from the dining table and sat.

'Look, years ago, things had happened here in Athens. Tragic events that made everyone crazy. Markos's whole world was destroyed and his mind was full with the need for revenge. He was fourteen and went completely crazy. I had no control.' Spyridon hid his face in his hands. 'I had a breakdown, lost my senses to worry and grief and fell into a bottle. I yelled at him and, I'm ashamed to say, I beat him too.' He touched his tiepin and stared at the floor. 'So he ran away and joined the communists.' Spyridon paused; when he spoke, his voice was thick with emotion. 'He couldn't talk to me. I didn't care how *he* felt, I was too wrapped up in my own misery. Perhaps if I'd listened . . . but as a father, I failed him.'

We were silent for a moment, then I had to ask.

'What did you mean when you said he destroyed my family?'

'Do you have any alcohol?'

I shook my head, suddenly realising I'd never seen Spyridon drink so much as a glass of wine.

'Oh God! Why did I have to say that to you of all people – about your family? I'm mindless with worry, he's been gone longer than any time before. Bloody rebels! He risks his life, you know? The thing is, he doesn't do it for himself – it's always for other people!'

He was stalling.

'So, go on, what did you mean?'

Spyridon glanced into my eyes, then stared at the window.

'That night, when the theatre blew up . . . It was the communists who set the bomb. It was Markos who crawled down the sewers from an alley behind the theatre. He set the detonators in the dynamite under the stage. His leader, Sotiris, was killed by the explosion. "A martyr for the greater good". Markos told me once. Eventually, he stepped into Sotiris's shoes.'

My body went cold. I stared at him, couldn't blink, couldn't think. My world was breaking up, crumbling apart around me.

Mama, Papa, my brothers . . . all those people that lay on top of me. The bodies that shielded me from the blast and saved my life. Big Yiannis's wife. The line of corpses in the street. All dead because of Markos? The memory of that night returned with all its terrible sounds and smells, noise and pain.

Mama, Papa, Ignatius, Pavlos . . .

I had a sudden memory: standing in the alley, my skirt hem caught in the stage door. Feeling foolish, I glanced around, hoping nobody saw my silly situation. Then, I'd hammered on the door for help, conscious that a group of boys not far away were watching me. I had forgotten that ragged group until now. Was Spyridon telling me one of those youths was Markos? They must have seen Mama come out and laugh, seen how alive she was, how perfect. I touched my cheek, felt her kiss, and remembered running to the theatre front.

Markos knew she was in there. He knew all those people were in there. Yet he still set the detonators.

'Leave,' I said quietly.

Spyridon paled. 'You promised. Look, I'm sorry, it wasn't personal, he was just . . .'

'Not personal!' My distress turned to rage. I slapped his face. 'Go! Get out of here! Get out! Get out!' I screamed.

I didn't realise how hard I was crying until after I'd closed the door.

* * *

Broken-hearted for all those I'd loved and lost, I hid myself away and refused to answer the door. My head was full of Markos. Everything he had ever said floated around me like dandelion seeds, spiralling away when I tried to grasp hold and make sense of things. I hardly ate or slept. On the third day, light-headed, my breath stale, I bathed, dressed and went to see Madam Magdalena.

'Will you take me back to work for you, Madam?' I asked.

She primped her dyed raven hair and sniffed. 'I don't know that I can afford you now that you're rich and famous.'

I almost laughed aloud that she thought I was rich.

'Make me an offer,' I said boldly.

'I can't give you more than fifty drachmas a night.'

'Make it fifty-five and I'll start tonight.'

*   *   *

Later, I lay in bed, rubbing the cramps in my calves, reliving that night in the theatre. I imagined Markos crawling through detritus to set that ton of dynamite. He knew innocent people would die. And he had lied to me, too. I'd told him the very first day we met, under Lord Byron's statue in the park, how my parents had died, and he'd said nothing. All these years we'd known each other, and still he'd said nothing. How could I forgive him for what he had done? My heart was breaking. I could no longer stand to lay eyes on the man I loved.

Later that morning, Spyridon came to my apartment with a box of chocolates.

'It's a peace offering,' he said. 'I *am* sorry, Sofia, but it's been difficult hiding the truth. In the end, it's better that you know now, rather than find out after you're married. It happened ten years ago, in wartime. He was young and hot-headed. Things were different then.'

I turned away from him. 'Do you think chocolates will compensate for the death of my family? Or all the lies Markos has told me? Go away. I never want to see you or your son again. Nothing you say will make me change my mind. It's over between us, Spyridon. I've got my old job back with Madam Magdalena, and you know what? I'm earning a lot more than you ever gave me!'

CHAPTER 21
MEGAN

Manchester, present day.

'I'M GOING TO FIND MY MOTHER,' Megan explained to one of the volunteers at the Salvation Army. 'I'll probably go back home to London, so I won't be back.'

'We hope to hear that every day,' the woman said, smiling. 'Stay safe.'

Megan found the Cherry Tree Hotel and stood on the street corner for a few minutes, watching the entrance, struggling with her emotions. She didn't *have* to go back to London with Mum. She could still go to Crete. But at the same time, she knew she should make contact. The note her mum left on the window had shaken her – if her mum had really missed her that much, was really that desperate to find her, that surely meant something.

'I'm looking for Mrs Johnson,' she said nervously when she reached the front desk.

The receptionist tapped her computer keyboard.

'Ah, Mrs Johnson checked out this morning.' She frowned for a moment. 'Oh yes, I remember. It's her son's birthday tomorrow. She's gone back to London today.'

Megan sighed. She glanced at the computer and then the receptionist.

'I'm her daughter,' she mumbled, and turned for the door. Her daughter, but not as important as her son.

'Wait!' the woman called after her. 'She's coming back. She's booked in for Monday night. She's looking for you – she told me so. She's really desperate to find you.'

Megan grinned and, without turning around, called, 'Thanks!'

So, her mum really was looking for her, really did care. A weight had been taken from her. Somehow things would work out.

If it was Josh's birthday tomorrow, she should phone him. Another thought hit her – her own birthday was a week before Josh's. She had missed it. Sadly, she realised that would have been a big thing for her mum. She had always made such a fuss: a ridiculous cake that Megan loved, surprise presents, blowing out candles and making the birthday wish.

A sudden thought lifted her melancholy. Her mother's birthday was the first day of November. Megan would turn the tables and prepare a surprise celebration for her. A cake with candles and everything. The thought made her smile. Mum deserved it.

Megan decided to celebrate her own birthday with a chocolate bar and a Coke. Why not? She was seventeen. She could sit on the canal bank and not worry about anything for half an hour. She thought back to the dingy room, the fire and Pissed George. She needed to clear her mind. As she passed the station, she saw a massive queue at the taxi rank. Another rail strike, she guessed. Never miss an opportunity. She delved into the deep pocket of her camo pants and pulled out the juggling balls.

Two hours later, Megan had an amazing fifty pounds in change: the most she'd ever made in one go. It brought her up to her target amount for Crete. Now all she had to do was get her passport back and buy a ticket.

She'd had this plan for so long, but now she felt hesitant. Should she contact her mum first, or go to Granny Anna? She closed her eyes and thought of the day they had sailed to Balos Bay: the iridescent turquoise water, white sand, islets that she and Josh had walked out to. She remembered the clean air, the warm sun on her face.

She was happy there. It had been the summer holidays, free from the worries and pressures of school and her parents' plans for her future. It was before that awful party, before seeing her dad with that woman. And she could be happy again in Crete with her grandmother. After all, it was only a few hours away. It would be easier to get her life on track if she had her own base and wasn't reliant on others.

If she could get a job, have a proper place to live, then her parents would realise she was a responsible person, not a child. They couldn't tell her what to do with her life; they'd accept that she could make up her mind for herself. They'd be free to get on with their own busy lives. Also, with Granny Anna on her side, Megan could work out what to do about Dad, could talk to her parents about her mistakes and set the record straight. She could start afresh as an independent adult.

Yes, she should stick to the original plan, make her parents proud, hug Granny Anna. She closed her eyes. She missed her grandmother so much.

A hand gripped her shoulder, pulling her back to reality with a start.

'Megan Johnson?' the policeman said. 'We'd like you to accompany us to the station.'

'Hey, leave her alone, she ain't done nothing but entertain us!' someone shouted from the slow-moving taxi queue.

* * *

197

At the police station, Megan was afraid, although she could not figure out what she had done wrong. Then she had the horrible thought that someone had told the police about that party, the drugs people were taking. Did anyone know her father was there? She feared that would be the end of his career. Or perhaps her name had been given by one of the others. She was hoping and praying it was something else entirely. Something to do with Emily, perhaps.

She asked if her mother was there and was told Mrs Johnson had returned to London, just as the receptionist in the Cherry Tree had said. Megan's prints were taken, and she was told to empty her pockets. She placed her juggling balls in the grey metal tray, along with the Ziploc bag containing her savings. They counted it in front of her, wrote the amount down, and she signed the bottom along with two policemen who had acted as witnesses. A policewoman asked her a sheet of questions. Then a man came into the interview room.

He glanced at the form. 'Megan Johnson?'

She nodded.

'I'm DI Fenwick. Do you know your mother's trying to find you?'

She nodded again.

'Good. Do us all a favour and go home when you've helped us with our enquiries, will you? Your mother's frantic.' He didn't wait for a reply. 'How did you get all this money?'

'Busking. I juggle. Am I in trouble?'

'I don't know – are you?'

She shrugged.

'We need to clear up a few points. Where did you get your juggling balls?'

'The pound shop.'

'And your friend, Emily – did she juggle too?'

'How do you know about Emily?'

DI Fenwick ignored her. 'Just answer the question.'

Megan struggled. 'She had some balls, but she couldn't do it. I was trying to teach her.'

'Did Emily get her balls from the pound shop, too?'

'No, she said she got them from a boyfriend.'

'Tell me about her boyfriend.'

'I don't know him. I've only known Emily a week. I don't know anything about her, really, just that we got on well until she nicked my bag.'

She decided not to mention what had happened outside the chip shop: how she'd pulled Emily's hair, been pushed over, twisted her ankle. What difference did it make to anything?

'We'd like to run some tests on your things – will you sign a consent form?'

'What will happen if I don't?'

'We'll arrest you.'

Megan swallowed. 'I've done nothing wrong. I've got nothing to hide.'

'Where did the money come from?'

'I told you. Juggling. I've been saving to go to Crete. My grandmother lives there.'

'How did you get so much?'

'I've been saving hard for months. Juggling in the mall, the station, the taxi rank, you know, around.'

Another policewoman came in and put Megan's rucksack on the table.

'This yours?' Fenwick asked.

Megan's eyes widened. Would they give it back? She nodded. 'Emily nicked it.'

'I'm going to place the contents on the table and I want you to tell me which of the things are yours.'

Megan felt her heart racing when he placed her passport on the table, followed by the photo of her family. Besides her things, there were several packets of McDonald's sugar and salt, a plastic fork and spoon, two juggling balls in a Ziploc bag, a dog-eared copy of *Eighteen*, and half a tube of wine gums.

'Just the photo, birth certificate and passport,' she said. 'The rest is Emily's. Is she here, Emily?'

Fenwick and the policewoman exchanged a glance before he said, 'Never mind about that for the moment. Just answer the questions.'

The policewoman picked up Megan's juggling balls with a plastic bag, turned it inside out and zipped it shut.

'Can we take these to test for prints?' Fenwick asked.

'Sure, but you've already got my prints.'

'Don't worry about it. Now, can you tell me your movements over the last forty-eight hours?'

Megan told him about her night at the building, about fearing she was being watched, someone hammering on the door, and about the fire. She showed him her mother's note, and said she left to try and find the Salvation Army shelter so she could clean up before going to her mother's hotel. When she got to the Cherry Tree, her mother had already left.

Fenwick seemed satisfied. He was about to leave the interview room when he turned and said, 'I'm sorry to inform you, but your friend Emily was the victim of a fatal attack. PC Davis here' – he nodded at the woman – 'will answer any questions and make an appointment for you to talk to a counsellor, if you wish. However, in my opinion, you should go back to your family, young lady.'

'What? Emily . . . dead?' Megan whispered. 'But why? How?'

'That's what we're trying to find out,' Fenwick said, leaving the room.

Stunned by what had happened to Emily, Megan said nothing. PC Davis filled her in on the details of her friend's death, and Megan realised the car backfiring that she'd heard was actually a shot. However, she kept the incident to herself; she had seen nothing that could possibly help the police. Still, the news made her feel so heavy inside she could not even cry. Crazy, thieving Emily – gone, just like that.

Two hours later, Megan was given her possessions and told she could leave. She delved inside her rucksack and pulled out her precious passport. Finally! She could go to Crete. She could stay with Granny Anna and get a proper job; the sooner she was sorted, the sooner she could call her parents and put an end to the mess she'd caused.

*   *   *

Megan entered the travel agency and took the nearest vacant chair.

'Can I help you?' the assistant asked, appearing startled.

'I need to get to Crete as soon and as cheaply as possible.'

'Passport?'

Megan handed it over with a sad smile, thinking how much Emily had wanted it. The woman flicked through it, introduced herself and started working on her keyboard. Thirty minutes later, thanks to a last-minute cancellation, Megan left the shop with a boarding pass for a flight to Crete in six hours' time. The ticket included transfers to Chania, which was where she wanted to be, and accommodation at Rent Rooms Maria. She'd managed to get an amazing deal, which her savings just covered. She'd have a week at the Rent Rooms while she found her Granny Anna. Hopefully, she would earn a little more juggling at the airport. She headed for Centrepoint, a hot shower and some charity clothes.

As she rummaged through the rail of free clothes, she heard a familiar voice.

'Hi there. Can I help you with anything?'

It was Pam, the woman Megan had spoken to in the Tourist Information Centre. She remembered the ginger biscuits and smiled.

'I'm looking for shorts and T-shirts. I'm going to fly over to Crete to see my granny in a few hours' time, and I've got nothing to wear.'

'That's great. Let me help. Size ten, yes?'

Megan nodded. 'By the way, erm, I wanted to thank you for the biscuits, the other day. I was . . . well, it was a difficult day.'

'Ah, no worries, you saved me a few calories. I'd have scoffed the lot if you hadn't.'

'How's your son?'

'We're talking, so that's an improvement. Thank you.'

Their eyes met, and Megan felt she'd learned some kind of lesson, though she wasn't sure what. As she was leaving the shelter, Pam called her back.

'Here,' she said, reaching for the shelf of bric-a-brac. 'A good luck gift from me. Stay safe, Megan.'

She handed over a little red travel alarm clock.

Forty-five minutes later, Megan was on the airport bus with a hardly used backpack stuffed with shorts and T-shirts, two pairs of sandals, one picnic place setting, the alarm clock and her juggling balls. She placed her boarding pass between the pages of her passport and grinned.

I made it. I'm behaving like a responsible adult. Mum and Dad can finally be proud.

Suddenly, she had tears in her eyes. She wanted to go home.

She had been confused about what she should do ever since she discovered her mother had come up to Manchester. It had all been so clear in her head since she ran away. Her parents hadn't cared about her. They hadn't cared that she wanted to go to performing arts school, not university. They hadn't cared about what she wanted for her future. And when the pressure had led her to drink, to drugs, to parties, to *that* party, the night she'd seen her dad . . . she had been certain that she could never go home. But after the last few days – her mum, Emily, the fire and the police – she was all mixed up.

She should stick to her plan, get to Crete, and then get in touch with her parents. Everything would work out. It would. Especially with Granny Anna at her side.

CHAPTER 22
SOFIA

Athens, 1955.

THE BELLS OF ATHENS WERE ringing the New Year in. I walked home from Madam Magdalena's establishment, nervous as always to be in the streets on my own. The distance was too short to warrant a cab, and usually I walked with a couple of the other girls, who also finished their shift at midnight. Tonight, I seemed to be the only one going home, too tired to party.

I turned the corner, and there on my doorstep stood Markos. For a second, my heart soared. I wanted to rush into his arms, kiss him, give myself to him . . . but how could I? This was the very man who had killed my mother. I despised his grin, hated him, loved him, cursed him, all at the same time.

I took a breath and approached my door. Seeing the expression on my face, Markos dropped the smile.

I couldn't look at him.

'Why didn't you tell me?' I said quietly.

'I've just got back. Haven't even been home yet. I wanted to surprise you.'

'No . . . why didn't you tell me about my family? Mama, Papa, my brothers, all the other people in the theatre?'

The colour drained from his face. 'Sofia, I—'

'Was a British politician fair exchange for five hundred Greek lives? Were my family so worthless to you?'

'No, listen to me—'

I held my hand up, lost in my own pain. 'How could you hide the fact that it was *you* who killed my mother, father and brothers for so long? All those times we spoke about my family . . . Have you asked yourself how many other Greek children lost their parents that night, left to struggle on alone? Innocent lives suffering miserably in the cruel and abysmal orphanages? Painfully caned for the slightest misdemeanours. Frightened and alone. Didn't you think you owed me the truth before you asked me to marry you?'

I saw him swallow. 'Sofia, I wanted to tell you, believe me, but I couldn't find the right words. That explosion was a terrible mistake, and a long, long time ago.' He placed his hands on my shoulders. 'I was just a boy.'

'Don't touch me!' My tears spilled over. 'I *hate* you. I can't even stand to look at you. Go away. I never want to see you again. Markos, it's over between us.'

The church bells stopped ringing.

He shook his head, a confused frown on his face.

'But I love you. You love me,' he pleaded, but his words seemed stale, detached in the silence of the street. 'I can't change what happened, but not a day passes when I don't regret it.'

A couple came down the street, laughing, dressed in party clothes.

'Happy New Year!' they shouted, their words hollow in my ears.

'You took everything from me, Markos. You've known it since that day in the park, the first time we met. You destroyed my family and now you've destroyed the love I had for you, too. Did you think you could marry me, have children together, and keep such a terrible thing secret for the rest of our lives?' He stared at me, at a loss for what to say, and I pushed past him. 'I never want to see you again.'

205

I closed the door behind me and rested my back against it. He didn't knock, or try to come in. I stared down the dark corridor for a long time, trying to make sense of my feelings. The only sound I could hear was the beating of my broken heart. It was too much to bear. Was I destined to lose everyone I ever loved?

* * *

I struggled through the next week, trying to plan my career without the man I had wanted to spend the rest of my life with. Markos had destroyed my childhood, but why should I let him wreck my future? There were other record producers, other agents. I would start putting myself about.

Yet the more I thought about it, the more I realised this was hardly Spyridon's fault. He would be humiliated if I went elsewhere. He had been pushy, and cared about the money above all else, but he did look after me to a certain extent. Who was to say my next agent wouldn't be worse?

On Friday night, after a lot of soul-searching, I went into El Greco's and sat at Spyridon's table.

'I've been waiting for you,' he said. 'Knew you'd come back eventually. I presume you've come to your senses?'

I was so angry I could have hit him again.

'I want fifty per cent of the net profits from my performances and records.'

He frowned. 'Thirty per cent, and not a penny more!'

'Forty per cent, and one full day a week off!'

'Thirty-five per cent, one week in hand which you'll lose if you ever drop me in it again, and one and a half days per week off!'

'All expenses?'

He nodded.

'Done!' I said coldly.

We shook hands, and I ordered the dish of the day, moussaka.

'Look, I'm sorry about you and Markos.'

'Like you said, it's better I found out now. I don't want to see him again.'

'He's devastated. He does love you, Sofia. I'm sure you know that.'

I shrugged, not trusting my voice. The wounds were still too raw. The moussaka was tasteless.

* * *

By mid-May, I was back on the old circuit of cutting records, writing new songs and performing. My piano lessons resumed on a Sunday afternoon and I befriended my tutor, Aphroditi. She had a husband, and a son who was a year older than me. She adored them both. On a Sunday evening, we would go for a bite to eat at El Greco's and I would sometimes sing a song as I practised on their old piano.

Word spread that Alexa Bambaki's daughter was singing in the taverna, and by the summer, El Greco's was packed every Sunday night. Now and again, I thought I caught a glimpse of Markos and my heart would break.

'Sometimes you look so sad while you're playing,' Aphroditi said one evening.

'It's the music ... it reminds me of times gone by, brings things back. The war – and everything that went with it.'

She smiled softly. 'It's hard, isn't it? I lost my eldest boy in the December protest. Did you know? He was shot from the Grande Bretagne Hotel. Some say it was the British military, others say it was the Greek police. I don't know who to blame.'

I shook my head. 'I was only ten. I lost my family when the theatre exploded a few weeks later.'

'Tragedy. I'm always afraid for Theo. He's in with the communists – my husband, too. I'm scared to death most of the time.'

'Does Theo know Spyridon's son, Markos?' I asked, unable to stop myself. 'We were engaged once.'

She nodded. 'I'm sorry. Sometimes they're away for weeks. I swear they'll be the death of me. I get frantic, but they always come home in the end.'

'I can imagine how awful it must be,' I said, thinking about Markos again.

'In 'forty-seven, when the Communist Party was outlawed, I hoped they'd give it up. They say there are almost forty thousand communists in special prisons, though God knows how many are still alive. The civil war's supposed to be over, but it's still going on under the surface.'

She rubbed her tired eyes, the skin on her face etched with worry.

'Perhaps it's just as well it's over between me and Markos,' I said, the words seeming flippant and false in my mouth. 'I'd go mad with the stress. It must be awful for you.'

She frowned, stared at the floor. 'I see pictures in the papers. Leaders laughing, smoking cigars, drinking brandy – and freedom fighters hanged in public. It makes me spit. And there's no one to talk to. I daren't open my mouth. You never know who's listening these days.'

I can't say what made me look up at that moment, but there was Markos at the window. I gasped. Aphrodite turned to see what had caught my attention.

'Ah, speak of the devils. They're back, then. I'd better go home.' She picked up her handbag. 'Keep practising those finger exercises. I'll see you next Sunday.'

I glanced at the window again. Markos had gone.

* * *

Eager to get home for some much-needed sleep, I hurried out of El Greco's, but as I turned the corner, a hand grabbed my arm.

'Markos!'

'I have to talk to you, Sofia.'

'Get off me! I don't want to listen! It's over between us, Markos. We can never be the same. Never. Please, leave me alone.'

'There are things you don't know. Let me explain. Then, if you want me to go, I will.'

I hesitated. How could anything justify what he'd done to my family?

'Why can't you understand? Nothing you say can make it all right.'

'I know that. I can't tell you how sorry I am, or how much I regret what happened, but please, give me a chance to clarify.' He stepped back. 'Just half an hour. Is that too much to ask?'

My heart begged me to listen, forgive, take him back . . . because, oh, I loved him. My head condemned all thoughts of forgiveness and demanded that I hate the murderer who stood before me. My fists clenched knuckle-white, my heart bleeding for all those I'd loved and lost. That I loved Markos was the truth, and because of that love, guilt joined the battle and fought inside me. Damn him! I dared not look into his eyes, because then I'd be defeated.

'No. I'm sorry, but no.'

I walked away, tears hot on my cheeks, my heart in splinters.

209

CHAPTER 23
ZOË

Manchester, present day.

'WHAT DO YOU MEAN, *you let her go?*' Zoë yelled.

She was standing in the police office in front of DI Fenwick, incensed. When he'd called on the train to say they were holding Megan to question her in relation to Emily's death, she had been frantic. Desperate to see her daughter at last, she'd got off at the next station, got the next train back to Manchester and rushed to the police station.

Only to find that Megan had already left.

'How could you do that? I've been searching for her for over six months!'

'She answered all our questions, Mrs Johnson. The only fingerprints on the illegal juggling balls were from the other girl. We had no reason to hold your daughter here against her will.'

'Did she get her passport back?'

'I think you know very well we have no right to keep her passport.'

'So, she might not even be in the country? How do I know where she is now? What if she's in danger? The ones who killed Emily – they're still on the loose, aren't they?'

He rubbed his forehead. 'Mrs Johnson, please. Let us do our job. Go back to your hotel and wait for your daughter. She already knows you're coming back to Manchester. You might find she's there already.'

* * *

Zoë returned to the Cherry Tree Hotel and found a different receptionist behind the desk. She recounted a short version of what had happened and asked if they still held her room and if there were any messages. They had kept her room, but there were no messages for her.

It was Friday night. Zoë had hardly slept in three days and she ought to go down to Centrepoint, but she was drained. Megan knew where she was. She asked reception to call her if her daughter turned up, no matter what time. Then she lay on the bed, her neck and shoulders stiff with tension.

* * *

Zoë woke in the dark room, her skin dry and itchy, eyes gluey, tongue swollen as if she had been on a drinking binge. She should shower. After pulling off her clothes, she lay down again, woke at dawn, and felt like she hadn't slept at all. Another day to drag her weary body through. Another search. And at the end, probably another failure.

She dropped her lifeless legs to the floor and stared at the opposite wall, waiting for a plan to form. The urge to lie down again and pretend she didn't exist was gaining momentum. At eight o'clock, she phoned Centrepoint.

'Hi, I'm looking for my daughter, Megan Johnson. She may have slept at the shelter last night. Seventeen, slim, dark curly hair.'

'Hello, Mrs Johnson. We're not supposed to give out information . . .' The woman hesitated. 'Listen, I spoke to you before when you came in with Megan's friend. I can tell you, Megan didn't sleep here last night.'

'I know it's against the rules, but if she does come in, could you call me?'

'If she lets me, yes. I'll do what I can to help.'

* * *

Before Zoë took a shower and put on the same stale clothes, she phoned Josh, hoping to catch him before school. He had picked up before she realised it was Saturday.

'Happy birthday, son!' Zoë cried into the phone.

'Thanks, Mum . . .' he said flatly. 'And thanks for the tickets to Silverstone. I'm really looking forward to going with Dad and . . . Trisha.' Zoë heard the deep disappointment in his voice.

'Josh, I really am sorry.'

After a long silence he said, 'Mum, it's my birthday. I'm fifteen. Couldn't you have even tried to be here? It's always Megan. How many times do I have to tell you? She left of her own accord. It was her choice.'

Zoë felt suddenly full of remorse. 'Oh, Josh, I'm so sorry! It's just that she was here – she came to my hotel. I was halfway home, but I had to come back. We're so nearly there. I'll make it up to you, promise.'

'No, Mum, there's no need.' There was a pause. And then, 'Look, I've decided to go and live with Dad, then you'll be free to search for Megan for as long as you like. But I want you to know that I miss Megan too, Mum, and I keep telling you – she'll come home when she's ready. And the other thing is, I miss *you*, Mum. You don't seem to realise that *I* need you as well.'

Then the line went dead.

Everything he'd said was true. At that moment, she felt certain Megan had been in contact with Josh. How else could he be so certain that she'd come home when she was ready? He must have been in turmoil, keeping a promise to his sister and at the same time trying to reassure his mother.

Zoë sat on the edge of the bed, feeling miserable. She glanced at the clock. Only minutes had passed, but she felt trapped in the same tragedy, reliving it again and again. Was she making the same mistakes with Josh as she had with Megan? There was only one solution: she had to abandon her search, return to London and convince her son she loved him just as much as she loved his sister.

*   *   *

Zoë paid the receptionist and left the Cherry Tree Hotel. At the train station, she bought a ticket to London, found a quiet corner on the platform and waited. Her heart was so heavy she could hardly think straight. Poor Josh. Stable, trustworthy, no trouble at all. He had hardly ever worried her. Now she thought about it, she had taken his stability for granted when she sank into her frantic search for Megan. She had pushed him away, just as she'd pushed Frank away. How could she not have known how much he was hurting, how much he was needing her? She had failed everyone.

CHAPTER 24
SOFIA

Athens, 1965.

TEN YEARS OF FAME, CONCERTS and even a few television appearances flew by. Flowers were thrown at my feet, men tried to romance me, and although I did go out once or twice with the nicest of them, I never fell in love again. Dreams of Markos stayed in my heart and memories of the love we'd had refused to leave my mind. Spyridon kept Markos out of my way, and for that I was grateful, but occasionally I'd spot him in the audience and for a second, I was jubilant – and then all the reasons why we broke up came flooding back to me, and I tried to dismiss him at once. There was no point in having these hurtful thoughts and foolish wishes. I turned to my fans, gave them the best of me. Only in my bed at night did the dull, loveless life that lay ahead daunt me, without Markos or the children we had hoped for.

I had cut nine records, and further concert bookings rolled in. Fans presumed that wealth went along with fame, and I didn't want to dull the shine of their adoration, but it was difficult to keep up appearances, and sometimes I could hardly afford to meet my utility bills.

* * *

'Come to the Igloo Club on Fokionos Street,' asked Antonis, handsome editor of the *Athens News*. 'They're playing the new

Chuck Berry and Rolling Stones music, you know? There's an amazing guitarist . . . Eric Clapton, they call him. Plays the blues. You'll love his riffs. So intense he's always snapping guitar strings.' Antonis laughed. 'Makes the audience wait while he replaces them. Cool, baby! You ever heard of him?'

'Of course,' I replied, indignant, though I rarely went to clubs. I had no time or money for a social life.

We went to the Igloo, which was packed. Antonis had phoned the manager ahead, and he met us at the door and ushered us to an empty table near the stage. We had hardly taken our seats when Spyridon joined us.

'Ah! Here you are!' He grabbed my hand. 'Sofia, I have news for you. You've been shortlisted for the Eurovision Song Contest! This is it – I feel it.'

I grinned, pleased. I was very well known in Greece, but the idea of being an international star excited me.

A woman had come onto the stage and sang 'The White Rose of Athens'. The audience joined in, many linking arms and swaying to the music.

As they sang, Spyridon glanced around, his eyes sparkling.

'Look what the Eurovision did for Nana Mouskouri. I hear she's cutting this one next.' He nodded at the stage. 'I'm betting there's a gold disc at the end of it. That competition made Mouskouri into a worldwide star!'

Two young women came over. Flushed and nervous, they thrust ornate little notebooks and a pen forward and asked for my autograph. Smiling, I complied.

When the song ended, the singer recognised me and bowed, holding her arms out. I closed my eyes and the past rushed towards me. The smell of cigarette smoke, thunderous applause, and then the white vacuum of the explosion sucking me in.

When I opened my eyes, Spyridon and the club owner had their heads together. They seemed to reach an agreement, shook hands, then Spyridon turned to me.

'You're on in two minutes, Sofia.'

'You're joking! Spyridon, I've just finished a show. Give me a break!'

He leaned and whispered into my ear, 'Do it!' He rubbed his thumb against his fingertips. 'He knows someone who can pull strings for the Eurovision!'

'But my throat's sore. I put everything I had into the concert, but it's never enough, is it? You go too far!'

'Just this once, Sofia, I promise. Clapton and his band seem to have disappeared. There'll be a riot if the spot isn't filled.'

'Damn you! How much is he paying you?'

Spyridon looked sheepish and hesitated, so I leaned across and spoke directly to the owner.

'How much is he getting for this?' At that point, Spyridon made a choking noise, but I told the owner, 'I'm not setting foot up there until I know!'

After a heated discussion, I agreed to sing three songs on condition I received the entire fee. The only way to get through to Spyridon that my time was my own was to hurt his pocket. He'd taken me for granted and overworked me for too long.

I was into the third song when my voice broke on a high note. I struggled to the end. The burning in my throat was unbearable. Spyridon, realising I had a problem, had a glass of iced water waiting for me. He ordered Antonis to take me home.

Poor Antonis – he'd been trying to get me to go out for months.

* * *

The next day, feeling wretched, I could hardly speak. Spyridon had me gargling with salt water, and then olive oil. Eventually, he called the doctor.

'Acute laryngitis,' the doctor told us. 'Total rest for your voice, and plenty of fluids. You'll be fine in a week or two.'

Spyridon, who was pacing like an expectant father, stopped in his tracks.

'Total rest! A week or two! She's got a show the day after tomorrow!'

The doctor shook his head. 'If she performs now, she'll do permanent damage to her singing voice. I've seen it happen to Callas. Her voice was never quite the same after she went on stage too soon. It's not worth the risk.' He turned back to me. 'Plenty of fluids, avoid cigarette smoke and smog. Don't talk unless you have to. No humming or whispering. Definitely no singing.'

* * *

Spyridon came round every day. He had searched for a temporary replacement for me, but with no luck. Shows were cancelled. He was not a happy man.

'Sofia, you've had a week – you must be okay by now. I need you back on stage, and your fans need you, too, in these troubled times.'

Athens was still in political turmoil. George Papandreou was ousted as premier by King Constantine, and the students were organising a massive protest. On 21 July, when the city was thronged with holidaymakers, more than ten thousand rioters clashed with the authorities. Steel-helmeted, club-swinging police tried to keep control. Many people were injured, and one student died.

I knew all this, but I shook my head, not wanting to speak unless necessary.

'I'll get the doctor and see what he says.'

'I don't want to risk it,' I said quietly.

Spyridon squared his shoulders. 'I don't want to risk it either, but the doctor said you'd be better in a week! What am I supposed to do?'

'He said, "A week or two", remember?'

'Come on, Sofia, give it a go. Just do the Friday-night concert. You can stop if you feel any discomfort. Sing the songs you're comfortable with. The longer you put it off, the harder it'll be to get back to the top, and you don't want to be labelled as unreliable.'

'All right, all right, no need to get dramatic. I'll do one concert – if, and only if, the doctor thinks it's okay.'

His shoulders dropped and he rubbed his forehead. 'Thank you.' He glanced around the room. 'Have you eaten?'

I shook my head.

'I'll fetch something from El Greco's. Sofia! Are you listening?'

But the TV behind him had caught my eye.

'Spyridon, look at the news!'

He turned and stared at the screen. Another protest reared in the city. People scattered under a fierce baton attack from the riot police. What poleaxed us both was the leader of the insurgents in the unfolding scene.

'No!' Spyridon cried. 'Markos!'

I clasped my hand over my mouth. Markos, wild-eyed like a trapped animal, was quickly surrounded. He was trying to break out of a tightening circle of aggressive men in uniform. The police charged. He seemed so powerful one moment, then utterly vulnerable, overcome by six baton-wielding police thugs. His wet vest turned red and stuck to his chest as they

218

hammered into him. For a moment he was hidden. Batons were raised and flailed. Then, satisfied, the police stepped away.

Markos lay curled on the ground, hands over his head. The police laid into him with heavy boots, kicking so hard they almost unbalanced themselves. Markos grabbed a foot that was heading for his face and pushed. The uniformed thug fell back, instigating a shocking retaliation by the riot police. Indignant, their truncheons hammered down again until Markos's body lay limp on the road. Although he was clearly unconscious, one of the police ran at him with a final kick of revenge to his chest.

My heart was bleeding.

'Sofia!' Spyridon shouted. 'Did you catch where it was?'

'Omonia Square.'

'Not again! Damn it, how many times do I have to go through this? He's all I've got left, and he has no regard for his own safety or my peace of mind. That boy will be the death of me. I've got to go!'

'Spyridon, I . . . Oh, God!'

He glanced at me, sympathy flickering over his face for a second.

'Believe me, I know it's hard for you too, Sofia. I'm sorry for you. I'll get back to you before the night's out.'

He rushed away, leaving the door open.

Should I follow him? I hesitated. *Damn.* My heart hammering, I snatched my cardigan and raced out. Spyridon always parked his beautiful car in the alley behind my building and he was pulling out when I caught up. He braked, and I clambered inside.

'I shouldn't have come,' I muttered. 'I must be crazy. Where are you going?'

'Police station. Let's hope I've got enough money on me.'

'Money?'

'It's the only way I'll get him out.'

A youth rolled across the bonnet and disappeared down a side road. Startled, Spyridon slammed on the brakes and my head hit the windscreen. I fell back heavily onto the seat.

'Are you all right?'

I rubbed my head and nodded.

Before he had a chance to pull off again, another young man, pursued by two policemen, ran across the road.

'Virgin Mary! I wish they'd give it a rest, *malaka* thugs.' I didn't know if he referred to the protesters or the police. He was already searching his pockets. 'I'll have to call back home to get more cash.'

We drove across the city. In all the time I'd worked for Spyridon, I'd never been to his home. When we pulled up at a block of apartments, I was shocked.

'You live here, in a small apartment like mine?'

'Yes, of course. What did you think – a mansion?'

'But the suits, the car, flashing the money . . . I thought, you know . . .'

'That I was filthy rich? No, Sofia. The fact is, people think that if you're a success you have big money, so I keep up a front. Most of my money goes on getting Markos out of trouble over and over again, and keeping up appearances. Stay here, I won't be a minute.'

* * *

Outside the main police station, Spyridon took a deep breath and exhaled slowly. He let his hand fall over his face, wiping away the frantic father, replacing it with a look of wealth and power. He squared his shoulders and walked purposefully into the police station.

I watched him shake hands with the man on the desk, who I noticed immediately slid his hand into his pocket.

'My son is in here?' Spyridon asked, squaring his shoulders again.

The desk sergeant confirmed he was.

'Then let's speak to the chief superintendent.' He jerked his thumb at me. 'You know who this is? Sofia Bambaki.' He turned. 'Sofia, give this fine young man your autograph.'

Spyridon was shown into an office. Half an hour later, he reappeared and said, 'Come on, we're going home.'

'But what about Markos?'

'Never mind about Markos. They'll let him go in an hour. You're sworn to secrecy about this, okay? I don't want him to know I bailed him out.'

'But—'

'End of subject!'

His brusqueness shocked me. 'Is he all right? He took a severe beating.'

'Perhaps a couple of cracked ribs, but he's alive. Theo was not so lucky.'

'You don't mean Aphroditi's son? That's why she didn't turn up for piano practice. Blessed Virgin! Poor Aphroditi, she must be going crazy.'

'He was killed today. Just remember, I don't want you telling anyone about this, Sofia. All right?'

*   *   *

The following Friday, I waited in the wings, even though I still had doubts about my voice and hadn't sung a note since the onset of my laryngitis. In the dressing room, I had hummed my favourite warm-up exercise and left it at that.

'You'll be fine,' Spyridon assured me. 'Just take it easy – don't push it.'

The compère introduced me: 'And now, the moment you've been waiting for . . .'

All the familiar emotions gathered in my chest. An adrenaline rush that whipped up my heart rate, a ripple of anxiety and such a heightened sense of self, I was even conscious of my blink rate. I placed my hand flat on my middle, closed my eyes and calmed down.

Everything will be fine.

From the audience, there was thunderous applause as the band played the introduction. I started with a gentle love song, and by the third song, my fear had gone. I sang in full voice, projecting across the theatre and loving every moment. The audience clapped along and the thrill of performing erased every other concern. I could only see the front row; the rest was darkness, apart from the pop of an occasional camera flash. I glanced over the theatre, then returned my attention to the front.

Markos!

I stared at him, conscious of his black eye and bruised cheekbone. I hadn't seen him for over a year, and he had changed dramatically. Now, gaunt and wild-looking, he had a haunted air about him. Lost in the memory of our love, I stopped singing and gazed. I was only looking at Markos. He gave a sharp nod.

I took up the song again and put everything I had into it. My throat and neck began to burn. Then tears pricked the backs of my eyes.

The song became so poignant that I struggled not to cry for my lost love, my dearly departed family and Aphroditi's poor son.

The rhythmic clapping stopped and my mood seemed to ripple through the theatre. My voice became hoarse, and my neck felt as if I had swallowed a sea urchin. At the end of the song, I wiped my tears away and bowed. The auditorium was silent for a moment, then the applause broke out and I swear I felt the vibration of those clapping hands in the air around me. I bowed to the left, the centre and then to the right, disappointed to see Markos's seat empty.

I bowed again and exited the stage. The lights went up and my audience were crying out: *Encore! Encore!* to a slow handclap. Spyridon grabbed my wrist and tugged me back on stage. The pain in my throat was so intense, I could not voice a protest.

'Ladies and gentlemen, Sofia is not well,' Spyridon said into the microphone. 'But rather than cancel the show, she insisted on coming here to perform for you tonight.'

The audience went wild. I clutched my throat and nodded. It was then I saw Markos standing at the fire door. I wanted to sing to him, pour my heart out, perform my mother's song. Tears of sadness, for all the wasted years, rolled down my cheeks.

I shooed Spyridon away, acknowledged the audience again, nodded at the band and said, "'Life's Sweet Song'."

They struck up the melody and I sang directly to Markos.

At that moment, I knew – it was like a light going on – that I had to have this man by my side for the rest of my life. The past did not matter. I loved him too much. Despite my burning throat, when I came to the end of the song, I held onto that last note just as my mother had, holding my arms out towards the man I loved.

* * *

That night, Markos ate with us in El Greco's. His eyes hardly left me. Although euphoric in the theatre, I felt shy in the taverna. Spyridon was in the worst mood ever and we ate in silence.

'I can only manage the soup, Spyridon,' I whispered. 'I'll have to see the doctor in the morning, my throat's killing me.'

'Get a good night's sleep and then we'll see,' he said.

Markos frowned at his father. 'Don't be ridiculous, Papa. Clearly there's something wrong with her throat. Don't you ever think of anyone but yourself?'

Spyridon gave me a warning glance, so I kept my mouth shut.

'She's got an audition for the Eurovision in three weeks. We've got the song, but it'll be hard graft to be ready on time!'

My heart did a little skip. 'You should have told me, Spyridon. That's exciting news!'

'You need to trust me – both of you!' He threw some money on the table. 'Get some rest, Sofia. I'll be round with the doctor in the morning.'

He got up and marched out of the door.

Markos watched him. 'I don't know how you put up with his bullying. Anyway, I thought your boyfriend would have joined us.'

'Boyfriend? What boyfriend?'

Markos seemed confused, then frowned at the empty doorway. '*Malaka!*'

* * *

Markos walked me home. We stood on the doorstep and he stroked my hair.

'I've missed you. It's been ten years since I stood here last.'

'Ten years. Can it really be so long? What a waste of time.'

'I thought you were with somebody else.'

'No.'

'I love you.'

Oh! It was all I wanted to hear. In a moment of overwhelming joy, I threw myself into his arms. He cried out, toppled back and cracked his head on the doorpost.

'My ribs! My head! Ouch!'

'Sorry! Your broken ribs, I forgot.'

'I'd better lie down right away, in case one of them punctures a lung.'

I stepped back, hands on my cheeks, horrified for a second that I might have caused such a thing. Then I saw the old twinkle in his eyes.

'You'd better come in then, lie down for a while.'

He nodded. 'Mmm. I might need some support.'

'You can lean on me, Markos. You can always lean on me.'

'Likewise,' he whispered.

* * *

'You've got nodules on your vocal cords,' the doctor said. 'I'm sorry, Sofia.'

'What do you mean, you're sorry? How long should she rest her voice?' Spyridon said angrily.

The doctor smoothed his moustache.

'For a good while, at least until we've seen the results of the tests. One of her lymph glands is swollen. I'm a little concerned. We'll send her for a biopsy this afternoon.'

* * *

225

Frightened of what the future held, frightened for my life, I tried to put on a brave face. Markos stayed with me, holding my hand, his big brown eyes bathing me in calm while the biopsy was carried out. This protocol was not usually allowed and I wondered if Spyridon's pocket was a little lighter as a result.

Two days later, we received the result, the three of us sitting in the specialist's office.

The doctor cleared his throat, his reluctance to speak quite clear.

'There is no easy way to say this. You have a tumour, Sofia. I'm sorry.'

Stunned, I stared at the specialist. He glanced at his notes.

'Luckily, we've found it in the early stages. We'll operate to remove it and then give you a bout of radiation therapy.'

'You mean I've got cancer?' I whispered. 'Oh my God, am I going to die?'

He shook his head. 'You're very lucky we discovered the growth this early. If it hadn't been for the laryngitis, it might have been another story. I doubt it will affect your speaking voice a great deal, but you'll have to accept that it's the end of your singing career. Your vocal cords will be weakened by the surgery, and they'll be prone to further damage should they come under any strain. If this happens, in a worst-case scenario you may lose your ability to speak completely.'

'What . . . no voice at all?'

Markos squeezed my hand.

'They say Mouskouri only has one vocal cord,' Spyridon said.

'Stop it, Papa!' Markos shouted. 'It's over – get used to it! Find yourself another singer!'

'Gentlemen,' the specialist said. 'Sofia needs our support. I'm going to admit her now and operate tomorrow.'

I clutched my throat, imagining the scalpel. One slip . . .

'I'm frightened.'

'There's no need to be frightened. It's not a difficult procedure. With rest, and the right care, you'll be fine.'

'I'll stay with you,' Markos said. 'You won't be alone.'

When we arrived home to pack my things for hospital, I pulled Markos towards me. I had longed to be on my own with him, and I needed all the comfort he could give me now.

'How long will it take for your ribs to heal? Are they terribly painful?' I asked.

'Six weeks, but they're not too bad now so long as I don't make any sudden movements.'

'Perhaps you should lie down while I put some things together.'

He took my hand and led me into the bedroom. 'Rest with me for a short while?'

He lifted my chin and kissed me.

I looked at him, the man I loved. We had wasted years already, and who knew what would be the result of my surgery?

I followed him into the bedroom.

CHAPTER 25
MEGAN

Crete, present day.

MEGAN FOLLOWED THE OTHER passengers queuing at passport control, showed her documents and was frisked by security. She'd slept on the plane and arrived at Chania airport just after 3 a.m. Greek time. It was a comfort to be part of the crowd. Here she was just like everyone else – not a runaway, not a thief, just a young woman going on holiday.

To arrive in Crete at last was her greatest achievement. She had dreamed of it for a long time. Megan thought of Granny Anna's surprise when she would turn up in the little village of Kissamos, just to the west of the city. Megan imagined hugging her frail body. She would buy her grandmother a small gift, and maybe she would make enough money to take her out for a proper Cretan meal, cooked on the coals and served by a fat, grinning taverna owner. Her priority would be to get a regular job. She'd try at the theatre first, then at the tourist office. She could do these things in the city, and also busk to make extra cash if things didn't go to plan.

When she'd first started performing in the streets of Manchester, it had felt daunting. People had rushed past Megan and hardly glanced her way. If she tried to observe the commuters, she usually ended up dropping her balls. Now, her concentration had shifted. She knew what she was doing. She could juggle without thinking about it, focusing on the passers-by.

Women with young children and old folk were the most generous and appreciative. She found that the more she smiled, the more money she received. Each day was a challenge she rose to, and apart from when the worst weather struck, her daily profit increased.

Occasionally, she had been heckled by shopkeepers, or asked to move by the police, but in general, street arts were welcomed in Manchester. However, it would be another thing altogether to perform on a real stage, or even before the camera, with an audience that had paid to see her.

Megan had juggled in the departure lounge while they waited for boarding and made a tidy sum. At first, she'd noticed the ground staff put their heads together for a discussion, glancing her way. But what was the worst that could happen, she thought to herself? They could ask her to stop, and she would. Despite her fears, everyone seemed to appreciate her, especially when the smallest children stopped chasing each other around the stark seating area and sat before her, captivated.

It wasn't just the money she got from busking; she loved it when people clapped. Something deep inside her seemed to rise, and she always made a bow, grinning to herself.

* * *

As she boarded the coach outside Chania airport, the dawn sky brightened in the east. Her excitement rose when the coach stopped and dropped her, along with a couple of lads, outside the apartment block, Rent Rooms Maria, just outside the city walls. The rep got off the coach with the driver to lug baggage onto the pavement.

'Mine's the orange and blue backpack,' Megan said – and then, because this was her new start, her opportunity, she asked if there were any jobs going as holiday reps. 'Where would I apply?'

The rep ticked Megan and the two lads off her clipboard list and laughed.

'Are you completely mad? It's the worst job in the world.' Nevertheless, she handed Megan a card. 'That's our office phone number. Give them a call. I'll bet there'll be a vacancy or two by the end of the month. You're room eight. Key's in the door.'

Megan lugged her backpack into the first-floor apartment. A spotless room, the whitest sheets and an immaculate tiled bathroom, all to herself.

* * *

The chirruping that filtered through Megan's fly screen woke her. She lay naked under her clean white sheet, enjoying a moment of luxury before she opened her eyes. Food, a bus time-table, a walk around the harbour and a visit to the travel rep's office were on her agenda for the day.

A knock sounded on the door.

'Who is it?'

'Gary and Jeff, from the airport coach last night.'

Megan grabbed a T-shirt and shorts from her backpack, pulled them on and opened the door.

'Hi, what can I do for you?' she said to the two good-looking guys.

They were clutching a paper carrier with *ΨΩΜΙ* on the front. Megan didn't speak or read Greek; her mum had moved to England so young that she'd never learned to read in Greek and though she could speak a little Greek, she always felt more comfortable using English. Granny Anna hadn't taught her either; she always said that speaking Greek made her sad, made her think too much of her past. Still, Megan had been to enough bakeries on holiday to recognise the Greek word for 'bread'.

'I'm Gary. We've bought some fresh cinnamon rolls. Care to join us?'

Even as he spoke, the sweet spicy aroma of the buns filtered into the room.

'And I'm Jeff. You brought a kettle?'

Megan shook her head. 'Didn't think.'

'Take milk and sugar?'

Megan nodded, smiling.

'Then join us for breakfast on the roof in ten. Okay?'

* * *

Gary and Jeff were all smiles. The chunky, good-looking pair were from Brighton, and both seemed friendly. They had also come to Crete to look for summer work. Gary was taking travel, tourism and ancient history at uni, and Jeff dreamed of working in a London theatre. He had helped, via the internet, to design floats for Chania's upcoming carnival. Megan liked them immediately.

From the top of the three-storey building, they looked out over the rooftops and enjoyed the view of Koum Kapi beach.

'You coming to the beach later?' Jeff asked. 'We're planning to learn snorkelling.'

Gary's eyes widened as he pulled his chin in. 'That's the royal "we", Megan. I'm absolutely terrified of putting my face under water!'

She laughed; they were like a double act.

'I wish I could,' she said, 'but I've got to get a bus timetable, and go to the travel office today.' She explained that she was trying to get a job.

'We're in Chania for the carnival,' Jeff said. 'I'm dying to see the floats. Then next week we'll start looking for work.'

'Sounds like fun,' Megan said. 'I'm hoping to perform in the carnival, too. I'm longing to see the parade, but my priority is to find my granny and get a job.'

And call my mum, she thought, but didn't say. That was far too long a story.

CHAPTER 26
SOFIA

Athens, 1967.

Markos told me about everything that had happened to make him set off the dynamite under the theatre. One moment he was shearing sheep with his father; the next, he was helping to pull his dead mother and sisters out of his bombed house. I cried when he described their burial in a nearby field. Spyridon had been a simple family man once, and Markos an innocent boy. Their lives were changed forever by the actions of a distant government.

I knew what it was like to lose everyone you loved at a tender age. If I had had the chance, just after my parents' deaths, to kill the people responsible, who knows what I might have done? If I had been older when it happened, still a child at heart but old enough to act, or if it hadn't been for Mr Zacharia, who knows what I might have been driven to?

Although it was hard at first, although I could not forgive him straight away, I did come to understand his actions. That fourteen-year-old child that I had come to love so deeply needed to blame someone, and needed balance in the scales of justice. He had acted out of an overwhelming desire for retribution. He had believed then that what he was doing was right, and knew now that it was wrong.

* * *

Spyridon, although disappointed I could no longer sing, found himself another soloist. She blossomed under his promotion and earned him plenty of money. We still met every Friday night at El Greco's. Markos kept his word, determined to show me he could change. He found a proper job working for a section of the agriculture administration, travelling to various islands, counting goats and olive trees that were eligible for government subsidies.

I went back to work at Mr Zacharia's bakery. I'd missed him, and he was glad to have me back.

Every weekend, I accompanied Markos to his favourite *kafenio*, where the *Andartes* gathered. They often sang dissident songs, or quoted rebellious *mantinades*, the older ones banging their sticks on the wooden floor to keep the rhythm of the four-line poems. I joined in these vibrant verses of protest, softly. But I missed singing so much!

Sometimes, when I was alone at home, I would play one of my old records and stand in front of the mirror and mime. 'Life's Sweet Song' was my favourite, of course. It brought back all those old memories of my mother and her last rendition. I even found myself curling my fingers around Big Yiannis's barley sugar, and wondered what had happened to that great bear of a man. Inevitably, I would end up in tears.

To compensate for not being able to perform, I wrote defiant songs for Markos's communist friends, testing the tunes on an old piano before Markos played them on his beloved *lyra*. Sometimes, the *kafenzies* locked the door and his young grandson would come out and play his long-necked *baglama*, too. The men drank, and sang, and railed against the government. When feelings escalated, tables were pushed back and the men would vent their emotions by dancing. Arms across shoulders, they would stamp and leap to the beat as passions rose.

Markos and I talked about getting married, about having children together. We made plans to be wed the following spring. Spyridon gave us his blessing, and for the first time, a kind of harmony developed between the three of us.

*　*　*

Zacharia and I started to work shifts. One week he would start at 1 a.m., kneading, rising and baking, and I would come in at 7a.m., open the shop and serve the customers while he slept. The next week we would reverse roles. One morning, at 7 a.m., already late for work, I hurried towards Syntagma Square, thankful that the city seemed quieter than usual. In fact, there was nobody about at all. No pedestrians, no traffic on the roads. It felt strange, almost dreamlike.

As I walked, the ground stared to vibrate, and a great roaring and clanking filled my ears. I remembered the Kefalonia earthquake of '53 and looked up, terrified, expecting to see the buildings swaying. The noise grew, until a great tank rolled right in front of me.

The monster was followed by an armoured car. A soldier leaped out of the vehicle and yelled at me. 'You, stop! Papers, ID!'

Shaking, I delved into my purse and handed him my ID card.

'Hands against the wall!' he ordered, roughly turning me around. He snatched my handbag and rummaged through it. 'Where are you going in such a hurry?'

'I work at the bakery. I'm late, sir.'

His glare frightened me. A bully for sure. Arrogant and in authority: a dangerous combination.

'Raise your hands above your head, I'm going to search you. Resist and you'll be shot!'

'Shot?' I squeaked.

My tormentor was a man you wouldn't cross. My insides curdled and a pulse throbbed in my temple. He patted me down, squeezing my breasts, cupping my mound and stroking my buttocks with unnecessary fervour. My face burned.

'Go!' he said. I was shaking so badly I couldn't move for a moment. 'Go!' he repeated.

I picked up my handbag from the kerb and ran. More tanks were rolling into Syntagma from all four corners of the square. The military were lined up outside the tomb of the unknown soldier and parliament buildings. I seemed to be the only citizen on the street. I was desperate to continue running, to get out of there as soon as possible, but I did not know what might happen. Though I held my head high and marched with an air of authority, my insides were quaking.

Mr Zacharia stood in the shop doorway, his face a mask of concern.

'You're late, Sofia!'

'Sorry,' I sobbed, still feeling the soldier's hands all over me. 'They searched me, the military. Touched me all over. I'm so shaken, so ashamed.' I pushed past him, covered my face with my hands and wept. 'What's going on?' I asked when my composure returned.

'Don't you listen to the wireless, Sofia? Not that you can now. We've got a media blackout and a military coup. You need to go to the police station and get a special pass to be on the streets at this time of the morning. I'll come with you. The constitution has been suspended. Those *malakas* out there can arrest anyone they like . . . or shoot them if they resist. They've arrested the army's commander-in-chief. As a country, we're powerless, crippled.'

236

I stared at him, wishing I'd paid more attention to the political situation, but it all seemed so complicated.

'They're rounding up the communists, shipping them out like the Jews in wartime. Parliament and the royal palace are in military hands. They're arresting people. Flour-man Fannes told me they've commandeered his boat and packed it with communists, shipping them off to the prison islands – Makronisos, Gyaros, and the like. It's another holocaust! Holy Mother, haven't we suffered enough?' He slapped his forehead, leaving a floury handprint. 'The country's in the grip of the Colonels. The prime minister's disappeared! Some say he's been assassinated – others claim they're holding Kanellopoulos captive, or he's run away. Who can know? *Malakas!*' He blew at the ceiling. 'Anyway, get the bread into the shop, then put the *paximathi* into the ovens to dry out. People will want rusks to hoard – they always do when crisis threatens. Quick as you can, Sofia.'

Markos was in Kos, counting goats. Would he know what was going on?

'What about Markos? Do you think he'll be all right?'

Zacharia frowned. 'If anyone knows he's a commie he's in danger. The powers that have this country in their clutches are shooting renegades or shipping them out to God knows where. Prison islands. You should warn Markos to hide, and you must stay away from him.'

'But who's behind it all? Why is this happening to us?'

'The Yanks – think they can rule the world. I suspect the British are secretly behind it, too. Afraid of the Russians, see. Desperate to stamp out the reds.' He shook his head. 'If Markos phones, tell him to be very careful. More than three men together are counted as a subversive group and liable to be shot on the spot! I'm going to turn on the radio in the back of the shop so we can keep up to date with what's going on. Only the military channel's broadcasting, but at least it'll keep us informed. What *malaka* hell has this country turned into?'

Markos was due home later that day, and the overwhelming need to protect him filled me with panic. Both Zacharia and I worked in silence all morning, concentrating on the radio. The military music stopped every hour to publicise the latest list of rules for the general public. We were both shocked to hear: *Army Decree number 13: playing or listening to music that is not broadcast by the military is forbidden.*

I swallowed. Music was so great a part of my life. Even when I could not sing, I loved to listen to it. And poor Spyridon – it was his livelihood. What would he do?

* * *

When my work at the bakery was done, I rushed home, only to find my door broken open and the contents of my apartment scattered. Afraid, I rushed to the *kafenio* where I knew I would find Markos's friends. But it was empty and locked. I peered through the window, and there, painted on the white wall, was the quote from Che Guevara that had become the group's slogan: *If you tremble with indignation at every injustice, then you are a comrade of mine.*

I hurried back towards Syntagma Square. By this time, the sun had gone down and the street lights were out. In the twilight, I heard a terrible wailing that somehow seemed familiar. Filled with dread, I turned in the direction of the voice. There was Aphroditi, chained to a lamp post in the centre of the *platea*. She clutched her husband's severed head.

Unable to breathe, I almost collapsed. After a second, I rushed towards her, but a guard stepped in my way and grabbed my arms.

'Leave, or it'll be the worse for you,' he said.

'She's my friend!'

'Woman! I'm telling you, get out of here. I'm just doing my job!' Although he held himself stiffly, his eyes were wild and sparked with fear. 'This is a friendly warning, daughter. If you're seen showing compassion towards her, you'll succumb to a worse punishment yourself. Go now, vamoose, scoot – remove yourself!'

I ran back to my home and phoned Spyridon.

'They're rounding up the communists. They've killed Aphroditi's husband, you won't believe what they've done. It's too terrible.' I could hardly speak for sobbing. 'I'm afraid for Markos!'

'Where is he?'

'Kos. He's due back on the ferry at 4 a.m. My home's been broken into. Everything's thrown about.'

'Is there anything to connect you with the communists, Sofia?'

'No, of course not . . .' Then I remembered my book of rebel songs. 'I'm not sure. I need to check.'

'Get out of there – you're in danger! Go and stay with a friend. I'll collect Markos from the ferry. Go, do it now – the situation's critical!'

I grabbed clothes and stuffed them into a bag. I searched for my songbook, and it seemed to be the only thing missing. What was going on? Surely they didn't think I was a threat to the government. I was only a singer – an ex-singer. I pulled the door closed, even though the lock was smashed. I kept to the backstreets and alleys until I arrived at the bakery. Mr Zacharia was there.

'My home's been ransacked. Can I sleep under the counter like in the old days?'

He looked gaunt and grave. 'No, you can sleep in the cellar. Much safer. Help me move the counter.'

We lugged the heavy timber bench forward and I saw there was a trapdoor in the wooden floor. He went into the back and returned with a small torch.

I followed him down some wooden steps and found a room the size of the shop above. There were ten mattresses covering most of the floor. Nearly all were mouldy. There was a coal-chute leading up to the backstreet, with a grille above letting in the only light and air.

'What is this place?'

'We hid Jews here in the war. Spyridon and Theo's father would smuggle them out of the city at night.'

'So you knew Markos before?'

Zacharia nodded. 'I went to school with Theo's father, flour-man Fannes, and Spyridon. Between the four of us, we managed to save over two thousand souls. Markos and Theo were very young, but they delivered essential messages for us. Without the boys' help, our work would have been impossible.' He stared at nothing for a second, his mouth turned down. 'One of them would drive the flour van over that grille. The van had a trapdoor in the floor. At the port, they were loaded onto ships in flour sacks, just a few at a time.'

'Oh. You did that? *He* did that . . . ?'

'Keep it to yourself, Sofia. I have no wish to end up like Aphroditi's husband.' At the surprise on my face he said softly, 'The woman I loved was Jewish.'

I was afraid to speak, afraid of saying the wrong thing, but there was no need; he answered my unspoken question.

240

'She never came back from Auschwitz.'

'Oh, Mr Zacharia, I'm so sorry.'

He looked away, then glanced up at the grid as a vehicle drove over it.

'There's a tap and a latrine behind that curtain.' He pointed to the corner. 'And a candle, but try not to use it. We don't want to attract attention when it's dark outside.' He fumbled in the pocket of his grey trousers and produced a box of matches. 'Here, take these.'

From the faint light that filtered down through the floor-boards from the shop, I could see there was writing all over the peeling whitewashed walls. Different sizes, notes, small drawings.

He turned away. 'I must go. They'll come here looking for you. I'll drop a loaf down the coal-chute in the morning.'

He hurried up the steps, lowered the trapdoor, and I heard the old counter being dragged over the floor above.

In the dark, I tried to remember which was the cleanest-looking mattress, and finally lay down. With no watch or clock, I wondered where Markos was, and prayed Spyridon found him before the police did. I don't know if I slept. My thoughts drifted through my life: my parents, the orphanage, the starvation that followed, Markos, my singing. Those glorious songs would have uplifted me now. Even to hum them would have given me cour-age, strength. But in the silence and darkness of the cellar, I was overcome with fear for Markos, and for myself.

After what seemed like an endless length of time, I opened my eyes and realised I could make out the shape of the coal-chute. Dawn had arrived. For a moment, I was disorientated. I blinked rapidly, staring at the floor, then I realised ... The moment I moved, a crackling sound came from the cement. A thousand cockroaches disappeared in an instant. I stared at the bare concrete and whimpered.

As the light strengthened, I could hear Mr Zacharia above me, going about his morning toil. I recognised the sound of the back door, then a shower of dirt came down the chute as the grate was lifted for the first time in who knew how many years. I hurried over, desperate to catch the bread before it hit the floor. It was so hot I almost dropped it.

Where was Markos? I glanced around, wondering where the roaches had gone, dreading the night ahead. The only indication of time passing was the length of the shaft of light shining down the coal-chute, moving as slowly as the hour hand of a clock.

* * *

I stood in the beam of light, my face turned up, feeling the sun's warmth on my skin. Time crept by and I guessed it was early afternoon. The light-shaft grew longer again and slipped towards the left. I jumped every time I heard footsteps above, or whenever someone walked over the grate. The walls seemed to be closing in, the spacious cellar becoming smaller. I was trapped in a room with cockroaches waiting for darkness to descend. The peeling walls drew my attention, and while there was enough light, I decided to read the scribbled notes on the walls.

I am with Mama, Papa, and my baby brother. Soshi Munkle. 8½ years old from Aristotle Street.

Dear Sister, stay safe in Canada. Nana, Josh, and Sarah are with me. We will meet again. Kala Menzies.

I have a toothache! It stinks in here! David Cohen, 15.

242

There were hundreds of messages. Some were sad, while others were full of hope. I thought about the poor wretches who had passed that way and wondered how many had survived the war and come back to thank Mr Zacharia, or Markos and his friends.

The sound of heavy stamping above took me out of my brooding. Soldiers' boots, muffled shouting. Trouble. Wide-eyed, I stared at the ceiling and followed the footsteps across the floor above, blinking away the dust and flour that sprinkled down with each stomp.

Something heavy fell to the floor, followed by banging and clattering. Zacharia warning me? Should I climb out through the coal grid? What if they discovered the cellar? They might kill Mr Zacharia like Aphroditi's husband. I imagined his severed head and started shaking.

Then Zacharia's angry voice boomed from above. 'If you find her, tell her from me she's lost her job! I need somebody I can rely on!' he thundered. 'Any of you got a sister who can knead bread dough?'

The ruckus seemed to calm down. I wanted to hug him. Dust continued to rain from between the floorboards as they marched out of the shop.

* * *

The sunlight had gone and with the dark came my dread of the cockroaches' return. I sat on the bottom stair, my skirt tightly wrapped around my legs. To my relief, the shop above became quiet, but in the silence, every small noise seemed to pierce my skin. If only I had washed myself while the basement was lighter. My unease picked up every rustle, amplified the faintest sounds, and my eyes strained to detect movement across the dusky floor. Soon it would be night and I would not be able to stay awake.

Footsteps in the backstreet drew my attention. The grid screeched as it moved. I dipped into the space under the stairs, pressed myself into the corner, felt cobwebs on the back of my neck, and held my breath. A fat paper bag, two corners twisted into tight ringlets, slid down the chute and landed on the floor. I realised it was food from Mr Zacharia. I leaped up to retrieve it, catching a whiff of the delicious olive bread.

'Thank you,' I whispered as I bent.

Suddenly I was splayed on the floor with no notion of what had hit me. Something big and heavy, filling the coal-hole, had followed the bread. In a terrifying second, I realised a man had come down the chute. Trapped in the dark, I fought with all I had, kicking and scratching and biting. He groaned, fended off my blows and tried to catch my wrists.

'Stop! Stop, it's me!' he whispered urgently.

Markos!

I pulled back, gasping, then crying for joy in his arms, pressing myself against his chest. Like a bolt of lightning, he filled the room with energy.

'Oh, Markos! I've been so worried. What's going on? The police – or the army, I don't know – they came looking for me. They broke into my home and ransacked the place.'

He rocked me, smoothed my hair and whispered endearments until I calmed down.

'It's the junta,' he explained. 'They're rounding up the communists. Some traitor has passed them a list and we're on it.'

I tucked my head under his chin, squeezed my knees together and buried my face in his chest. I fitted perfectly into that innocent place against him and, for a few seconds, I believed everything would be all right. We were safe for the moment.

'We'll stay here for a couple of days, while my beard grows enough to disguise me – and then Zacharia will take us to Piraeus for the dawn ferry to Crete.'

'We're going to Crete?'

Images raced through my head, lifting my spirit. I had seen a little of the island while working for Spyridon. Life consisted of eating, sleeping, preparing for the theatre and singing, but between events, we had travelled from one end of the island to the other on winding roads through quaint towns and villages. My first appearance was always in Chania and I loved that town above all others. Then I would perform in Rethymnon, and after, on to Agios Nikolaos, where we would return on the ferry to Athens. Ag. Nik., as the new breed of hippy tourists called it, heaved with discotheques, gift shops, and resonated with a popular wave of protest music that came from America. This had swept through Europe: Joni Mitchell, Bob Dylan. Songs of peace and freedom.

'Come and lie with me,' Markos said, easing me towards the mattresses.

'God, no! The place is teeming with cockroaches. They make my skin crawl. I'm staying on the stairs. There're thousands of them, Markos, the floor was completely covered.'

'Ah, you poor old thing. What time does Zacharia come back to work?'

'Between twelve and one.'

*   *   *

We sat on the stairs for six hours, dozing in each other's arms, whispering plans for our future, until I must have fallen asleep.

A noise woke me suddenly and I realised Zacharia was unlocking the back door to the shop.

'He's here, Markos,' I whispered, as pinpricks of light filtered down from between the floorboards.

Markos made three sharp knocks in the boards and the light above us went out. I could hear Zacharia moving the counter and soon we were standing in the dark shop.

'What is it? You shouldn't come out, it's too dangerous.'

'The cellar's full of cockroaches,' Markos explained.

'Right, well, I can't have them coming up into the shop. You know what to do.' He lifted a couple of white bags from the shelves. 'Baking soda and sugar, mix them together and place a plate of water next to it. The roaches'll be done for by tomorrow night. Hurry now, Markos. I'll keep a lookout out front. The military police are in the streets.'

'I'll go in the back and start the dough, shall I, Mr Zacharia?' I asked.

'Good plan.'

Ten minutes later, with the shop lights still out, Zacharia and Markos were shifting the counter back in place. Then Zacharia delved into his pocket and pulled out a key on a string, which he handed to Markos.

'Go to my house,' he said, nodding at the back door. 'You'll find clothes in the wardrobe. Disguise yourselves. I'll pick you up at half five and take you to the port. The ferry leaves at six. Be ready. Get in the back of the van as soon as I pull up.'

Markos nodded, took my floury hand and tugged me through the back door.

* * *

I woke, curled into the contours of Markos's body. He, propped on one elbow, gazed lovingly at my face.

'We have to go soon,' he whispered. I wanted to stay where I was. 'Come on, let's shower,' he said. 'We'll be a long time on the ferry.' He pulled me to him and kissed me softly.

We made love in the shower, dressed hurriedly, waited just inside the front door. When Zacharia pulled up, we tumbled into the back of his van. At the port, Zacharia got our tickets to Crete, then drove to the boarding ramp. Luckily, he knew the stevedore and asked about his family while we scurried up to the passenger deck. There was barely time to thank him properly.

I gave him a fierce hug. 'You've been like a father to me, Mr Zacharia, and I love you for it. Please stay safe!'

'Go, go!' he said. 'The bread's in the oven, I have to get back!' His voice was gruff, and his damp eyes avoided mine. 'Here, this is yours.' He pushed an envelope into my hand. 'All those years you worked for nearly nothing – well, I always put something aside for you for when you needed it. Use it wisely.'

Then he turned away and was gone.

A breeze, soft as the breath of spring, made the tears prickle on my cheeks.

'Come on, let's find a comfortable place to relax,' Markos said. 'We have plans to make. This is a historic day for us. A fresh start, Sofia.'

I hoped with all my heart it was. A cottage, steady work, children: these were my dreams and I felt myself on the verge of them.

In a matter of minutes, we were settled in a quiet corner at the back of the middle deck. Markos spread a blanket we had brought with us. Under the rear stairway, we sat on the floor with our backs against the wall.

He slid his arm around my shoulders. 'I'm hoping it's going to be third time lucky,' he said, as the ship rocked gently and I knew we were pulling out of Piraeus harbour. 'Sofia, I'm asking you again – will you marry me?'

I smiled inside, but kept my face straight. 'You know my answer, Markos. As soon as you have a regular job. As soon as we're safe. I want us to have children, and I know you do too, so let's set the foundations for a family in Crete, and once we've done that, I'll say yes.'

He rolled his eyes. 'You're so practical. Can't you just do something spontaneous occasionally? Let's go for it, live dangerously.'

'Go for what? I've had enough danger to last me a lifetime. I want to feel secure. Bliss for me is you coming home from work and me serving up your favourite food, putting the kids to bed and then watching television with you, listening to music on the record player and singing along. I'm not a complicated person, am I?' I smiled with the thought. 'I dream of you putting your knife and fork together and saying, "God, that was good!" I imagine bathing our children, telling them bedtime stories until they fall asleep with smiles on their faces.'

Even as I spoke, I was lost in my imagination and hadn't realised I had closed my eyes. Silent for a moment, content with my dreams, I embraced this new beginning on the island of Crete.

'What's your vision of the future?' I whispered.

'The same as yours,' he whispered. 'But I want our children to grow up with the freedom to be themselves, in a country where the government isn't telling them who they can speak to, or what they should or should not wear, or which songs they're allowed to sing.' He started humming a Bob Dylan melody.

'Markos, shush! You'll get us into trouble!'

My dreams shrank within me. Would he ever give up the fight?

* * *

Night had fallen by the time we arrived at the bustling port of Heraklion, capital of Crete. Wagons of live sheep and pigs rattled down the ramp. Impatient travellers pushed and shoved to get off the ferry, while others hurried on board to collect cardboard boxes that had come from Athens. Students also came on the ferry to collect carpet bags sent from home. Clean underwear, freshly baked biscuits from *Yiayá*, cassettes for their tape players and the latest music and messages from girlfriends. Short, strong Cretan men pulled trolleys aboard to collect stock for their gift shops, and women stood on their toes, searching for family members.

Several stevedores swiped their arms through the air, shouting '*Ela! Ela!*' as if it would make anyone move faster. A loud whistle came from beyond the crowd, making Markos stretch his neck.

'They're here,' he said. 'Come on.'

We rounded the throng and found a man with red, swollen eyes, Yosef, and his son, Andreas. The son was about the same age as Markos. They stood by a battered pickup with no doors or tailgate. We got in the back and sat on the rolled-up blanket with our backs pressed against the cab.

'What are we waiting for?' I asked, as cars and trucks disappeared into the city.

'He's picking something up off the ferry.'

I stared when Yosef and two stevedores appeared with a pine coffin, which hardly fitted in the centre of the pickup. Markos and I squeezed into opposite corners while they tied it down.

'Can't they turn it on its side?' I asked Markos. 'Give us a bit more room?'

'No, of course not – she'll roll over, and the flowers will be crushed.'

'You don't mean there's somebody in there? You're pulling my leg.'

Markos laughed, shaking his head. 'The grandmother. She died in an Athens hospital, but they have to bury her in her own village with her ancestors.'

We clung onto the coffin handles to stop it slipping from under the ropes as we climbed a steep hill.

'Where're we going?' I asked, trying not to think about the poor woman who lay between us.

'Zoniana, in the mountains. We'll be safe there even if somebody comes looking for us. The locals are a fierce lot, and there's always a couple with Kalashnikovs guarding the village.'

I wasn't sure the information made me feel any better.

CHAPTER 27
SOFIA

Crete, 1967.

AT FIRST, I WAS AFRAID of these fierce fighting men in their beige jodhpurs, black shirts and polished knee-high boots. They wore crocheted scarves around their heads, the fringes falling over their foreheads like random curls. Determined, bold eyes shone from tanned, rugged faces. I glanced at the daggers with ornate bone-carved handles tucked into their blood-red cummerbunds, wondering if they ever used them.

But my fear was unfounded. The villagers knew of Markos and treated him like a hero. They made us very welcome. After a night sleeping at Andreas's house, we were given a small stone cottage on the outskirts. The village nestled in the shadow of the great snow-topped mountain, Psiloritis. The locals shared what they could with us; soon, we had old but clean blankets, badly fitting curtains, odd plates and dishes. Touched by their kindness, I wanted to give something in return, but it was impossible. They knew so much more than me.

Markos worked for the shepherds, slaughtering and skinning sheep and goats and helping to plant the hemp fields. At night, he played his *lyra* in the smoke-filled *kafenio*. Village men sang rebel songs and passed around a joint or two. For the women, evenings were spent in the street spinning wool, or embroidering elaborate clothes which were taken down to the next village, Anogia, and sold to the street traders.

When the village priest, who was also the baker, broke his wrist, I offered to help in the bakery. There was something therapeutic about the kneading of dough and I found peace in the back of the kitchen.

For months, life was almost idyllic. I was content until one evening in October, when Markos didn't come home for his evening meal. I placed the plate of *pasticcio* on a pan of hot water, with an upturned plate on top, then hurried to the *kafenio* to ask if anyone had seen him. The sight that met my eyes was all confusion. The room, packed with village men, stank of cigarette smoke and alcohol, and they were all drunk. The older men banged their sticks on the floor, while they shouted the warrior *mantinades*.

I listened for a moment as they chanted and banged the tables uproariously; the little glasses and *karafākis* leaped to the rhythm.

My Cretan knife held
As the funeral bell's knell
For Che was our brother
And a fighter as well!

We cry for our comrade
Our hearts truly sad
They killed Che Guevara
In black we are clad!

On the peak of Psiloritis
A little bird sings
But deep in our hearts
Guevara's death stings!

From that day, when Markos received the news of his idol Che Guevara's death, he not only wore the black beret, he also donned the black shirt and jodhpurs of the Cretan fighting men.

* * *

One morning, several weeks later, Markos came rushing into the bakery, sheep's blood staining his hands.

'I have to leave!' he said. 'Right now. I must return to Athens. Manno is waiting to take me to the port for the night ferry.'

He started washing his hands urgently.

My first thought was the marijuana fields outside the village, which I'd come to understand were the village's main source of income. I'd heard there had been trouble before. Someone was shot when the police raided the village. Several men were arrested and taken to Heraklion prison. In retaliation, the village men had kidnapped the chief of police. Nobody would explain how the matter was resolved, but somehow it was. Soon, the hemp fields with their central crop of cannabis were re-planted, and the local marijuana trade continued to flourish.

'Markos, what's wrong? You're frightening me.'

'The *kafenio* had a phone call. Papa's had a stroke. They don't think he'll survive.'

I felt sick. 'Oh, Spyridon. Oh, God. I'm so sorry, Markos. You must be frantic. Of course we must go.'

'You stay here, Sofia. I'm going on my own.'

'Like hell you are. I'm coming with you.'

He marched to the cottage, hurriedly pushing a few things into a bag. I was behind him.

'You're not going without me!'

Two hours later, we arrived at the port of Heraklion. The ferry was late, which made Markos nervous.

'I don't like standing around here. Someone might recognise me.' He grabbed my hand. 'Come on, let's go into the fort – at least we'll be able to see the ferry before it arrives.'

I stared at the enormous sandstone blocks of Fort Koules, then at Markos as he peered out to sea. In Crete, we had set solid cornerstones on which to build a marriage and start a family, and I had been looking forward to our future. Now, I had a feeling those foundations were about to crumble, and felt the world shift from under our feet.

When the ferry arrived, we hurried out of the shadows, heads down, nearly the first people to board. Once the ship had weighed anchor, we stood at the back rail, eyes fixed on the city of Heraklion as it slipped towards the horizon. Later, while I dozed on the upper deck, Markos joined a group of men. They talked quietly with their heads together. When I woke, I found him alone at the front rail. He stared across the sea, towards Athens.

'Sofia, listen,' he said, when I reached his side. 'I don't want to frighten you, but there've been developments in Athens. We're in greater danger than I first thought. It's better if you stay on the ship and return to Crete.'

'No, I won't hear of it! What's happened?'

'The communists were promised amnesty and inclusion in the country's politics, if they surrendered their arms. Yesterday, all over the country, my comrades complied. Thousands threw their weapons to the ground in Syntagma Square, and others did the same in the centres of the other mainland cities.' He rubbed his hands over his face. 'It was all a government lie. My comrades were cheated. Now – defenceless – they're being rounded up and sent to prison camps all over the country to be "re-indoctrinated".'

I stared at him. How were the people supposed to have faith in their government, when they lied and cheated so openly? I wanted to share his concern, talk about the injustice and our predicament, but I didn't know what to say. We sat shoulder to shoulder, waiting for the ship to dock.

I had fallen asleep when the loud rattle of the anchor chain woke me with a start.

'Come on,' Markos said tenderly, his face pale from lack of sleep and worry. 'Let's go and see how the old goat's doing.' He smiled sadly. 'You realise he'll probably ask if you can sing yet?'

'It will be all right,' I said, hugging his waist.

'One of my comrades from the old days is meeting us. Let's go to the back rail and look out, see if we can spot him as we dock. They won't let us off before the biggest wagons have gone ashore.'

Everyone pushed and shoved towards the disembarkation ramp, with such determination you would think the ship was sinking. We stood at the empty rail overlooking the quayside while Markos searched for his friend in the dawn miasma. I stared out towards the city, hoping to catch a glimpse of the Parthenon on the horizon. As the sun appeared, the Acropolis was bathed in golden light, and beyond it, Mount Lycabettus. Memories returned of my walk up there when I was a girl. I'd thought about that day so often. How much I enjoyed the afternoon with my family, having no knowledge of the horror that awaited only hours later.

'There he is!' Markos cried, pointing to the throng of people waiting to board. 'He'll take us to the hospital.' He waved both arms over his head and after a moment said, 'He's seen us, and look, the passengers are leaving. Let's go down.'

When we got to the bottom of the ship's stairway, Markos pulled me into a corner.

'Listen to me, Sofia. If anything happens to me while we're here, I want you to run, okay? Don't hang about, just run! Run for my sake. Give me your word, now, before we get off the ferry.'

'But—'

'Just give me your damn word, now!'

Startled by the fierceness in his voice, I felt tears in my eyes.

'I promise,' I whispered. 'You know I'll do anything you want.'

'Well, know this – I love you more than life itself. No matter what happens, I love you that much. Always remember it – even if you don't understand my behaviour, even if I seem cruel and uncaring, *I love you*. Now and forever, for always.'

'I will. But Markos, you're frightening me. Whatever happens, we're in this together.'

'Don't be stupid! You're not listening, damn it! We're not in anything together. At the first sign of any danger, you get as far away from me as possible. If the authorities catch me, they may hang me, or shoot me, or hack off my head. If you're with me, you'll suffer a worse fate, right in front of me, until they eventually kill you, too. That's the way *they* work.'

I wanted to ask who *they* were, but he continued quickly and there was a sense of urgency about him.

'So, you *will* get away from me. Otherwise I will suffer tenfold, once for me and ten times more for you.' He rubbed the furrows in his forehead. 'I shouldn't have let you come.'

'I had to be with you.'

I was filled with foreboding and more afraid than I had ever been in my life.

256

'Now you get off this ship without me and follow the other passengers out of the port. At some point, we'll pull up beside you, and you'll get into the car as quickly as possible. Go!'

In a few minutes, Markos had become a different person. A fierce soldier. A leader who gave orders. I had never seen him like this before and became very uneasy. I pulled his face towards me and kissed him hard, then turned and ran from the ship.

The sun rose quickly. I followed his instructions. Once outside the port, I walked towards the bus station. A black car pulled up alongside me. I dived in and the vehicle pulled away before I had closed the door.

We drove to the hospital, but it was all in vain. Spyridon was gone; he had died in the night. I cried for the martyr behind the showman – the man who performed for his own audience, while grieving for his beloved family, and always fearing for his much-loved son. Markos seemed so desolate, blaming himself for not getting to his father's side sooner. We stayed by the bedside for half an hour, then there were forms to fill in. Spyridon would be buried the next day.

We were taken to a friend's house outside the town, on the outer fringe of the suburbs. They presented us with a room barely larger that the bed it contained, then invited us to their table. Our hosts shared their bread, village sausage and a jug of the indigenous Savatiano wine. We ate and drank hungrily before they left us alone.

'I love you,' I whispered later, lying in Markos's arms. 'I'm so sorry for your loss, my darling.'

He squeezed my hand, but it was a long time before he spoke.

'Don't forget what I said. We are both in danger while we're here. The military are trying to purge the country of communists and the might of America's behind them.'

257

'I feel safe with you.'

'My family felt safe, too. They lived not fifty metres from this place. From the window, you can see the field they're buried in. You can't imagine how awful it was.'

'I *can* imagine,' I said, my anger rising. 'I suffered the same loss, remember?'

Once again, he was silent for a long time.

'Can you ever forgive me?'

I held his hand. 'I don't have to. When I think about it, it wasn't actually you that killed them, do you see? The real culprits are those who manipulate the political situation for their own gain. The murderers were the politicians, the ones who gave orders to bomb your family's area just because they wanted to show the communists they were in control. They are the killers. You're no more guilty of killing my family than the British pilots are guilty of murdering your mother and siblings.'

'Thank you,' he whispered, and I heard how much it meant to him. He stared at the ceiling. 'I'm going to have to dig them up.'

'Oh, God, no. Markos, no. Let them rest in peace.'

'Papa would want it,' he whispered. 'He loved my mother and my siblings so much. He would want them to be buried with him. I'll go before daybreak, take a sack and a shovel. It's been so long, there'll only be bones.'

He turned and hid his face in the side of my neck. His breathing was deep and laboured, his face wet. I held him tightly, my heart breaking for him.

* * *

I woke alone, the sun streaming through the window on a glorious day. Then, my surroundings brought back the reason why we were there. Oh, Spyridon ... May his soul rest in peace. But where was Markos? I wondered if he was having breakfast with our kind benefactors? I rose, stretched every sinew, and reached for the window to let in some fresh air.

Although the house sat in the suburbs, it turned its back on the city and a picturesque country scene lay before my eyes. Distant olive trees, carefully pruned into silver-green lollipops, stood in straight rows. A vineyard followed the contours of the gentle hillside like the tines of a fork. Next to the grapevines, a wheat field rippled in the gentle breeze like creamy ocean waves, and in the foreground, a flock of sheep grazed in a lush meadow. Then, my eye was caught by an odd patch in that field. Something jarring, not right. A square of brown earth.

Markos had committed himself to reuniting his family in death. I watched, desperate to go down and support him, but knowing it would be wrong to invade his sadness at that private moment. I imagined the tears on his face, and the pain in his heart, as he recognised and pieced together his mother and siblings. As the weight of grief fell on me, Markos straightened and turned to face the house for a moment. He could not possibly see me from that distance, but it seemed as though he knew I was there.

An hour later, head bowed and shoulders slumped, he returned to the house. The family were together, awaiting reburial.

After the funeral, we gathered outside the cemetery and received condolences from lots of people in the music business. Spyridon's neighbour gave out spoonfuls of *koliva*, boiled wheat and nuts sweetened with honey and cinnamon. Several of Markos's friends and fellow communists came to support him, although the junta had placed a ban on more than three people gathering together. They all came back to the house where Markos and I slept.

Zacharia hurried over. It brought tears to my ears that he had come.

'Condolences to you both. Sorry I can't stay – there's bread in the oven. I went to visit Spyridon in hospital and he gave me this for you, Markos. He said it was the only thing of real value that he had left.' He reached into his pocket, and when he opened his great fist, the small gold locket that had always been fixed to Spyridon's tiepin lay in the palm of his hand. 'I believe it was your mother's.'

'It should be buried with him,' Markos said.

Zacharia shook his head. 'No, he was insistent that you should have it. He said it was his most precious possession and he could not bear the thought of it being buried.' He handed it over. 'The little clasp is broken off, but you can probably get it open with a knife.'

'There's no need. It probably contains a photo of my mother.' He slipped it into his jacket pocket.

'Your father was much liked, Markos,' I said, trying to ease his pain although my own grief was intense. 'Look at all these people, paying their respects.'

'They should go away from here. They put themselves and us in danger.' Markos glanced around nervously. 'I'm going to ask the men to leave now. Do me a favour and go around the women, will you?'

He had hardly uttered the words when military vehicles roared in from both ends of the road. People started running, rushing into each other. Soldiers leaped out of Land Rovers. Rifles were pointed skywards, boots stomped menacingly as a team of military men surrounded the house. We were trapped, penned in. A baby cried, a woman yelled, 'Get off me!' Somebody was shoved to the ground, his arm twisted up his back until he cried out. The tray of *koliva* scattered.

Everyone was forced into the small house.

'We fell into their trap,' Markos muttered. 'They knew I would come to my father's funeral.' He breathed in. 'I have to give myself up before they start killing people.'

Before I had a chance to argue with him, one of the police yelled through the door.

'Silence!'

We pressed against each other as the room became more crowded. Children wailed and the air became unbearably stuffy with the cloying smell of sweat and the dry, brittle stink of fear. A table was dragged to the front door and one by one people were questioned and their identity cards scrutinised. They were either set free or handcuffed and shoved into a van.

An air of panic filled the room. Most of the men were bundled into the van. One of the young men hurled abuse, swearing and kicking as the police tried to manhandle him into the vehicle. He pulled a knife. There was a gunshot, a woman's scream, and the protester's boots left two furrows in the earth as his limp body was dragged away.

The terror was palpable. Nobody spoke. People were trembling; everyone stared, white-faced.

'Stop it!' Markos yelled at the military. 'It's me you're looking for! These people have just come to say goodbye to my father. They're not guilty of any wrongdoing!'

A soldier pulled Markos roughly through the door. I moved so that I could see what was happening to him. He was shoved so fiercely he fell sprawling to the ground, catching his head on the corner of the van door. Blood spurted from a cut over his eye and ran down his face. Without thinking, I leaped to help him.

One of the officers made a grab for me, but I managed to wriggle free and threw myself at Markos, who was getting to his feet.

'Get lost, you filthy slut! It's over between us!' Markos yelled, before slapping me so fiercely across the face I fell into the dirt, stunned. 'Stay away from me, you bitch!' He turned to the officer checking documents. 'Do us all a favour, shoot this festering *poutana* – she's given everyone around here the clap!'

I listened to his words in a daze of horror. Shamed, my face burned from the force of his hand and the shock of his words. Even though I saw what he was doing, I couldn't help the sobs escaping me. He was trying to save me, I knew that. If they knew that we loved each other, they would have tortured me in front of him. That was what he'd been trying to tell me before. I opened my mouth, longing to shout after him as they bundled him into the wagon and slammed the doors, knowing it would risk both our lives if I did.

'You! *Poutana!* Where's your ID?' the one at the table yelled at me, his lips curling in disgust.

I scrambled to my feet, resisting the urge to run, knowing I would be shot if I did. He peered at my face for a second.

'Pity,' he muttered. 'We'd have put you to good use.'

After taking my identity document, he ordered me into the next van, which was already half full of locals, all of whom had attended Spyridon's funeral. There were three other women: Agapi, a working girl, from Madam Magdalena's; Thina, the local midwife; and Honey, a cook from El Greco's.

Eventually, we were driven away. Our van was crammed with frightened mourners. Nobody knew where we were going. We all remembered earlier times in Athens's history when the people suffered one horror after another, so nobody wanted to speculate. We knew if we resisted, we would be shot without question.

Honey was a big woman. She wept quietly, her flesh trembling with each sob. She slipped her arm around my shoulders and we cried together. Agapi, who was not used to being awake in the daytime, remained quiet, her eyes fixed on nothing. Thina the midwife had been a close friend of Spyridon's for many years. Nobody knew the extent of their relationship, but I suspected it was more than platonic. Although she was not a woman to show her emotions, her white face and red-rimmed eyes told me she had spent the night in tears. I heard that she had also been on the team that had tried to save Spyridon's life.

'Girls,' Thina said, 'when they ask what you do, say cook and nurse. That way there's a chance we'll stay together.'

Twenty minutes later, we were dripping with sweat in the back of the airless van. Sickened, I started to think of the ovens of Auschwitz. Many of those poor devils met their end when the exhaust pipe was fed into the vehicle that they travelled in. Suddenly the air seemed rancid, poisonous, and I feared we were being exterminated. The stories in the press had been horrific; nobody even talked about them.

Then, with a lurch, we pulled to a halt and the rear doors were opened. I gasped for air, filling my lungs. We were at the port of Piraeus.

As we were pulled out of the van, I caught a glimpse of Markos, his back turned to me. I longed to rush over to him, but Thina held me.

'You'll only make more trouble for him, and for yourself. Whatever you do, don't let anyone know about the two of you.'

* * *

263

We were herded into small rooms and interrogated, one at a time. When it was my turn, I was shoved towards a desk and told to sit. After filling a form in, declaring my name, address, religion, and so on, my songbook was thrown in front of me.

A man in a smart grey uniform asked if the book was mine.

'It looks like a notebook I had . . . but how can I be sure?'

'Did you write the songs and poems inside?'

'I . . . I've written hundreds of songs and poems for many people. I can't remember most of them. They tell me what they want, and I think something up.'

'Write down the last song you remember!'

I'd written nothing but rebel songs for longer than I could recall, both in Athens and Zoniana in Crete. For a moment I couldn't think straight. I picked up the pen, my hand shaking, and then I wrote my mother's song as Mr Zacharia had translated it into Greek. I felt a wave of relief as I put the pen down and smiled up at him.

'Well done,' the officer said, with a sneer. 'But you made one mistake.'

I stared at the paper; there was nothing to connect me with the rebel songs.

'You forgot to change your handwriting.' He turned to his assistant and said the words that filled me with dread: 'Take her!'

'Where? No, no! I'm not a communist, I swear I'm not!'

His face did not change. 'You write rebel songs, and you're on our list of dissidents.'

*   *   *

An hour later, I found myself shoved into another overcrowded truck that belonged to flour-man Fannes. My only relief was that my friends were with me: Honey, Agapi, Thina and I clung together in a corner.

'Don't forget, separate when we're leaving the wagon, but when they ask what you did, what you were, say cook or nurse. That way we'll have access to food and medicines. We'll be better treated, too.'

Several of the women were wailing and the racket added to everyone's discomfort. Thina took control of the situation. I guess as a midwife, she was used to dealing with distressed women.

'Listen, everyone – we need to unite as a team if we're to survive this shit. So, let's get to know each other right now. I want everyone to say their name, where they're from and what they do. Then touch the person next to them, and they continue. Got it? I'll start. Thina Portokali, Pláka, midwife.'

She touched me.

'Sofia Bambaki, Syntagma, ex-singer.'

I touched Honey, and so it went on.

* * *

We stood in the cramped, windowless space for a long time. Silent, each with our own thoughts, our own fears. I began to wonder if we were all destined to suffocate. Then, the door opened and flour-man Fannes slid a bucket of water in. Everyone pushed forward, whimpering and trying to grab the bucket. Thina took charge again.

'Two swallows each. Then, if there's any left, the bucket will go round again. Now push back and I'll come round with the water.' The midwife squeezed between us. 'Heaven help any bitch that tries to cheat! 'Cos if you do, it'll be a broken nose you'll be nursing before we get out of here!'

The blast of fresh air when Fannes had opened the door dissipated the stench of urine and sweat for a while, and the tepid water refreshed us all. After several hours of confinement, we were unbalanced as the vehicle slammed to a halt. Dusk was falling by the time we jumped off the tailgate towards the unknown. Fannes was standing at the side of the wagon.

'Where are we?' I whispered, staring at the high fence and spotlights.

'Korydallos Prison. I'll tell Zacharia.'

I wondered why we had been in the truck for hours, when Korydallos was on the outskirts of Athens. Then, I realised it was probably because they were processing the men. There was no sign of them now.

Then I noticed the high barbed wire fence. Through that stark boundary, I stared at what seemed to be an endless, windowless cement building, and once again I recalled newsreels of Auschwitz.

We were marched towards the prison. I glanced over my shoulder at the city lights, reluctant to drag my eyes away from the free world. Once inside the tall gates, the place seemed deserted.

And then, a terrifying scream reverberated over the land. My blood chilled, and several of the others started to sob. What sort of hell were we going into?

CHAPTER 28
ZOË

Manchester, present day.

ZOË STOOD TOO NEAR THE platform edge and peered along the track. She tilted forward slightly in expectation, then dropped back onto her heels with the dullness of defeat. Anyone could see she was a smart, good-looking career woman dressed for work in high-quality clothes and shoes. Nobody would begin to imagine the pain in her heart, or the desolation that filled her mind, day after endless day. The constant feeling of failure as a wife – as a mother – had destroyed the bright, effervescent person she once was.

Zoë Johnson's soul was trapped in the dark, dank basement of life, and she wanted out.

Oblivious to the bustle of early-morning commuters, she shut out Manchester, the station and her misery. Determined to raise her spirits, she closed her eyes and invoked the island of Crete. Memories flooded back. Warm sunlight caressing her sun-bronzed shoulders. Lazy breakfasts on the quayside. Chania's charming waterfront. She remembered gazing over colourful wooden boats to the solid lighthouse, a beacon that told fishermen of a safe haven to its right and dangerous rocks to its left. One wrong decision, one mistake, and a terrible fate awaited the lonesome skipper.

On nearby tables, tourists had admired the picturesque harbour and smiled at little Josh sleeping in his pushchair.

'Enjoy the peace,' one woman said. 'It doesn't last long.'

'I know,' Zoë replied, nodding at Megan, who skipped and danced a few feet away. 'I have an overactive four-year-old too. She never sits still!'

They laughed together.

A night fisherman returned and chugged up to the quayside, metres from where they sat. Zoë remembered the cheeky wink of a waiter when her husband wasn't looking, and how good she'd felt in herself. So much had happened since that perfect day thirteen years ago.

* * *

Zoë glared at the train tracks and rocked slightly. Tears spilled from beneath her dark lashes. Somewhere in her life she had taken the wrong turn, missed the warnings and crashed onto the rocks.

She needed harmony at home, and she thought she'd had it. Now she realised the foundations of her marriage had been crumbling away for years, and nobody had noticed, until the entire fabric collapsed. One week's holiday, when they were all together, talking to each other and sharing dreams, was not enough to cement them together for the rest of the year.

Now, the very structure of their family life was utterly broken, beyond repair.

It was her fault. She had never concerned herself with the maintenance. There had always been her mother to take care of everyone's home life. And Zoë rewarded her mother by fulfilling her dreams of succeeding in a highly prestigious career.

She needed Frank's arms around her so badly, but if he was with her, she knew she would be pushing him away, frantic with worry about Megan or Josh.

The noise of the morning's commuters faded as she hugged herself. Withdrawing into the silence of her mind, she remembered the precious day when her baby girl was first placed, protesting loudly, on her chest. The full force of Zoë's love poured towards the tiny newborn. Her daughter would be amazing. She would be responsible for the next inventions – or become a doctor, saving people's lives, or enter politics like her father, making the world a better place. Her daughter's generation would change the world, choose kindness and love over hate and prejudice. Baby Megan was precious beyond belief and that conviction had never wavered.

Zoë heard the distant rumble of the next train. Commuters moved forward. Her weight shifted over one foot. She balled her fists, but the moment she closed her eyes the scene at that Cretan harbour returned. She and Frank were eating delicious eggs, on bread still warm from the bakery. Her chest expanded as she recalled the aroma. And there was Megan, in her new yellow sundress and sandals, fascinated by the gently bobbing boats.

She heard herself calling, 'Be careful, Megan!' as her little girl ventured closer to the water.

Her daughter looked back, grinning, and then returned to her parents.

Frank's fingers sought Zoë's across the table and, even before looking up, she knew he was smiling. They had so much to be thankful for. The perfect family, with perfect lives.

* * *

Zoë returned to the present and tried to forget her bitterness, his betrayal, how much she had loved him . . . and for a short while, hated him. When he first announced he was moving out, she hadn't been able to believe it. Angry, she had said 'Good!' Now, she was numb, despairing. She had lost the path back to his love. Megan had left her. Frank had left her. And now, so had Josh. If only she could talk to her mother . . . but that was impossible too.

She glanced around the platform. Under the glare of artificial light, people raced against time. There was no hint of happiness, friendship or support for each other in that place. Everything was unfriendly, cold and scentless. Nothing would change in the world if she was no longer a part of it.

In the echoing station, Zoë knew she could not live without the people she loved. They had been the sunshine of her life. Mama, Frank, Josh and Megan. All gone.

A computer-generated voice announced the next train. Only the vending machines, filled with junk food, stood still.

In just a second, Zoë's pain would be over.

* * *

Someone grabbed her arm – the shock made her jump out of the fog of desolation.

'Lady, can I help you?' the guard asked, pulling her back, then stepping away, keeping a safe distance.

Zoë flinched, blinked at the small Asian guard, then turned her back and fled towards the station exit. The train arrived and screeched to a halt.

The guard hurried after her and shouted, 'Madam, you dropped something!'

She hesitated, then took the business card from his out-stretched fist.

Samaritans.

Horrified, unable to respond, her mind was on rewind for a second. She had come so close. Filled by a compulsion to explain, she stared at the guard and searched for the right words.

He nodded at the card. 'They can help.'

She slipped it into her pocket, took a sideways glance at the train and groaned.

'Thanks,' she whispered, her voice trembling. 'I . . .' She gulped, frowning. 'It's my fault, you see. All my fault.'

The enormity of what might have been hit her. She placed her hands on her cheeks, her mouth falling open. Then she spun on her heels, about to disappear into the throng of Manchester's rush hour, lugging her turmoil with her.

'Would you like a cup of tea?' the guard called after her. 'I've finished my shift. It would be my pleasure, madam.'

Zoë pulled her chin in and stared at him incredulously, pushing her trembling fingertips over the lines in her forehead. She took a breath, her shoulders slumped, and she nodded.

They found a vacant corner in the bustling station café.

'Sometimes, it is necessary to talk to a stranger in order to get things straight in the mind,' he said. 'I am Dalip, madam.' He placed two steaming mugs on the table.

'Thank you, Dalip. I'm Zoë.' She sighed and tangled her fingers. 'I was going to . . .'

He lifted his hand in a halting gesture, shaking his head slowly like a tired horse.

'And I would be sitting here all alone right now instead of drinking Darjeeling with you.'

Zoë smiled sadly.

'Why not tell me about it? I have plenty of time, and sometimes it's easier to talk to a stranger. It can help to share your troubles. I am thinking that despite the hurt you are feeling, if you look at your situation from a fresh perspective, you will see it is not so bad after all.'

'Not so bad! You can't imagine ...' She sighed. 'It's such a long story, I don't know where to start.'

'At the beginning is certainly the best place. I am, as they say, all your ears.'

She stirred her tea in silence, gathering her thoughts. It took a few minutes for her insides to stop shaking.

'The last seven months have been hell. First, my daughter disappeared. She left a note, saying she had run away, but we had no idea why. I took it out on my husband and made his life hell, God knows why. In the end, he moved out, and I suspect he's having an affair with his secretary. My mother, who lived with us, returned to her homeland, Greece, without telling me she was dying. She was so ill, and I didn't even notice. I was hardly coping myself, too busy searching for my daughter, Megan. And now my son's had enough of me too. He's moving in with his father because he thinks I only care about his sister.' Her voice shook. 'It was the final straw, simply too much for me to lose, too much for anyone. And there's worse ... Because of my bad judgement, a young girl the same age as my daughter has been killed. She was seventeen, Dalip ... seventeen.'

Zoë's grief seemed to stick in her throat. Unable to speak, she sipped her tea. When she found her voice she asked, quietly, 'How did you know that I ... ?'

'We are trained to watch for these things. You see, the catastrophe is not only for the troubled person, like yourself, or their family. The poor train driver – it's terrible for him too. Even the passengers, over a thousand commuters on that train.' He lifted his chin towards the platform. 'They feel it, and when they realise what has happened, they get very upset. So many lives are changed by that one act of despair.'

'I didn't think . . .' She tried to imagine. 'Oh God, I didn't even think! I'm so ashamed.'

She looked up, glanced into his kind eyes, placed her palms together and made a little dip.

'This is my job,' he said. 'To spend eight hours a day trying to save people's lives and helping the aged or confused. It's an honour to be given such high responsibility.'

Zoë's tension lifted a little and she smiled. 'How long have you worked here?'

'Six months now. I'm from Bangladesh. My family is still there, four boys and three girls. They're very happy with the money I send home. My eldest son wants to play cricket for our national team. It's his dream.'

'You're very proud of them.'

'Yes, of course.' He smiled. 'It must be very hard for you, to have lost so much of your family.'

'I was heartbroken when my mother passed away. She'd always been there for me. An anchor, amazingly supportive when Megan went missing . . .' She stopped, suddenly wondering, hoping. 'Oh, Dalip, maybe you have seen her on the platform. She juggles.' Zoë reached into her bag, pulled out her phone and showed him her photographs. 'This is Megan when she first disappeared.' She scrolled down. 'And this is a recent passport photo. Do you . . . ? Have you seen her? Perhaps she came to the station last night, or this morning?'

Her jaw stiffened. Hope was always there, in the back of her mind. The begging sort of hope that gripped her whenever she showed anyone the picture of her daughter.

He stared at the photographs for a minute, then shook his head.

'I don't recognise her, but that doesn't mean you should give up. Someone will have seen her. Someone, somewhere can help you find her.'

CHAPTER 29
SOFIA

Korydallos Prison, Athens, 1968.

THEY SAID THE PRISON HOUSED two thousand wretched souls, perhaps two hundred of whom were women who were put to work. I worked with Thina in an overstretched hospital ward. Honey was working in the kitchens. The three of us shared a room with Agapi, who had been Madam Magdalena's most popular hostess. She was forced into working as *personal assistant* to several of the commanding officers.

'How come you didn't get a job in the cookhouse, Agapi?' Honey asked.

She shrugged haughtily. 'I failed the test, if you must know.'

'What was it?' I asked.

'They asked how long to boil an egg. Three minutes, I said. I know that much.'

Honey frowned. 'So how come you failed?'

She shrugged again. 'They asked how long to boil three eggs. Nine minutes, I said. I'm not stupid, you know – but they still failed me.' She breathed on her nails and polished them on her thigh. 'I'm assisting the officers.'

We all slaved a twelve-hour day and swapped stories whenever the four of us were together in our room – which wasn't often. Men were tortured and brought into the hospital, battered, broken and sometimes dying. Their terrible suffering broke my heart. I longed to see Markos, yet hoped he had escaped and was somewhere safe.

* * *

Three months passed. I had worked through the night shift and, at 10 a.m., Thina waddled into the ward on her flat feet. The first eight hours of my shift were hectic, but for the last four, time had dragged.

'You look distraught,' she said. 'What's the matter, doll?'

'We lost bed seven. His ribs had punctured his lungs and he drowned in his own blood,' I muttered. 'I've filled the forms in. They took him away in a body bag. Bastards.'

'We can't save them all, Sofia – but we can ease their suffering. That's why we're here.'

Thina was right, and that angered me further.

'You won't believe how busy I was. Four broken thumbs to set. I'd like to use the thumbscrews on that bastard officer's cock!'

'Wouldn't do any good. Bet he's never had a boner in his entire life! Soft as butter on a summer's day.'

Our eyes met and, feeling better for the rant, we smiled together.

'Now I'm bored, with only the worst of everything to think about,' I said. I looked more closely at her. 'You look different. What've you been doing to yourself?'

'Agapi's teaching me her make-up tricks. She shaved my bushy eyebrows off, then showed me how to draw perfect ones.' Her grin showed the gap in her strong teeth. 'One of her visitors left this behind.' She waved a thick black pen. 'A kind of marker, but it's perfect for the job. Let's have a go at yours.'

I folded my arms across my knees and leaned forward.

'There, perfect!' she said after a few minutes of her face close to mine. 'I need more practice, though.'

'You could do moustaches too,' I joked. 'Tidy up the camp commandant's nose-broom.'

'Okay,' she said, laughing. 'Let me try one on you. A Charlie Chaplin, here we go . . .'

'Don't you make me look like Hitler!' I said, before she shushed me and started drawing. This kind of manic comedy helped alleviate some of the horror we had to deal with.

We were still giggling when the door swung open and I felt the pen jerk up my cheek. The officer in charge marched into the ward. I slapped my hand across my top lip.

'Have you got a spare bed in here?' he said. 'And why have you got your hand under your nose?'

'I've got a cold, sir. I don't want to breathe germs on you.'

He looked at me suspiciously as Thina busied herself with the bandage tray.

'Put a surgical mask on. I've got a prisoner coming in. Prepare a bed,' he ordered.

'Yes, sir!'

Once he had gone, I tried to remove the moustache with rubbing alcohol, but it wouldn't go. The redness of my skin only attracted more attention. I was stuck with Hitler on one side, and Salvador Dalí on the other. I don't know why we continued to laugh. The situation was ridiculous, but something crazy ran through us, as if we sensed the horror that lay ahead. Thina stuck a strip of plaster over the offending moustache, which stiffened my top lip and made me talk like an aristocrat.

We were still giggling when two guards arrived. They hauled an unconscious man into the ward by his armpits. The prisoner's boots dragged along the floor. His head, covered in limp, matted hair, lolled down. They tossed him onto an empty bed and the moment I saw his face, all the mirth left my body.

Markos!

To see him like that – battered and broken and on death's doorstep! My first reaction was outrage. I wanted to get hold of the pig who had hurt him so badly and stick a scalpel into his gut.

Seconds later, this need for revenge turned to intense sorrow. Tears stung my eyes, making it difficult to see as I started cutting away his clothes and washing the filth from his body.

'Markos, what have they done to you?' I whispered when the soldiers had gone. Thina rushed to my side.

'Dear God! Is that Markos? He's hardly recognisable.'

Unable to speak, I nodded.

'Right, let's do what we can for him. The doctor won't respond if I call him out for dressing wounds. He'll just say that's our job, so I'm going to give him a shot of morphine myself and put it down as going into the patient who died.'

I mixed a dish of saline solution and tried to clean his wounds. He had what appeared to be swollen, infected burns all over his body. Horrified, I realised some of the sores were maggoty. I couldn't imagine what had caused such terrible injuries. I cut his rags away, killed the grubs wriggling from his wounds and spoke tenderly to him as I worked. With every festering sore, anger rose in my throat. I wanted to kill those responsible. How could they do this?

As I bathed him, I tried to remember happier times, and thought back to the moment I knew my heart belonged to him. We had taken the bus to our special little cove near Piraeus, and dismounted on the promenade. Markos jumped down onto the sand, turned and lifted his arms towards me. His face lit up, eyes full of laughter as he gathered me towards him, pulling me against his chest and kissing me before my feet even touched the ground. When he put me down, I was somehow changed – we both were, as if we held a secret that needed no words. My heart was his, and his was mine.

When Markos regained consciousness, the morphine had started to take effect.

'Markos, it's me, Sofia,' I whispered. 'I'm taking care of you.'

'You want some melon?' he asked deliriously, staring into the space between us. 'Hey, scruffy street kid, you look starved.'

I thought back to the alley behind the bakery.

'I can't remember when Mama hugged me,' he mumbled. 'I can't remember and I can't ask anyone.' His voice was that of a young boy. 'Papa slept with her body in his bed last night. I could hear him talking, talking, talking, all night long. I slept on the kitchen floor because my brothers and sisters were in my room. We have to bury them in the field today, Papa said so. Can you be sure there's a Heaven, nurse? There is a Hell, I know that much.'

'Markos, it's me. It's Sofia!'

'He doesn't know where he is,' Thina said. 'We need to get him rehydrated. Damn it, maggots! He must have been out there at least three days, probably longer. Bastards. Looks like they've given up on converting him – now they're just using him as an example to the other prisoners.' She fixed up a saline drip. 'Let's cut the last of these rags off.'

We worked together, one either side of Markos, until he was naked. As I gathered up the tatters, something fell to the floor. Recognising it, I slipped it into my pocket.

'Look, you can stay here for a few hours, Sofia. Help me wheel his bed into the corner, then pull a chair up and sit with him.'

I threw my arms around her neck and wept.

* * *

Three days later, most of the wounds on Markos's body were healing. I learned they had wrapped barbed wire around him to make a cage, so that he couldn't move. Then, they left him out in the heat for his fellow prisoners to see. In the intense sun, the wire had roasted into his skin, then the blowflies found his bare flesh and laid their eggs.

'Renounce communism now, and we'll set you free!' blasted through the loudspeakers every hour, and a ladle of water was thrown over Markos's face to return him to consciousness.

Markos had refused, so the torture continued.

* * *

'Please, Markos,' I begged, when he returned to his senses. 'Give up the cause. It's enough now. You've done enough. I love you so much, Markos. Please, just say whatever they want. I'll do the same and we can get out of here.'

A pained expression dulled his eyes. 'I can't. Too many of my comrades have died fighting for the freedom of our people – how can I betray them all? Besides, we'll never be free. The KKE will find me and kill me for betraying the party.'

'Then we'll escape them too, leave Greece.'

'No. I'm not my father. How could he change sides like that, go over to the capitalists and the monarchy? All he loved was money! And now we're in this situation because we came back for his funeral. Fools that we are.'

'No. You misunderstood him. Look, I can prove it.'

I went to the surgical tray and brought a scalpel back to his bedside.

His eyes widened. 'What are you going to do?'

'When I cut your rags off, I found this in the hem of your trousers. It must have fallen through a hole in your pocket.' I withdrew Spyridon's tiepin from my pocket. After sliding the scalpel in where the clasp was missing, it popped open. There was a faded sepia photo of Markos. 'You see why he didn't want it buried with him? Because he wanted you to live. He'd worn that picture of you over his heart since the day he lost the rest of his family.'

Markos held out his scabbed hand and I placed the tiny locket in his palm. He stared at it for a long time before he spoke.

'I don't understand. If he cared, why didn't he support me?'

'He did support you. Always. Markos, he made me swear I'd never tell you this, but I must. Your father used every penny he had to bribe people to get you out of trouble, out of prison. Then, he stood back – frantic with worry – while you went on and fought for the cause you believe in. You see, you always had his backing, but he was consumed by fear that if you continued, he would lose you too.'

'What . . . ? He did that?' He stared at the ceiling. 'Why?'

'Because he loved you. You were all he had left. He told me that whenever he saw you, he was reminded of Isabella and how much he loved her.'

'Why didn't he want me to know?'

'Because he believed if you knew he was behind you, you'd never give it up and you'd always be in danger. He was very proud of what you did.'

Markos screwed up his eyes and lay stiff and silent for a while. I understood how much pain he felt.

'He wouldn't like to see you in this place. It would break his heart.'

I saw his eyes fill with tears. 'When I was in the wire cage,' he said, 'I remembered every moment of you, every inch of your body, every word you ever said to me. Even that terrible day behind the theatre when I wreaked revenge for my family's deaths, and you lost your family. The day I lost my comrades, and in a way, lost my father too.'

'Your father loved you more than you knew.'

He nodded, tried to squeeze my hand. 'I know that now.'

CHAPTER 30
MEGAN

Crete, present day.

OUTSIDE CHANIA BUS STATION, Megan juggled while she considered her plan. The depot was busy due to the upcoming carnival. That morning, she'd had an interview at the tour office. The area supervisor seemed to like her, and had asked if she would return the following Tuesday for an interview with the area manager.

Now, she just had to get to her grandmother's village. Granny Anna would help her work out what she ought to say to her dad, how much she ought to tell her mum – and how to apologise for all the worry she must have caused.

If only Megan had paid more attention to Granny Anna, listened to her on those rare occasions when her grandmother had talked about her village home in Crete. They had visited as a family, of course. Great-aunt Calliopi, Granny Anna's older sister, lived in the cottage, the small stone house her great-great-grandfather had built that could never be sold. On their last holiday, Granny Anna said, 'One day this place will belong to you and Josh, Megan.' It was a surprise to them both.

She closed her eyes and saw the stone building in a flash, while continuing with the rhythm of her juggling.

Up and over. Up and over.

The cottage had gigantic beams, dark honey in colour. 'Eucalyptus tree trunks,' Granny Anna had once explained. Above them, pale as parchment due to their age, was a sheet of closely packed bamboo. The walls inside were roughly plastered, and a stone fireplace filled one corner. Outside, there were neat rows of cabbages and beans, and a giant, shady fig tree with huge leaves. A few chickens always pecked around a neat stack of olive wood that dried in the sun. The logs would be ready for burning in the cast-iron cooking range by winter.

At the back of the building lay an olive grove, the trees over five hundred years old. Some of the trunks were like gnarled caves and she remembered playing hide-and-seek in the grove with Josh when they were younger. The cottage lay on the outskirts of Kissamos village, with a clear view down to the sea. Megan was sure she would find it.

She glanced at coins thrown onto the pillowcase at her feet; she had enough for her return bus ticket to Kissamos, plus a little extra.

'Hi, Megan. How's it going?' Gary and Jeff grinned at her.

She juggled two balls in one hand and tossed the third to Jeff. He popped it against his bicep, then to his hand before pitching it back.

Megan laughed. 'You've done this before!'

'A dubious past,' he replied. 'Come and have a cold beer. Our treat.'

She thought about her quest, and her mother. Perhaps she had earned enough for the day.

* * *

The three sat together at a pavement café. Condensation trickled down the outsides of their beer glasses. Megan guzzled the small bowl of crisps placed in the centre of the table, then stared at the pale gold Mythos and licked her lips. This was a real treat.

'Cheers, guys!' she said, lifting her glass.

'*Yammas!*' they cried, grinning at each other.

'Learning the language, are we? How's it going? You two having a good time?'

They glanced at each other again and grinned.

'I think the locals have clocked we're gay,' Gary said. 'But they keep calling me "*Ela!*" and I keep saying, "No, it's Gary!"'

Megan, about to sip her drink, blew a raspberry into her beer and then hooted with laughter.

'*Ela* means "Hey!" or "Come here!", nothing more.'

They laughed together in the warm Cretan sun and Megan buzzed with happiness. This was how she'd always dreamed it would be, living in Crete, happy, normal. These guys knew nothing about her or her past, and didn't care. She could be who she wanted to be.

* * *

At ten o'clock the next morning, Megan was on the bus to Kissamos with her newly found friends.

Gary, eager to see a famous mosaic in the small town, enthused about the history of Kissamos.

'See, it's got a *great* past! Mid-1600s, the governor, Geovanni somebody, opened the city gates to the Turks. The richest Cretan families, who lived in the magnificent Venetian mansions, went and converted to Islam. Can you believe that? But, the less fortunate families were oppressed, practically turned into slaves by the rich.'

'Boo!' cried Megan and Jeff, grinning at each other.

'Then . . .' Gary continued, realising he had the attention of several tourists around them. 'In the early 1800s, the new Commissioner of Crete landed at Kissamos with six hundred Cretan fighters.'

'Yay!' Jeff punched the air and everyone grinned.

'The commissioner and his men laid siege to the fort and the Turks surrendered. *Hurrah* for the Cretans!'

'Hurrah! Hurrah!' Jeff and Megan cried together.

'But then, in the last war . . . the Battle of Crete . . . Well, that's another story and I'm saving it for the trip back.'

A tourist tapped him on the shoulder.

''Scuse me, mate. Could you tell us what bus you're getting back, 'cos we'd all like to hear the rest of the story too.'

The three grinned at each other.

* * *

By midday, Megan was frustrated and sweltering. She had trekked up and down streets around the village, to no avail. The town was larger than she remembered. Gary had lent her his watch, so they could all meet up at three o'clock at the harbour. They bought bottles of cold water and sat on a bench watching fishermen moor up or prepare for night fishing. Jeff noticed a nearby *kafenio*, a place where the local men gathered.

'Come on, time for our daily beer. Let's go and ask about your nana in there.'

Inside the *kafenio*, men played cards and backgammon. Megan chose to sit outside, under the shade of an enormous mulberry tree. The *kafenzies* placed their beers and a bowl of peanuts on the wooden table.

'Where you from?' he asked.

'England,' Megan replied. 'But my grandmother's from here, Kissamos. I'm looking for her.'

'Ah, welcome, welcome!' He beamed from ear to ear, his face shining with joviality. 'Tell me the name of your grandmother. I know everyone here, everyone!'

'She's Anna Despotakis. She has a sister called Calliopi. They live in a stone cottage with an olive grove out back.'

The smile left his face. 'Anna Despotakis? The hunter's wife?' He stepped towards the road and spat.

Startled by his change of mood, Megan stumbled on. 'I don't know if she was married to a hunter. She lived in England for a long time, but came back here recently.'

An elderly man came out of the *kafenio* and a heated exchange took place between him and the *kafenzies*. Megan didn't understand everything they said – her Greek was so limited – but she caught the words, *malaka*, hunter and Despotakis several times. Then the other fellow spat dramatically into the road. He scowled at the three of them before marching away.

'Why do I get a horrible feeling we're not as welcome as we thought?' she whispered to Gary.

The guys shrugged. 'Seems that way. Best we drink up and leave.'

'Can we pay?' Jeff called out.

The *kafenzies*, who had stood in his doorway since the exchange, made a definite 'tut', raised his eyebrows and said, 'You no pay me nothing, I no want your money.'

There was no generosity in his voice. He flicked his jet worry beads over his hand and returned indoors.

* * *

287

'Why don't we ask at the police station?' Jeff asked. 'We've got an hour before the bus leaves.'

'I don't understand why he got so angry. She's just an old woman. She's lovely, really gentle and kind.'

'It's a mystery to me,' Gary said. 'Do you know much about your grandfather?'

Megan shook her head. 'He died when my mother was a little girl. Mum hardly remembered him.'

They found the police station but had no success.

'I know nothing,' the policeman in the front office said. 'Leave your details and come back tomorrow.'

*   *   *

The next morning, they went to the bakery together and feasted on doughnuts, cinnamon rolls and strong Greek coffee.

'What's the plan for today?' Jeff asked.

'I've got to find my grandmother,' Megan said. 'I'll busk at the harbour, to earn my bread, then go back to Kissamos.'

'I'm up for a day on the beach,' Gary said, with a grin. 'I need to get a tan and with my fair skin, it's a slow process.'

'So why don't we tan and juggle this morning, and do Kissamos this afternoon?'

They nodded in agreement.

CHAPTER 31
SOFIA

Korydallos Prison, Athens, 1972.

I HAD SEEN LITTLE OF MARKOS for the past three years. Then, a new junta officer, Despotakis, took over the camp. Efforts to convert Communists into Royalists escalated, and Markos was singled out as an example to those who stubbornly stuck to their ideals. When they dragged him, unconscious, into the ward, Thina kept him there as long as possible and we cherished every moment together.

As spring approached, I realised my life was about to change. Tender breasts, no period and debilitating tiredness told me I was pregnant. I was both horrified and elated. Markos's child grew inside me, the living proof of our future. I longed to tell him about the baby. If there was anything in the world that would make Markos renounce communism and get out of Korydallos Prison, surely it was this.

I hadn't seen him for three months, but the memory of our last encounter was still fresh in my mind.

'I love you, Sofia. You are my life, my all,' he had whispered. 'You make anything bearable. When they inflict their torture, I thank them because I know they are bringing me back to you.'

My beautiful, wonderful man. In those moments of turbulent passion, he was restored to the handsome Markos I had fallen in love with. All the scars and disfigurement of junta torture disappeared in the dark, behind the hospital screen.

I calculated that our baby was due in early November 1972. That left me with six months to try and persuade the love of my life to change his priorities.

Yet weeks passed with no sign of Markos. Every day stretched out. Every time the hospital door opened, I was overcome by both hope, then fear, that I would see the father of my baby, near death once again.

'I'm desperate to send him a message, Thina,' I told the midwife. 'But the junta are cunning, and the prison's riddled with informers. It's too much to risk.'

'You do right, Sofia. Nobody knows who they can trust.'

* * *

I stood on a chair and peered out of the high hospital window. The glass had long since gone, but thick bars blocked any chance of escape. April turned to May, and the wasteland outside the prison fence became an undulating blanket of wild iris. The frilly, pale blue flowers uplifted me. New growth and hope. A shadow dashed past, making me flinch. I turned my eyes up to the cobalt sky, where the first swallow of the year did its aerial dance to celebrate the season. It soared, twisted and dived in an aerobatic display of freedom. I wanted to weep with joy. But then, overcome by sadness, I placed my hand on my swollen belly. Would my child ever run free in such a meadow?

The prison loudspeakers came on, blasting the creed of the Colonels. The statement droned on, but always ended with the same words: *The government is good, communism is bad; admit to the error of your ways and return to freedom!*

I peered up at the blue sky of summer and whispered, 'One day *we'll* be free as a bird, small baby. If it's the last thing I do, I'll get us out of here.'

The door opened and I jumped down, almost tipping the chair in the process.

'What on earth are you doing, Sofia!' Thina cried.

'Sorry, sorry – I was just chasing a wasp.'

She wasn't fooled. 'You know you'll get punishment if you're caught looking out of the windows. Watch it, Sofia!'

I nodded rapidly.

'How'd the shift go? Any more patients?' she asked.

I shook my head.

'How are you feeling in yourself?'

'No change here, Thina.' I sighed. 'I don't know what to do. I'm three months pregnant and Markos has no idea. I don't even know where he is. And we hear such awful things . . . like that poor seven-year-old boy. A junta officer ordered his name tag to be stitched to his bare chest! And that old man they lowered into a barrel of water by his feet. Dipping him until he gave up struggling and drowned.'

Thina frowned. 'It's all so awful, but what can *we* do?'

The swallow flitted past the window again. I wished I could climb on its shoulders and fly away, like one of Aesop's fairies.

* * *

A month later, Markos's body was dragged in and thrown onto a bed. They had beaten the soles of his feet until he was unconscious and beyond revival. When the officers had gone, we rearranged the beds and pulled a screen across the corner. I bathed Markos's feet with cold water to try and reduce the swelling, then I sat beside him.

They had kept him awake for days, tied to a table, whacking the soles of his feet with a pole every time he closed his eyes.

Constantly reminding him that he only had to renounce commu-nism, pledge allegiance to the new government and they would set him free. Of course, Markos refused until eventually, with many bones in his feet broken and his clothes stuck to his body by urine and defecation, his tormentors had given up on him.

The doctor, a stern, unreadable man who came to the prison twice a week, kept Markos sedated for four days. For most of that time, I sat next to his bed. Sometimes he muttered incoher-ently; other times he screamed and, terrified, I would burst into tears. But there was nothing I could do to stop the demons in his head. On the fourth day, Thina reduced the sedative. As he returned to his senses, I took his hand and arched over the bed, my face close to his.

'Markos, love, before I say anything else, I must tell you I'm having our baby.'

For a moment, his eyes lit like street lamps, then they dulled as the situation dawned on him.

'You can't have a child in this place. I'll not have my son or daughter born here. Oh, God have mercy on us.'

He was silent for a long time, holding my hand, his eyes on me. A fledgling of hope fluttered in my chest – if only we could be free. I knew he was thinking the same. Then a frown fur-rowed his brow and I realised he was thinking of all those who had died so that he could continue fighting for the cause.

'I know what you are going to say,' I said, 'but I swear I'm not leaving this island without you.'

He was silent for a long time again.

'We must escape,' he said eventually. 'Leave it with me. I'll make a plan, get help, get us out of this hellhole.'

'There are only two ways out of here,' Thina interrupted. 'You renounce communism and do whatever they demand, or you die and leave in a body bag.' She had a dish of black water and two cotton balls. 'Place these on your closed eyes for ten minutes. They'll stain your skin black, make you appear ill. Hopefully the doctor will keep you in for another couple of nights.'

'What is it?' I asked.

'Water and mashed walnut husks.'

As the door into the ward opened, Thina came over with a mug of tea. She discreetly whipped a thermometer out of the drink and stuck it into Markos's mouth. His blackened eyes widened, and I guessed it was hotter than Thina had anticipated. Straight-faced, she picked up Markos's wrist and took his pulse.

'This way, doctor. Prisoner 83247 has an infection. His temperature's up and down, and some of his lesions are infected.'

We had moved the steriliser and desk across the corner of the ward, so that I could stay behind it whenever an official entered. We didn't want anyone to notice my expanding waistline.

The doctor whipped the thermometer out of Markos's mouth and stared at it.

'He certainly does have a temperature.' He pulled his eyelid down. 'Odd discoloration around the eyes, too. Might be a liver infection.' He pulled the sheet back and pummelled below my man's ribs, ignoring the white scars from past tortures. 'Might need a B_{12} shot.' He scribbled on a prescription pad and handed it to Thina. 'Call if he gets worse. We don't want something contagious spreading through the camp.'

He moved on to the next bed and twenty minutes later, left the ward.

I returned to Markos's bedside.

'Are you all right?' I whispered.

'Apart from a scalded mouth.' He stuck the tip of his tongue out. 'I've probably lost my sense of taste altogether. Come here.' He placed his hand on my belly. 'We're really having a baby? I'm amazed. I'm happy. So happy. We'll find a way to get out of here, Sofia, if it's the last thing I do.'

I nodded. 'Tell them you'll give up fighting for the communists – that you see the error of your ways. That you were misguided and misled.'

He turned his head away from me, and my heart was breaking for him. After all he had gone through, it was a hard decision, but for the sake of our child, we had no other option. I, too, wondered why we had to suffer so much, when deep down we both loved our country with a passion. Perhaps this was my punishment for breaking my promise to Mama so many years ago. I gave my word that I would never get involved in politics, yet here I was in a political prison, having the baby of a man who had brought about my mother's death: a communist freedom fighter.

As I looked down on the man I loved, I longed to absorb his pain. We had known each other so long, meant so much to each other for so many years, that nothing could break us apart now. No matter what the junta threw at us, we would always love each other.

After kissing him softly, I whispered, 'Remember Zoniana? We can find that village happiness again, Markos. I love you so much.'

He raised his eyes to mine and, in a moment of understanding, he tried to squeeze my hand.

'I'll find a way,' he whispered.

Thina came over. 'You're booked out of here after seeing the doctor tomorrow morning. I've asked if Sofia can help me through the night shift, and he's agreed she can.'

She turned to me. 'You'd better oil the wheels on the screen ...
– we may have to pull it around Markos's bed in the night. I don't
want to wake the other patients.'

She raised her eyebrows, a knowing glint in her eye, and
I understood.

'Thank you,' I whispered.

* * *

I spent the night in Markos's arms. We made love in the ward,
behind the simple cotton screen. Silently, hardly moving, yet
filled with love and tenderness. Neither of us knew when we
would see each other again.

Hope grew in my womb alongside our baby. We talked
through the night, making plans for the future, yet both knowing
we were dreaming. Unless we could get out of there, we had no
future at all.

The next morning, he was taken back to the prison where his
torture would continue as an example to other communists. It
would break his heart to abandon the cause, but now we had
more important things to consider.

When he had gone, I sat behind the screen in the corner of
the ward and wept.

* * *

As the weeks and months passed and my child grew inside me,
I was torn over Markos. I longed for his return to the hospital –
yet I dreaded it, too, always hoping I would not see him again
until we were free. Agapi had given me a long, pale silk dress,
and I spent every spare moment carefully unravelling it in order

to crochet my baby's layette. At least I would have a special shawl for swaddling.

I tried to gather information about Markos from other prisoners. One day, an elderly man from the cookhouse was admitted to the ward with severe burns.

'You Sofia?' he asked gruffly, while I concentrated on removing the dead, white skin from his palms.

I nodded.

'Markos is your man, isn't he?'

I nodded again, my hand trembling at the mention of his name.

'He's asked me to give you something. It's in my back pocket.' He went to retrieve it but winced with pain.

'Wait, I'll get it. You keep your hands still.'

The paper was crumpled. I smoothed it and read the creased words.

My one and only love. My thoughts are always with you. Soon, we will be together forever, I promise. You must trust me, whatever happens. All my love, XXX

'I wrote it for him 'cos he can't use his hands right now.'

I clutched the letter to my heart as if it were my beloved Markos.

'How is he?' I asked.

'He's havin' it hard all right. Don't know how he stays on his feet the way he does.' He looked at my swollen belly. 'That his?'

I nodded. 'I'm so afraid for him.'

'I reckon he'll be in here soon enough.'

'Why? Oh God, I can't stand much more of this.'

'Of course you can, young woman. If he can put up with what they're throwing at him, at least you can be strong when he needs you.'

'What are those bastards doing to him now?'

'They's using the thumbscrews. Busting his fingers. Poor bastard. He'll be good for nothing if he ever gets out of this place. You'll see him soon enough.'

* * *

The old man was right. The next afternoon they hauled Markos in. Thina rushed over to the officers who dragged him to a bed.

'Leave him,' she ordered, drawing their attention away from me, and giving me a sideways squint of warning.

I understood. She did not want them to know I cared about this man. If they discovered he loved me, they would torture me in front of him. I stiffened my back and stood behind the desk so they couldn't see the advanced state of my pregnancy. The moment the officers had gone, Thina pulled the screen around his bed and ordered me to take care of him.

I rushed to Markos's side. Barely conscious, he mumbled incoherently.

Every finger on his mashed hands was broken several times. His arms were bruised black to his elbows.

'Can't you give him a shot to relieve his pain?' I asked her.

'I can't. I've used up our supply. We're waiting for a delivery tomorrow.'

'But he's in agony. It must be unbearable!'

'Look, the body has a way of taking care of itself. If the pain is indeed unbearable, he would be unconscious. Now go to his bedside and remind him why he needs to get off this island.'

She nodded at my full belly.

* * *

A few weeks later, I was cringing with a backache that had bothered me all night.

'Let me listen,' Thina said, indicating the examination table.

I struggled onto it, cumbersome, yet oddly energised.

'I'm betting before midnight,' she said. 'Try to take it easy today. No heavy lifting. We don't want your waters to break until the last minute. Sit behind the desk and crochet your baby blanket until I need you.'

I placed my hand on my belly and thought about Markos.

'Do you think I can get a message to him, Thina?' I asked, climbing off the table and smoothing my uniform.

'I don't know. Perhaps someone's going off the ward – they could let him know it's time.'

The door opened and Colonel Despotakis barged into the room. His petite wife, who was heavy with child, was trying to keep up with him.

'Where's the doctor?' he demanded.

I ducked behind the desk.

Thina answered, drawing the colonel's attention away from me.

'Dr Orpheus has gone into Athens for supplies, sir. I suspect the storm has hindered his return. They say the road's collapsed under a landslide. I'm in charge. Can I help you?'

'My wife Anna should have returned home today, but she has the same problem. Communications are down. Transport of any sort is impossible, and the wind's almost reached hurricane level. Have a look at her – she's not feeling well and the baby's due in a few weeks.'

'Yes, sir, of course.' Thina quickly assessed the small woman, who looked exhausted. 'I'm actually a midwife, sir. I have all the skills to take very good care of your wife.'

'Good. You'll come and examine her in my quarters.'

Thina shook her head. 'All our equipment's here, sir. Better for your wife if she could stay overnight. That way I can keep a close eye on her.'

The colonel considered this for a moment. He flicked a glance around the ward, hardly seeming to notice me.

'All right then. But get the men shifted out of here – I don't want them near her in this situation. Let me know how she is when you've examined her, and if there's any change.'

Thunder cracked outside, and lightning lit up the ward as the storm raged on. The colonel stared at the window for a moment, then turned and left.

* * *

We moved our four male patients into the operating room next door. They had almost recovered from their injuries but, if we could, we always kept patients in until we needed the bed space. We knew what we would be sending them back to.

'Write a note for Markos, Sofia,' Thina whispered. 'Tell him the baby's on its way. Perhaps he can get in here tonight or in the morning.'

A surge of excitement rushed through me. Despite the horror around us, my child – *our* child – was about to be born. I started writing a long love letter to Markos, begging him to come. My heart was breaking. Tears fell onto the paper as I pleaded with him to accept the junta's creed and sign their paper renouncing communism.

Thina and I helped Mrs Despotakis out of most of her clothes and onto the examination table. She seemed a kind woman, although small, fine-boned and rather timid.

Thina placed one end of the Pinard horn to Anna's full belly and her ear to the other, as she had often done to me, to listen to the baby's heartbeat. Her eyes met mine and she looked away quickly. She replaced the horn with her stethoscope, and after listening again, returned to the desk. Anna watched her intently.

'Is everything all right, nurse?' she asked me quietly. 'I haven't felt any movement for a few days now.'

'Don't worry, that's normal. There's no room, you see.'

She breathed in deeply. 'My previous two were stillborn,' she told me, tears coming into her eyes, 'and this is my last chance. I'm desperate for everything to turn out well.'

I removed the blood pressure cuff from her arm and patted her shoulder.

'I'm sure everything will be fine. Don't worry.'

Thina came over with a syringe. 'I'm just going to give you an injection to help with your vitamins, Anna. We need you to be healthy for the delivery, don't we?' She tapped the vein in Anna's wrist. 'And a little gel to keep your uterus in peak condition. Just pull your knees up. Now relax.'

I watched, interested in the procedure.

'Right, all done. Now, I want you to take a mild sedative, to give you and baby a good night's sleep, Anna.'

Thina left the bedside and returned with a couple of tablets and a glass of water.

Just as she returned, I felt a clench deep inside me. My first real contraction.

Thina glanced at my face and knew.

'Can I have a word at the desk, nurse, when you have a moment?' she said.

I couldn't walk for a minute, and pretended to take Anna's pulse until the overpowering feeling faded. Then I pulled the screen around Anna's bed and followed Thina across the room.

Thina moved her head close to mine. 'Look, I've just realised: Anna's husband, the colonel, is the junta officer who rules the prison. Her baby's due a couple of weeks after yours, Sofia.' Thina shook her head sadly. 'There's no heartbeat,' she said in a low whisper. 'The baby's dead in the womb. Poor woman. She's forty, lost babies before . . . and with her medical history, there's no chance of another child. Also, her blood pressure's up. We should abort the baby as soon as possible. There's a chance of eclampsia, and then Anna might die too.' She glanced at the screen. 'I've induced her labour. It's her third confinement, so she shouldn't be too long.'

'She doesn't know, does she?'

Thina shook her head. 'I'm not going to tell her just yet. I want to talk to you first.'

I stared at Thina for a moment. She was biting her lip, a new light in her eyes.

'What is it?'

'I was thinking, at least we could get your baby out of here. You're about to give birth, and I can induce her labour with a shot. If we get the timing right, we can swap the infants.'

I stared at her. 'Are you mad?'

'Keep your voice down. Think about it, Sofia!' she said urgently. 'It may be the only chance you get to give your child freedom. I don't believe Markos will ever abandon his fight, and deep down you don't either. You won't leave here without him, will you? And what sort of a life will your child have on the island? Can you imagine stitching a name tag to its little chest, for God's sake? They'll take your baby away from you, and you'll never know what's happening to it. It's atrocious, the things they do here.'

I cowered as another contraction loomed and faded.

'You're condemning him or her to this hellish prison. Your child deserves freedom, an education, parents who can afford to take care of him properly.'

I stared, not wanting to consider her suggestion. Thina's words were all the more shocking because I knew they were true. I had to admit that I would not leave the island so long as Markos remained a captive of the colonels in Korydallos Prison, and I knew he would never truly turn his back on the cause that meant the world to him.

'Sofia, listen to me!' Thina whispered. 'I'm risking my life for you. I could be shot for this, but I don't want to see a child born into this hellhole. I've heard that things have improved back home. The colonels may be hated, but they've brought some stability to Greece. There's work, there's food – people are going back to the type of life they had before the war.' She put her fists on her hips and continued. 'There's a storm raging out there.' She nodded towards the high window. 'They say it'll last for three days or more, so the doctor's stuck in Athens with his supplies, and Anna's staying here for her confinement.' She paused, giving me time to consider the facts. 'Don't you see, Sofia? This could be your only chance. It must be God's will. At least think about it.' She touched my arm. 'The Fates appear to be on your side. They've given you this opportunity to get your baby out of here and into a better life.'

I sat on the stool behind the desk, my knees apart, my swollen belly between my thighs. This life inside me was the only blameless thing coming from my turbulent past. A child, born of love, innocent and pure. I recalled all the horror I had seen here – the pain, torture, grown men crying for their loved ones. Did I want my baby to experience this hell on earth? I reached for Thina's stethoscope, put the buds in my ears and the diaphragm on my belly. My baby's heart beat quickly, with an urgency only known to him or her.

To hear my baby's pulse, beating much faster than my own, independent and unique, was the deciding factor. That heart must continue to flourish inside my baby, my child, my adult son or daughter. No matter how independent my baby became, part of it would always be me, and part of me would always be it.

CHAPTER 32
ZOË

Manchester, present day.

ZOË SAT ALONE IN THE station café and watched Dalip as he left. This stranger had given her hope. Although life was irreversible, the future was open to change if Zoë chose to instigate it. She would go back to London, make sure Josh understood how much she loved him, and then she would talk to Frank about Megan, find out if he knew more than she did about why their daughter had left home.

She walked out onto the platform and saw the next train to London would arrive in fifteen minutes. She wondered where Megan was at that moment and suddenly remembered Centrepoint. Perhaps the day staff had seen her.

She gave them a call.

'My name's Pam,' a woman said after Zoë had explained the situation. 'Yes, your daughter was here yesterday. She was getting some things together for her trip to Crete. She had a ticket booked for yesterday afternoon.'

'Crete! She's really gone to Crete!'

'Yes, she had a last-minute flight. Said she was going to visit her grandmother.'

Zoë's heart plummeted. Poor Megan didn't know Mama had died. Her daughter was heading for such heartbreaking disappointment. She returned her attention to Pam.

'I can't thank you enough.'

'Please keep in touch. We always hope to hear of a happy ending.'

'I will, I promise.'

Zoë hung up, watched the London train pull in and decided she was going to Crete. It was impossible to keep trying to divide herself between her children, searching for Megan while feeling the guilt of abandoning Josh. But in the end, this might be her last chance to find her daughter.

She would tell Megan about her grandmother, and they would go to the cemetery together, supporting each other in their grief. Zoë felt her jaw stiffen. She hadn't had a moment to mourn her own mother. She missed her terribly, but even that heartbreak had been overshadowed by her desperation to find Megan.

She remembered seeing a travel agent opposite the station and hurried towards it.

* * *

Outside the shop, Zoë checked the time and realised Josh would be on his break. She called him. He didn't answer – his choice of weapon – and she understood he was still hurting, so she sent a text.

Need to speak to you, URGENT, need your help. Love you. Mum XXX

She waited five minutes, then called again, determined to get him on her side, determined to make him realise she was on his side.

'Hi, Mum,' he said flatly. 'What can I do for you?'

'Hello, darling, how was Formula 1?' She projected warmth into her voice. 'Did you enjoy it? I was thinking about you all day.'

'Yeah, it was cool, we had a good time.' He was silent for a moment. 'How's the Megan search going?'

'Josh ... it's terrifying, to tell the truth. I haven't wanted to worry you, but I'm at my wits' end now and I need someone to talk to. I don't know what to do or which way to turn. Have you got a minute?'

Silence again. Then, 'Sure, tell me about it, Mum.'

'A friend of Megan's was shot, killed. The police think she was involved in some heavy drugs, but the trouble is, she was the double of Megan and I'm afraid there will be an identity mix-up and the thugs might go after her. That's why I couldn't come home for your birthday.'

'What? Blimey, Mum, killed ... You should have said. I had no idea it was that serious.'

'I didn't want to worry you. Anyway, that's not all. Megan slept at the top of a derelict office block, which was set on fire. She managed to get out, and also rescued an old man – saved his life – but then she disappeared again.'

'And now you don't know where she is?'

'That's the thing – I do. Megan caught a flight to Crete yesterday afternoon – she's planning to go and live with Granny Anna. I guess she doesn't know that her grandmother has died.'

This time Josh didn't answer.

'When was the last time you spoke to her, Josh?' Zoë was careful to keep any animosity out of her voice.

After another silence, he spoke softly and Zoë could hear the regret in his voice.

'She made me promise not to tell, Mum. It was the week Granny left for Crete. I'm sorry. What are you going to do?'

'I don't know. Should I go after her? She'll be devastated when she learns about Granny Anna. Or, should I give up and come home? I'm too exhausted and worried about everyone to make a decision.'

'Surely you can't give up now? Not after everything that's happened.' She heard him take a deep breath. 'Mum, I really do think you should go to Crete. If she calls me, which isn't likely, I'll tell her you're on your way.'

'Do you know why she left home, Josh?'

He sighed. 'It's difficult to say when I gave my word, but if she's in danger . . . Well, I guess these are extenuating circumstances and it's okay to break my promise.' He sighed. 'I don't know all of it, but I know she didn't want to go back to school . . . And there was this guy she was seeing, and . . . and I think she was partying too hard, you know? Drink and . . . weed, and stuff. She was ashamed and afraid you'd find out. She thought she'd jeopardised your job and Dad's reputation.' He swallowed. 'The thing is, she thinks she's let you down and needs to prove herself. I told her that was bullshit but she wouldn't have it.'

'She could never let us down. Nor could you,' whispered Zoë. 'We love you both, Josh.' She took a deep breath. 'How's your father?'

'He's working all the hours.' After an awkward pause, he said, 'You should call him.' Then, more strongly: 'Call him from Crete, Mum. Please.'

She heard the heartbreaking hope in his voice.

'Thanks, Josh, you've been a big help. I'll phone you tomorrow evening with an update. Love you.'

'I love you too, Mum,' he said, for the first time in his life.

* * *

Zoë hurried into the travel agent's. Before anyone could ask if they could help, she said, 'I need a ticket to Crete, quite urgently.'

'Blimey, it's a stampede!' one of the assistants joked, staring around the empty shop. 'Take a seat while I see what I can do.'

'I think my daughter took a flight to Crete. Megan Johnson. Is there a chance she booked her ticket here?'

One of the others smiled. 'That's right, she did. I remember her. She's going to visit her poorly grandma. What a considerate young woman. You must be very proud.'

Zoë's profound joy was quickly enveloped by sadness.

'But the tragedy is, she doesn't know her grandmother died a couple of months ago.'

'Good lord, that's so sad.'

'She'll be so upset.' Zoë sat down heavily. 'I have to get to Crete as soon as possible.'

The woman nodded. 'It's carnival weekend, so there might be a problem, but don't worry, we'll get you there somehow. I'll just check which accommodation your daughter was allocated and print it off.'

* * *

Athens, present day.

The next few hours flew by. Zoë found herself in Greece, after taking the only available flight: Manchester to Athens. At the Olympic desk in Athens airport, she hoped to get an internal flight to Crete, but there was none available.

'There's a shortage because of the upcoming carnival,' the Olympic rep explained. 'Same every year. Most of the seats are taken by Greek students studying at British universities. Carnival weekend's the highlight of their year.' She nodded at a row of filled seats near the desk. 'Look, there's already a queue waiting for no-shows.'

'Please, it's urgent,' Zoë pleaded.

The rep looked up, and as if seeing Zoë for the first time, her face softened.

'I shouldn't say this, but why don't you take the overnight ferry? If you get a taxi to the port of Piraeus right now, you'll catch the last boat to Crete, and you'll be there by six in the morning. At least you'll get a good night's sleep on board.'

*   *   *

The ship was full of students, tourists and Greeks, all heading for Crete. To make matters worse, every cabin was taken. She found herself an armchair in the front lounge and made herself as comfortable as possible. The noise was almost unbearable. Young children raced around; older ones played on their tablets with the sound up high. Men clacked their *komboloi*, and all the Greeks seemed to be shouting above the racket of two blaring TVs.

She glanced across the room and saw a very elderly woman asleep across three cushions. She must be deaf, Zoë thought, to sleep through all that din. She took her jacket off and left it on the seat while she queued for coffee and doughnuts. After eating, she dozed, and woke with a jerk at three o'clock in the morning. The lounge was still and quiet. Everyone slept, except the old woman, who now appeared to be scribbling on bits of paper. Zoë resisted the urge to ask her if she would swap seats for a few hours, as she longed to lie down.

She wondered how the woman came to be travelling alone at such an age. At the counter, she bought a warm cheese pie, a coffee and a glass of water. She asked the man behind the counter to give the same to the old woman, who was now busy with her crocheting.

'No need to say it's from me,' she said, thinking of the woman's pride.

Zoë ate, and dozed again, imagining her daughter asleep in a hotel bed. Dreaming of the moment she would hold her again.

As the passengers disembarked at Chania, the old woman was waiting near the exit. She gave out slips of paper to everyone that passed, and Zoë took one. It was in Greek. Guessing she was begging, Zoë placed a few euros in the woman's wrinkled hand and wished her good luck. The old lady bowed.

* * *

Crete, present day.

Zoë stood in a taxi queue for half an hour before she got a ride to Megan's Rent Rooms Maria apartment block. She knocked on every door, but with no luck. Hardly anyone was in, and those who were hadn't seen anyone of Megan's description. She had seen a bakery on the opposite corner of the street and bought herself a spinach pie and a couple of bottles of water, then returned to Megan's accommodation. By one o'clock, the sun had moved around and, sweltering in her court suit, Zoë wished she had bought a change of clothes. She walked across to the shady side of the street and sat on a low wall facing the building. An hour later, doubt started to set in.

And then, just about to give up hope, she saw three young adults walking around the corner towards the apartment. One was a young woman.

Megan!

Zoë almost collapsed. She kicked off her heels, abandoned her bag and raced towards them yelling, 'Megan, Megan!'

In moments, they were in each other's arms.

Zoë pushed Megan's hair back, ran her hands over her face, down her arms, confirming she was real . . . unharmed.

'You don't know how afraid I've been. God, I can hardly believe I've found you at last. Are you all right?'

Megan was crying. 'I'm sorry, Mum. I'm so, so sorry. What are you doing here?'

Zoë's heart was so full, her emotions so high, for a moment she struggled to speak.

'I came to find you, Megan. I've been searching . . . so long. So very long.'

Megan threw her arms around her mother's neck.

'Mum, I'm sorry, really sorry. I didn't realise how worried you were. I thought you didn't care. I thought—'

'Megan, please, please never run away from me again. Whatever happened to make you leave home, we can tackle it together. Do you understand me, Megan? Was it me? Did I do something to push you away?'

'No! No – it was me. My mistakes, my messes and . . . Oh, Mum, I've been so stupid, so self-centred and thoughtless. Can you forgive me?'

'I'm so relieved to have found you at last, Megan. There's nothing, nothing to forgive, but I do need to understand.'

In her excitement, she had barely noticed the two young men behind Megan, until they began to drift away, and one said gently to Megan, 'I guess we're not searching for your granny today then?'

Zoë lowered her head. 'Darling, listen, I have to tell you something.' She struggled, grief filling her up and making it impossible to speak for a second. 'Granny Anna – Mama – passed away a little while ago. She had cancer – that's why she left London. She didn't want me to stop searching for you, in order to look after her. Your poor grandmother had battled with her illness for some time, but kept it to herself.'

As she told Megan, Zoë felt she had been given permission to grieve for her mother, now that she had found her daughter. How she wished Mama was with them to see this day. She glanced up at the sky, and as her sadness grew, she felt Megan's arms tight about her.

'I'm so sorry, Mum. I'm going to miss her.' Megan was crying again. 'I came here to look after her. Josh said she'd been poorly. I thought Granny Anna would help me get back on track, too.' She stared at her feet. 'You see, Mum, I sort of lost my way for a while.'

* * *

Zoë slept in Megan's room, where there were twin beds. She spent a large part of the night propped on her elbow, gazing at her daughter. Occasionally, she felt a twist of anger at the girl who had given her so much grief. If Megan hadn't run away, would she and Frank still be together? Would she and Josh not have lost their footing for a while? Though their relationship was strong once again, Zoë had learned some painful, and important, lessons. She reminded herself, although it seemed like an eternity of turmoil, it had only been seven months. Megan had just been a kid then, but clearly, she had matured a great deal while learning to stand on her own two feet.

Zoë knew she could never rectify the upheaval that had gone on between them all, or bring Emily back – no matter how hard she tried – but they could put the chaos and heartbreak behind them and move forward with lessons learned. Their future was as yet unwritten. Tomorrow they could all start afresh.

CHAPTER 33
SOFIA

Korydallos Prison, Athens, 1972.

THE WORST STORM EVER RECORDED continued to rage. Day or night, we could not escape the deafening roar of the wind.

My contractions were every five minutes. The fiercest cramp I'd ever experienced multiplied by ten, but just when I feared I couldn't take any more, they would subside. I walked up and down the ward, and leaned against the wall as I felt the next pain building.

'I can't take much more, Thina,' I said when the contractions were coming three minutes apart. 'I just want it all to stop.'

'You can't guess how many times I've heard that said.' She smiled encouragingly. 'You're doing great, Sofia. Not much longer now. Just remember, every single person on earth arrived in this same way. You'll be fine, and it will get easier when you start to push baby out.'

'Anna's out for the count,' Honey said, appearing from behind the screen. 'What do you want me to do next?'

She primped her hair and stroked the bib of her nurse's apron, pleased to be helping Thina with the deliveries. She had four grown boys herself, all of whom had escaped to Crete, where she hoped they would keep a low profile.

I sensed a change in my next contraction. As the pain became unbearable, I squatted down with my forehead against the wall. When it was over, Thina and Honey helped me onto the examination table.

'I can't take much more,' I whispered.

'Of course you can, you're doing fine, Sofia,' Thina said.

I balled my fists, seriously wanting to throw a punch her way.

Thina examined me and turned to Honey. 'Sofia's fully dilated. She'll want to push with the next one. Just nip next door to make sure the patients don't need anything. I can't be in three places at once.'

Honey scurried out of the ward. She returned red-faced and excited.

'Markos is in there! He wants to know how Sofia is. Can he come in?'

Markos!

'Not now,' Thina said. 'It's not as if he can help with those smashed hands, and the fewer people in here the better. Go back and tell him we'll call him in when it's time, but reassure him everything's perfectly normal.'

Thina turned to me and put her stethoscope to my belly.

'You're doing great. Good strong heartbeat.' She nodded towards the fabric screen that stood between the only two beds. 'I'm going to increase Anna's medication, keep her asleep and give her another shot to induce her contractions.' She glanced at my exposed belly. 'Try not to push yet.'

I had made the hardest decision of my life: to let our baby go to Anna and escape this hellish place. To say my heart was in splinters was an understatement. My baby was a part of my body, my life. The infant that represented the union of Markos and myself. It seemed obscene to give this embodiment of our love to another woman, and to the evil monster who kept us imprisoned here. The depth of my grief was absolute, and yet I knew it was the right thing to do. I had yet to share this decision with Markos.

If our lives were over, ruined, at least our child could live and flourish. At least he or she could grow up in peace and safety. I had no idea what Markos would think, though he had left me no choice. My body tingled with the onset of another contraction and as it built, the urge to push was almost overwhelming.

'Pant,' Honey instructed.

I felt like my middle was a wet towel being wrung out and twisted against itself. I panted against my hand, trying not to cry out. From behind the screen, on the verge of losing control, I heard the door bang open, and then an officer's voice boomed into the ward.

'Colonel Despotakis wants a report on his wife's condition.'

I bit my lip, drawing my knees towards my chest, desperately, desperately wanting to push.

'Look for yourself – she's sleeping peacefully,' Thina replied. 'Tell the colonel there's nothing to worry about. We're taking good care of her. There will be a nurse at her bedside all night.'

I heard the door close as my contraction faded. Sweat greased my brow. Exhausted, I could not take another contraction.

'You're doing well, nearly there,' Thina said matter-of-factly, placing my foot against her shoulder and leaning towards me. 'Come on now, take some deep breaths – it's time to start pushing this baby out.'

* * *

'Here it comes, Sofia,' Thina whispered. 'One big push now.' She turned to Honey. 'Go and get Markos, quickly!'

I pushed with everything I had, from my neck down, and from the soles of my feet up. I clenched my teeth and felt the sinews in my neck strain, as every molecule of strength in my body went into forcing our baby out.

'Well done, Sofia. Now, breathe. Open your eyes and say hello to your child.'

I lifted my head and looked down between my legs. There was my baby's head, slippery, black-haired, eyes scrunched and seconds away from birth. Oh, the joy that filled me in that moment was beyond description. The aching and exhaustion that had built over the last hours disappeared. Too tired to laugh or cry, I was simply filled with wonder. Then I realised Markos was beside the bed, staring at his child. Clearly, he had a broken nose, and I wondered if he had done it to himself in order to get into the hospital at this important time. He dragged the beret from his head and twisted it in his fists. As the cramps across my middle intensified again, he took my hand and watched his baby being born.

'Another push, Sofia,' Thina said. 'Here she comes.'

And in one swift motion, as the contraction climaxed, she lifted our baby.

'A little girl,' Markos whispered. 'Zoë,' he said. 'Life. She has life.'

In a flash, Thina cleared out the baby's airway and she cried, a sound that made my body contract again. Thina tied the umbilical and placed our baby on my chest.

'Darling, Markos . . . say hello to your daughter.'

Tears filled his eyes.

'I'll clean her up in a minute,' Thina said. 'Just relax, Sofia, and concentrate on the infant while we finish our work down below.'

Markos replaced his beret, reached over and touched the baby's cheek with his shattered fingers.

'I wish you a big life and freedom, my baby,' he whispered. 'You have *life*, and I swear to fight with mine to give you the *freedom* that you deserve.'

As he spoke those heartfelt words, life and freedom, I knew he would never renounce his struggle for the Greek people. With his own child in the world, how could he stop fighting to make it a better place? He would be a champion for his daughter, and his determination to fight for liberty in his beloved country was only going to increase.

Honey came around the screen and smiled at the baby before she said, 'Anna's contracting, and she's coming to. Are we ready to make the swap?'

No! No!

I wanted to stop the world turning. I had to hold my precious little girl a while longer.

'What do you mean, the swap?' Markos asked.

I hadn't realised I was crying until I tried to speak.

'It's our only option, Markos. Anna's baby is dead. We can swap the children – no one will ever know. It's our only chance to give our baby the freedom, *Eleftheria*, that she deserves. She didn't ask to be born into this hellhole, and we have no right to keep her here, my darling.'

Markos's face showed his heartbreak. 'You mean my child will go to a junta officer? No! *No!*' His head dropped into his hands and his shoulders shuddered. 'This has to be the worst torture . . . I can take anything but this – I won't allow it!'

'But my love, don't you see? I have kept my pregnancy hidden, but how could I hide a child? They will torture me to make me say who the father is and then they will torture our baby in front of you, to get you to sign. God, Markos, can you imagine? It's our only way to know she's safe.'

His hands were over his face, hiding his tears. Then, as if he realised he hadn't long to see his daughter, he took our naked little baby from me and held her gently to his chest. She opened her eyes and gazed curiously into his face. Markos stroked her cheek, brushed her cherub lips with his little finger. She latched on and sucked, her eyes never leaving his. The moment was too beautiful to bear.

'She looks like my baby brother who never received a name,' he whispered. 'We must name her now.'

'You've already done that, Markos,' I said. 'Life and Freedom. Zoë Eleftheria.'

We both wiped our tears away.

As our baby peered into Markos's eyes, he blessed her.

'Zoë Eleftheria, I wish you a long and happy life. May you have your mother's courage and your father's strength. May you find peace, and love, and good health. May you never know the sorrow of war, and may your children live in contentment and one day learn of their grandparents' great sacrifice.'

He kissed her forehead and then kissed mine.

Thina broke the moment. 'Keep hold of her until the time we have to make the swap – but then you must hand her over immediately. Do you agree to do that, Sofia? There's no going back now.'

My heart was in bits. I'd lost my family, everyone from my past, and now they were going to take away my child, my future.

'Sofia, we're all risking our lives for your baby's freedom. I need your word, now!'

'Markos,' I murmured. Tears raged down my face. 'It's the right thing to do. If we love her enough, we must set her free, give her the chance of a good life in the free world.'

'To a junta officer? To the very people that have caused us so much pain? The ones that take me to the brink of death over and over, and just when I'm on the steps of Heaven, bring me back to this hell?'

'It's the greatest gift we can give her, Markos. Freedom! Life! Isn't that what you've been fighting for?' The more I tried to convince him, the stronger became my own conviction that this was the right thing to do. 'Now's not the time to be selfish. Our sacrifice is for her. Whoever she is with, wherever she lives, will not alter the fact she's *our* child.'

While I said all these things, the tears flowed hard down my cheeks. This was my child, our child, our little Zoë Eleftheria.

I nodded at Thina, then turned to Markos. He breathed in hard, then nodded.

We both knew this was the best recourse for our child.

Markos leaned over the bed and put his forehead against mine; his tears and mine mingled in my eyes and then streamed into my hair. We had no use for words. He rested a mangled hand on the wondrous infant that snuggled against my breast.

* * *

While we held our child, Markos and I listened to the sounds coming from the other side of the screen.

'What's happening?' Anna Despotakis mumbled.

'You've gone into rapid labour, Anna. Everything's in order, don't worry. I'm going to put a surgical screen up, below your chest. I don't want you to get anxious about anything that's happening down below. It's a new way to help the mother in childbirth. You just concentrate on pushing when I say so.'

'Please don't let me have another stillbirth. Please, I'd rather die.'

'Your baby is fine. She'll have life, don't worry. In fact, isn't that the perfect name? If it's a girl, why don't you call her Zoë, or perhaps Eleftheria? Life and Freedom. They're two beautiful names. Now I come to think of it, isn't that what you were mumbling in your sleep half the night? *Zoë Eleftheria.*'

'I was? They *are* beautiful names, aren't they? I'll see what my husband thinks. If it's a boy, he'll be named after my father-in-law, of course.'

'Zoë Eleftheria,' Honey repeated, with a smile. 'What perfect names, Anna. I heard you saying them in your sleep, too. Just keep repeating them as your little one comes into the world.'

* * *

I lay on the hospital bed with Markos in the chair beside me. Before dawn, my newborn baby girl would be taken away. My eyes fell on the man I loved more than life itself. He had our daughter in his arms, holding her clumsily, his broken fingers sticking out awkwardly. Grief shredded every part of me.

Markos placed Zoë back on my chest. With her eyes closed, she opened her little mouth like a baby bird, searching for a nipple to latch onto. Filled with the magic of new life, sparkling hope, and the proof of new beginnings, I gazed at our baby. She was everything good and lovely in this hate-filled place. It was impossible to gaze into the face of our tiny infant without feeling a rush of joyful emotion.

'Darling, Markos,' I whispered, searching for the right words to say to this man that I had seen so little of for the past nine months, while his child turned and kicked and grew in my belly.

When we arrived at Korydallos, he had still been unbearably handsome. Now, the scars of his constant wounding were ripe and swollen. And yet he was still beautiful to me. I could see there was no sweeter moment on earth than the one in which a grown man melts after meeting his child for the first time.

'Isn't she beautiful?' I whispered, the knot in my throat making every word painful. 'She looks like you, Markos. There's no mistaking she's your daughter, is there?'

Markos nodded and I saw his tears still wet between the scars on his face. Recently, they had wrapped him in barbed wire again, his screams a warning to other dissidents: *renounce communism now or this fate will befall you too*. They had smashed the fingers that held his baby girl so tenderly. And yet beneath it all, I saw his smile, his eyes, his tenderness, his courage, all shining down on the infant that he placed in my arms. Our baby girl, Zoë, born in the Athens prison of Korydallos, on 1 November 1972.

At that moment, Thina appeared and gently took baby Zoë from my arms. I gasped and panted to prevent myself crying out *Stop!* Markos put his head against mine, and we wrapped our arms around each other.

'Oh, God help us,' I whispered, my body trembling with silent sobs.

* * *

Drained and aching, I slept like a corpse and woke hours later. Thina and Honey had managed to wheel my bed into the opposite corner, and I woke to find the screen around me. Markos was back with the male patients.

I heard a man's voice, then a baby's cry. My womb contracted so violently with that sound that I gasped, then pressed my hand across my mouth to stop myself crying out.

'What's going on behind the screen?' I heard Colonel Despotakis say. 'I told you I wanted my wife to be alone.'

I shifted so that I could see him through a narrow slit between the fabric and the frame. Dark hair, but pale skin like he never saw daylight.

As he came towards me, Thina said, 'It's Sofia, the nurse who's been with your wife for eighteen hours, sir. She's devoted herself to giving Mrs Despotakis and baby Zoë the best possible attention, and refuses to leave her alone for a moment.'

He stepped around the screen and seemed to be studying me. I kept still, seeing him only as a blur under my lowered lashes. After a moment, he seemed satisfied and nodded.

'Baby Zoë?' He turned to Thina. 'When was this decided?'

'Ah, sorry, sir. It's a nickname that seems to have stuck. Mrs Despotakis kept saying *Zoë* and *Eleftheria* while she was in labour. I guess after the last two births, it was the only thing on her mind – that she gave birth to a child with life and freedom. Anyway, the names seem to have stuck. They are beautiful, like your daughter, don't you think, sir?'

He grunted and stood a little taller.

I watched him through the narrow gap. He held Zoë awkwardly, and although he was reputed to be a hard, vicious man, he looked down at her with tenderness.

'I wanted a son,' he said. 'But she's a pretty little thing, don't you think?' He smiled. 'When can they leave?'

Thina glanced at the screen. 'It was a sudden birth, and your wife is quite exhausted. She needs a few days' recuperation, to build her strength a little.'

He passed my baby over to Anna and then smoothed the front of his uniform.

'I'll make sure you're not disturbed. Anyway, it will be a few days before the road is repaired. Ensure my wife's comfortable at all times, and never left on her own.'

'Of course, sir.'

At that moment, I knew Zoë would be loved and well cared for, and the thought made me want to weep again.

He turned to his wife. 'Well done, darling. We'll get you and baby Zoë back home as soon as this storm abates and the road's passable.' He straightened and turned to Thina. 'If you need anything, be sure to let me know. I'll have special food sent in for my wife.' He nodded towards the screen. 'When she wakes, thank her for a good job.' Then he left the ward.

Thina came round the screen and stuck her thumb up.

'Did you hear that, Sofia? Seems the bastard has a heart,' she whispered. 'Looks like it's going to be Zoë Eleftheria, then.'

She smiled and returned to the bedside of Anna Despotakis.

I felt crushed, but knew I had to get through the pretence of a working day. Once I had rested, I was overcome by the hopelessness of it all. Thina caught me behind the desk in tears.

'You have two choices, Sofia. Don't see the baby again – which will be easier – or spend every moment with her until she leaves. Whatever you choose will be almost unbearable, but I'll support you.'

'Are you mad? Zoë is *my* daughter. I have a right, a need, to hold her, care for her, simply look at her, for as long as possible.'

'Okay. I've made a plan,' Thina said. 'Everyone says the storm will be raging for another two days. I'm going to swap the beds around and put Anna in the operating room with an empty bed. I'm ordering you to stay with Anna and *her* baby at all times, so she gets the best possible care. Understood? If you agree, I'll inform Colonel Despotakis, and start moving the patients out of the operating room.'

It was an effort to stand up, never mind walk. I wasn't in pain, exactly; it simply felt as though I had pulled every muscle in my body, and then gone under a steamroller. I was no use to Thina, so she called Honey in again. At six o'clock, the cook came with a mountain of the most delicious food for Anna. She ate a little and left the rest for us. I don't know how Thina stayed on her feet, but she did. After we had all eaten, she and Honey rearranged the beds, and I was alone for the night with Anna and baby Zoë in the operating room.

* * *

I sat next to Anna's bed, holding my baby and watching the fine-boned woman who believed she had become a mother. Anna was exhausted due to the medication administered to induce labour. I reminded myself that she had gone through labour too. Her dead child, a little boy she had never seen or held, was bagged and hidden in the rubbish, to be disposed of in the prison landfill.

I thought about the colonel who believed he was Zoë's father. A man responsible for keeping thousands of people incarcerated, though all we wanted was the best for Greece and her people. Anna was innocent of these political crimes against us. She told me she was only sixteen when her arranged marriage had happened. Her meekness and timidity, her silence around her husband, did not speak of a happy marriage. All she wanted now was to love and care for her child in the best possible way.

I was mentally and physically drained. I knew that in just a few days, I would lose Zoë forever, but I tried to dismiss the future and focus on the joy of the present. That special moment when Zoë was first placed on my chest – my love poured out in a second that could never be surpassed. Feeling the weight of my treasured newborn against my breast, my thoughts were full of hope and love. I felt humbled, overcome by awe, and in shock that I had produced such a beautiful little creature.

I had no concern about what the future held for me, only that Zoë would be happy and safe in a free world. Her baby cries called to my heart, and my womb cramped painfully, nailing the bond that had formed between us while she was still in my womb. Those ties would only get stronger. I felt more love than I'd thought possible, and I knew I could never, ever forget her.

We had rigged up a cot from a drawer placed on two chairs, between our beds. When I found myself nodding off with the baby Zoë in my arms, I knew I had to put her down. Reluctantly, I did so, and caught a few hours' sleep. On waking, I felt a pang of jealousy to see Anna sitting up with Zoë on her breast.

I resisted the urge to snatch her away, swallowed my animosity and injected kindness into my voice.

'How are you feeling, Anna?'

She never took her eyes off baby Zoë.

'I finally know what unconditional love is, Sofia. I seem to have grown another heart in my chest and it's filled with all the love I have for my beautiful daughter.' Tears trickled down her cheeks. 'I can't explain more than that,' she continued. 'All I can say is that I love my daughter more than anything or anyone I know, and I will always do so.'

CHAPTER 34
MEGAN

Crete, present day.

THERE WERE SO MANY THINGS Megan wanted to say to her mother. Often, she hesitated, ashamed of her behaviour, or appreciating how foolish she had been. How could she have ever doubted that her mum cared about her? It was only now she understood the heartache she had caused. She knew she owed her mother the unabridged truth of her past.

They had walked to the seafront together, and her mother bought them lunch, lamb chops off the charcoal and village salad, at a beachside taverna. Megan couldn't stop apologising. She explained that she'd never realised how her family had fretted over her and, in the back of her mind, she even feared they had forgotten her. Since she and Simon had broken up, life had been filled with earning enough money to eat, and worrying about where she would sleep.

Her mum reached out, curled her fingers around Megan's hand and held on.

'Darling, I have to ask – what made you run away in the first place?'

Megan looked away. 'I'm so ashamed.'

'It doesn't matter. You have to tell me. Megan, I need to know where I went wrong.'

'Mum, you didn't do anything wrong. It was me, I completely messed up and made some stupid decisions. I never talked to you about anything.'

'Then tell me about it, and don't spare the details.'

Megan knew she was defeated. She had to explain what had happened or else it would always be between them.

'I'd been unhappy for months, Mum. I knew how much you and Dad wanted me to go to uni, study for a career that I really wasn't interested in. I don't take after you or Dad. Your skills are not my skills. I hated school. I always wanted to be a singer or a dancer or an actor. A performing artist, doing something on stage, no matter what. Even camera work, stage props, or costumes. I don't know. How could I talk to you about it, when I didn't even know exactly what I wanted to do myself? You'd think I was being childish, being naïve, and it just kept eating away at me.' She stared at the horizon. 'I had this overwhelming feeling I was letting you both down.' Megan turned and faced her mother, shocked to see the intense sadness on her face. 'I'm terribly sorry, Mum. I realise how wrong I've been now that I *am* talking to you about it. That's why I was desperate to talk to Granny Anna. I knew if I did, then I would see everything more clearly. I don't know why I didn't realise I could have simply come to you. I guess I didn't want to disappoint you.'

'You haven't disappointed me, Megan. Worried me, yes – disappointed me, no.'

Megan smiled faintly. She had better get it all out now.

'Anyway, I got mixed up with the wrong sort, kids that were older than me, who did drugs and drank too much and . . . Well, there was this guy, Mum. Simon. I never told you about him, but I was seeing him for a while. I thought he was really cool. I thought I was in love . . .

'There was a party. You thought I was on a sleepover, revising with my friends, but me and Simon and some of the girls

328

from school went to this house . . . I'd never seen anything like it. People were doing drugs and practically having sex in public. There was so much booze. It was like an X-rated movie.' She paused for a moment, not wanting to tell. 'Dad was there.'

She hesitated, not sure what else to say.

Her mother was astute. 'With another woman?'

Megan's eyes widened. She nodded.

Her mum sighed. 'Tell me the rest.'

Megan swallowed. 'She was all over him, and I . . . I was so angry, and I didn't know what to do. I didn't want Dad to see me, so we all went down to the pool and I kept drinking and . . .'

'Go on, Megan.'

'I smoked weed, Mum. I got so drunk I could hardly stand up. And then me and Simon started – you know – in the pool, and Dad came past and he saw and . . . and he got so mad. He went ballistic. He said my behaviour could damage your good reputation as a family lawyer and youth magistrate, beyond repair. He said having a daughter who was involved in drink and drugs would destroy his career if the press got hold of it, too.' She felt herself close to tears. 'Dad said I was reckless and irresponsible, that I should grow up and stop being so selfish. He reminded me how hard you both worked in order to give me and Josh everything we wanted.'

Her mum's mouth hung open for a moment.

'I begged him not to tell you, and swore I'd never, *ever*, let you down again. And Dad promised he wouldn't tell you. Did he?'

Mum shook her head. 'Your father always keeps his word.'

'Dad brought me home, dead drunk, and I just . . . Well, after that, I just couldn't bear it. I couldn't stand the idea of facing

Dad again, after what he'd seen me do, after what he *knew*. And I'd seen him with that woman, too, and I couldn't bear to ask him, to confront him – and I couldn't have told you about me without telling you about him, and I was so scared that if I told you about the woman I'd seen him with, he'd tell you everything. So I just ran. The next morning, I got up and I left that awful note . . . Mum, I'm so sorry. I bunked off school and went round to Simon's – he had a flat. I couldn't think straight. He said I could stay for a bit if I wanted, and he'd look after me. That evening, I thought maybe I'd made a mistake and I came back to the house, but there were police cars outside and I thought it was about the drugs. I got scared and I ran.'

Mum shook her head and dropped it into her hands.

'When the school phoned and said you hadn't arrived that morning, I went up to your room and found that note. I was out of my mind with worry – of course I called the police. Your dad had gone to Brussels that morning with work and I couldn't get hold of him. I was so scared.'

'I had no idea what to do.' Megan shook her head. 'I went back to Simon's. See, Mum, I thought I was in love.'

Her mum smiled softly.

'It was great at first. Fun. He was nice to me, and I felt grown up, keeping the flat nice, cooking meals. But then he started using more and more drugs, not just weed, but heavy stuff. He was dealing, too. It was all such a mess. Anyway, his flat was raided by the police, while I was at the shops one day. I was too scared to go back.'

'You should have come home.'

'I couldn't, don't you see? It had been months by then. And if the police had followed me, that would have been the end for you and Dad. I mean, Simon was drug-dealing, in with all sorts of bad people. What could be worse? And Dad would see how much I'd failed – how much worse I'd got. No, I couldn't.'

Megan sighed. 'I thought if I could do something good, to make you proud, then everything would be all right. I tried to get a job, but I had nowhere to stay and nothing seemed to work out. I managed to earn some money juggling on the street, but I was always afraid that someone I knew would see me, so I thumbed a lift up north. I was there for a few months, sleeping rough, trying to make money. I knew Granny Anna had gone back to Crete, so I thought if I could earn enough to go and see her, then she could help me talk to both of you, to make things right. She looked after me all my life, so I decided to go and look after her for a while, now that I'd got the hang of cooking and cleaning at Simon's. Granny Anna would tell me what to do about Dad. You see, I love you both, and it was all so confusing.' Megan trailed off, her eyes full of tears. 'I can't believe she's died.'

'Me neither. It's very hard to accept. Did you really think our careers were more important to us than you?'

Megan shrugged. 'You help a lot of people. And you've always been dead passionate about your work. It made me proud, you know, and I couldn't stand the thought of disrupting everything. And Dad, too – all those refugee kids. He's done amazing things for a lot of families. Where would they be without him? I could have ruined his reputation, put an end to his political career. I couldn't bear the thought. At the time, running away seemed the best thing to do. Instead of the slur of a daughter involved with drugs, you'd have everyone's sympathy.'

Her mother looked as though she were about to cry.

'It was a stupid idea. I'm so sorry, Mum.'

Although it was difficult, Megan was relieved to be able to talk and felt a great weight lifted from her shoulders. Her mother was really listening, for the first time in years.

'No, it's me that's sorry, Megan, darling. I should have made it clear that you can always count on me. I should have listened more. I should have been there for you.'

* * *

They talked all afternoon. It felt good to share, to talk about their lives and the past year on equal terms.

'I've caused all this trouble, Mum. I shouldn't have put Josh in such a difficult position either, making him promise not to tell that I'd called. And Dad, too – I'd made him promise not to let on about the party, and I guess he must have known that was sort of why I'd run away.'

'Megan, we all make mistakes. You're nearly an adult now. It's okay to learn some lessons.'

'I have – especially after hearing about Granny Anna. She was so wonderful, wasn't she? I can't believe she moved away when she was ill, just to spare you the worry and the strain.'

'She was a wonderful mother. I miss her so much.'

'What happened to Emily, Mum? I was devastated when the police told me she'd been killed.'

'Poor Emily. I don't believe she was a bad kid either. She was just struggling and alone. It's a sad story, but she'd become involved with drugs and a gang were searching for her. I was so afraid they'd mistake you for her, you looked so alike.'

'Emily and drugs? I don't believe it.'

'Her juggling balls were stuffed with heroin worth thousands. They found one in the room you slept in. Thank God your finger-prints weren't on them.'

'You're kidding me!' Megan thought for a moment. 'So that's why the police were so interested in mine. I'm sure Emily had no idea. She stole the balls from a guy she was living with for a while. I told the police when they interviewed me. Just goes to show . . .' She trailed off, realising things could have been a lot worse for her. 'Mum, I've been such an idiot.'

They sat in silence for a while, each with her own thoughts.

'Can we call Josh and Dad?' she said, wanting to change the subject.

Her mother nodded, and opened her handbag to search for her phone. It had slipped down the other side of the lining. As she pulled it out, a sealed envelope came with it. Mum frowned.

'What's that?' Megan asked, seeing the foreign stamps.

'It came on your birthday, from my mother's solicitor here in Crete. I'd forgotten about it.'

Her mother tore it open.

CHAPTER 35
SOFIA

Korydallos Prison, Athens, 1972.

I HANDED BABY ZOË TO ANNA DESPOTAKIS and asked how she was feeling.

'When your child is born, Sofia, you'll understand,' she said softly, nodding at my swollen belly. She didn't seem to notice that my waistline had been wider the day before. I tried to smile, not trusting my voice. Anna stroked my baby's cheek. 'My first two infants died in the womb. A little girl and a little boy. I blamed myself for their deaths, of course, always looking for things I must have done wrong. You see, I'd felt the life in them. I'd seen little elbows or knees poking up and moving across my belly as they turned. At night when I slept, my dreams of holding them were so vivid that I'd woken expecting to find my baby in my arms.' She kissed Zoë's head. 'Those dreams were all I had, until now.'

Her eyelids drooped and I understood her fatigue.

'Why don't you pass baby over to me and get some rest?'

'Just another minute.' She sighed. 'I know I'm lucky in these difficult times, because the colonel will make sure we have the best of everything. Zoë will have a nursemaid, and the finest schooling in Greece. She'll have ballet lessons, singing lessons, piano lessons. She'll learn to speak any languages she wants, choose any career, always with our support.' Her face crumpled and, for a moment, I thought she was going to cry. 'I've never been as happy as this in my life, Sofia. I can't describe the rush of emotion I felt when Thina placed her in my arms. Now I'm responsible for loving her, teaching her and guiding her through life's ups and downs. I know I'll always protect baby Zoë with my life.'

* * *

That night, I thought about all the things Anna could give my baby that I could not. But I also knew my child could be happy, and want for nothing, in the simple village life we had planned on the slopes of Mount Psiloritis. I dreamed of Markos, healed and healthy, playing with Zoë in the orchid meadow. She would help with the olive harvest and orange-gathering, and wear the national costume for the Zoniana cheese festival. Zoë would grow strong and healthy, with an outdoor life away from the smog of the city. She would dance while her father played the *lyra*. Life could be perfect.

Except, of course, Markos would probably never play the *lyra* again.

When I woke, dawn was pushing back the night in Kory-dallos and I had been crying in my sleep. On this day I would say goodbye to my baby – and who knew when, or if, I would ever see her again?

At least my daughter would be away from the cursed prison and in the safe hands of a good woman.

I held Zoë at every opportunity, snuggling her close to my chest. I told her to listen to my heartbeat, to remember it, in the hope that one day she would hear it again.

Later that day, as the roaring wind outside abated, a swallow flew in through the high window, explored the room in a darting

335

flight, and then returned outdoors. It seemed like an omen. Anna needed the bathroom, and for a few precious minutes I was left with Zoë. I did not know if I would ever be alone with her again, and I had so much to say.

'My dearest darling daughter, I love you with all my heart. Be good for Anna. She'll make a wonderful mother. I feel it. Take my blessings for a good, happy life. That is all I can give you.

'I want you to know that in the few hours we've had together you have changed my life, and the life of your courageous father. He loves you so much. He'll always fight for your liberty, for a free world for you, where swallows duck and dive over the orchid fields, and men sing whatever they like in the *kafenio*. Keep me in your heart, my beloved baby, until we meet again.'

Tears pricked the backs of my eyes and I had to swallow hard to stay in control.

When Anna returned, she could see I was emotional.

'I'm sorry,' I said, forcing the words through the pain in my throat. 'I've grown so attached to her that I don't want to see her go.'

'She *is* precious, isn't she?' Anna smiled. 'You've been so kind, Sofia. I couldn't have wished for better care. I'm sure my daughter owes her life to you. If ever you're in Athens, please come and see us. I'll give you my address and telephone number. You'll always be welcome.' She glanced at the bed. 'I guess I'd better shower and dress, ready for when the taxi arrives. Will you look after her for another half an hour?'

'Of course. It's my pleasure.'

I glanced at Anna and for a second, God forgive me, I wanted to kick the legs from under her. I longed to smash down the prison gates and run, as far and as fast as I could, with Zoë grasped tightly against my chest.

Yet I had to be strong, for everyone's sake. For Zoë, above all.

When the hour came, I handed over my child. Thina was at my side and I sensed her concern. She feared I would break down and not let go of my baby – or worse, claim she was mine. For my daughter's sake, with my heart like lead in my breast, I placed her in the arms of Anna Despotakis.

When the door finally closed on the colonel, Anna and my baby, I stared after them, my vision swimming. Cold and stiff, I was filled with a sense of awful shock. I thought a condemned woman must feel the same when she put her head on the block under a guillotine, accepting the inevitable.

I had already died inside.

'Go and change your uniform, quickly,' Thina ordered, staring at my chest.

I looked down and saw two round, wet patches over my breasts. My milk had come in.

CHAPTER 36
SOFIA

Korydallos Prison, Athens, 1972.

A WEEK AFTER I HAD given up Zoë, they dragged Markos into the ward, unconscious and dehydrated.

'What have they done to you?' I asked, after we had pumped him full of fluids and he regained consciousness.

'I signed the papers,' he said.

I was so amazed, so pleased, that I began to cry.

'I swore allegiance to the bastard government and said everything they wanted me to say – but still it's not enough! They've ordered me to inform on my comrades. Me, a traitor. I can't do it, Sofia.'

'Oh, Markos!'

'We have to escape,' he said, slowly. 'I can't bear it any longer. I want to be with you, in the real world. And maybe, just maybe, we can find a way to get Zoë back.'

I said nothing, and stared at the floor. I knew this was impossible. It was a heartbreaking thought that we had no proof she was ours. However, in the outside world, we could have more children and live the life of a normal family.

'I'm making a plan,' Markos whispered. 'You won't leave unless I do, right?'

I shook my head.

'Going together is doomed to fail. So, you must go, and I'll follow.'

'*No*, Markos! Don't ever suggest such a thing again! You go first, and then I'll find a way to be released. I've already got the colonel on my side – he appreciates everything I did for Anna. I think he'd be lenient if I confessed to my wrongs and swore allegiance to the government. Besides, I'm up for a review at the end of the month. I just have to sign the papers and swear an oath that I'll never write subversive songs again.'

Markos was silent for a long time.

At last I asked, 'How do you intend to escape this hellhole?'

'With the help of flour-man Fannes.'

'There's no way you can get outside the fence – it's too heavily guarded.'

'You're right . . .' He glanced at the window. 'That's the difficult part.'

* * *

A plan was hurriedly put into action. Fannes delivered the flour at noon on a Friday. He dropped the full sacks off at the gate, where the empty ones were stacked and waiting for him. A note was placed in the pile telling him that Markos would be hidden in the next stack of sacks.

It was a wild plan, incredibly dangerous if he got caught, but we could see no other option. Markos was desperate.

I could hardly breathe for excitement. Markos and I would soon be free. Markos dreamed of finding a way to get Zoë back, and though I knew how near impossible that was, his hope was infectious. I began to plan out all sorts of possibilities. I had Anna's address, after all. I could get a job in her household as a nursemaid, and spend as much time as possible with Zoë; then, one night, I could take her from the house and we would run as fast as we could, Markos and our child and me.

But what a wicked thing to do to Anna. If I committed such a terrible act, caused so much pain, then I would be no better than the bastards that tortured us all.

The ward was full, but I was in no state to look after anyone. When I dropped the bedpans, Thina rolled her eyes and told me to concentrate on my job. When I messed up a catheter removal, and ended up drenched in a patient's pee, she became angry, even though the patient found it entertaining.

'Sofia! Concentrate, will you! I'm trying to teach you, and we've got a job to do.'

I glanced at the window, wondering where Markos was. His plan to cut through the wire fence was weak, but we couldn't think of another way to get outside the prison. It was pitch-black outside and had been for the past hour. I heard gunfire just after dark. Although that was nothing unusual, the horror of what might be made me gasp. I turned towards Thina, wanting to share my fears, yet afraid to do so.

'Listen – did you hear that, Sofia? It sounds as though we're in for a busy night.' She studied me for a moment. 'Are you all right? You seem upset.'

'Sorry, sorry, it's just that . . . Oh, Thina!'

'What's going on?'

I hesitated, but couldn't keep it secret any longer. Thina was my friend, and I owed her a lot. We went to the desk, out of earshot of the patients, and I told her about Markos's planned escape.

'I'm so afraid for him!'

'Let's sort the casualties out, and then I'll see what I can find out from Agapi. There's nothing you can do but get on with your job.'

Later that night, the priest came into the ward hugging his arm. Thina examined him. 'A distal radius fracture,' she said.

I frowned at her.

'A broken wrist, Sofia. You know this stuff. A break in the larger of the two bones in his forearm. They seem to be aligned, so we can deal with it if you get your head into gear.'

The old priest was ashen. Thina tried to take his attention away from the pain as she splinted his arm.

'Any gossip from inside, Father? Do you know what the gunfire was about?'

'Another soul gone to meet his maker. Someone was trying to escape.'

I gripped the bedhead.

'They didn't make it, then?' Thina asked casually.

'Patrol caught him the other side of the fence. A guard shot at him, but another got caught in the crossfire. The inmate caught a graze, but the guard's dead.'

'Do you know who it was?' Thina asked, still keeping her voice calm. 'Where's the inmate? If he's injured, they should bring him in.'

'No point, is there? He'll be in solitary now and they'll put him before the firing squad on the morrow. No getting away from that. Poor fool. May God save his sorry soul.'

My knees buckled and I struggled to say upright. Thina pulled the screen around the priest and told him to try and rest.

'They can't shoot him, Thina,' I hissed, as she pulled me out of earshot. 'My God, what have we done?' The panic was frothing up inside me. 'How can we save him?'

She took me by the shoulders and shook me. 'Stop it, Sofia! Pull yourself together. He's a grown man and he's made his own decisions – and you're no use to him in this state!'

Although she spoke severely, I saw pity in her eyes, but then a spark of fear. I too would risk death if my relationship with Markos was revealed, and Thina and I would both face the firing squad if the truth about the colonel's baby came out.

'I've got a bit of coffee stashed,' she said, her voice softening a little. 'I'm going to make us a drink. We must calm down and try to work something out, all right? Hysterics won't get us anywhere.'

I watched her make the drinks, but my mind was on Markos, agonising over his fate. I turned to the window. The night was a black abyss staring back at me. Then, clutching at straws, it occurred to me that we didn't know for sure that the man who had been shot was Markos. My man could be in the back of the flour truck right at that moment, heading for Piraeus and a ferry to Crete.

My spirits rose. 'Thina, perhaps it wasn't Markos. Have you thought of that? He might not have been the only prisoner planning to escape tonight.'

She passed me a tiny coffee cup and frowned, her drink halfway to her mouth.

'Get that inside you while I talk to the priest.'

'I'll go!'

'No, you won't. You're too emotional. Besides, we don't know if he's working for them or not. Think about it – who better to gather information for the junta than a priest? All those last words spoken in confidence. No, I don't trust him. I'll go.'

She hurried across the ward and disappeared behind the screen.

I glanced around the ward, checking everyone was asleep, and then moved closer to the priest's bed. I found the chink in the screen's fabric and peered through. The patient's sad face was illuminated under the bed lamp. Thina had propped him up with extra pillows. She had a wonderful way with patients, her voice steady, authoritative yet sympathetic. I felt a tug of impatience as she made small talk, but still I listened eagerly to every word that passed between them.

Thina was gaining the priest's confidence by telling him why she was imprisoned. Her brother, a dissident, had disappeared and she had refused to give the junta information as to his whereabouts. She didn't know where he was, but they refused to believe her.

'May I ask what brought you here, Father?' she asked.

After a long silence, lost in his own thoughts, he said, 'I made a mistake. I thought they would respect a man of God. I thought I was immune to their evil. I came to the prison of my own free will, to help the dying – to try and bring them a little peace in their last moments. The junta saw me as a communist sympathiser and decided I should stay.' He pushed his sparse hair back. 'They tried to turn me into an informer, but I refused. They beat me and threatened to kill me, but I have no fear of death. I've earned my place in Heaven. Eventually, they gave up.'

'Do you know the man they caught trying to escape tonight?'

'They call him Che Guevara on account of him looking like that poor devil from the Cuban revolution. Now he'll end up in the same situation, poor soul.'

I bit on my knuckles to stop myself crying out.

'He's had a terrible time of it,' the priest went on. 'They use him as an example to the other prisoners, so for all his fighting against the junta, in the end, most men see what punishment he takes and decide to give in. Not what he was suffering for, was it?'

I crept back to the desk, tears on my face. They couldn't take Markos away from me. Without him, without Zoë, I was nothing.

The muffled voices from behind the screen continued, but I was lost in my own misery. I could think of nothing but my dearest love, the father of my child. The man who would face a firing squad unless a miracle happened.

* * *

I woke when a hand touched my shoulder. I saw Thina's sorrowful face and the desolation in her eyes. I pressed my hands on my belly, slack and flabby now the fruit of my womb had left the prison with another woman. A spark of self-pity reared. What had I done to deserve all this? Everyone I loved seemed destined to face death. Why not me? It would be so simple to save someone's medication, such a relief to fade into nothing. I wanted to die before Markos, to be waiting for him in some idyllic afterlife with my arms outstretched at the pearly gates.

'You have to be strong,' Thina whispered, as if reading my mind.

'I've got no strength left in me. Why, Thina? Whose bastard plan is this – to cause so much pain in one lifetime – and for what purpose?'

'Come on, let's squeeze another coffee out of those grounds. I've got something to tell you.'

* * *

Markos's trial was the following afternoon, but I knew the sentence and execution were already written. Thina made me take some pills before walking back to our room with me. Agapi returned just after us, dishevelled and smelling of sex.

I sat on the edge of the bed, fighting sleep, exhausted. Agapi and Thina had their heads together, whispering, glancing at me.

'For God's sake, at least share what's going on. Give me that much, please!' I cried. 'What do you know, Agapi? Tell me!'

Honey turned in her bed, opened her eyes and sat up. 'What's happening?'

Nobody answered.

Agapi sighed and stared at me through her smudged mascara.

'The guard told me that Despotakis himself is heading the trial, but they've hoisted the black flag over the exercise yard already. It's a foregone conclusion.'

'I want to kill Despotakis!' I cried. 'Can't we do that, inject him with something lethal?'

Honey swung her legs out of bed and blinked at me.

'Don't talk crazy,' Thina said. 'We'd all end up as target practice, and what good would that do?' She sat next to me and slipped her arm around my shoulders. 'Listen, Sofia, I had a long talk to the priest. He's a good man. I told him you and Markos were engaged, nothing else, and I asked if he could marry you before . . . you know.' She squeezed hard as the hopelessness of the situation overwhelmed me. Unable to speak, I nodded. 'He said he'd sort something out for tomorrow afternoon, immediately after the trial. It's all been arranged. Agapi used her charms on Markos's guard. He's agreed to bring Markos to the ward just long enough for the ceremony.' She squeezed my hand. 'I'm so sorry, Sofia. There's nothing else I can do.'

* * *

The patients of our small ward were hurriedly discharged, or moved into other wards. Together, my friends dressed me for my wedding. Agapi gave me her best dress, a long, cream lace gown with a scalloped neckline. I tried to concentrate on my

345

wedding vows to Markos, but nothing could take my mind away from the inevitable. Soon, Markos would be dead. The wedding ceremony itself was dangerous – if any of the other guards saw, save the one Agapi had persuaded to help us, then they would know what Markos and I were to each other. But my man was already doomed, and I did not care now if they killed me. However, my amazing friends were putting themselves at incredible risk, for my sake. Their loyalty and friendship filled my heart and uplifted me.

Agapi applied my make-up and added a dab of perfume to my wrists. Honey managed to smuggle in two wine glasses and a posy of artificial flowers that started life as a table decoration in the officers' mess. It was all ridiculous, and yet it made the day bearable.

At four o'clock, my friends made me stand behind the screen in the corner of the ward. Holding the stupid flowers, I waited. The door creaked open. Determined to be strong for the man I loved, I took a deep breath and stepped out.

Markos, unshaven, wearing a white shirt, stood next to the priest. I could not remember the last time I had seen him without his precious beret on. He dropped his head to one side and, though his hands shook, he reached out for mine and smiled. All the love he had for me shone from his brown eyes. I could barely stand for my grief and love of him, but I managed to walk to his side and passed the posy to Thina.

The priest cleared his throat.

'Do you, Markos Papas, take Sofia Bambaki to be your wife?'

'Yes, I do,' he said, gazing into my eyes.

'And do you, Sofia Bambaki, take Markos Papas to be your husband?'

I swallowed a sob and whispered, 'I do.'

The priest delved into his pocket and produced a ring that appeared to be made of bone. He placed it on the open page of his prayer book, blessed it, and continued.

'Markos Papas, state your wedding vow to your new wife.'

Markos turned to face me and took my hands in his. I could feel his gnarled and twisted fingers and longed to kiss them, to heal them.

'I'll always love you, Sofia,' he whispered. 'Be sure of that. Don't ever forget me, my darling. When the sun comes up, say good morning and think of me. When you raise a glass, call my name – and, one day, find our precious child and tell her that I will always love her, too.' He was silent for a second. 'I know I have not been able to give you the life you longed for, and I regret that, but I have always loved you, more than anything else in all the world. In spirit, I'll always be with you and our daughter. I swear this on my wedding oath.'

'Sofia Papas, state your wedding vow to your new husband.'

I lifted Markos's broken hands and kissed them tenderly, then took a deep breath to steady my voice.

'This is my oath to you, my beloved husband. Whatever I do, whatever I see, wherever life takes me, you will always be with me in my heart, Markos. I swear that I will try and find our child and tell her how you loved us both. No other man will ever share my love. I was always yours, and I always shall be.'

'You may place the ring on Sofia's finger,' the priest said.

Markos lifted the ring with his thumb and his little finger and awkwardly tried to slip it onto my hand. Everyone leaned in, willing it to fit, but it fell to the floor and broke.

'Oh, sorry! Sorry!' I cried, bending down to scoop it up.

The ring had broken clean in two, and on examining it, I saw the words engraved on the inside: *Life* and *Freedom*. Markos took one half, *Freedom*, and I held onto his, *Life*.

The priest blessed us, and then the guard escorted us next door, into the operating room. My mind spiralled. These seconds had to last forever; they were all we had. Our child was out there in the free world and my husband's life was about to end. I had lost everything I loved – but now, just for now, we were together.

'You have thirty minutes to say goodbye,' the guard said, with a glance over his shoulder at Agapi. 'I'll be outside.'

I had so much to say – a whole lifetime of words to squeeze into minutes. Yet I found myself unable to speak. At that moment, words didn't matter; they were nothing but noise, and silence seemed more sacred.

We held each other. 'Markos, I wish—'

He placed a finger on my lips. 'Wishes are no use to us now. Let's not waste our last moments. Kiss me hard, a kiss I'll never forget, and I will take all your love with me into the ever-after. Tell my daughter about me, Sofia. Find her for me and perhaps, one day, bring her to my graveside to weep for her father.'

'I don't want you to go!'

'Quiet now.' He placed his mouth over mine.

I opened his shirt, and my dress, and pressed my naked body against his. His heart beat against my breast, and our tears mingled as we made love with all the passion and tenderness time allowed.

When that final knock sounded, Markos whispered, 'Turn yourself away from me. I don't want you to see me go.' He took me by the shoulders and turned me around, so my back was to the door. From behind me, he whispered into my ear, 'Remember this moment, Sofia. Know that I love you more than life. I will always be near, on the other side of the door, behind a tree, around the corner, somewhere just out of sight. If you need me, you'll always find me in your heart.'

I felt his sigh, warm on the back of my neck. I breathed in deeply, hoping to take some of his breath inside me, to keep alive forever. Then, I heard someone enter, a few quiet words, and the door closed.

I was alone, and Markos was gone.

* * *

The whine of the old bus to the execution site filtered through the hospital window. I climbed on the stool and peered out. As it came level, I saw an arm come out of the back window, and Markos's beret flew through the air as he slung it towards the hospital building, crying 'Eleftheria!' Freedom!

I wanted so much in that second. I thought back on our many years together: the first time I had ever seen him – that school-boy at the marble statue who offered me food; that proud face in the audience at so many of my concerts; that brave, brave man who had fought for a better world.

And I thought of our daughter, Zoë Eleftheria, the beautiful child we had made together. A part of him that would live on.

The beret landed on the barbed wire and hung there like a lost soul in purgatory, neither free nor imprisoned. My heart ached.

When the bus had passed from view, and I knew I would never look upon him again, I stepped off the stool and pressed my back against the wall. My eyes, blinded by tears, fixed the ward clock as the second hand ticked towards the execution hour.

Thina came over and tried to place her arms around me, but I shrank from her embrace.

'Don't touch me. Leave me alone with this moment. Let me have this pain, raw in my heart for the rest of my days!'

I stood in solidarity, just as Markos would, straight and strong and proud of the life he'd led. Triumphant for all the poor souls he had saved. Rejoicing that Zoë would live on with his blood flowing through her veins, and his love in her heart.

Thina stepped away, out of my line of vision.

My concentration returned to the clock until the face of it was all I could see, and the sound of each tick all I could hear.

The second hand passed the halfway mark and moved towards six o'clock. Each of my breaths was a deep, hard celebration of life, as I knew were Markos's. We were one person as that hand hit the hour. Our souls united in the dark, to embrace one last time.

Through the broken window, the sound of gunfire reverberating over the prison camp reached me. I fell to my knees, weeping. From that moment on, I was to live the rest of my life without the man I loved.

* * *

The following evening, Agapi used her charms once again and got me a pass out to visit the cemetery. I knelt at Markos's freshly dug grave, my hands flat on earth that was still warm from the heat of the day.

My heart, like our wedding ring, was broken in two. I rose to my feet and let my emotions take over. Facing the rising moon, I filled my lungs with what I imagined to be Markos's last breath, then I sang at the top of my voice:

My child, you were life's sweet song,
Though you were not with me for long.
I glimpse your empty chair,
Through tears, see you there,
Lullabies are now your sweetest songs.

Oh, lover, you are life's sweet song,
I'll see you again before long.
Angels, wings give you flight,
Every star-spangled night.
My love, you are life's sweetest songs.

They could shoot me. At that moment, I didn't care.

And then I thought of Zoë, a part of Markos who would go on to achieve great things. His love lived in her heart. His bravery and selflessness would give her the strength of spirit to help so many, and make the world a better place.

Markos lived on in his daughter.

CHAPTER 37
ZOË

Crete, present day.

'Come on, sleepyhead. Let's go and get some breakfast,' Zoë said. 'Time for coffee and eggs on fresh bread at the harbour. Just like the old days. And then we'll head over to the solicitor's office to go over those documents they mentioned in the letter.'

Megan mumbled something incoherent.

'I'll get the first shower then, while you wake up.'

Soon, they were walking around the marina towards the harbour.

'Tell me about Granny Anna, Mum,' Megan said.

Zoë smiled. 'Granny Anna was an excellent mother to me, quite strict sometimes, but only in my best interests. I don't think I've ever told you this, but I was her third child. Her other two babies died before term.'

'So that made her cherish you even more?'

Zoë nodded. 'She was married to a soldier, some sort of colonel in the Greek army. She never wanted to talk about my father. I sometimes wonder if theirs was an unhappy marriage. She said he was a good man, doing his duty for his country. He had a heart attack and died a few years after my birth.'

'How awful.'

'I never really *knew* him. I do have vague recollections of his return home for a few days, bringing me new dolls, and flowers and chocolates for Mama. But that's it, really, and Mama said her photographs were lost when she moved.'

Megan's chin rested on her fists as she gazed at her mother. Zoë smiled.

'I don't remember much else about my childhood in Greece – except that I had a nanny that I adored for a while. She taught me to paint, always one picture for Mama and one for her. Once, she put blotting paper around the inside of a jam jar and we grew beans. I asked if she could put blotting paper on my bed, so I could grow faster.' Zoë smiled. 'We laughed and laughed, and then she started crying. She was always crying. I think she must have had great trouble in her life.'

'What happened to her?'

'We moved to England and I never saw her again. I often think about her, though. I called her Aunty Sofie, though she was no relation, just an old friend of Mama's.'

Zoë took Megan's hand. 'Greece was going through troubled times, both politically and financially, in the seventies. After Papa died, my mother managed to claim some sort of refugee status.' She frowned, wondering if that was really possible. It didn't sound right now that she said it out loud. 'We moved to England so that I'd receive a better education.'

'It's such a pity you never got to know your father, Mum. It must have been quite hard for Granny Anna to bring you up as a single parent in those days.'

'It probably was, but she always managed. She received financial help for my education right up until I finished university.'

'What, from the army?'

'Yes. Well, I suppose so. I never questioned it.'

They walked along the promenade until they arrived at Zoë's favourite taverna, near the marine museum.

'Let's sit here and eat breakfast together.' Zoë smiled. 'I dreamed about this moment so often while you were missing.'

Megan glanced at her guiltily. 'What do you want to do today?'

'I'd like to take flowers to the cemetery. We could go together.'

Megan nodded sadly. 'Do you think she was happy, Mum?'

Zoë nodded. 'Isn't it terrible that I never thought of that until after she died? She always *seemed* happy. Mama loved us all, didn't she? She gave me the freedom to continue with my career, and she adored you and Josh.'

The taverna owner came rushing out.

'*Ela!* Welcome back, *Kyria* Zoë! Why you stay away so long? Where is *Yiayá* Anna?' Without waiting for an answer, he turned to Megan. 'No! I do not believe it. This *koukla,* this little doll, cannot be your daughter – but wait, yes, I see she has all the beauty of her mother! We must lock up our sons, those dark eyes will break many hearts!' He turned to Zoë. 'How did she grow up, yet you become no older? Praise the Blessed Virgin, it's a miracle!'

Zoë laughed. It seemed almost impossible that her dreams had really come true. Megan was here with her. As the clouds of the past months dissipated, she thought about Frank and Josh, and wished they were there too.

Megan broke into her thoughts.

'Can we go to Granny Anna's cottage tomorrow? I got the bus to Kissamos with Gary and Jeff, and we all searched, but we couldn't find the house.'

Zoë nodded. 'Of course. In fact, why don't we go today? We can go to the solicitor's tomorrow. I only need to collect some documents – Greek bureaucracy, I guess. I'm not looking forward to that, so let's just go to Granny's first.'

'Great. Can we try Josh and Dad again? I can't believe neither of them picked up yesterday.'

Zoë nodded, and took out her phone. Truth be told, she was a little nervous about speaking to Frank. She hadn't yet got up the courage to tell Megan that she and her father had split up. She could barely trust herself to speak to Frank without shouting at him, now that she knew he must have had an inkling of why Megan ran away.

She tried Josh's mobile, and Frank's, but both went to voice-mail again.

An old woman, dressed in black, shuffled up to the table and smiled at them both. Zoë recognised her as the one on the ferry from Athens. Oddly pleased to see her again, she dipped into her purse and gave her a ten-euro note.

The old woman tapped her heart and bowed. Their eyes met and Zoë felt an aching sadness for the woman, who placed another slip of paper on the table beside her.

'I wonder what her story is,' Zoë whispered, as she moved on to the next table.

A draught caught the paper and blew it onto the quayside.

'Poor old thing,' she whispered as the breeze lifted the note into the harbour. 'She seems so alone.'

She watched the slip float for a moment, before it sank out of sight.

CHAPTER 38
SOFIA

Crete, present day.

I WANDERED AROUND THE QUAYSIDE tables, giving out slips of paper until I had to take the weight off my feet. From a pavement café I watched the woman who had generously given me ten euros. The girl opposite her must be her daughter. They were happy, excited; the mother took her daughter's hand and kissed it. And though I was smiling, my emotions were tangled and my heart sore. If things had turned out differently, that could have been me and my daughter.

My darling Markos was waiting for me in the afterlife; I felt it in my heart. Weary from the search, I longed to join him. My tears rose, and I felt them trickle down my cheeks.

The café proprietor knew me and brought a Greek coffee and a thick slice of bread sprinkled with olive oil and oregano. When I tried to pay, he passed me a napkin and said, 'Dry your tears, *Yiayá*, this one's from me.'

I bowed in thanks, then pulled the baby shawl from my bag and started crocheting. This month, surely, I would find my baby. She was here for the carnival; I felt it in my bones.

Someone had left a local newspaper on the seat. I put my handicraft to one side and studied the tabloid, though I hardly understood what was going on in the world.

The woman and her daughter were deep in conversation. The mother lifted her hand and ran it down her daughter's hair in a gesture of affection. I remembered Markos doing the same in our last moments together and my heart squeezed.

I miss you so much, Markos.

And I miss you, my love.

Bored with the news, I turned to the obituaries and memorial services. Anna Despotakis's name leaped off the page. My heart pounded dangerously. Anna Despotakis, my old friend, guardian of my daughter, had died more than a month before.

I took some calming breaths, but my tears returned as I recalled the events that had brought us together so many years ago. Such joy. Such heartbreak.

For all these years I had searched Greece for Anna and Zoë. I wiped my eyes and returned my attention to the announcement; it contained a lawyer's address and phone number. At last, I had discovered the linchpin to my past.

I wrote a note for the proprietor of the café and he kindly phoned the lawyer, making an appointment for that afternoon.

* * *

On the other side of town, weary from the walk, I found the lawyer's office. The heavy glass doors proved a challenge, pushing me back onto the pavement like the flippers of a pinball machine, just when I thought I was making headway. Eventually, after conquering the door, I faced steep marble steps.

I filled my lungs, gripped the handrail and started up. One step at a time. Halfway to the top, thigh muscles I didn't know I had protested. I ground to a halt, legs trembling, forehead greasy. Halfway up – halfway down – I turned and sat on the stair. Would I ever reach my goal? A young woman, skinny as a sparrow, flicked the entrance doors open and skipped up the stairs in her short, tight skirt and spiky heels. I quashed a sudden temptation to stick my foot out.

'You all right, *Yiayá*? Can I give you a hand?'

I smiled, and struggled to my feet. With my arm looped into hers and my heart thumping, she whisked me up to the lawyer's office.

Relieved to find Anna's old lawyer, Mr Rodakis, nodding off at his desk, I tapped on the wood to wake him and handed him a note I'd written earlier.

He read it, then stared at me, clearly surprised by my state of shabbiness.

'*You* are Sofia Bambaki?'

I nodded, touched my mouth and made a sawing motion under my chin.

'You can't speak?'

I nodded again.

'You've come about Anna Despotakis and Zoë Eleftheria?'

I had never wished I had my voice more than at that moment. Tears of frustration pricked my eyes. I balled my fists and thumped myself in the chest in an act of pure frustration.

The lawyer was my age: a bespectacled man with a worried face. He called the woman who had helped me up the stairs and introduced her as his granddaughter, Mimi.

'This is Sofia Bambaki,' he explained. 'A famous singer in my day, but now she can't speak.'

Mimi made a little bow, smiled kindly and shook my hand.

'Sofia has been a client of mine since the seventies, but we lost touch when our office moved to Chania. Can you retrieve her file, and bring us coffee?' He turned to me. 'Sweet?'

I nodded.

'We tried to contact you when we moved,' he said as the door closed, 'but the telephone number you gave us was no longer in use. We wrote, but never received a reply.'

I left home to search for my daughter, I wrote.

'The money you set up for Zoë Despotakis's education ran out, not long after she completed her university degree. She studied to become a lawyer herself, as it happens.'

I filled up with pride, and my tears finally overflowed. With a kind smile, Mr Rodakis drew a box of tissues from his desk drawer and handed it over.

Mimi returned with the coffees as I started writing another note. Mr Rodakis stopped me.

'Mimi, bring your tablet in for *Kyria* Bambaki, would you?'

After a shaky start, I got the hang of typing my words on the tablet.

Where is she?

'You mean your daughter, Zoë?'

I nodded, dabbing at my tears with a tissue.

'I went to see Anna just before she passed away. She was my cousin, you know. Zoë was with her.'

I gasped. He'd seen my daughter! My grown-up daughter. Did he shake hands, hug her, kiss her cheeks? I felt myself turning inside out with emotion.

He paused and sighed. 'Neither of them know the truth, Sofia, and I thought it was best to leave it that way, at least while Anna was alive. Near the end, Anna said she would like to see Zoë. Her sister telephoned London, and Zoë came straight over. She returned to London after Anna's death, where I believe she is happily married with two children.'

Filled with the greatest joy and sadness, I tried to take it all in. I did not have the strength to travel to London, and I could not speak English. My darling daughter was well and happy, and what more could a mother ask for? Of course I longed to hold her once before I died, but that was pure selfishness.

I reached for the tablet.

Please describe my daughter for me. I have not seen my child since she was a little girl.

He nodded. I closed my eyes and, with the lawyer's help, I built an image of my girl.

'She's quite tall, perhaps five eight. Dark, curly hair, as you would expect, past her shoulders, I think, but clipped up the way you women do. Beautiful features, even without make-up. Perfect skin. Full mouth. Medium nose. Brown eyes with gold flecks.'

Markos's eyes. I'd seen eyes like that recently, but I couldn't remember where. Rodakis continued.

'Slim, but not skinny. What I believe are called "child-bearing hips". A very eloquent talker as I remember. Stylish, even when dressed casually. Despite her intense grief, she looked very beautiful at Anna's funeral. Everyone wanted to know who she was.'

I found myself smiling.

* * *

The time had come to end my search for the baby I had given away all those years ago. My love for our child had never died; I remembered every moment we had spent together, and recalled Markos's tears as he held our daughter, moments after her birth. His words came back to me: *She will have life and freedom, Sofia.* And it seemed his prophecy had come true.

What more could we ask for, Markos? I'm so tired, my love. Can I give up this search?

Wherever Zoë is, she is still our child, Sofia. Nothing can change that. You are free, my darling.

Finally defeated, I wept with the futility of it all, and with my tears, I felt a great weight lift from me.

Once I'd pulled myself together, I decided the time had come to end this search and go back to my little room in Athens. I would leave immediately after the carnival. Mr Rodakis and his daughter watched curiously as I pulled an odd assortment of things out of my travel bag. The shawl, my half of the wedding ring, Spyridon's gold locket, a crumpled nursery painting and a brown envelope. I placed these things in a line on the desk and thought I should write a letter to Zoë. There was so much I wanted to say. But then I looked at the brown envelope that Markos had given to me and, remembering the contents, I considered it was enough.

I tapped a message on the tablet:

I am giving up my search for Zoë. If she ever gets in touch with you again, please give her these things.

Then, relieved of my life's baggage, I got to my feet and left the office.

*   *   *

Back at the harbour, while walking past the fort, I slipped a hand into my pocket and rolled the sea glass between my fingers. I reminded myself that although there was no clue as to what it had once been, it was unique, changed, but still a thing of beauty and value.

In a shady corner under a tree near the fountain, in Talos Square, I rested on a bench. The public swimming baths were nearby. I could get a shower, much needed after my long walk from the lawyer's office. On my travels, I usually bathed in the sea, but it would be nice to wash the salt from my long hair. Sometimes, people left shampoo or shower cream behind, and such a luxury added to my pleasure.

A couple of children ran about the grassed square in their fancy-dress costumes. I wondered if the children in England dressed up for carnival week as they did in Greece. Had Zoë been a fairy, Cinderella, or perhaps when she was older, Athena, or a pop singer? Had Zoë's children, my grandchildren, dressed up too? I hoped so.

My thoughts drifted back to Markos. Closing my eyes, I recalled standing at his graveside, singing my heart out.

CHAPTER 39
ZOË

Crete, present day.

THAT AFTERNOON, ZOË TOOK MEGAN to Granny Anna's cottage, but they found it empty and the outside defaced with graffiti. Black swastikas, *KKE* daubed in red and hammer and sickle signs spoiled the flaking outside walls. The door was unlocked, but they had to put their shoulders to it because grit had blown under the doorjamb.

Inside, although covered in months of dust, the contents seemed undisturbed. Great-aunt Calliopi and Granny Anna had clearly spent much of their time on crocheting and embroidery; the cushions, curtains, tablecloths and bed linen were all handmade. A shelf of painted plates surrounded the room and, at the far end, stood an enormous bed, the honey-coloured wooden spindles supporting an embroidered canopy above the mattress. Against the back wall, in the cave-like sleeping area, another shelf was laden with handmade linen. Garish icons adorned the walls; their solid-gold haloes glinted in the dull light. Plastic flowers in yellowing cut-glass vases, and varnished seashells, were displayed atop the mismatched furniture.

Above a bow-fronted walnut sideboard, the 3-D silver foil image of New York's Empire State Building made such a bizarre contrast. Next to this, adding to the surrealism of the room, a cream plastic relief of Rembrandt's *Last Supper* hung in a resin frame of fairies and bluebells.

'This is soooo cool!' Megan said. 'I'd completely forgotten what Granny Anna's looked like inside. Nobody could actually *make* a place like this. It's a museum packed with generations of personal memorabilia. Can you take lots of photos while I go to the loo, Mum?'

The bathroom was a small, brick cubicle outside. A faded brocade curtain hung in the doorway and inside, the corners were lost in a candyfloss of cobwebs. The smallest room, lit by a bare bulb, contained a peach toilet with no lid or cistern, just a bucket of stale water beside it. Over a small washbasin was a well-worn tap. Burnished brass showed through the chrome. From this, a cheap rubber hose and showerhead looped around a nail in the wall. Drainage was a round grid in the floor.

Outside, the olive grove and the garden were overgrown, and although the place should have had an air of abandonment, it was vibrant with colour and wildlife.

Morning glory tangled through a lemon tree near the door. The purple trumpets were a startling contrast to the vivid lemons and white, waxy blossom. Zoë plucked a couple of the dark, leathery leaves and passed one to Megan. They snapped them, inhaling the zing of citrus oil.

With their backs to the graffiti, Zoë sat with her daughter on the patio bench, a white-painted scaffolding plank on four cinder blocks. They rubbed the citrus oil onto their ankles to keep away mosquitoes. Zoë gazed over the tousled garden and spotted a brilliant-green lizard with a yellow throat waddling along a stone wall. The reptile stopped to stare at them, bobbed its head a couple of times, then disappeared over the other side.

'Did you see that?' Megan whispered.

Captivated by the moment, they sat still, wondering what would appear next. Cicadas sawed through the silence, building to a climax, then suddenly fell quiet. Moments later, the insects started again with the solitary call of the ringleader.

At the gate, a sunflower taller than either of them hung its heavy head as if staring at its roots. On the patio table, which was nothing more than a painted cable reel, stood a blue wicker basket full of more sunflower heads.

'Granny Anna ate sunflower seeds like you eat crisps,' Zoë whispered. 'She loved them.'

They stared at the giant seed-heads with delicate shrivelled petals. A blue tit flew in from the lemon tree and artfully plucked a seed from the spiralling centre, cracked it and feasted on the contents. Another joined it, then another. The tiny blue, yellow and black birds skipped back and forth like pixies in a fairy tale. Striped seed husks were scattered among dried petals on the tabletop.

'It's so beautiful and undisturbed,' Megan said quietly. 'Makes me feel a little drunk – do you know what I mean?'

Zoë nodded.

'I want to come here and write poems and paint, Mum. I feel like it's shimmering inside me – the ability, I mean, the need to do something.' She met Zoë's eyes and blushed. 'Take no notice, I sound completely mad.'

Zoë shook her head. 'You've always had a way with words. I know you used to write songs and plays when you were a child – and when I see you juggle, I know you'd be amazing on a stage.' She delved into her oversized, cluttered handbag and pulled out a small package. 'This is for you. I bought it at the airport when I was going up to Manchester.'

Megan undid the gift-wrap and stroked the A5 book full of blank pages.

'It's perfect, Mum, thank you. The best present I've ever had.'
Zoë glanced sideways at her daughter and smiled.

* * *

It was clear that Aunt Calliopi had not lived at the cottage for some time. When Zoë phoned Mr Rodakis to make an appointment, she asked about her aunt.

'I'm afraid Calliopi had a stroke not long after Anna died,' he said solemnly. 'I'm sorry to say they turned off the life support last week. I tried to call your landline in London but there was no answer. That's one of the reasons I wanted to speak to you.'

* * *

Back in town, they had just ordered iced coffee at a pavement café when Zoë's phone rang. She saw Frank's number and felt her heart flip like it hadn't in months.

'I missed a call from you earlier,' Frank said. 'How's the search going?'

Zoë breathed in deeply. 'Frank, I've found her.'

She heard a gasp, then a long moment's silence on the other end of the line.

'At last. I always knew we'd find her. Tell me she's okay . . .' His words were husky, emotional.

Zoë tried to keep her voice steady. 'She's sitting opposite me right now. We're in Crete.'

'In Crete? What . . . ?' Frank's voice broke. 'God, I've missed her. I've missed you too, Zoë. Please, come home – both of you. Josh is driving me mad, and . . .'

Zoë stood up, and walked a few feet away from the table. This wasn't a conversation she wanted to have in front of Megan right then.

Zoë held her breath. 'Look, Frank, there's something I have to ask you. Megan said that she was at a party the night before she left and that she—'

'She told you?' Another long silence, then, 'Is that why she ran away? Zoë, it's been eating me up for months, but I gave my word not to tell you because she didn't want you to judge her. I put myself in a difficult situation. If I didn't keep my word and honour my promise, how could I ever expect her to do the same?'

'She said she saw you with another woman.'

A moment's silence. 'Did Megan think I was *with* somebody? It was a fundraiser, an art auction with a party after, but I knew they were a pretty wild crowd – you know the sort of thing, you've been to enough of them with me in the past. They work hard, but they play hard too. Bearing this in mind, I didn't want to go alone. You were busy with your new partnership deal and couldn't go, remember?'

Zoë had vague recollections of trying to work through the contract she'd been offered.

'A colleague of mine offered to accompany me, but after a few drinks, well, it was clear raising funds for the refugees wasn't the first thing on *her* mind. Very embarrassing. She's moved on, thank God. Don't tell me Megan thought I was up to no good? Good grief!'

Zoë felt her shoulders drop.

'Listen, Zoë, these last few months have been a terrible mistake ... Walking out on you and Josh – it's something I've regretted more each day. We've had a trial separation and I've never been more miserable. I went to the solicitor's yesterday and cancelled the petition for divorce. I can't live without you, Zoë. I want to come home, go back to how we were.'

Zoë was almost speechless. 'After all you've put me through? You're the one who walked out just when I needed you most, Frank. It was you who filed for divorce!'

She had raised her voice too much and saw Megan turn and stare at her from the table.

'You drove me out, Zoë. I'm not blaming you, but you did. We were both so fraught about Megan leaving, we did nothing but hurt each other.'

Zoë sighed. 'What happened to us? Why are we blaming each other? We were so happy once.'

'I still love you.'

She swallowed hard. 'Oh, Frank.' She looked back towards the table and saw Megan's wide eyes. 'Frank, this isn't the time or the place.'

'I know, I know. You said Megan's there? Can I speak to her?'

Zoë crossed the café quickly, flipped the phone on to speaker and placed it on the table before Megan.

Megan's eyes were full of questions. 'Dad, it's me.'

Even from across the table, Zoë heard his gasp before he responded.

'Megan!' A pause. 'Are you all right? Your Mum said—'

'I'm fine, Dad. I've made such a mess of things. I didn't realise how much you both cared.'

'Never mind. Oh, thank God, thank God! Are you sure you're okay?'

'Dad, I'm so sorry, really – I didn't mean to cause so much trouble. I thought . . . Well, perhaps I misunderstood everything.'

He sighed into the phone. 'Look, I'll call you back in a few minutes,' he said huskily before ending the call.

Megan's jaw dropped. 'I didn't expect him to be so upset, Mum. I feel terrible. I'm so ashamed to have caused all this distress.'

'Neither of us have stopped loving you, Megan.'

She thought about Frank. All she had been thinking about these last few days was how angry she was with him. He'd known more about why Megan might have run off than he'd told her. It had only now occurred to her just how guilty he must have felt all these months.

For so long she had been thinking about how he'd left, just when she needed him most. But she had pushed him away, just when he needed her, too.

'Megan, I should have told you before. Your father and I – I'm sorry, but we're living apart.'

'What? No, Mum, that's crazy. You can't split up! You and Dad love each other. I know you do.'

'He moved out,' she said, and couldn't quite keep the bitterness out of her voice.

'But that's nuts!' Megan's face fell. 'Was it because of me?'

'No,' said Zoë softly. 'It was because of me. I drove him away. And you're right, we do still love each other. I think we do. Perhaps, when we get home, we can try again.'

* * *

Later that afternoon, after Megan had had another long phone call with her father, she and Zoë got a taxi to the solicitor's office and climbed the steep marble stairs to the first floor. The solicitor was an old man, and it was his granddaughter who now ran the business. Zoë learned from the granddaughter that despite his eighty-five years, Mr Rodakis insisted on going into the office for a couple of hours every day and continued to take care of his old clients.

'Ah, Mrs Johnson? Please, take a seat. I'm very sorry for your loss, both your mother and your aunt. What can I do for you?'

'Please, call me Zoë. You sent me a letter saying you wanted to speak with me about an investment my mother made. I'm quite surprised, Mr Rodakis. My mother was almost penniless when she died. She hardly managed on her small pension, so I sent her a little money each month to help. I don't think she had any investments. She would have told me.'

'Not Anna, no, but . . .' He hesitated, and shuffled his papers. 'There is something I have to tell you, Zoë. Anna Despotakis was not your biological mother.'

Zoë stared at him, incredulous. 'What are you talking about? Of course she was.'

'There are some things you don't understand about your past. Your parents are not who you thought they were.' He sighed. 'I have kept this secret for a long time – your biological mother wanted it that way. She came to our office in Heraklion many years ago to make financial arrangements for your education. She paid money to you and to Anna for many years, in order to make sure you were always well provided for. Our offices have moved twice since, and now we practise under my granddaughter's married name, so your biological mother lost touch. When I sent you that last letter, the investment had just matured, but I had no way of contacting your biological mother. It was only very recently, when she saw the announcement of Anna Despotakis's demise in the paper, that she got in

370

touch with us again. She was here this very morning. She left a letter from your biological father, and a few items of personal significance. She wants you to have them.'

'B-but,' stammered Zoë, 'I don't understand. How is this possible? Why did nobody ever tell me?'

'Your biological mother wanted to protect you, to keep you happy – and Anna, too. You see, Anna really believed that you were her own child.'

Zoë blinked disbelievingly. 'But how could Anna not know if she and my father had adopted me?'

'You weren't adopted. The circumstances of your birth are quite sad, but if you have time, I'll tell you what happened.'

* * *

Once the solicitor had voiced the facts relating to her birth, Zoë sat in stunned silence. She felt Megan press her hand as she tried to imagine this woman who had given her away, and everything she must have suffered through the decades. Zoë had searched for Megan for little over six months; she could hardly imagine her own mother's heartbreak after a search that went on over many decades.

'So, my birth mother gave me away in order to protect me?'

Mr Rodakis nodded. 'The saddest thing is, it was Anna's husband who ordered your real father to be executed.'

Zoë felt her jaw drop.

'You see, Anna's husband was one of the junta colonels. He never knew the facts behind your birth either. He always thought you were his child.'

'Excuse me – what was that you said?' Megan asked. 'The *hunter* colonels?'

'Ah, no, not *hunter* – that's just how it's pronounced in Greek. The hated *junta* colonels.'

'So that's why the taverna owner in Kissamos was so aggressive?' Megan asked. 'Granny Anna was married to one of the junta colonels. It's all beginning to make sense.' She turned to Zoë. 'You said Granny Anna never talked about your father, Mum, and didn't have any photographs.' She frowned for a moment. 'Just a minute, was it called the *Regime of the Colonels*? Martial law, like? We did all this in history at school. They were sentenced to death, weren't they, the colonels? Crimes against humanity?'

Rodakis nodded. 'You're right, young lady. They all received the death sentence originally, but then it was commuted to life imprisonment.' He turned to Zoë. 'Anna Despotakis's husband died of a heart attack after only six months in prison.'

'I never knew any of this,' Zoë said. 'Mama just told me that my father was an officer in the army, and he died when I was little.' She breathed out, still shaken. 'What can you tell me about my biological mother? Do you have her name and address? Can I visit her?'

Mr Rodakis shook his head again. 'She's from Athens, but she's been roaming the streets for years, looking for you, thinking you still lived in Greece. Young people think she's just a homeless old woman, but older folk know who she was. They say she's lost her mind due to her tragic life.'

The solicitor gazed at Zoë sadly. 'Sofia Bambaki is unable to speak. She was once a celebrated singer, but her voice failed her. Life has been very hard on her. Her husband was killed by the pitiless regime, and I know her decision to give you up always pained her. After she was released from prison, I believe she did once manage to find you – but when she saw how happy you were with Anna, she made the biggest sacrifice anybody could, and decided to remain in the shadows of your life, helping you from a distance. Sofia became comparatively rich because her singing career took off again. She sent most of her money to Anna, through me, for your well-being. When you were little, Anna was persecuted for being the wife of a hated junta officer, and when she took you to England, Sofia and I both lost sight of her.'

Zoë and Megan stared at each other.

'These items,' the solicitor continued, pulling a box from beneath his desk, 'Sofia asked me to pass them on to you one day.'

He pushed the box across his desk towards Zoë.

'There's a letter from your biological father in here. I took the liberty of translating it into English on the back. There are also some sentimental items that she wanted you to have.'

The solicitor pinched the bridge of his nose.

'I'm sorry to throw so much upon you at once. I know it is a lot to handle.' He struggled to his feet and grasped his walking stick. 'I am afraid I have another meeting now. Please get back to me if you need anything more.'

'Wait! At least tell me their names,' Zoë cried. 'You said my mother was Sofia Bambaki – was that my father's name? I know Greek women often keep their maiden names.'

Rodakis nodded. 'It's all in the box, Mrs Johnson.' He moved a step towards the door, then turned back. 'Wait – there is one more thing. Anna bequeathed the cottage to her grand-children. It belongs to your children now. You must come back and make arrangements for the transfer of deeds for the house in Kissamos.'

* * *

Outside the office, with the box under her arm, Zoë squeezed Megan's hand.

'What a day . . . Come on, let's get back to our apartment and see what we've got here.'

Megan frowned. 'Are you sure you want to find out, Mum? I mean, the truth might be much worse that you imagine. If my grandfather was in prison, who knows what he might have done? Oh, Mum. Please tell me Granny Anna will always be your mama – she will, won't she? No matter what. I loved her so much.' Megan's face scrunched up and suddenly she was in tears. 'Why did I run away, Mum? If I hadn't, she wouldn't have left and we could have been with her when she died. I feel so awful about that. It's no good being sorry – it's too late to change anything, and I'll regret it for as long as I live.'

Zoë put her arm around her and pulled her close.

'Of course she will always be my mother, and your Granny Anna,' she said softly. 'She was a wonderful, selfless person and I'll always love her, but that doesn't mean I don't want to find out who these people were who gave me up. Sofia Bambaki has been searching for me for so long, and I know how hard that is.'

Megan sniffed hard. 'I can't believe Granny Anna's gone. I've been planning to come and see her for so long. I imagined collecting olives, making candied peel, learning to sew with her. I never thought, not for a moment. It just feels as though people like her live forever.' She wiped her eyes. 'On top of that, you and Dad separating. It's such a shock. You seemed so happy together. I mean, you're my *parents*, for God's sake! Is this all down to me, causing everyone more stress than they can handle? I'll never forgive myself, never. Poor Granny, and I never got a chance to tell her how much I loved her or say goodbye. I'm so sorry. I know I keep saying it, but I'm heartbroken, Mum.'

Zoë struggled to stay in control of her emotions.

'Darling, your granny knew how much you loved her. She loved you too, and she had faith in you. She kept telling me you'd come home one of these days. "Nothing will keep our Megan away from your shepherd's pie for too long," she would say to me when I got depressed.'

Megan smiled through her tears, then pulled back and stared at her mother.

'You got depressed?'

'Well, a bit.'

Zoë remembered the station platform, closed her eyes, tried to block out how close she'd come to taking that last step. Thank God for Dalip. She promised herself, when they got back to England, she would find him and thank him properly.

'I wonder where Sofia Bambaki is now,' she whispered.

CHAPTER 40
SOFIA

Korydallos Prison, Athens, 1972.

As I STOOD AT THE side of Markos's grave, singing my heart out, I heard the prison patrol approach. Their heavy boots crunched a menacing rhythm in the dirt. The moon crept higher; its silvery light shimmered through the darkness towards me. I felt Markos reaching out from Heaven and sang the final lines with all the power I had.

> *Angels, wings give you flight,*
> *Every star-spangled night.*
> *My love, you are life's sweetest songs.*

I hung onto the last word, my face turned to the night sky, my feet planted firmly at my love's graveside. There was no point trying to outrun a bullet. And even if there was, I had nowhere to go. I had no one left. They cuffed my hands and marched me back inside. I expected to be thrown into a solitary cell but instead I was trooped down a corridor of offices. A door was knocked, 'Enter!' called from inside, and I was thrust into a grand room.

Behind the desk sat Colonel Despotakis.

The colonel was working through a sheaf of papers, ticking boxes and scribbling notes in red ink. He glanced up, then back at his papers for a moment. Then, as if remembering something, his head jerked up.

'Aren't you the nurse that took care of my wife?' he demanded.

'Yes, sir.'

'What in the name of God were you doing? You could have been shot!'

'I wasn't trying to escape. I only wanted to say goodbye to a dear friend, sir. He had been in the ward so many times. I had become rather attached to him.'

'Where did you learn to sing like that? I could hear you in here.'

'I was a singer, sir.'

He stared at me; his brow furrowed. 'What's your name?'

'Sofia Bambaki, sir.'

'Sofia Bambaki – *the* Sofia Bambaki?'

'Yes, sir.'

He leaned back in his chair and folded his arms.

'My wife will be thrilled. She has all your records – wait till I tell her you delivered our child!' For a moment, he appeared human. Then, his authority reared. 'Why are you imprisoned here?'

'They said my songs were subversive because they were sung by some of the communists, sir. But they were just songs and poems about the war, and love.'

'Do you support the communists, Sofia Bambaki?'

I thought of Markos and I wanted to say I'd support anyone who stood against you, Colonel Despotakis – but then I thought of Zoë, and freedom.

'No, sir. I love my country with a passion.'

He stared at me, tapping the ballpoint on his desk like a metronome.

'May I speak, sir?'

'Go on.'

'How is your wife and your little baby, Zoë?'

'You remember her name?'

'They are both precious to me, sir. Zoë was my first delivery. I hope I might meet her again one day. And your wife was so brave – after everything – so I'm filled with the greatest admiration. I think about them all the time.'

He lifted his hand and hooked his fingers towards himself.

'Come forward. Sit down, Sofia.'

I felt Markos guiding me, giving me strength. I wanted to cry his name as I stepped towards the chair.

'Thank you, sir.'

'Guard!' he yelled, making me jump. 'Take the cuffs off this woman,' he ordered when the soldier appeared. 'Do you know who this is?' He didn't wait for an answer. 'Sofia Bambaki, one of Greece's greatest singers.'

When the guard had gone, he turned to me.

'Look, Sofia Bambaki, I'm grateful for the way you took care of my wife. You didn't have to stay with her day and night. I'm going to try and help you.'

'Thank you, sir.'

'We use entertainers to lift the morale of the troops. You can star in the shows. Sing for the soldiers. Manage their spirits. Start here in Korydallos, then perform in barracks all over Greece.'

I thought about my friends, Thina, Honey and Agapi. Could I do anything for them, help them in any way? They had supported me through my most difficult times.

'Why are you hesitating?' Despotakis asked abruptly.

'I'm thinking about my friends, sir. I owe them a lot, it's difficult to abandon them for my own good. If they hadn't supported me the way they did, I couldn't have given my undivided attention to your wife. They're very loyal women, not criminals.'

'Why in God's name can't people just be grateful for what they're given?' he muttered.

Because as communists, they believe we're all equal and have the same rights, I wanted to reply – but I bit my lip.

After a long silence, he shouted 'Guard!' and I was escorted back to our cell.

*   *   *

In our room, after midnight, Honey yawned and flopped onto her bed.

'I've got to be back in the kitchen in four hours. Go for it, Sofia. Don't think about us – take the opportunity to get out of here. You'd be mad if you didn't.'

'I agree,' Thina said. 'It's a chance to return to the outside world. You've got to take it, Sofia.'

Agapi staggered in, smeared lipstick and messy hair.

'I hate the bastards!' she complained, peeling out of her close-fitting dress and leaving it like a puddle on the floor. 'What's going on? Have I missed something?'

She threw herself on the bed.

'Sofia has a chance to get out of here,' Thina said, hanging up Agapi's clothes. 'You shouldn't leave your frock on the floor, you'll have roaches in it by morning.'

'I've had roaches in it all night, dirty bastards!' Agapi muttered. She turned to me. 'I hope you're not hesitating. Christ, I'd be out of here in a flash!'

'You don't understand. It's my voice. If I go back to singing, I might destroy my fragile vocal cords permanently. I'm not just talking about my singing, but my actual voice would be lost forever.'

'What? You'd be a mute?' Agapi clutched her neck, looking horrified.

Thina frowned. 'Nicely said, Agapi.'

I nodded. 'Putting it bluntly, yes. I'm not sure I want to risk it.'

* * *

I woke to the sound of Thina's voice.

'Come on, Sofia, time to go.'

A deep, dreamless sleep left me feeling heavy and cotton-mouthed. Agapi, dead to the world, muttered and tossed about, giggling and panting. Honey had gone already. I washed and dressed quickly, then left for the hospital with Thina. On the ground, outside our door, lay an unopened packet of cigarettes. I slipped them into my pocket.

'Must be Agapi's, I'll give them to her later.'

Unlike most inmates, because of our particular jobs in Korydallos, we were not locked into our room. However, we had to pass across the main yard and through one set of security gates to get to the hospital.

The sun broke over the horizon as we left the building, throwing our long shadows across the concrete. For a moment, the grey drabness of Korydallos was painted with gold. The air felt cool with the freshness of dawn. Inspired, I wanted to stand in the middle of the exercise yard and sing. I thought of Markos. I had a reason to move on, to try and live, not because he had died, but because of a powerful feeling that I was living for both of us.

* * *

At noon, Thina was teaching me a new procedure. With a scalpel in my hand, I was about to lance an angry carbuncle on a guard's posterior. My patient, on all fours on the bed, had his trousers around his knees, his bottom and the angry swelling close to my face. The neighbouring patients, both prisoners, were up on their elbows, looking at the guard's arse and exchanging gleeful glances.

A soldier barged into the ward and yelled 'Sofia Bambaki!' startling both me and my patient. He hunched and jerked back, straight onto the knife's tip. Yellow pus squirted from the pierced carbuncle right into my face.

Thina blew a raspberry into the palm of her hand and, with her shoulders jiggling, passed me a fistful of gauze. Both neighbouring patients collapsed onto their beds in stifled hysterics. The visiting soldier stopped dead, stared in horror at the tableau before him and pulled in his chin with disgust.

'That's sorted then. Clean yourself up,' Thina ordered in a strangled voice. 'I'll take over.'

The soldier followed me to the sink.

'I have to escort you to the colonel's office.'

'Go for it,' Thina said. 'What have you got to lose?'

As I left the ward, I bumped into the priest.

'One moment,' he said to the soldier. 'I need to speak to the nurse about a private matter.' He turned me away and spoke quietly. 'I found this on the ground, after . . . He would want you to have it, to complete the circle of never-ending love.'

He placed the other half of the wedding ring in my palm.

I followed the soldier down the corridor and into Despotakis's office, where he ordered me to sit opposite him at the desk.

'I've spoken to Athens,' Despotakis said. 'They have agreed to put you on the "Morale Team". This officer will escort you to your cell. Gather your belongings and go straight to the main gate. The rest of the team are in Patras. You will join them this afternoon.

If you try to escape, you will be shot. If you *should* manage to escape, which is practically impossible, your friends will be lined up and executed. Do you understand?'

I squeezed the broken ring. 'Yes, sir.'

The rest of the day rushed by. I never got the chance to say goodbye to my friends. A guard escorted me to the gate. Once outside the wire fence, I stopped and looked back at the prison. Something caught my eye on the fence, and I realised it was Markos's precious beret.

I touched the guard's arm. 'Please, could I get that?'

He frowned and shook his head.

I no longer cared what happened to me. I could not leave Markos's beret behind. 'I'm begging you. It's my husband's hat. He was executed the day before yesterday. I have nothing from him. Please!'

I delved into my apron pocket and thrust the cigarettes towards him.

'Women!' he muttered, snatching the packet of Camel. 'Stay by my side.'

We hurried to the fence, where he jumped up and caught the beret.

'Here,' he said. 'Now don't give me any more trouble or you'll be back inside.'

I stuffed the beret inside the bib of my apron and, with my hand pressed against my chest, hurried along to the second gate. Once outside, the guard pulled the cigarettes from his pocket.

'I'm going to have a smoke. Make one step in either direction and I will shoot you. Got it?'

I nodded and watched him step towards the perimeter wall, out of sight of the inner guard.

Flour-man Fannes was unloading his sacks. He ran an eye over my nurse's uniform, then my face.

'My God, it's Sofia! Virgin Mary, we thought you were dead! Wait until I tell Zacharia – he'll be ecstatic.'

'How is he, Fannes?' I asked quietly, swivelling my eyes towards the guard, who glared at me.

Fannes frowned, then nodded. Lowering his voice, he replied.

'Struggling on, baking his daily bread, sad that so many of his friends have gone. How's Markos?'

He glanced at the guard, clearly uncertain of whether it was safe to ask more.

The question came suddenly and hit me so hard I couldn't answer. I pulled the beret from behind my apron and held it to my face. My sorrow poured out in a torrent of tears.

Fannes crossed himself and stared gloomily at the road.

'May God forgive his sins,' he muttered.

CHAPTER 41
MEGAN

Crete, present day.

BACK AT THE APARTMENT, MEGAN watched her mother's face as she opened the old metal box. Mum's hands trembled as she lifted a brown envelope and placed it on the table.

'Why don't I make us a cup of tea, Mum? We're both hot and tired, and it's been quite an emotional day.'

Her mother blinked at her, and Megan could see surprise in her eyes.

'Look at you,' she said. 'You're all grown up. I'd love a cup of tea, thanks.'

The words swelled in Megan's chest. It seemed strange that such a small gesture could impress her mother – and yet she knew it wasn't the sort of thing she'd ever done at home. She smiled and kissed her mother's cheek.

'Listen to me, Mum, it doesn't matter what we find out. I love you, okay? So does Josh, and I believe Dad does too, no matter what's happened in the past. Promise me you'll talk to him, please?'

Someone knocked the door. 'Anyone home? Gary and Jeff here!'

Megan's spirits lifted, glad of some moral support. She dreaded the idea that her mother might start crying or something. As much as she felt they'd made progress, things were still a little awkward between them.

'Hi, come in!' Megan called, throwing the door open. 'We're having an exciting moment. Mum's about to discover stuff about her parents. It's all a big mystery.' She glanced at her mother and saw her shoulders drop. 'Oh, God. I'm sorry, you'd rather be alone, wouldn't you, Mum? I didn't think.'

Zoë nodded. 'Actually, yes, if you don't mind, boys.'

They both shook their heads. 'We've been helping with the carnival floats all day. Now we're going on the roof for a beer – just came to invite you along.'

'Very kind, thank you,' Mum said. 'Megan might be up shortly.'

When they had gone, Megan said, 'Sorry again, of course you don't want strangers around right now. I've got a lot to learn, Mum, but I *am* trying.' She glanced around the floor, feeling awkward. 'I'll make the tea while you read the letter.'

Her mother dropped her head to one side and smiled in a proud sort of way, and Megan smiled back, overwhelmed by the need to give her mum a hug.

Megan concentrated on the welcome tray. They'd bought the travel kettle, coffee and sugar sachets earlier – the first time in ages they had done anything together. What were the right words to comfort and support her mother? She had zero experience of dealing with her parents in a grown-up world. For the past few months, she had thought of no one but herself.

She could change – she knew she could – but she hoped her parents could be forgiving when she made mistakes along the way. She had a lot of growing up to do.

She glanced over her shoulder as she waited for the kettle. The letter was trembling in her mother's hand, and the silence seemed dense in the room. As Megan dropped teabags into the mugs, she heard a sob. Should she give her mother space, or another hug? Confused, she hesitated, then flicked off the kettle and went to her mother's side.

Megan could see her mum was reading down the page. She pulled a chair to her side and squeezed her shoulder. Her mum got to the end of the letter, folded it in half and slipped it back into the envelope. It was all right. She would give it to her to read when she was ready.

Megan watched as she delved into the box and pulled out a dusty black beret with a narrow leather trim. She stroked it, her eyes brimming. When she ran her fingers around the inside, a tightly rolled piece of red paper fell out. They stared at it, and when Mum unrolled it, they saw it was filled with tiny Greek letters.

Μην με ξεχάσεις ποτέ, αγαπημένη μου. Όταν βγει ο ήλιος, πες καλημέρα και να με σκέφτεσαι. Όταν σηκώνεις το ποτήρι σου, να λες το όνομά μου. Και πες στο λατρεμένο μας μωρό, τη Ζωή, πως θα την αγαπώ για πάντα.

'I wonder what it says,' her mum murmured.

Megan reached for her mother's phone, opened Google Translate and tapped in the letters.

The app answered her question.

Don't ever forget me, my darling. When the sun comes up, say good morning and think of me. When you raise a glass, call my name, and tell our precious baby, Zoë, I will always love her.

Mum's tears brimmed. Megan tried hard to stay strong, but her tears were close, too.

After a long silence, Megan got up to make the tea. When she finally turned and placed the drinks on the table, she realised her mother had waited for her before investigating further. It was a considerate gesture.

'I love you, Mum,' she said.

'And I you, darling.'

Their eyes met and they smiled at each other for a moment. It was no big deal, really – and yet Megan felt changed, as if in that second, her mother had welcomed her into the adult world.

Mum returned her attention to the box. 'Let's see what else we have in here, shall we?'

The rest of the box seemed to be filled with knitting, but when they spread it on the table, they realised it was a pale lemon triangle of crocheting, unfinished, the last loop still around the crochet hook.

'That's bizarre,' Megan said. 'I wonder what it is.'

'It's a baby shawl. I guess it has significance. Perhaps it was for me, her baby.'

At first, they thought there was nothing more in the box, but then Megan noticed a bump in the cardboard lining.

'Look, something's gone underneath.'

'Pass me a knife from the drawer, Megan.'

Mum poked at the paper until it lifted, and they found what looked like half an ivory ring.

'It's got writing on it. What does it say?' Megan asked.

Her mother peered at it. 'On the inside, it looks like my name, Zoë, which means *Life* in Greek – I know that much. Granny Anna told me a long time ago. I wonder if it said *Eleftheria* on the other side. That means *Freedom*, my middle name. I guess we'll never know. There's a date on the outside.' She took it to the window and examined it in the bright sunlight. 'Two weeks after my birthday. I wonder if it's a wedding ring. Maybe that's when they got married.'

'So romantic,' Megan whispered. 'I want to write all this down, the great love story of my grandparents. It would make a great play – or a song, maybe. It would suit a song.' She peered into the box. 'Look, there's something jammed into the corner.'

Her mother prised it free with the tip of the knife.

'It's a little locket.'

She eased the small gold heart open with the knife. Inside was a sepia photo of a long-haired boy, but what made them both gasp was the Che Guevara beret on his head.

'Oh!' murmured Zoë. 'Perhaps it's a photo of my father, your grandfather – look, he's wearing this same beret. He's so young. I wonder if the photo was taken around the time they first met.'

They sipped their tea in silence, until Megan said, a little timidly, 'All this has made me want to see Dad. I thought I wanted to stay here, Mum, but I'm desperate to go home to Josh and Dad, at least for a while.'

Her mother smiled. 'I miss them too. We've got so much to put right. Come on – the travel agent is open until nine. Let's go and see if there's any last-minute seats – and we can pick up a couple of *giros* for supper on the way back.'

They freshened up and walked into the city, entering the first travel shop they came to. Three women sat at their desks in the empty shop. Two were painting their nails. The other spoke to them in Greek.

'Sorry, do you speak English?' Mum asked politely.

'Should do, I'm from Blackpool,' the woman said, with a laugh. 'Married a lazy Greek for my sins, over thirty years ago. Shirley Valentine, eat your heart out.'

The three of them grinned at each other, though Megan couldn't say why she thought it was so funny.

'We wondered if there are any last-minute flights to London, say tomorrow or the day after?'

'Sure – the planes are half-empty going back. Everyone's coming in for the carnival and staying for a long weekend.'

Megan looked at her mother, and beamed.

'Okay, let's do it,' she said. 'Soon as possible.'

The woman tapped her keyboard. 'Noon tomorrow?'

Mum nodded.

'Passports, please.'

Megan handed hers over proudly, glancing at her mother, who was rummaging in her cluttered handbag. As the assistant opened Zoë's, a slip of paper fell out.

'Is this important?' the assistant asked.

Mum peered at it, frowning, then she shook her head.

'I don't think so. An old woman gave it to me on the ferry from Athens. What does it say?'

'Ψάχνω την κόρη μου, γεννήθηκε στις φυλακές Κορυδαλλού την 1 Νοεμβρίου 1972.'

'I don't understand,' Mum said.

'Ah, sorry: "I am searching for my daughter, born in Korydallos prison, Athens, 1 November 1972",'

Megan gasped. 'Mum, that's your birthday!'

Her mother had her hand over her mouth. After a moment, she said, 'I can't believe this. The solicitor said she came over for the carnival every year, hoping to find me. Oh my God, Megan,' she muttered. 'Perhaps I met my own mother and didn't even know it was her. Wait! We saw her again at the harbour this morning, giving out her bits of paper. Do you remember? The woman who couldn't speak. I thought she was begging and gave her some money.'

'Some? You gave her ten euros, Mum. I saw.'

'Let's say I was celebrating in my own way, after finding you.'

The older assistant screwed the top on her nail polish and looked up. 'You must mean Sofia Bambaki,' she said with a heavy Greek accent.

Mum gasped. 'It *was* her! We have to find her.'

She got to her feet and stared around the room.

'She was a famous singer long ago,' the assistant went on. 'My own mother was a big fan, bought all her records. Sofia lost her voice and was unable to perform for her public, or even speak. Unfortunately, she seems to have lost her mind, too. She's wandered around Greece for many years, claiming to be looking for her daughter – though by all accounts, she never had a child.'

Mum sat down again and took hold of Megan's hand.

The travel agent continued. 'She's been in here a couple of times, hoping for a cheap ferry ticket.' She crossed herself. 'Poor old dear. I think I have one of her notes, too.'

She pulled her desk drawer out and tipped it onto the counter. It was in the same state as Mum's handbag.

'Here it is,' she said, after a moment.

Megan went to the desk and took the slip back to the woman from Blackpool.

'Ah – it's not quite the same. I'll translate: "*I'm looking for my baby, Zoë Eleftheria, born 1 November 1972*".'

Megan gasped. 'That's you, Mum! The old woman – it was her, your mother! Oh! My! God!' She scratched her head. 'I'll call Gary and Jeff. They're working with the carnival people. They can put it all over social media. Leave it with me! I'll find her, don't you worry!' She turned to the assistant. 'We don't need the flight now, not just yet – but thanks for all your help.'

'Do you really mean it?' the woman from Blackpool asked. 'Sofia Bambaki is your mother? Look, my name's Pauleen, I'd like to help. My husband's friends with the guy who owns the Cretan radio station. I'm sure he'll be interested in helping to find her. Shall I ask?'

Her mum, who had always been the backbone of the family, now seemed in shock. After a moment of surprise, Megan spoke for her.

'Yes, please do everything you can. My mum's never knowingly met her biological mother – she didn't know who she was until today. It would be wonderful if you could help bring them together.' She unzipped the front pocket of her mother's handbag and pulled out her mobile. 'Here, take our phone number, please, and get back to us the moment you hear anything. Honestly, we're so grateful for your help – all of you.'

She turned to her mother. 'Look, Mum, let's go back to the taverna where we had breakfast. She was there this morning. Perhaps the owner knows her and can tell us where she's staying.'

Her mother nodded slowly. 'It's such a shock. I can hardly believe what's happening.' She turned to the travel agents. 'Thank you all so much.'

* * *

Night had fallen by the time Megan and her mother returned to the apartment.

'What a day – I'm exhausted! Do you want to go for a beer with your friends, Megan? I'm going to shower and sleep.' She pulled a twenty from her purse. 'Here, go and relax if you want.'

As Megan went to take the money, she noticed her mother's frown, and she withdrew her hand.

'I don't need it. I've got my own money, thanks.'

If they were to be on equal terms, if she were to prove that she could be an adult, she shouldn't be financially dependent on her mother. In fact, she promised herself that she would get lunch tomorrow.

Then she hoped they wouldn't be too hungry.

Mum shook her head. 'No, sorry, take it. I was just thinking of Emily. I gave her a twenty to get some chips. Then she walked out of the door and I never saw her again.'

Megan pressed her mum's hand. 'Are you sure you'll be all right by yourself, Mum?'

'To be honest, after all that's gone on, I'd be glad of the space. But if you'd like to stay in, that would be lovely too. Will you take my phone? Just in case you need me. I'll put the apartment phone number on it – you just have to remember to ask for room eight.'

Megan grinned, longing to know how Gary and Jeff had got on. She had called and updated them after leaving the travel agent's.

'Thanks, Mum. I'll make you a coffee, you must be gagging. Then I'll find my mates.'

* * *

The guys were having a beer at a pavement café near the apartment, both thumbing their phones.

'Hi! How's it going?' Megan cried, relieved to see them.

'Good. How's it with you? What's the story behind all this then? Sounds fascinating.'

'I don't know all of it myself.' She sighed. 'The truth is, I ran away from home months ago, and Mum found me here, when you first saw her. She's just discovered her mum wasn't her biological

392

mother, and that her biological mother was this famous Greek singer called Sofia Bambaki who gave her away at birth. But – you could make a film of this, I'm telling you – her biological mother actually spoke to her on the ferry from Athens yesterday. Well, didn't exactly speak to her, but that's another story. But neither of them knew who the other one was. Now I'm trying to get them reunited.'

'Dramatic!' Jeff said, still typing on his phone. 'You're right. Sofia Bambaki was pretty famous – so was her mother. Seems Sofia was in prison for years for writing rebel songs, while the country was under martial law. *Her* mother was killed in an explosion while singing on stage in the city, at the end of the war.'

'I didn't know that,' Megan said. 'What a tragedy.'

Gary lifted his phone. 'Give me a sad puppy-dog look. Nice!' He took a photo. 'That'll go with the story.'

Jeff's phone vibrated. He picked it up and stared at the screen.

'Holy shit! Antonis from the carnival put it on a Greek site. He's got so many replies he can't read them all.' He stood up, grinning. 'Megan, it's gone viral. Come on, he's two minutes away.'

They met Antonis at a café bar near the ancient city wall. He shook hands with Megan, which she thought was pretty cool. In fact, she thought he was pretty gorgeous, too, with his almond eyes and sweeping lashes. Weird. She couldn't remember finding anyone attractive since Simon.

They were all deciding what to do next, when Megan's phone rang.

'That'll be Mum.'

'Mrs Johnson?' a man's voice said.

'No, sorry, this is her daughter. How can I help you?'

'This is Kreta FM, the radio station. I believe you have an interesting story for us and want help in finding Sofia Bambaki?'

'Absolutely. She's actually my grandmother, though I've never met her myself.'

'I wondered if you and your mother could come into the studio tomorrow morning and take part in an interview?'

CHAPTER 42
SOFIA

Athens, 1974.

ON STAGE IN ATHENS'S BIGGEST prison, I was halfway through singing the last record I'd cut with Spyridon when the camp colonel came on stage and stopped the performance with an announcement. The concert was over, and soldiers were to return to barracks. All leave was cancelled and anyone trying to leave the camp would be dealt with severely.

The audience murmured as the lights went up. There were police with pistols drawn at the exits. Back in the dressing room, I asked the other artists what was happening.

'Who knows?' one of them said. 'There's a media black-out, and a nine o'clock curfew. It's like the war all over again.'

'I heard the colonels have been overthrown by a new government,' another said.

'Does that mean we'll be released?' I asked, thinking at once of Zoë and Anna Despotakis.

The first one shrugged. 'Possibly. We can hope, I guess.'

* * *

The following months passed in chaos. Nobody seemed to know what was happening. The colonels were held in that same prison, and each of the many thousands of people they had incarcerated were having their cases reviewed. I was one of them.

Eventually, I was freed and immediately headed for Zacharia.

* * *

It was eleven o'clock in the morning by the time I reached the bakery's street. People were buying the last dozen or so of Zacharia's loaves outside the shop. My heart leaped to see him. He looked older, but his face was still the one I knew and loved.

'Zacharia! Zacharia!' I yelled, my arms outstretched as I ran towards him. He dropped a loaf, abandoned his customers and hurried towards me.

'Sofia, Blessed Virgin – is that really you, Sofia?'

We fell into each other's arms and I wept against his neck. He held me vice-like against himself, his wide chest shuddering with sobs.

'Glory to God! I've missed you so much,' he mumbled.

'And I you, Zacharia.'

We turned back to the shop, his arm about my shoulders, the customers taking everything in. When we reached them, they broke out in applause. Wiping his eyes, Zacharia boomed, 'I'm not selling any more bread today!' The people looked crestfallen until he continued, 'It's all *free*! Take it!'

I laughed, mad with joy.

'Come inside,' he said, steering me through, locking the door and then flipping the 'open' sign to 'closed'. 'When did they let you go?'

'This morning. I came straight here. I feel like it's my home, you know.'

'It is your home, and always will be,' he said. 'This calls for a celebration! Raki!'

'It's eleven o'clock.'

He shrugged, grinning. 'Might be midnight in China. Now come and tell me everything.'

We talked all day and late into the night. Seven long years had passed since I saw him last. We talked about Spyridon, Markos, and the tragedy of his death, both of us weeping. I told him of the joy of having our own child, and when I told him her name, Life and Freedom, he stared at the ceiling for a moment.

'That is just like Markos. I loved that boy like a son, you know. He saved many people in the war, always putting their welfare before his own safety. Such selflessness and bravery – he should have been given a medal by his country, not executed. But where is your child? Is she safe and well?'

I recounted the facts behind Zoë's escape to freedom and told him how much I longed to hold her again. When I showed him the baby shawl I had crocheted and unravelled each month, swearing I wouldn't finish it until the day I had her in my arms again, he smiled and nodded.

'We need to sleep a while if you're weighing dough for me in the early hours,' he said. 'Where are you staying?'

'Under the counter?'

He laughed with a great bellow.

'I won't hear of it. Come to my house and sleep in the back room.'

* * *

In Zacharia's spare bedroom, dead tired after a long and joyous day in the bakery, I recalled that last time I had been there, with Markos. I placed his beret on the pillow next to me and lay propped on my elbow, facing it. I told Markos about my day and my hopes for the future, until sleep took me away. When my head finally fell onto the pillow, the beret slipped forward and seemed to kiss my forehead.

Goodnight, Sofia. Sweet dreams.

Oh, Markos.

* * *

I worked for Zacharia for the rest of the week, but often my thoughts were pulled towards Zoë. How would I find her? What would she look like now? Sometimes I thought about my friends and wondered what had happened to them.

One evening, we went over to El Greco's where they told me Honey had been released a year ago, married, and gone to live in Thessaloniki. They had no address or contact with her. Madam Magdalena had died, and her establishment had closed. I hoped Agapi had found herself a man and settled down to a normal life. Thina would probably be working in a hospital, and I promised myself I would try to find her one day. I owed her so much.

'Sofia, concentrate!' Zacharia yelled, hurling a dough ball back onto the scales. 'You're well off the mark!'

'Sorry, I keep thinking about my baby. What am I going to do, Zacharia?'

'Why don't you try to find Anna, and call on them? You said she gave you her address and told you to visit. How old is she – almost three? Perhaps you could watch them in the park, first. See if Anna is taking good care of her. Take it from there. Even if your daughter has another mother now, it doesn't mean you can't be part of her life.' He stared at me for a minute before he said, 'There's something else I wanted to ask you. How's your voice these days?'

'I sang all right at the prison concerts, but I did have a good rest between each one, with changing locations after each show. And to be honest, I never gave a hundred per cent. It wasn't as if I had Spyridon pushing me to do two shows a night, seven days a week. Why do you ask?'

'The entrepreneur who took over Spyridon's singers was asking about you. Do you want to meet him?'

'I suppose – but only if you come with me.'

'Then I'll arrange a meeting in El Greco's.'

* * *

At noon the following Wednesday, I sat on a bench near Anna's house. My eyes itched. I'd been staring at Anna's house since nine o'clock that morning, watching the door, waiting. Twice, my emotions reached breaking point and holding back tears was a struggle.

Surely Anna would take Zoë for a walk before lunch and siesta. I half hoped she didn't – I was too jealous to bear the idea of her being a good mother. I wondered if she had gone to visit family in Crete, the island of her birth, if I was waiting for her like a fool in Athens. I was about to walk over and ring her bell, when the door opened and Anna appeared.

I gazed at the little girl holding Anna's hand.

Look, Markos, it's our daughter. She's so beautiful. My face, your eyes and hair. Oh, how I love you both.

They walked towards the park, a hundred metres away. Anna hardly took her eyes off Zoë. I waited until they were out of sight, then hurried after them. When I reached the park, Zoë was in a baby swing, and Anna pushed her gently while singing the nursery rhyme, Κούνια – μπέλα, *Swing, my pretty one.*

I watched, captivated, until somebody said 'Excuse me!' and I realised I had stopped in the middle of the path.

At a park bench near the swings, I continued to observe. Anna lifted Zoë out of the swing and followed her. My child toddled to the slide with her arm outstretched. Surely Anna wasn't going to let her go down the slide? Zoë was too young. I started forward, then held back.

'Mama! Mama!' Zoë cried, pointing, trying to drag Anna towards the four steps of the baby slide. After a moment, Anna picked up Zoë and climbed the baby slide herself, sat Zoë in her lap, and started down. My heart melted to hear Zoë's cries of glee.

Anna's hips were wider than the chute. One metre down the gentle slide and I could see she was stuck. With her arms wrapped around Zoë, she tried to yank herself down using her heels. Zoë laughed loudly, entertained by it all. Anna glanced around, her face turning redder by the second. I swallowed hard, then walked over.

'Do you need some help?' I called. 'Oh, goodness, it's Anna Despotakis, isn't it? Do you remember me? I was your nurse. Here, let me take Zoë while you get yourself free.'

I reached for my daughter.

Anna's face blanked – and then she recognised me.

'Oh, yes, of course. Sorry, I've forgotten your name. It seemed a good idea at the time, but now I can't move.'

'I'm Sofia. Hey, Zoë, come to Aunty Sofie while Mama gets out of there.'

I held my arms up to my daughter, and Anna passed her over. I clutched her to my chest.

In that moment, a mad thought overtook me. I could run. I could take my child and run and not look back. I had time to get away, and Anna was stuck – she could not follow. Zoë was young; she would soon forget Anna existed.

Run! the voice in my head yelled. *Run! Get away now while you have the chance!* It was now or never.

Markos! What shall I do?

Stand still. She's our child, no matter who she's living with. Think of Zoë. She loves Anna as her mother.

I want her all to myself.

'How embarrassing!' Anna said. 'Thanks for coming to our rescue. It was a reckless thing to do, perhaps, but she can be such a determined little monkey.' She held her arms out towards Zoë. 'Come on, give the nice lady a rest now – you're too heavy to be carried all the time.'

Zoë shook her head stubbornly and clung to my neck. I was in Heaven.

'Shall we sit on the roundabout, Zoë?' I suggested. 'Look, there it is. We can all have a nice ride while I talk to Mama. Would you like that?'

She nodded and gave me a kiss on my cheek as I put her down. *Oh, Markos.* We walked over to the roundabout with Zoë between us, holding both our hands.

'She's my husband's pride and joy,' Anna said. 'Nothing's too good for her.'

She looked into my eyes and for a second I saw terrible despair.

'Is he home?' I asked.

She shook her head. 'You haven't heard? They say the trial's set for next summer. He and the other colonels are detained in the very prison where my daughter was born.' She stared at the ground. 'They're not holding out much hope. It's all too awful'

The irony of the colonel's incarceration in Korydallos Prison, the place where Despotakis had sentenced Markos to death, struck me at once. I should have been rejoicing. What terrible suffering and heartbreak that man had caused. Yet I was filled with great sadness for my new-found friend. And for Zoë – had she learned to love him as her father? Would she miss him dreadfully?

'I'm sorry, Anna.' I knew what she would suffer, and that wasn't fair. 'How will you manage with Zoë?'

'Money won't be a problem, at least. My husband is due a grand pension, and we have the house.'

Zoë sat in the centre of the roundabout, with her arms sticking out and a smile on her face.

Then Anna said, 'Tell me about your baby. I remember you were pregnant in the hospital. What did you have?'

'I . . .'

'Mama! Mama!' Zoë cried, crawling over the top of the roundabout.

I turned at the call, but of course she did not mean me. She pulled Anna's hair so her head tilted back, and then kissed her face again and again. Zoë giggled and clapped her dimpled fists. Then she repeated the procedure.

'Zoë, stop it, you little devil!' Anna laughed, although Zoë tugged hard and it must have hurt. After a moment lost in pleasure, Anna turned to me, beaming with happiness.

She must have read the desolation on my face, because her grin fell and she reached out and touched my arm.

'Sofia, I'm sorry. Your baby – what happened?'

I took a deep breath. 'I had a little girl, but . . . I lost her.'

As if I had something contagious, she drew her hand away quickly and placed it over her mouth.

'I'm so sorry. I know how painful that is. It's almost unbearable. So unjust. God knows what I would have done if . . .' She stopped, shaking her head sadly. 'You know, you're always welcome to come to my house, Sofia. In fact – forgive me for the abruptness, but I have been looking for some time – I don't suppose you'd like a job, nanny to Zoë, just a few hours a week?'

Before I could think about it, Zoë turned her attention to me and, to my great joy, I got the kissing treatment too.

'I must apologise – it's her latest game.' Anna smiled fondly. 'Last week it was taking her shoes and socks off at every opportunity.'

My feelings were in disarray. This was *my* child, a part of *my* body, and Anna had her. It was clear that Zoë was well looked after, happy and unconditionally loved. And it was clear too that she adored Anna. Could I really bear to be so close to my daughter, to work in her home, and hear her call another woman 'Mama'?

'Look, Anna, I have a few jobs in the air right now. I'm working full-time at the bakery, and I might be able to go back to singing. Can I meet you again next week and let you know?'

'Of course you can. Did my husband tell you I was a great fan of yours? I have all your records. I wondered . . .' She hesitated, suddenly appearing shy. 'Next week, after the park, would you come to my house and sign them for me? I'd be so thrilled.'

* * *

While Zacharia and I prepared the bread in the early hours, I told him all that had passed between Anna, Zoë and myself.

'What should I do, Zacharia? I want so badly to be near Zoë. It's a longing that's gnawed away inside me since the day she was born. But I'm not sure I can stand it, being so close and yet so far from her.' I threw a dough ball on the scales – perfect. 'Even if I did have the money to support her, there'd be no way for me to prove she's my child. Anna is the only mother she's known.'

'Why not try the job? If it's too hard for you, give it up.' He sighed. 'I think it's good you're making friends with Anna. She's not your enemy. As far as she's concerned, Zoë is her child, and she loves her dearly.' We were silent for a while before he spoke again. 'Remember I told you about the music entrepreneur?'

I nodded.

'We're meeting him tomorrow evening. Let's see what comes from that, shall we?'

* * *

Vagellis Gregorio was a tall, imposing man who knew what he wanted. With his Churchill cigar, pale grey trilby and black pencil moustache, he gave the impression he had just walked off a fifties film set.

'The public are hungry for pop music after the military regime,' Gregorio told us. 'Across Europe, the bell-bottom brigade's fizzling out, Motown is old town, and the Beatles have broken up. We need new stars and a mixed bag of music. Sign with me, Sofia, and I'll make you a star – not just here, but across the continent and beyond.'

We talked for two hours. I agreed to think about his proposal and meet him again the next night.

Zacharia seemed to think Gregorio had put a good deal on the table, but my concern was how hard he would work my voice once I signed on the line. I hadn't sung since the prison concerts, and although I felt ready to start again, if he pushed for more concerts than I could handle, the consequences might be devastating.

Nevertheless, I signed a contract and started out on a fresh chapter in my life.

I cut a new record straight away and, thanks to the advancement of the industry, most of the time at concerts, I mimed to my recordings. This saved my voice from being overworked. My fame spread, new fans idolised me and my old fans returned, too. I acquired a small apartment of my own and moved out of Zacharia's, but I still tried to help him once a week, and sometimes cooked a meal for us at his home or mine.

On 28 July 1975, the trial started for the instigators of the 21 April 1967 coup. Ironically, the trials were held at Korydallos Prison. I bought a TV for Zacharia's shop and we had the live programme on as we worked.

Over twenty defendants were charged with acts of high treason and mutiny. Security surrounding the trial was heavy. A thousand soldiers armed with sub-machine guns stood guard at the jail's perimeter, and tanks patrolled down Solomou Street and the main roads surrounding the prison.

We watched Despotakis as he took the stand. Like the other colonels, he seemed to think he had served his country and done nothing wrong. He refused to defend his actions and was completely unemotional.

The trials finally ended on 23 August, with the death penalty by firing squad for mutiny sentenced on all the major players in the coup.

I had mixed feelings about the trial. I wanted the murderers of my beloved Markos to suffer as we had, but it was painful to see Anna's distress, and to know Zoë would be without a father. I understood what Anna was going through and my heart ached for her.

The colonels' death sentences were changed to life imprisonment. The news angered me, because nobody could change Markos's death to life, but I saw Anna's relief.

Wednesdays were the highlight of my week. I went to Anna's house and played with Zoë while Anna shopped and had her hair done. On one of these occasions, I sensed something was wrong the moment I arrived at the house and saw her dishevelled state. After a few months behind bars, Colonel Despotakis had a heart attack in prison and died before they could get him to the hospital.

Death was too good for him – but still, I felt sorry for Anna. Devoid of make-up, in her drab, black widow's weeds, she looked tiny and lost. Zoë had caught her mother's mood and had no appetite for play.

'I won't need you for the thirty days of mourning, Sofia. I'll be home by myself – and, to be honest, I'm not sure I can afford to pay you. I'm so sorry. I don't know how my finances stand, now that I'm a widow.' I could see she was fighting tears.

Zoë pulled the head off her doll, and started crying. I scooped her up and said, 'Let's fill the sink and play with water, shall we?' That did the trick.

'But you'll still get an army pension, surely?' I asked, as I sat Zoë on the draining board and ran the tap.

'I hope so. Nothing seems certain.' She hung her head. 'I loved him, you know? He was a difficult man at times – harsh and determined, but he was my husband, and he adored our child.' She turned towards the stove. 'Coffee?'

'Thank you.'

We were silent with our thoughts for a few minutes, until she said, 'It's all too upsetting, Sofia. I have a sister in Crete. She lives in our grandfather's property in a little village called Kissamos. I was thinking I might go and spend some time there.'

My heart lurched. She couldn't move away.

'You shouldn't leave your home, Anna. You belong in Athens. Would you like me to find out about your pension for you? I've got a quiet week and I'd be happy to help if I can. Listen, you don't have to pay me to come and play with Zoë on a Wednesday. It would be my pleasure. I'm really fond of her.'

Anna gave me her details and I spent most of the afternoon on the phone. I made notes and discovered her army pension was about to stop. The meagre widow's pension from the government was not enough to keep Anna and Zoë in the lifestyle they were used to, especially in the city.

I tossed and turned in bed that night until, unable to sleep, I pulled on my clothes and went down to the bakery.

'Need a hand?'

Zacharia closed the door behind me and we worked in silence for a while. Then I told him what had happened.

'Stop fretting about the problem,' he said quietly, 'and concentrate on a solution.'

The silence returned, and I made a plan.

*   *   *

The following year passed quickly. Zoë learned to count to ten and write a few letters. Anna slowly got over the death of her husband and was overjoyed to discover from her solicitor in Crete that an anonymous supporter of the junta had bequeathed a substantial monthly sum to Colonel Despotakis's widow. This was primarily for the education of their daughter.

That was the story I insisted Anna was told, and her solicitor obliged. Knowing I was responsible for my daughter's education and welfare made me feel good. I was doing something – the only thing I could. My Wednesday visits grew from a few hours to most of the day, and Anna and I became good friends.

My career escalated. By the end of the year, I had a large amount of money in the bank. I called the solicitor in Crete and told him I was doubling the money, and asked him to invest some in Zoë's name.

I bought Zacharia a modern, automatic bread-making machine which thrilled him. Installed in the back of the shop, the stainless steel monster did everything on a timer, and although there was no need for him to get up at one o'clock in the morning, we both went down to the bakery and watched the mixing, rising and baking go though its process every night for a week.

CHAPTER 43
ZOË

Crete, present day.

WHEN MEGAN HAD GONE TO meet her friends, Zoë opened the box again. She held the infant's painting, having no memory of it, yet understanding it was her own work. Was it possible that Aunty Sofie was her biological mother, and that she had treasured a painting Zoë had done as a little girl for all this time? She tried to recall the woman, but her memories were vague. She took her father's letter out of the brown envelope and read it again.

My dearest Zoë Eleftheria,

You will not remember me, your father. On this very night, I held you for the first time. I want to tell you that your mother and I love you more than life itself. I hope you can forgive us for giving you away. It is the only safe way we can get you out of this hellish place and secure a safe future for you.

Our hearts are broken that you are leaving us, but we were lifted up to Heaven by your arrival into the big, wide world. I was with your mother when you first drew breath and made your first cry, a sound that was sweeter than any other in my entire life.

When your mother placed you in my arms, I cried with joy. You seemed such a small, helpless little girl, but I know in my heart you will go on to do great things. Your mother is an amazing woman and I have always loved her above all others.

I have written this letter to you because I don't know what the future holds. I have spent my life fighting for a better world, a place where you can grow and be happy. I love you, Zoë Eleftheria.

The strength of my love will always be within you, in your heart and all around you, now and forever.

Your father,

Markos Papas

CHAPTER 44
SOFIA

Athens, 1976.

GREGORIO AND HIS CREW WERE hurrying me along.

'Come on, Sofia! We'll miss the flight at this rate!'

My excitement was beyond the sun. We were heading for London, the first stop on my big European tour. Two nights performing in each major city, eight countries, six months of concerts with magazine features, radio and TV interviews – the whole works. Pop music was multinational, great hits topped the charts. One of my favourites was Elton John's 'Don't Go Breaking My Heart', and out of Sweden had come a new group that everyone loved, Abba, with 'Dancing Queen'.

Zoë's favourite was 'Save All Your Kisses For Me', and we would sing it together and try to kiss each other's necks in between the lines, which always resulted in a bout of tickling and hysterical laughter. Anna had asked me not to telephone while I was away; we both knew it would only upset Zoë.

The Olympic Airways Boeing 737 climbed above Athens. I glanced down from the window and saw the Parthenon lit up, reminding me of the night I ran away from the orphanage. I thought about my daughter and wondered what she would think when I didn't visit on Wednesday. Anna was right, and I knew it. Zoë had just started school, and there was enough unrest in her life without me phoning. I would miss her terribly.

The tour was a huge success, but near the end, my throat started to give me pain. Remembering the old days with Spyridon, I often found myself looking for Markos in the audience. Oh, how I missed him. At my suggestion, the grand finale of the tour was back in Athens. It would be a free concert in Syntagma Square in honour of my mother, Alexa Bambaki. It would take place on Easter Monday, the following year. A cunning ploy, Gregorio claimed. The show would put me back at the top of the Greek charts, replacing Nana Mouskouri, who was still going strong, and Demis Roussos, who was at his best.

I insisted Gregorio sent a couple of front row tickets to Zacharia and another two for Anna and Zoë. We only flew in from Milan that morning and, although exhausted, I was looking forward to the event. Gregorio had organised a dress the same as the one my mother wore on that last night, and my hair was to be styled the same way too.

On the evening of the concert, the memories of that terrible day came back, vivid and terrifying. Still, I was determined that this would be a joyous occasion in memory of my family and Markos, the only love of my life. Gregorio had acquired some old black-and-white film of my mother, taken by a Pathé News reporter who had fled the theatre moments before the explosion to meet a deadline. The film was bought for an extortionate price to play on the backdrop before I sang.

Six months away had seemed like an eternity, and I was longing to see those I loved in the audience. I knew I would see a big difference in Zoë, and that a young child's memory could be short. I was worried that she might have forgotten me, but I could work on our relationship once again.

Someone knocked on the dressing room door and the hairdresser answered it.

'Flowers for Sofia Bambaki.'

I turned to see the owner of the vaguely familiar voice, but he was hidden behind a huge bouquet.

'Thank you,' I said. 'Who are they from?'

'They're from me, Sofia,' he said, lowering the flowers.

It took a moment before I recognised the old man.

'Oh, Mr Yianni! My goodness, how are you?'

I stood as he wrapped me in one of his bear hugs.

'I brought you something else, for luck.'

He dipped into his pocket, held out his fist and placed a barley sugar in my palm. Our eyes met.

'Your mother would be proud,' Big Yiannis said quietly, before he kissed my cheeks and left.

I sat for a moment, staring after him, wondering how he had fared after that terrible time when our lives crossed.

* * *

Once I stepped on stage, I was in another world, lifted away from everything. Each song had its own particular poignancy, taking me back to another place – but the highlight was my finale. Moments before the last song of the concert, 'Love's Sweet Song', the lights went down. An air-raid siren wailed and searchlights, set at either end of the stage, played across the night sky. The air-raid warning faded. In front of me, beyond the crowd, stood the beautiful Grand Bretagne Hotel; to my right, the tomb of the unknown soldier with two *evzones* guarding the area, and the houses of parliament. Beyond those iconic buildings, Mount Lycabettus and the little chapel of Saint George on the summit were illuminated in the black sky.

413

On the backdrop behind me, Mama sang the first few lines of her final performance, then the spotlight came over me and I continued. My tears rose, my heart breaking for all those I had loved and lost. The words of the song seemed so poignant.

Mother, you are life's sweet song,
Without you, it's hard to be strong.
But you live in my heart
Even though we're apart

As I sang, I could see my family at the top of Lycabettus – me, a ten-year-old, waving at the marines out at sea; and then Markos, holding Zoë in his distorted hands. Tears of emotion ran down his face. My tears fell too as I sang for them all.

Overcome by the moment, I held the last note far longer than I should have, holding out my hands as my mother had, towards the empty seat reserved for Zoë. I closed my eyes and saw my mother, nodding in approval.

Even though my eyes were closed, I was aware of flashbulbs, thunderous applause, and a sudden weakness in my knees. I clutched the microphone stand, felt myself falling as the uproarious applause filled Syntagma Square. Someone caught me. I tasted blood in my throat and the world turned black.

* * *

I woke in hospital. Zacharia and Gregorio were at my side. Zacharia placed his finger across his lips. I became aware of a pipe down my throat.

'Don't try and speak, Sofia. You've had an operation.' I noticed his eyes were red-rimmed in his unusually pale face. It was then I realised he was holding my hand. He squeezed gently. 'You have to be strong now. You've overcome much greater tragedies than this in your life, Sofia, but you'll find what I am about to tell you hard to accept.' He glanced at Gregorio. 'Could you leave us for a minute?'

When we were alone, Zacharia continued.

'I'm sorry, Sofia. I wish I could take this from you, but I can't.' Pain seared my throat. I lifted my hand to my neck and found it bandaged. Zacharia stared at me with a look of utmost devastation. 'You've had a total laryngectomy. You had cancer on your larynx, and they've had to remove your voice box. You won't be able to speak, let alone sing. I'm so sorry. They had to remove your vocal cords in order to save your life.'

A cold moment passed, a few seconds with nothing but the facts. I waited for some other emotions to arrive, but I guess I was in shock. I had no voice box. There was nothing to heal, no medicines to cure me. I would never make another sound.

* * *

The days merged into each other. I got used to writing things down, but I did so with the greatest sadness and impatience. I felt crippled, imprisoned, isolated and terribly lonely. I could not even laugh, and only demonstrated my pleasure or displeasure by turning my mouth up or down. People felt strangely embarrassed to talk to me, almost as if they were ashamed of their own voices. Others seemed to think I was deaf, too, and shouted. Despite all these awkward situations, I longed to be talked to. It broke my heart that I would never be able to speak to Zoë again.

One of the first notes I wrote was to Zacharia: *Where are Anna and Zoë?*

'After you left on tour, there was some trouble from the KKE party. They targeted Anna as a wife of one of the hated colonels and publicly asked how she was living in what they saw as luxury, when she was supposed to have no visible means of support. In the end, one of her windows was broken and she received a nasty cut from flying glass. She feared for Zoë's safety. They went into hiding.'

But how will I find them?

'I think you will have to leave them for a while, until things calm down. You know Zoë is being well cared for, thanks to your generosity, and Anna is a good woman.'

My grief was beyond measure, but I knew Zacharia was right.

He visited me every day. He tried hard to cheer me up, but I gradually slipped into the depths of despair.

* * *

My career was over, my life of luxury ended. Anna and my daughter had disappeared, and even her solicitor did not have her address. I still had royalties coming in from my records, but once my payment towards Zoë's education was taken out, there was hardly enough left to live on. I moved into a bedsit and lived as frugally as I could.

I went back to working for Zacharia, though with his auto-mated bread-making, he no longer needed me to come in at night. People were kind. For years, they brought records into the bakery for me to sign.

* * *

Old age finally caught up with Zacharia. His lungs gave him trouble after years of breathing in flour dust.

On Christmas Day 1986, Zacharia died peacefully in his sleep. This gentle giant, one of life's unsung heroes, had saved many Jewish lives in the war. He had provided people with their daily bread for over sixty years, and been a father to me for most of my life.

He left the bakery to me.

Fannes and I washed this humble man and dressed him in his one and only suit. On Saint Steven's Day, we led the mourners from the bakery to the church. Fellow shopkeepers took time out from their Christmas celebrations to act as coffin-bearers as we progressed on foot to the local cemetery.

We all stood in silence.

* * *

I struggled on with the bakery for another ten years, but with the arrival of cheap supermarket bread, trade fell off. Eventually I sold the premises, along with the wonderful bread-making machine, to Petros, Fannes's son.

All through those long years, I had never stopped thinking about Zoë. At last, when I had a little money in the bank again, I decided to concentrate on finding her. Lent approached and it occurred to me that Anna might have returned to her family home in Crete. I would go for the carnival. Surely, they would attend the celebration too. I was reaching for a small bag to take on my journey when an old box tumbled off the top of the wardrobe. Inside, I found the precious, yet useless, mementoes of my life: bits and pieces of sentimental value that I had kept over the years.

Here was the lemon baby shawl I started when I was in labour. Of course, I had never given it to her, and she was too old for such

417

a thing now. Spyridon's locket was there too, which I opened and then wept over.

My darling, Markos. How I miss you.

My broken wedding ring reminded me of our wedding day and my beloved husband. And the tightly rolled piece of paper on which Markos had written his poignant words. Long ago, I had discovered it inside the rim of his beret, which still lay on the pillow next to mine every night. A red and yellow painting of a matchstick woman with the words, *AUNTY SOFIE* painted below it and *Zoë 1976* written in the corner brought tears to my eyes.

These were the treasures of my life, valuable beyond measure, and I decided they would go wherever I went. I packed two changes of underwear, all the cash I had and set off on a journey that I hoped would bring my daughter back to me. On the bus to the port of Piraeus, I decided on a diversion. My first stop at the outset of this adventure was to the prison outside Athens.

I wrote a note to the bus driver: *I'd like to get off at Korydallos cemetery, please.*

He frowned and nodded sadly.

I sat in the front seat and remembered the first time I had made that journey, inside the truck of flour-man Fannes. Afraid, I had clung to my friends, Thina, Agapi and Honey. I wondered where they were now.

Shortly, the cream cement prison came into view, running parallel with the main road. The area was now highly developed with houses and businesses crammed around the tall perimeter walls.

I realised I had my hand over my mouth, my cry of anguish silent, yet intense. Events that took place behind those walls returned to me – images of Markos's tortured body, my baby still slippery from the womb, the warm earth of my husband's grave. When the bus stopped, the young driver read my expression, gave me a sympathetic look and waited patiently as I climbed down.

I walked to the burial area and stared at the cemetery, which was much larger now. I remembered that they had buried Markos in a barren corner plot alongside mounds of unmarked graves. Now, rectangles were neatly marked out by kerbstones and gravel paths. Marble headstones, ornate tombs and plastic flowers loomed around me.

Where are you, Markos?

I wandered around that labyrinth of death searching for his name, ignoring the monumental structures and concentrating on the simple graves. Defeated, I closed my eyes for a moment, and in that darkness, remembered the moon, the proximity of the prison, and found my bearings. A few steps to my left lay a simple stone bearing the words MARKOS PAPAS.

I hurried forward and my heart leaped.

Markos.

Yes, my darling.

Somehow his soul knew I was there. I fell to my knees – a mistake, as I felt them crack when I hit the dirt. Nevertheless, awash with joy and sadness at finding my husband's grave, I proceeded to scrabble in the gravel below his headstone. After digging a small hole at the head of the grave, I pulled the broken wedding ring from my pocket.

Freedom is yours, my darling, I whispered in my mind. *Until we meet again, I'll see you in my dreams.*

I kissed his half of the ring, dropped it into the hole, and quickly covered it.

How are you, my love? What a stupid question, Markos, but you know what I mean. I'm still trying to find our daughter. It's my quest. Once I have, I'm sure I'll be joining you.

I closed my eyes and saw him, complete with long hair and Che Guevara beret, nodding his head and smiling.

I think about you every day, Markos.

And I, you. I heard his words as clear as day.

Can you hold me for a moment?

I felt his arms slip around me, his breath in my ear.

I love you, Sofia.

I want to join you, my darling, but I must find Zoë. You understand?

Of course. I'll be waiting for you.

I found a piece of flint and scratched a few words onto the headstone. On my feet again, I gathered a handful of poppies that grew from the base of the stone wall and placed them at his feet.

Goodbye, my darling angel, until we meet again.

* * *

On my way back to the bus stop, my hand itched. I looked down and saw one of the red petals had stuck to my palm, like my mother's last kiss. Bright and red and fresh as the day. I closed my fingers around it and smiled. They would always be with me, the people I loved.

After taking a bus to Piraeus, I boarded the next ferry to Crete.

CHAPTER 45
SOFIA

Crete, present day.

I WOKE WITH A START as my head fell forward. Confused, I stared about for a moment, wondering where I was. Then my trek to Crete came back and I realised: Chania, Talos Square. The sea glass felt warm in my hand. I stared at it and remembered the poppy petal and Markos's grave. So many years had passed since that day when I first set out on this fruitless quest. All to no avail. I reached into my bag for the shawl, deciding to do a little crocheting; but then I remembered, the blanket was now with the lawyer. My mission was over.

I pulled myself up and headed for the public showers.

*　*　*

Later, refreshed, I continued along the edge of the sea, until I found myself back under the tamarisk tree on the beach. I would sleep on the sunbed again. Tomorrow, I would enjoy the carnival parade, and then on Monday, watch families flying their kites to mark the beginning of Lent.

Then I would return to Athens.

CHAPTER 46
MEGAN

Crete, present day.

MEGAN DIDN'T WANT TO WAKE. She allowed herself to drift and doze under the crisp white sheet. She could hear the shower running, so Mum was up. What time was it? Then yesterday began to come back to her, and she sat up straight in bed. She was about to do something marvellous for her mother.

'Ah, you're awake. Did you have a good time last night?'

Megan was almost too excited to reply. 'Mum, we're going to find her! You won't believe what's happened.' She leaped out of bed and headed for the shower. 'Are you ready to go, Mum? We have people to meet.'

Her mother blinked at her in confusion. 'What's going on, Megan?'

'Your story's gone viral. We've got an appointment at ten o'clock. What time is it?'

'Nine.'

'Great. Could you knock on Gary and Jeff's room, number fourteen, and make sure they're up? I'll be ready in five minutes. We can grab some cinnamon rolls and eat them as we walk into town.'

As she threw herself at the bathroom, Megan caught a glimpse of her mother's astonished face and smiled.

* * *

Megan and her friends were meeting the Kreta FM radio producer in a harbourside café. They watched him approach their table. He was a short, chunky man with wavy shoulder-length hair, pale jeans and a flowing white linen shirt.

'Mrs Johnson?'

Her mother nodded.

He shook hands with everyone. 'We're hoping to get this out on the one o'clock news, but it's tight, so we'd better set off to the studio right now.'

Twenty minutes later, they were working through a script with his assistant. At one o'clock, the broadcast went out. The afternoon was dedicated to a phone-in, interspersed by Sofia Bambaki's hit records.

The phones went wild. So many people knew the old woman who gave out slips of paper, looking for her daughter. Most of them had no idea it was the famous Sofia Bambaki.

Megan was thrilled that she had managed to spark all of this. She held her mother's hand as they listened to phone calls coming in, smiling all the while.

'We'll find her, Mum. Don't you worry.'

At an interval, when yet another Bambaki song played, the studio assistant popped in and turned to Megan's mother.

'You had a phone call. I hope you don't mind, but I answered it for you.' They'd had to leave their phones outside. 'It was your husband,' she continued. 'He's arrived at the airport with your son. He's left the name of his hotel and asked if you would get in touch with them when you can.'

'I'll handle it, Mum.'

Megan slipped outside to call her dad back. She came back into the studio a few moments later, smiling.

Together they worked their way through the script, live on radio. The producer asked questions and translated Zoë and Megan's answers. Then a call came in from a woman who claimed to have been imprisoned with Sofia Bambaki, who said she had delivered Sofia's baby, Zoë Eleftheria.

Megan had her new notebook out, scribbling notes as the programme developed, but looked up sharply at this. She could see tears in her mother's eyes.

When the producer played the next record, Megan leaned over and said, 'My mother's really tired. Could we stop now, and come back for the programme tomorrow afternoon?'

The producer nodded. 'One more ten-minute session, to wind it up, and we'll continue tomorrow?'

Megan nodded, and glanced over at her mother. She was still on the phone to the woman who had been imprisoned with Sofia, who knew a smattering of English.

Suddenly, her mother's hand flew over her mouth.

'Oh my God,' she gasped. Then, into the phone she said, 'We've got to meet – where are you?' She listened and then said, 'Don't worry, I'll pay your fare, just come to Chania as soon as you can.'

The producer played another record, then put the call on speaker.

He translated the caller's words.

'Your father was a martyr. They tortured him for years, then they put him before the firing squad, minutes after he married your mother.'

Mum sobbed, much to the producer's delight, but found she couldn't speak. Megan spoke instead.

'I'm Sofia Bambaki's granddaughter. Please, come to Chania and help us find Sofia Bambaki. Where are you?'

The woman was in the capital of Crete, Heraklion, less than three hours' drive away. The programme ran for another ten minutes, then the producer took a call and came back, agitated. The story had been taken up by Greek national television.

CHAPTER 47
SOFIA

Crete, present day.

I woke on the sunbed. My old joints protested, as usual, when I struggled upright. Today was carnival day, but my pleasure at the thought of this colourful occasion left me. Perhaps I wouldn't go into the main street; all that jostling for a glimpse of the floats was tiresome. Life was more peaceful on the beach.

As I had no intention of returning to Crete in the future, there was no need for my usual frugality. I could celebrate the holiday with a proper breakfast. After climbing the steps to the promenade, I leaned against a tree and emptied the sand from my shoes. The fisherman's wife was sweeping outside the taverna. I went over and sat at a table, shoulders back, long neck, smiling. Posture told a lot about a person; Mama had always said so.

Maria, the fisherman's wife, watched, hesitated and then came over.

'Good morning. What can I get you, *Yiayá*?'

I pointed at cappuccino on the menu. I'd always wondered what a cappuccino was; the name sounded exotic and romantic.

Maria raised her eyebrows and smiled, then disappeared into the kitchen.

The radio was playing one of my old songs from the time when Spyridon managed me, so many years ago.

Maria returned and placed the cup of creamy froth before me. I patted my chest twice and grinned.

'You're welcome,' Maria said.

Another of my old records came on the radio. I pointed at the speaker, then at my chest and nodded.

'It's Sofia Bambaki,' Maria said. 'She's a legend. I love her old songs. There seems to be some kind of revival – they were playing all day yesterday.'

I pointed at the speaker, and at my chest again.

'Yes, so you're a fan too. She was popular in your time, I guess.'

Exasperated, I scrambled in my bag, pulled out my ID card and handed it to Maria. She looked at it and smiled.

'Ah, you have the same name – how sweet!'

My frustration escalated. I got to my feet, swept up a ketchup bottle, held it like a microphone and mimed the song. Then pointed at my chest again.

Maria stared. 'You're not telling me that *you* are the singer, Sofia Bambaki?'

I nodded.

'Virgin Mary!' Maria crossed herself and went running into the back shouting, 'Ioanis! Ioanis!'

I sipped my cappuccino. If I could, I would have laughed. When the record finished, I tried to catch what the announcer was saying, but these days, my hearing isn't what it was.

* * *

Ioanis seemed dishevelled when he came rushing out of the taverna. A couple of tourists sat at a table and picked up the menu.

'Go and serve them and turn the radio up!' he yelled at his wife. Then he came to my table.

For a moment I forgot to sit up and slumped in my seat. I was still tired. Perhaps I needed another hour on the sunbed before I went for my morning walk.

427

'*You* are Sofia Bambaki, the singer?' Ioanis asked.

I looked up and nodded, pleased that somebody cared.

'Listen!' he yelled, pointing at the radio speaker.

I turned my attention to the broadcast.

'That's all we have time for on *This Morning Live*, my friends. Join us again at four this afternoon for the latest update in our search for Sofia Bambaki. Our lines are open now. If you have any information, call us on 2100 59368.' Ioanis reached for his phone. The broadcaster continued. 'Now, a last word from Sofia Bambaki's daughter, Zoë.'

Zoë? My mouth fell open in a silent gasp.

'Listen,' Ioanis said.

'The irony is, I've met my mother twice in the past week without realising it. Once on the ferry from Athens, and once at the harbour in Chania.' The broadcaster translated, then the woman continued, reading in Greek: 'Θα σε βρω. Σ'αγαπώ μαμά – I will find you. I love you, Mama.'

The world was spinning; my heart sang, and tears sprang to my eyes. I remembered the moment I passed my little baby girl to Markos and saw his tears fall. He held his daughter with such tenderness. I thought of Anna's complete joy and dedication, and my own never-ending sense of loss. My hope, and the fruitless search that had gone on for over forty years. Could it really be drawing to a close?

Although almost half a century had passed, the day of Zoë's birth returned with such clarity that I wanted to cry out. I found myself gripping Ioanis's shirtsleeve instead.

Markos, I've found her!

I always knew you would.

* * *

428

Ioanis was back on his phone outside, pacing the pavement and gesticulating wildly with one hand. Eventually, he returned to the taverna and I saw him have a hurried conversation with his wife. A few minutes later, his son and daughter were in the building, and new tablecloths were being whipped out of their cellophane and spread on the tables. Maria disappeared for half an hour and returned in her best church clothes. Ioanis dragged out a ladder and cleaned the sign hanging over the pavement, dust falling into the dregs of my cappuccino.

Zoë . . .

Soon the taverna was heaving. Word had spread. As new customers arrived, they came up to me and beamed, old fans with their adoring looks that brought back the thrill of the old days. I slipped my hand into my pocket and clutched the nugget of sea glass.

Changed, but still unique, still a thing of beauty.

Some people brought old records and asked me to sign them. Ioanis grinned and placed a tuna sandwich and a proper coffee before me.

'For my very good friend, Sofia Bambaki,' he said loudly. Then he turned to the crowd. 'Sofia Bambaki always eats fish at my taverna. It is the best in Crete.'

Shaken, yet thrilled, I waited for the moment I would hold my daughter. It seemed incredible that they were coming, but Maria reassured me.

'Your daughter's on her way, Sofia.'

I had almost finished the sandwich when I noticed a crowd approaching from the pedestrian promenade. My old heart raced. Was Zoë with them?

I don't know if I can take all this, Markos.

You'll be fine. Your public love you, and so do I.

429

As the people drew closer, I saw cameras on shoulders, fur-covered microphones on long poles, young, bouncy people clearly excited and loving their job.

Zoë Eleftheria, was all I could think. Was she among the strangers?

* * *

A BMW with tinted windows came down the seafront walkway, which normally only allowed for delivery vans. The vehicle disappeared around the back of the taverna.

Shortly afterwards, a suited man appeared and introduced himself to me as a reporter for Greek national television. He turned his attention to Ioanis and Maria and interviewed them with their backs facing the sea. I peered along the promenade, searching for the taxi that would bring my child.

The TV presenter spoke into the camera, before turning his attention back to me. I was amused for a moment, thinking it must be a reporter's worst nightmare to interview somebody who couldn't speak. I had to give him credit – he handled it well, telling some of my story while I nodded and smiled or looked sad in the appropriate places.

'So, Sofia Bambaki, famous singer and darling of the troops, you have searched for your daughter, Zoë Eleftheria, for forty-five years?'

I nodded, my heart exploding with emotion.

'Then turn around,' he said.

Oh, Markos, Markos!

I gasped, stumbled to my feet, turned and reached for my daughter.

Zoë rushed into my open arms. We clung to each other, sobbing, rejoicing, triumphant at last.

She was Markos's daughter as sure as the day, his smile shining from her face. Beside her was a teenage girl – the girl from the taverna with Markos's eyes – and a boy a few years younger. My daughter, and my grandchildren. They, too, rushed towards me. Everyone seemed to be applauding, crying, cheering.

As I felt the arms of my family around me, I imagined Markos's arms encompassing me too. We all wept unashamedly. The taverna music was turned up.

Angels, wings give you flight,
Every star-spangled night.
My love, you are life's sweetest songs.

And I felt Mama was also with us.

Gradually, we calmed down. Zoë, my darling daughter, sat beside me and held my hand. Megan and Josh – who were introduced to me as my grandchildren – sat next to Zoë. The presenter joined us.

'Sofia Bambaki, we have another surprise for you.'

Just as I was wondering if I could take any more surprises, three old women appeared, grinning at everyone. Thina, Honey and Agapi. I would have known them anywhere.

'We've brought you a present, Sofia,' Thina said, once we'd all hugged and kissed. 'It's a digital notebook that speaks the words you type in.'

I held my friends' hands as we all tried to blink away our tears, but failed.

The TV crew left, but my friends and family remained, gathered around the table. My heart was overflowing with joy. While the others were all chatting away, I closed my eyes for a moment.

My quest is over, Markos.

I'm glad. I've missed you.

EPILOGUE
ZOË

Crete, present day.

ZOË CLOSED THE LID OF her suitcase. The months had flown by, and now she was on her way to Crete once again. The day after finding her birth mother, she and Frank had patched things up. They had talked everything over: Megan's disappearance, their own stresses with work, how hard they had pushed each other away – and how much they still loved each other. They both wanted to give their marriage another try, take a step back from their jobs and dedicate time to fixing their relationship.

She remembered Frank's suggestion.

'Why don't we show the kids we're serious about restoring our family values?' he'd said. 'Let's renew our vows.'

Zoë thought for a minute, then agreed.

'Good idea – you're so romantic, darling. And to show we have every faith in them, we could ask Megan and Josh to organise the occasion.'

So now Zoë and Megan were about to leave for Crete. Frank would follow the next day with Josh, Trisha and Don. The ceremony would take place the day after that.

'All ready, Mum? Taxi will be here in ten.' Megan made another tick on her list. 'That's everything sorted until we get to Greece. Granny Sofia and her friends seem very organised. I just got a text to say Gary and Jeff are there and will meet us at the airport.'

'You've done a remarkable job, Megan,' Zoë said. 'Thank you.'

'It's been great, and I've learned so much. I've been talking to Gary and Jeff – they've been such a help.'

'Have you spoken to Mama today? How's the book coming along?'

'Sure, she's fine. I've sent an outline of her memoir to the publishers and they seem very enthusiastic. Being able to talk to Granny Sofia every day has been great. She keeps remembering the most bizarre things, and considering all she's been through, what a sense of humour she has. Sometimes I'm in fits! Honestly, the things she tells me – you couldn't make it up. She just loves her tablet. Her friends are a hoot, too. It's brilliant the way they take it in turns to stay with her, and translate our conversations. I mean, my Greek's coming on, but it's still not great. I make the most embarrassing mistakes.' She stopped and smiled at Zoë. 'You know what, Mum – even though Granny Anna never knew the truth of your birth, I think she'd be thrilled to know her good friend and your nanny, Nurse Sofia, now lives in her cottage in Kissamos. It's cool – sort of completes the circle, don't you think?'

Zoë squeezed Megan's shoulder. 'You've matured so much over the last few months. I'm really proud of you.'

Megan covered her mother's hand with her own.

'It's me that's proud of you, Mum. I know how hard it's been for you and Dad. We've done our best with all this, me and Josh, so I hope you both have a really fab week.'

They both heard the sound of the horn.

'Here's the taxi. Come on, Mum, time to go.'

* * *

434

At Chania airport, Gary and Jeff were all suntans and smiles. They whisked Zoë and Megan to their hotel in Kissamos, dropped the cases, then went on to the cottage. Mama Sofia was sitting on the front bench, waiting. Tears were shed and hugs dispensed, then Zoë and her mother found themselves alone. Sitting side by side, they drank strong Greek coffee and ate crumbly shortbreads covered in icing sugar.

Zoë glanced at the sky and, almost speaking to herself, said, 'I wonder if Granny Anna can see us? If so, then I hope she knows how much we all loved her.'

She did not expect Sofia to understand, yet her mother also glanced at the sky, smiled and nodded. Sofia crossed herself and pulled the little tablet out of her skirt pocket. Once she had tapped a few keys and pressed the 'speak' button, the woman's voice, adopted by Sofia, spoke her words.

'Anna was good.'

Zoë blinked with surprise. 'You understand English?'

Sofia tapped keys again. 'Little. Shy. I try speak more now, for you.'

Megan came out of the cottage with her phone in her hand.

'Right, ladies, tomorrow we're going to Athens for the day. Leaving here at ten, then an eleven o'clock flight, arriving in Athens at noon. We have the five o'clock flight back.'

'Can I ask why?' Zoë said.

Megan smiled. 'All right, then. We're going to see where you were born, Mum.'

* * *

In Athens, the crawling city traffic ground to a halt several times. Pavements thronged with midday pedestrians, café tables and street vendors. Eventually they squeezed down a busy street choked with traffic and came to a halt alongside a high cream-painted wall. A menacing flash of sunlight drew their attention to an endless coil of razor wire above.

'Korydallos Prison!' the bus driver cried.

Zoë, Megan and Sofia dismounted and stared at the imposing double gates that appeared out of place in the built-up area. One would expect them to lead into a city park, not a notorious prison. They approached the guard, introduced themselves, and Megan produced a letter. They were led through the first gates, then held in no-man's-land while a phone call was made. Embarrassed by the stares from passers-by, Megan, Zoe and Sofia were led into the prison yard beyond the bars. They were body-scanned, fingerprinted and their bags taken through security, then held.

Sofia squeezed her companion's hands as the three were then escorted to the prison governor's office. Zoë and Megan noticed Sofia's pallor and a certain reluctance to go ahead. They remained protectively either side of her. The place smelled of bleach.

'Granny Sofia, you don't have to do this,' Megan said softly.

Sofia stopped and turned to her daughter. Zoë saw her mother's face crumple and her eyes fill with fear. She pulled her old mother against her heart and as she did, felt her own emotions simmering.

'This must be terribly difficult for you, Mama. We can leave whenever you want – just let us know when you're ready to move on.'

Sofia was still; then she stepped away from Zoë. With a little shake of her shoulders, she nodded at the guard to continue. They met the prison governor. Then, with his secretary to translate Sofia's notes, they visited the places where Sofia had slept, worked and given birth to Zoë.

They visited the operating theatre where Sofia had spent her last moments in Markos's arms, after their wedding. Sofia stood for a moment, then gently pushed them out into the corridor.

Zoë swallowed hard and then whispered, 'You want to remember your last moments in my father's arms in private?'

Sofia nodded and stepped back into the room.

Zoë closed the door, pinched the bridge of her nose and turned to Megan.

'This is too tragic. My poor, poor mother. I want so badly to ease her pain.'

* * *

Emotionally exhausted, the three women left the prison and drank coffee on the corner of a side street, where Megan scribbled all that had happened into her notebook.

Zoë took her mother's hand. 'Thank you for taking us on this pilgrimage, Mama. I realise how painful it must have been to relive all those events from your past.'

Sofia put her shaking hand on her heart and smiled sadly.

'We're almost done,' Megan said, then, turning to her grandmother she asked, 'Are you sure you can do this last thing, *Yiayá*?'

Her grandmother nodded.

* * *

They stood for a moment, peering at the oasis of marble tombs and plastic flowers, until Sofia got her bearings. Then they followed her to a simple grave. A small headstone had the name MARKOS PAPAS cut into the marble.

'Dear God, it's my father's grave,' Zoë whispered, her eyes filling and overflowing.

Sofia crossed herself three times, then tugged on Megan's sleeve and pointed at the headstone. She made a clawing movement with her hand.

'I don't understand, *Yiayá*.'

'I think she wants you to dig, Megan. She's buried something there.'

Sofia nodded.

A few minutes later, the other half of Sofia's wedding ring was recovered. The old lady clutched it to her chest, and turned her gaze towards Heaven.

* * *

The next morning, all the women – Trisha, Thina, Agapi, Honey, Megan and Sofia – bustled into Zoë's room for the big 'dress reveal'. They cheered and clapped when the sheet was pulled away from the hanger, leaving a simple, full-length, white silk shift.

'Thank you darling, it's beautiful!' Zoë said to her daughter.

Megan handed everyone a glass of prosecco and told them they had one hour to get ready and gather on the first-floor landing. When they did, Zoë realised everyone was wearing white, even her mother.

As they started down the stairs, a bouzouki and a *lyra* player wearing the national costume played in the hotel lobby. Zoë noticed that the male guests, waiting at the hotel entrance, also wore only white.

Josh took his mother's hand and led her to Frank. In the forecourt, Don appeared leading a donkey laden with embroidered linen and crocheting. Silence fell as he made an announcement.

'My dear friends, in keeping with Cretan tradition, Anna Despotakis started sewing her daughter's dowry-linen shortly after Zoë was born. Sheets, pillowcases, tablecloths and napkins, carefully and lovingly crafted in preparation for the day her child would leave home to go and live with her husband and his family, after their marriage.

'As this is not a custom in England, Anna told me she was too shy to make the gift at Zoë's London wedding, where I first met her. However, Anna continued to add to her amazing collection of linen until the day she died. I think she would want Zoë to receive her dowry-linen on this special occasion, with all her love, blessings and congratulations. So, I would like you to join me and raise your voices in three cheers for Granny Anna, whom I feel sure is with us in spirit. Hip-hip . . .'

Megan cheered the loudest, then threw herself into Zoë's arms.

'Oh, Mum! It's true – don't you feel Granny Anna's with us today, smiling down from Heaven?'

* * *

The procession, led by the musicians, walked along the promenade towards the jetty. Delighted tourists and locals applauded and cars honked their horns in the traditional Cretan wedding salute.

The music provided by the local musicians stopped, and a few lines of Brenda Lee singing 'Always On My Mind' came from a ghetto blaster. Zoë and Frank turned in time to see Sofia, supported by her three friends in their white wedding outfits, come forward. Sofia handed a ribbon-tied box to her daughter. The song faded into a pre-recorded woman's voice that everyone realised was speaking for Sofia.

'This is for you, my darling daughter Zoë. The shawl I started to crochet on the day you were born. I swore I would find you before I cast the final knot. Today, my work here is done. The knot is tied.'

She lifted the crochet hook from the top of the filigree and tossed it into the sea.

'I'm so lucky to have you,' Zoë whispered, kissing her mother's cheeks. She lifted the silk shawl and draped it around her shoulders. 'It's beautiful, thank you.'

* * *

The ceremony took place on the white sand beach of Balos Bay. Megan and Josh had kept everything simple. Trestles on the beach set with picnic hampers of wine, water and delicious *mezze*. Frank made an amazing speech, saying how precious every second of marriage is, because you never know when it might end.

When Frank sat down, Josh rose and addressed his grand-mother.

'Dear Grandma Sofia, as *I* am the only male here who can proudly claim to have my grandfather's blood running through my veins, I believe it's my solemn duty to fulfil the task that Markos Papas started on your wedding day, shortly before his death.'

As Thina, sitting on the other side of Sofia, translated, Sofia's hand came up and covered her mouth. With eyes blurred by tears, she stared as Josh picked up Markos's beret, which lay on the table, and placed it on his head. He delved into his pocket and pulled out the repaired bone ring, then recited carefully rehearsed words in Greek.

'Εκ μέρους του *Markos Papas: Σου δίνω αυτό το δαχτυλίδι, Σοφία Μπαμπάκη, ως σύμβολο της ζωής, της ελευθερίας και της αιώνιας αγάπης του.*'

'On behalf of Markos Papas: I place this ring on your finger, Sofia Bambaki, as a symbol of life, freedom and his eternal love.'

There was a moment of silence, then everyone clapped. Josh replaced the beret next to his grandmother. Sofia's tears dripped onto the back of her hand as she stared at the bone ring. She struggled to her feet, remembering Markos's words: *Don't ever forget me, my darling. When the sun comes up, say good morning and think of me. When you raise a glass, call my name, and tell our precious baby, Zoë, I will always love her.*

Sofia lifted her glass towards the sky and mouthed, *Markos!*

The guests all stood, raised their glasses and called, 'Markos!'

* * *

'That was a perfect day, wasn't it?' Zoë asked Frank once they were alone in the peace of their hotel room.

'Perfect, indeed. Do you think the kids will be all right? Josh is a bit young for an all-night beach party.'

'Don't fret – they're with Gary and Jeff. Don and Trish are there, too. They'll keep an eye on them.'

'What about Sofia?'

'I've just settled her down. She's very tired, but extremely happy. The kids were so thoughtful, making the day special for her too. I'm proud of them. Do you know, she puts that beret on the pillow next to her each night and tells Markos what's been going on through the day?'

'I'll bet she doesn't get very far tonight. She must be exhausted.'

'I love you so much, Frank.'

'And I love you too. More than you could understand.'

* * *

441

In the next bedroom, Sofia turned to face the pillow supporting Markos's beret, and as she did, it slid forward and rested against her cheek. She smiled knowingly.

It's been a long day, Markos, but quite wonderful.

I see you're wearing our ring at last, my darling.

I am. Your grandson slipped it onto my finger on your behalf.

I've waited so long, Sofia, my love.

My task is over, Markos. I finished the shawl and today my child placed it over her shoulders. My dearest, I'm so tired of life without you.

When you are ready, darling Sofia, just say and I will reach for your hand.

Oh, Markos, I want to be with you so much.

Sofia felt her husband's fingers against her palm. They were no longer broken and deformed, but the strong, perfect hand of the man she loved before their troubles began. She hesitated.

But, Markos, I'm an old woman.

Nonsense. You have always been beautiful.

And it makes me sad to leave all those I love here, Markos.

You're not leaving them. A part of you will be in their hearts forever. Did your mother ever leave you?

Ah, you're right, she didn't. Give me your hands then.

Leaving a smile on her face for her precious family, Sofia Bambaki stepped into the afterlife to spend eternity with the only man she had ever loved.

AUTHOR'S NOTE

AS IS USUALLY THE CASE, a number of random events came together like pieces of a jigsaw and led to the story behind *Greek Island Escape*. To celebrate the launch of *Secrets of Santorini* in 2019, my friend Patricia Castle gave me a beautiful nugget of sea glass that my talented Zumba teacher, Jill Dodgeon, had fashioned into a dragonfly shape. I often looked at the glass and wondered what it once was. This led me to consider how much we all change, like the sea glass, on our journey through life.

At that time, photography and writer friends, Dave Hollis and Carol Gaymer, came to stay with me in Rhodes for a week. Carol, a natural chatterbox, had cancer of the throat and every day was a struggle for her. This made me realise how we all take our voice for granted, and how precious it is.

Then, a local taverna owner told me the sad story of a distant relative of his: a famous Greek singer in Athens who'd secretly had a baby. Broken-hearted, she decided to give her newborn to a childless couple on one of the Greek islands in order to continue working and make enough money to give her child a good life. This happened at a terrible time in Greece's history, when people actually succumbed to starvation and dropped dead on the streets of Athens.

Shocked to learn that fellow Europeans would stand by and allow such suffering and death to happen on their doorstep, I investigated further and read about the awful struggles that took place, particularly in Athens, not only through World War II, but right up until the mid-1970s. It was a dark time in Greece's history. However, it was a newspaper article about Manolis Glezos, who is often referred to as 'a man of humbling greatness', that influenced me more than anything else.

In the process of giving my office a spring clean, I found a flashcard that had fallen behind my desk drawer. I checked the pictures and realised it was from the time when I wrote *Island of Secrets*, my debut novel, in 2016. That novel was based in the village of Amiras, Crete, where I lived. I had taken photographs at the memorial service, which takes place in September each year, to commemorate the 525 innocent villagers who died there on 13 September 1943. In several of the photographs, sitting behind the president of Greece, the heads of the armed forces and the Church, was the man with an enigmatic face that I knew I had seen recently. I checked through the hundreds of sheets of research I had printed off for my 2020 novel, *Greek Island Escape*, and there he was again.

In *The Guardian* newspaper (online), I read an article entitled 'Athens 1944: Britain's dirty secret', and there was a photograph of this same unmistakable face, and finally a name: Manolis Glezos (born 1922), the oldest member of the European Parliament. As a boy, he had crawled through the sewers of Athens with fuse wire wrapped around his waist. In the newspaper article, Glezos also told of his brother's beret, which I thought was a most moving story. I must emphasise that *Greek Island Escape* is *not* about Manolis Glezos or his brother – it is a work of fiction – but how could a writer not be influenced by these things? Manolis Glezos clearly loves his country with a passion and, like many Greek soldiers and patriots, was prepared to risk his life and freedom for Greece. A martyr in every sense of the word.

Glezos was presented with the International Award of Journalism in 1958, the Golden Medal Joliot-Curie of the World Peace Council in 1959 and the Lenin Peace Prize in 1963. He has also published six books in Greek. Yet, Glezos has also been put on trial and sentenced to death several times in his political career.

It was in this same article I read that Lt Gen. Ronald Scobie, on 5 December 1944, imposed martial law and ordered the aerial bombing of the working-class Metz quarter of Athens. I found this piece of information quite shocking. That the British would bomb the homes of ordinary families while the menfolk of those very same homes were for the most part fighting on our side, sacrificing their lives in our struggle to win the war against the Germans. All these facts tumbled around in my head, until eventually *Greek Island Escape* revealed itself as my 2020 novel.

I must stress, this is a work of fiction and not a documentary. All the characters are entirely fictitious, apart from the mention in passing of a few famous artists and politicians. However, the locations are real places, and the story is based on historical facts and many real events. For those interested in the modern history of Greece, I recommend a simple Google search on: Manolis Glezos, a man of humbling greatness.

Last but not least, *Greek Island Escape* would not have come about without the help and guidance of my agent, Tina Betts, and the publishing team at Bonnier Books UK, mainly Sarah Bauer, Katie Lumsden, and also Martin Fletcher and Steve O'Gorman. Thanks also to Kim Pether for her legal advice.

It goes without saying that, as always, without my husband's constant support, I would not have been able to research and write this story. Thank you, Berty!

WHY I LOVE CHANIA

THE PREFECTURE OF CHANIA, on the island of Crete, is one of Greece's most spectacular and picturesque areas. The breath-taking Samaria Gorge, the magnificent mountains of Lefka Ori, and the laid-back villages where life stands still, all beckon me. On the west coast lie some of the most beautiful beaches on earth. Falassarna, Elafonisi and Balos Bay are dotted with tiny islets that seem to float on the turquoise crystal water. And there is more. So much more that every time I leave, I feel I've missed something essential and I *must* return soon.

The city of Chania is addictive. I relocated from the UK to Lassithi, east Crete, also a delightful area. But sometimes, on the spur of the moment, my wanderlust strikes. I grab a change of clothes and the car keys, lock the house, and head for the west of the island. Excited to revisit it, I sense a new adventure awaits, just over the horizon.

After a scenic, lazy, four-hour drive along the north coast, I book into a charming, rustic hotel next to Chania's maritime museum, on the harbour. Dusk falls. Lights are turned on, and from my pavement table I watch their reflections dance on the dark water. I order food. My attention is drawn to the opposite point of the quay, where the elegant Egyptian lighthouse, bathed in golden light, points to a darkening sky. Noisy, colourful fishing boats chug past, on their way out to sea. A rugged skipper stands at his tiller. I sense his hope for a good catch and wonder if I'll see his return at breakfast.

The waiter brings my wine, a robust local red. '*Yammas!*' he cries.

'Cheers,' I reply, lifting my glass.

A basket, covered with a white napkin, is placed on the table. I peek inside. The scent of freshly baked bread topped with toasted sesame seeds rises and fills my senses. It's still warm. I break off a crusty chunk, sprinkle it with rich olive oil and a little salt. It's hard not to eat the whole loaf before my meal arrives. The tables are filling now. My moussaka and Greek salad arrive, and another glass of red. The waiter winks. I smile, stick my nose up and turn away haughtily. He laughs.

'Welcome back,' he says. I don't even remember his name. 'This wine is from me.' He pats his chest and makes a little bow.

Church bells ring in the background, and I wonder if it's a wedding or baptism. The moussaka is magnificent! The finest minced meats baked with sweet, sun-ripened tomatoes, hidden below a thin layer of aubergines. This is topped with a thick layer of light, creamy sauce. Is the secret of a perfect moussaka in the faint scent of cinnamon, the fresh parsley, or the delicate cheese?

Two young boys come along the promenade. One has a bouzouki, the other a squeeze-box. They play *Never On A Sunday*. I give them a coin and they grin, before moving to the next table. Across the harbour, a bride and groom mount one of the open horse-drawn carriages. The pale mare, ears sticking up thought a straw hat, clops slowly around the quay-side. Waiters stop what they are doing, come to the front, and applaud the newlyweds, shouting 'Bravo! Bravo!' and 'Good life! Good life!' Sometimes the Greeks have to say everything twice. Greek diners clatter their forks against their wine glasses in a tinkling salute, and all the tourists lift their smartphones. The couple nod, lean against each other, and wave royally. I know it's a moment they will always remember. The carriage turns into town, and I find myself smiling again.

This charming city is steeped in history. I try to make a plan for the few days I am here, but I know this is futile. The fates will have something else in mind and my itinerary will be scuppered.

Last time I was at this end of the island, I planned a hike in the country. Five kilometres into the walk and I was distracted by an olive harvest.

'Ela! Ela!' Head-scarfed women and chunky, whiskery men beckoned me urgently, hooking the air with a raised arm. Thinking there had been an accident, I hurried into the deep shade of tightly packed olive trees in the grove, treading lightly on the spread, green, olive-nets.

'Where you from? Where you go?'

'From England. On holiday.'

'Come, come!'

They hurried me further into the grove, which grew so dark I had to remove my sunglasses in order to see where I was going. At this point, the olives were still on the trees. Branches heavy with bunches of fruit bowed almost to the ground, blocking the light. Then, suddenly, we stepped into blinding sunlight. In this vibrant green clearing, blankets lay on the ground. I saw dozen dishes containing every kind of local food, plates and cutlery, and a lamb on a crude spit over a fiery pit.

'Come! Eat, eat!' They pulled me down, gave me a bottle of water, shouted Greek words that I didn't understand. Then came the food, bread, cheese, chunks of hot meat and salads.

'Good, good!' I cried, at which they nodded and grinned at each other. The oldest man took a shovel to a heap of smouldering olive leaves and returned with half a dozen baked potatoes.

My thoughts return to the present. Perhaps on this visit, I'll hike the Omalos plateau.

In the morning, refreshed after a good night's sleep, I sit at the same table and watch the harbour wake.

'*Kaliméra*! *Kaliméra*!' my waiter cries, his grin even wider than last night.

I wonder what time he got to bed.

'Good morning to you too!' I respond, matching his smile. I order fried eggs on bread and study the harbour when he disappears into the kitchen.

The night fishermen are returning. Restaurateurs hurry to their moorings to pick the best of the fresh fish. Buildings around the harbour glow, golden, in the morning light. Turkish, Byzantine, and Venetian architecture stand side by side. Chania has its own airport and port, and provides good roads for the intrepid explorer. Also, there are boat trips to ferry tourists to secluded bays where absolute peace reigns. Add to this horse riding, scuba diving, rock climbing, water sports and peaceful walks through orange and olive groves. This area is one of my favourite places in the world.

Once the capital of Crete, Chania has a turbulent and varied past. Like most Greek cities, it has two parts. The old town is an ancient walled city around the harbour. The new town is designed to accommodate every type of shopping, holiday and entertainment.

I love to stroll along the horseshoe shaped quayside. Proud Venetian captain's mansions, with peeling paint and rusted balconies, remind us of the dramatic history of the city. Many of these imposing Venetian exteriors are restored, making it easy to imagine the prosperous, elegantly-dressed shipowners and their wives alighting from horse-drawn carriages on the cobbled front. Turkish houses are easily distinguishable by their boxed in timber balconies.

Chania's rich Turkish heritage is also very clear on the east side of the harbour. The Turks declared Crete an Ottoman province in 1646 after conquering the west of the peninsula. Nevertheless, the Venetians held on to the capital city of Heraklion (then called Candia) until 1669 when the Ottomans succeeded in taking the rest of the island.

The Mosque of the Janissaries was built in 1645. This religious centre, with its iconic pink domes, is the longest surviving Ottoman building on the island. Erected on the site of a small Christian church, the mosque stopped functioning as a religious building in 1923. Its beautiful minaret tower was destroyed by a bomb in World War II. The mosque has since been used as a café, and then a tourist centre. Now, the construction is used as an artist's exhibition centre.

The Janissaries started out as slaves in the Ottoman empire; originally boys from non-Muslim prisoners of war, they were chosen by the sultan himself. Once selected, they were kept under the guidance of prominent Turkish families, where they were taught Islam, and the language and customs of the country.

These boys became Janissaries, the most elite of all Turkish soldiers – strictly disciplined and finely skilled. They ruled Crete on behalf of the Sultan and were feared throughout the land. The Janissaries had their own social class; they were highly paid, and received a pension when they retired.

In order to preserve their power, the Janissaries opposed the renewal of the army, which led to their downfall. After defeat in the Battle of Vienna in 1683, the Sultan was overthrown. His successor fought the Janissaries and eventually destroyed them, taking their possessions and mercilessly slaughtering them all for their involvement in a rebellion against the empire in 1826.

Despite Chania's occupation by the Ottomans, the nearby islet of Gramvousa with its sheer, steep cliffs topped by a Venetian fortress, managed to hold its own. In 1715, this fortified, storm-worn castle, which is close to the most picturesque Cretan beach of Balos Bay, was also overcome by the Turks.

The Egyptian Lighthouse is a short walk past the Mosque of the Janissaries, and was originally built by the Venetians in the 16th century. It is known as 'Egyptian' because it was built when the Egyptians occupied the area, giving their support to the Ottoman Empire against the rebellious Cretan warriors. To protect Chania from pirates at night, a chain could be drawn across the harbour entrance, connecting the lighthouse to the Fortress of Firkas on the opposite side.

The lighthouse fell into disrepair during the Turkish occupation, but it was rebuilt in the 1800s in the form of a minaret.

The original Venetian base survives to this day, although the carving of the Lion of St Mark, similar to the one on Heraklion's harbour fort, has long gone. In the beginning, it operated with an open flame torch. In 1864, the French Ottoman Lighthouse Company initiated a new type of operation: the reflective lighting machine. Standing at twenty-one metres high and twenty-six metres above sea level, the light covers a distance of seven miles. The lighthouse is among the oldest in existence to have been preserved to this day.

Due to bombings during World War II, the lighthouse was leaning dangerously, but extensive renovations took place in 2005.

The old city is insanely pretty. I always make time to wander the narrow, shady, streets, avoiding the heat of the day, exploring the art and craft shops for unique ceramics and paintings. These charming lanes are full of hidden tavernas, kafenio and leather-goods stalls, and the local bakery. The market is also delightful and I always remind myself to go there and stock up with my favourite herbs and spices, especially the yellow Cretan saffron.

After breakfast, I decide to take a bus to Kissamos, then an excursion to one of the famous west coast beaches to snorkel. While on the hour-long boat trip to the island of Gramvousa, our skipper talks about its history. Proudly, he informs us that the area is so uniquely beautiful that Prince Charles and Lady

Diana stayed there on the Royal Yacht *Britannia*, while on their honeymoon. I am more interested in the wildlife.

The cape of Gramvousa and its surrounding islets are protected areas that host four-hundred different flora and over a hundred bird species. I want to stay, camp overnight, but this is forbidden. The island is situated on the bird migration path and protected under the Natura 2000 programme.

The Mediterranean seal breeds in Gramvousa's caves, and the endangered Loggerhead turtles feed here.

The island looms straight up from the sea and at first, it seems there is no way to get to the Venetian castle perched on the top, 137 metres above sea level. The boat ties up and I notice there is a gentler side to the island, and a path to the top. The walk takes fifteen minutes, but the view is worth it. I sit on the wall and look down at the dizzying drop, then take some pictures. Rumour has it that pirates buried great troves of treasure on this island. It's easy to believe. I glance around and wonder where it might be.

There is little time to speculate, as I wish to embark on another adventure while I'm here on Gramvousa island. I hurry back down the path and along the rocky shoreline, until I see the rusting hulk of a large ship looming up from the clear water. My excitement surges. In moments, I'm out of my clothes and into my snorkel gear. With fins in hand, I pick my way between black, spiny, sea urchins that cling to the rocks. The males are easy to spot, as the sea is clear as tap water. The females disguise themselves with small stones and seagrass, but I manage to avoid them all and slip into my fins when the water is waist deep.

The hulking wreck is only a few metres from shore, and I swim around it, looking down, observing the crustaceans, corals, and shoals of small, colourful fish that travers in and out of the portholes. It's magical! Shafts of light play over the orange hull and yellow sand like spotlights, and refracted, dancing over the surfaces. In some places I can stand on the bottom and look into the ship. I'm amazed by it all and wish I had my underwater camera with me. Suddenly, I realise I have lost track of time and may miss the boat.

I swim to shore and promise myself I will return better prepared.

The skipper is standing by the boat. He blows a whistle and peers up the path to the castle. I shout, wave, and jog towards him. 'Sorry, sorry,' I cry. 'I forgot the time!'

'*Ela, koukla mou*,' he says. 'No worries, I wait.'

Back in Chania, I take a walk around the harbour, then sit at my usual pavement table at the busy waterfront taverna. I order food and wine, and watch the colourful fishing boats return as the sun sinks into the Aegean.

'You had a good day?' my waiter asks, placing my Cretan sausage, tzatziki, and green salad dotted with jewel-like pomegranate seeds onto the table.

'Wonderful. I climbed Gramvousa and snorkelled over a shipwreck.'

'You didn't go to Falassarna beach?'

'Next time,' I say. 'I'll have to come back.'

He nods knowingly and glances at the empty breadbasket. 'You want more bread?'

I shake my head and laugh. 'It's too delicious.'

Night falls over the city and, contentedly, I think everyone should visit Chania once in their lives.

But be warned, once is never enough.